When I first read   prised to feel tears arise: tears of need, hunger, yearning, promise. ....ads that both drive us and inhibit us as Jewish activists run so deep. Penny offers us a pathway for facing these wounds, allowing more of ourselves and each other to come alive as we do so. Her book is filled with wild, truthful and exuberant voices, you can feel their spirits in their words. *Hope into Practice* welcomes readers to join the conversation and the song.

–Rabbi Margaret Holub

A *wonderful, gutsy, and inspiring book.* Penny Rosenwasser takes on the most explosive issues in American Jewish life today—racism and anti-Semitism, victimization and privilege, and Jewish politics around Israel and Palestine— and she does it with a generosity of spirit and a clear head. The voices at the heart of this book are those of women struggling to forge meaningful Jewish identities and political practices. Rosenwasser tacks back and forth between their testimonies and a sophisticated analysis of contemporary Jewish history and politics. This book has a wealth of discussion modules for groups and is also a good read. Either way, a vision of a progressive Jewishness for a multi-cultural 21st century comes through proud and clear.

–Karen Brodkin, author of *How Jews Became White Folks and What That Says About Race in America*

This work fills a gap in the Jewish studies scholarship that connects real world conflict with the larger affective processes that drive it. Based on the bold assumption that communal and individual healing is integral to justice work, Rosenwasser's multidisciplinary book is at once a memoir, a Jewish feminist treatise, and an activist guide. Written from a poignant, personal perspective, *Hope into Practice* allows readers to reflect on their own struggles with Jewish identity, queerness, and ethical commitment in order to imagine a better future. A must-read for all Jewish feminists!

–Alainya Kavaloski, Jewish Caucus Chair, National Women's Studies Association

The Jewish women you'll meet in this book will inspire you, make you laugh, and challenge you to be more fierce. This is a book about liberation from our narrow places and the power to change the world. No matter who you are, you'll learn something new about being human.

–Noah T. Winer, Cofounder, MoveOn.org; Board Member, Jewish Voice for Peace

In creating a path of liberation for Jewish women, Penny shows a way for any freedom-seeking person to move from the internalization of oppression into wholeness. She illuminates what it takes to heal—both personally and collectively. This is a teaching story for all of us.

—Akaya Windwood, President, Rockwood Leadership Institute

A powerful tool for today's Jewish activists. Rosenwasser writes at once the things we cannot bear to read and the words we have been yearning to hear. She challenges us to ask what Jewishness could be without suffering and victimhood – questions asked with joy, not shame. Rosenwasser guides us to value our Jewish selves as much as we value others, and to fully believe in our worth, recognizing that this is no small feat. *Hope into Practice* acknowledges that we cannot wait to heal all our wounds before we act, but cannot wait until our movements are successful before we turn to our healing.

—Marjorie Dove Kent, Executive Director, Jews for Racial & Economic Justice

HOPE INTO PRACTICE

JEWISH Women Choosing JUSTICE
Despite Our Fears

Penny Rosenwasser

Editor: Joan Lester
Primary Reader/editor: Sandy Butler
Copy Editor: Vicki Gibbs
Cover Design: Studiopacific.com
Interior Design: Linda Herman, Glyph Publishing Arts
Proofreading: David Sweet
Index: Irene Elmer

Photo Credits
Author Photo: Irene Young
Bay Area Women in Black (slightly altered): Copyright © 2011 by Joan Bobkoff
Gaza Vigil: Phylece Snyder
Kaddish: Liat Weingart
All other photos are by the author.

ISBN 978-0-9889187-0-2

Library of Congress Control Number: 2013902711

Contents

Introduction

"I meet a guy in a bar that's cute...He asks 'You're Jewish? Wow. You don't look Jewish. You don't act Jewish.' And he says it in this tone that sounds like he's complimenting me. And I say...nothing. I say nothing, which combined with a flirty smile translates to 'thank you.'"[1]

–Vanessa Hidary

PRETTY CLOSE TO MY OWN STORY. Only I *did* say "Thank you." To the kids in school, neighbors on the block. Me, the pudgy, curly-headed, super-sensitive girl growing up in (brand-new) white, Christian, middle-class suburbs in northern Virginia, in the 1950s-'60s.

All of my friends' fathers were majors and colonels in the army, working at the Pentagon, just down the highway. We were trained to live in fear of the Russians bombing us at any minute, so we wore ID bracelets; mine said "Hebrew," and I hated it.[2] I craved one that said "Protestant," like all my friends had. To look like them, I later ironed my rambunctious hair in a futile attempt to restrain it into a smooth pageboy.

"Thank you" is what I thought I was *supposed* to say when told I didn't "look Jewish." It never occurred to me to say anything else. At least not until my early thirties, when I strolled into Oakland's women's bookstore one sunny afternoon, and *Nice Jewish Girls: A lesbian anthology*, edited by feminist activist Evelyn Torton Beck, leapt out at me. And my life changed.

It took many more years to grasp what the "thank you" signified: the dominant U.S. culture's mindset inside me. This was my first clue about internalized anti-Semitism—the way so many of us, as Jewish girls, got the (ridiculous, toxic) message that *something was wrong with us*. That we just didn't fit the white Protestant mold this country valorized. That our bodies weren't svelte enough; that we were too outspoken or needy or intense. Maybe our anxiety showed a little too much. That we were just a tad repugnant: not okay.

I had to write this book to stop that inner monologue in its tracks, to turn it around. It's a devastating rant; and it is changeable. These internalized critiques, along with fear and grief, outrage and powerlessness, passed down through Jewish families for generations, are not personal pathologies; they are a communal response to anti-Jewish prejudice, persecution, genocide.[3] Just like Second Wave feminism taught us, the personal *is* political.

One of this book's key assumptions is that delving into our Jewish stories, ideally in community with other Jewish women—while absorbing historical and psychological information about how and why we have been hurt—can give us potent insights, fueling our drive to repair the damage. Grasping the connection between our histories and our present struggles, we can learn to recognize and confront anti-Jewishness, and how we internalize it. We can believe again in our innate lovability and value, renew our vibrance, treasure ourselves: countering past trauma and current bias.

Simply put, when we transform self-hatred, we accept and like who we are, and we treat others better, too. We stoke our natural empathy. As our activism is less weighed down by inner demons, we become more effective in changing systems that are short-sighted, immoral, unfair. We become savvier and stauncher allies. Anchored in Jewish ethical tradition, we bolster our capacity to create a just world: for Jews, for all the disenfranchised and abused on U.S. shores, as well as in the Congo, in Haiti, in Palestine.

This book is *about* Jewish women in the U.S., but it is *for* everyone who cares about Jewish women, about Jews, about women. As feminist scholar Carol Gilligan wrote, "Bringing the experiences of women...to full light, although in one sense perfectly straightforward, becomes a radical endeavor."[4]

❧

I was born four years to the day after the last death march left Auschwitz. My family? We wanted to Blend In and Belong, as white, especially as "American." Christmas was an American holiday for us; our menorah also shone in the front window.

I later discovered that my mother consulted the local activist minister about raising my brother and me Unitarian. "No way," he insisted. "You have a precious heritage, don't deprive them of that." Ally Number One. So I reluctantly schlepped to (Reform) Temple Beth El Sunday School until I was confirmed at sixteen, where to me the other kids were not cool. I remember thinking, "Get me out of here!"

In our sprawling housing development we had three other white Jewish families and two Japanese gentile families. As far as I knew, four of us were Jews in my high school graduating class of 450. At a recent reunion, one of them ambled over in the bar at 2:00 a.m. "How did we ever survive being Jewish in such a Christian white-bread-and-mayonnaise community?" L. laughed. Later, she forwarded an e-mail from a former neighborhood play-mate who remembered me as her "first exposure to a Jewish family!" Unbeknownst to me, we had been a phenomenon.

Working with the National Council of Jewish Women,[5] the League of Democratic Voters, and the PTA, my mother was constantly knocking on doors: to elect Adlai Stevenson as president, to support local liberals, to collect for the March of Dimes. Our home was the unofficial commu-nity center/crisis clinic; my mother listened and dispensed advice, putting visitors to work folding laundry or weeding the garden. I learned that you "help people"—that's what you do.

Growing up, the anti-Jewish prejudice I absorbed was subtle, but potent: I felt I never looked quite right, that I was somehow different, sometimes unwanted—even though I was elected to leadership positions, won awards, had dozens of friends and dates. Adaptive and resourceful, I figured out how to please, to give, to prove my worth. I don't remember overt anti-Jewishness until pledging a sorority at my Ohio liberal arts college, when I learned that one of my favorite "houses" couldn't decide whether or not to pledge "a Jew" (me).

In keeping with the times, I was radicalized, boycotting college classes to support Black Demands, braving Pennsylvania Turnpike blizzards to march in Washington, D.C. anti-Vietnam War moratoriums. Later, join-ing a political research collective, I organized with my Jewishness barely visible. Who cared? I was busy diving into feminism, coming out as lesbian, protesting the Chilean coup as well as D.C. police brutality, supporting farmworkers, playing my kazoo on the White House lawn when Nixon resigned, chasing the FBI from my door. Then, traipsing the country performing songs of struggle and celebration with my lover, spreading the socialist lesbian-feminist call, and later, developing nationwide cultural networks of women's liberation and empowerment.

When I finally picked up *Nice Jewish Girls*, I found a Jewishness I could relate to: lesbian stories, though from women all over the map of class, ethnicity, politics, age, religious observance (or not). For the first time, really, I began to feel Jewishly proud, engaged. My lesbian-feminism led me to Step One in claiming a rowdy, joyful, complicated visible Jew-ness — one that was antiracist, woman-positive.

Looking back, I realized that my granddaddy *Moishe* had modeled (his version of) being a Jew for me — exquisite love and warmth, generosity, self-taught education, humor, deep spirituality, care for family, and "doing the right thing." Fleeing extreme poverty in the *shtetl*[6] of Przemyslany, Galicia (then Poland, now Ukraine) after his mother died, he reached Ellis Island in 1900 at age twelve. On New York City's Lower East Side, he swept the floor of a necktie factory, sifting through ashes for precious lumps of coal, later sewing women's skirts twelve hours a day. Years later, his sister pawned her wedding ring to help him buy a dry goods store in Denmark, South Carolina, where he raised his five children, including my mom — one of two Jewish families in the town of 2,000 — driving his sons several hours roundtrip to Hebrew school each weekend, teaching Bible study at the corner church.[7]

It was such sheer relief for me to finally feel pleased about being a Jew, to build Jewish feminist political community — that when I began hearing about the Israeli occupation of the West Bank and Gaza, I turned away. The information didn't sit well with my newfound Jewish-positive mindset, so plugging my ears seemed like the best option. For a moment, I became Zionist, because for the first time I understood why Jews were desperate for a safe haven. I ignored the rest of it.

But the disconnect with my social justice passions loomed too large. After picking coffee in Nicaragua to support the *Sandinista* revolution, being thrown in jail more than once for civil disobedience while protesting against nuclear power and weapons, organizing to support women with AIDS, exploring women's spirituality and healthy uses of power—and especially, leading diversity trainings around race and class, while producing/hosting radio programs about all these topics—I had to face that Jews had not only been victimized, but we could (and did) also oppress.

Seven trips to Israel-Palestine later, four of them leading women's peace delegations, I published a book of interviews with Palestinian and Israeli peace activists and toured the country with my "Women Waging Peace" multimedia presentation on the (U.S.-funded) Israeli occupation. Ever since, I've organized events to raise humanitarian aid for children in Palestine, Iraq, and Lebanon. I also fundraise for Jewish Voice for Peace (JVP)—an organization supporting full human rights for Israelis *and* Palestinians, focusing on movement-building to end the occupation. I've served as founding national board member, infrastructure-builder, public speaker, and event-producer for JVP.

In my forties and wanting to dig deeper, I charged into an experiential doctoral program focused on transformational change, hoping to give my activism more impact. Bent on learning a non-Eurocentric perspective, I was generously accepted into a study group with four African American women, self-named Four Dreds and a Jew. They (rightly) found suspect my eager/earnest desire to act for racial justice, while seldom bringing my explicit Jewishness to the table: my own story, where I came from, who my people were. I could best fight racism, they said, by first loving myself as white and Jew—healing my own wounds, validating myself (rather than wanting them to heal/validate me). Coming from that solid, self-knowing, proudly-Jewish place, I could be the best ally.

Our entire student cohort grappled with racism experientially, profoundly, in separate white and African American groups and also together. Thrust into a sea of ambiguity, everything I thought I knew was up for grabs; my world split open. Over the months, my defenses and denial wore down. Exploring where I came from, I was hit in the gut with how assimilation into whiteness had robbed me of a precious sense of belonging to my people. Emptiness and self-loathing were a high price to pay for economic advantage and Americanization. For the first time, I realized how my white Jewish experience was different from that of white Christians.

Lenses shifted; from looking at my Jewishness through a white filter, I began to see my whiteness through the filter of being a Jew.

The Jewish Women's Council I colead is being filmed for Shakti Butler's video "The Way Home," about women, racism, and what holds oppression in place. Eight of us sit in a semicircle, microphones hovering, cameras rolling. We're surrounded by Seder plates, Haggadahs, photos: of Sarah's mother Bertha, Sephardic from Turkey, who grew up in Cuba when the U.S. wouldn't let her ship enter; of Yeshi's sister Ricky, who pioneered anti-oppression work before dying of cancer. On display are Eva's handkerchiefs, which she carried when fleeing Hitler at age three. Far less assimilated than myself, these women from Austria and Iraq, New York and Israel, hold their Jewishness with love and pride, despite hardship—whereas, although I am Jewishly visible and value my heritage, I still identify more with the white non-Jews around me.

With filming under way, Sarah pleads, "Will you just answer me this? How can Jews put every other issue before our own?" I blush, hesitate.

"You're talking about me, Sarah," I respond slowly. "I remember being twenty-four years old in Washington, D.C., in a political research collective, surrounded by posters of Che Guevara, and lesbians on horseback. We support-ed the Washington Post *pressman's strike. We marched in Greensboro, North Carolina, against the Klan. But march for a Jewish issue? If you had asked me then, I would have said, 'Why would I do that? That's not important!'"*

Suddenly, in this rarefied setting, a wall melts away. I'm disoriented, but also freed up. Words tumble out: my growing up feeling no emotional connec-tion to Jewishness. Like there was a hole in my heart. Like somewhere I lost my wail. Like the minor key of my Jewish song had been stuffed into a major key.

"But," I pause, "even though I often felt on the margins and didn't know why, I was also white, middle-class, in the center. My voice was heard."

Loolwa stops me: "Not your Jewish voice," she counters. "Your Jewish voice wasn't heard."

Whoa...until that moment, despite learning to connect emotionally as a Jew, and starting to grasp the cost of assimilation, I had still been operating from only part of me. The Jewishness had still been in hiding: that's the missing piece, the hole in my heart. Stunned, I take a few deep breaths, and wonder: what would it mean for my full Jewish voice to be heard? How does it sound?

"You've been searching for who you are," Laura looks into my eyes, "because

it was taken from you." I beg her to tell her story again, about growing up work-ing class on the Lower East Side. Carts of knishes, Jewish neighbors pulling her into their homes saying, "You're too skinny, you need to eat!" My eyes and throat and belly yearn for such connection, such belonging.

Only ten minutes left to film; Shakti says we need to talk about the healing, which involves, Yeshi suggests, bringing your whole voice in. My stomach tightens. "But how do you deal with the fear?" I ask. Before Yeshi can answer, Anna swings around.

"Penny, how would you answer that question?" Her face is open, caring.

Gazing around the circle, I feel completely held. Scared—but not fro-zen. "I don't know," I begin. "I'm just starting to feel the part of me that got cut off. If I let it out, I'm afraid of releasing some kind of monster." Trembling, I flash on images of New York relatives; I feel them like worms slithering over my skin, sliding through nails and hair. Desperately I brush the worms away, shoving off disgust at my "loudpushynewyorkrelatives." Frantically now I am brushing, crying, "Quick, get them off I have to get them off!" I want to throw up. Worms as harbingers of assimilation. Where did I learn to so despise myself, my people?

Now Laura holds me. "You absorbed this anti-Semitism in the air you breathed, in that middle-class-white-Christian suburb," she whispers. Anna's eyes are red. Beautiful, strong, Jewish women surround me; the room is full of our common grief, our shared love.

Something has changed. Ripping open my shame and self-disgust, under-neath I am discovering a new Jewish voice—recovering a deep bond to Jewish women, reclaiming my full and visible belonging. I am finding my story.

(Note: throughout the book I use italics to convey my personal stories/reflections that are most in-depth.)

Soon after, I agree to cochair the National Women's Studies Associa-tion Jewish Caucus (for the next five years). At the group's next confer-ence, I run around the hotel publicizing events I've planned, handing out bright purple fliers with big Jewish stars and robust women dancing: totally in your face. One hundred people join our inclusive, experiential *Shabbat* service. Afterwards, a Christian woman from Texas tells me it was one of the most spiritual experiences she has ever had. I organize a workshop with the Women of Color Caucus about internalized oppression—on race, class, anti-Semitism, and ableism—and later, the Latina presenter e-mails me to say, "This topic changed my life." A twenty-two-year-old white Jewish activist writes: "Your presentation made a lot of what I have been struggling to understand about myself and my issues seem a little clearer, to see my most intimate inner workings being described in someone else's mouth! A crazy, strangely liberating feeling…that I am not alone."

ॐ

Braiding the psychological and historical, the political and personal, *Hope into Practice: Jewish Women Choosing Justice Despite Our Fears* has three sections. Part One, "How Did Things Get So Hard?," examines major aspects and impacts of anti-Semitism—scapegoating, violence, and stereotyping (including what is misnamed anti-Semitic)—illustrating why our inner critics are so harsh, a reflection of the bigotry. I also shine a light on how the influence some Jews have can be exaggerated, given this country's overwhelmingly white Christian (and male) culture of power. Then there's the complicated interplay between white Jewish privilege and insecurity, given an often-brutal history—and also, Jewish racism, the construction of Jewish whiteness, and white Ashkenazi dominance of Mizrahi and Sephardic Jews and other Jews of color.

Part Two, "Wrestling with the Voices," is just that: the psychodynamics of how the trickster's voice lodges in our minds and won't budge.[8] Tapes that tell us we are either Too Much or Not Enough; that we must tone down our Jewishness if we want to be accepted; that we don't belong; that we must drive ourselves to achieve and accomplish perfectly, so that nothing (more) horrific will happen. I explore our worry, urgency, hypervigilance—all understandable responses to past persecution—and how this fear led to assimilation U.S. style, with both losses and benefits. Finally, I probe the way we've allowed ourselves to clutch onto a victim mentality that doesn't serve us or the world, a mindset justifying the subjugation of Palestinians, an attitude manipulated by Jewish and gentile leaders, that aids their agendas. This is not to cast blame, but it means we have some healing, some work, to do.

Part Three, "Creating a Future," offers strategies for recovery from internalized Jewish oppression, beginning with activism as empowerment/ therapy (my personal vignettes). Other chapters call for Jewish women (also trans/gender queer folks) to share stories together, not unlike the feminist consciousness-raising groups of the 1960's-'70's—reframing toxic messages; confronting prejudice; building community; reclaiming a loud-proud (not superior), joyful Jewishness. These chapters also insist on inclusivity of Jews of color and sharing power; honoring resistance heroes and noticing allies; bringing our bodies and whole selves into the act—releasing emotion, using movement, art, music, psychodrama, breath work, and sensation: liberatory healing…and situating this book's entire premise in context, into the mandate from our prophetic tradition: the call to pursue justice for everyone, including, but not only, ourselves.

The Reader's Guide at the end (especially useful for groups) helps readers experientially explore these ideas, share stories, and practice healing processes.

My emphasis is on U.S. Jews; and everyone quoted is Jewish, unless otherwise indicated in endnotes. Also significant: my Ashkenazi lens will be obvious. I am inching my way towards inclusivity, towards an accurate reflection of Jewish multiculturalism, but this book is clearly constrained by its dominant Ashkenazi focus.

May these pages provoke conversation, disagreement, insight…and also activism. If you have reactions, if you are confused/worried/delighted/pissed off/inspired, then I've done my job. Summon your curiosity, and while you're at it, consider reflecting on your own Jewish (or gentile) life. I invite you on this journey; see what happens.

∽

In the chapters that follow, you'll meet nine extraordinary women. Amy, Deena, Elly, Emily, Geri, Jessie, Judith, Kim, and Rani (all pseudonyms) are the diverse and lively crew I recruited for my doctoral work on exploring, resisting, and healing from internalized Jewish oppression. Meeting together over ten months, we generated much of the thinking in these pages, using an action research strategy called Cooperative Inquiry: democratic and collaborative, valorizing emotion, full participation, and experiential mult-dimensional learning—definitely feminist-friendly.[9]

I drew us all in, but we kept ourselves together. Passionate about exploring our dissimilar Jewish stories, we were nearly desperate to make sense of our lives, to understand our struggles, to find ways to ease the turmoil. At our first meeting in Jessie's living room, her step-grandmother's ancestral menorah on the mantle was a beacon for us: smuggled from Berlin to China via Siberia while fleeing Hitler, then to the States. We shared and challenged, *kvetched* and *kvelled*,[10] testing out ideas with actions—laughing, contradicting, resonating, drawing out complexities, creating meaning. Sometimes crying, defending, withdrawing. What worked for Amy didn't necessarily work for Elly and Rani, but somehow we made room for every voice. As Emily concluded, "Even in the midst of the pain, we had our eye on healing."

Who are the soulful, unruly, complex, and savvy women who emerge here?

Amy, 34 (white Ashkenazi, family from Russia/Poland/Germany): Her Marxist college-professor father was driven out of Canada by anti-Semitism; her mother is German gentile. Amy feels "less assimilated than not," and says her father "stood out as a Jew." Raised lower middle class in an upstate New York university town, she was the only Jew in her school. A committed activist, Amy's alternative Jewish spirituality feeds her; she brings a playful creative spirit, and has men and women partners. With a master's in counseling, she works as a psychologist and substitute teacher.

Deena, 26 (Mizrahi/Ashkenazi, family from Iraq/India/Russia): Her father is Iraqi, via India; her mother's family is from Russia. Raised middle-class, she grew up in California, in the Valley. Moving to Los Angeles, she battled severe anti-Semitism at school, eventually finding refuge in a socialist Zionist youth group, which was staunchly secular and materialistic. Later, she found a niche in her campus *Hillel*. Deena's keen perspective and lightness of spirit combine with a deep pool of emotion; her partner is an African American Jewish man. Working in a multiracial nonprofit, her Judaism grounds her peace and social justice work.

Elly, 43 (white Ashkenazi, family from Russia/Lithuania): She grew up on Nazi Holocaust stories. Her grandmother knew former Israeli Prime Minister Golda Meir; her grandfather was a major player in Jewish education. Growing up working class on Chicago's South Side, she went to Hebrew school daily, and her "totally unassimilated" family kept strict kosher. An unapologetic, wise, and confident risk-taker, Elly feels ambivalent about her Jewishness. She is a social worker, married to a gentile African American woman.

Emily, 41 (white Ashkenazi, some Sephardic, family from Russia/Poland/Latvia/unknown): She has a seven-year-old daughter adopted with her white Catholic female partner. A working-class musician from New York City, she went to Hebrew school and was *bat mitzvahed*. In her late teens, when asked if she was Jewish, she replied "My parents are, but I'm not," yet admits she has "always felt Jewish from the get-go." An abuse survivor, she teaches therapeutic uses of music. Her spirit is earthy, energetic, spilling over with *l'chayim* (joy of living).

Geri, 46 (white Ashkenazi, family from Russia/Poland): She experienced "fierce anti-Semitism" in her mostly non-Jewish New York City suburb. After her *bat mitzvah*, her family moved to an upper-middle-class Jewish neighborhood. Her father was the only one of his siblings who "made it," which created class tension with Geri's cousins. Although her parents are very assimilated, Geri "always thought I was Other." A fundraiser for a health care corporation, she has a master's degree and brings a witty, hungry intellect. Her grandmother is her model of social justice activism. Geri's partner is a white Ashkenazi woman and they attend the lesbian/gay synagogue.

Jessie, 50 (white Ashkenazi, family from Russia/Poland/Germany/Finland): She is a working-class lesbian who grew up Reform in Sacramento. Her grandmother's people fled to the U.S. from pogroms, and, after the 1906 earthquake, they lived in a tent in Golden Gate Park. Her father died when she was a child; her stepfather had been imprisoned by the Nazis as a Berlin teenager but escaped to South Africa, while most of his family was killed in the gas chambers. Her great-uncle was a (gay) film director who discovered Greta Garbo. Jessie grew up "pretty assimilated but with a strong Jewish identity by the time I was five"; the upper-middle-class Jewish kids she went to Hebrew school with "were vicious" to her. Jessie did not go to college. She is a professional voice actress and battles Crohn's disease. Her honesty is disarming, her eloquence heartfelt.

Judith, 29 (white Ashkenazi, family from Germany): Her father's grandparents were the only Jewish family in their Kentucky town; her mother converted to Judaism. She grew up very assimilated and upper middle class ("I've always had everything I need") in Cincinnati, and was the first in her family to have a *bat* (or *bar*) *mitzvah* in one hundred years. She feels a "strong sense of Judaism," but questions the significance of internalized Jewish oppression: "Everybody has problems." An activist with a women's studies background, Judith has a master's in organizational development and is Executive Director of a Jewish Renewal synagogue. She brings openness, depth, vulnerability. Her first girlfriend was Palestinian, her current girlfriend is white, Catholic, Italian American.

Kim, 43 (white Ashkenazi, family from Hungary/Czechoslovakia): She was raised in a wealthy, materialistic, loving Jewish community in Denver, "very concerned about survival." She lost dozens of relatives in the *Shoah*. Her home was upper-middle-class, "hypocritical, Conservative, kosher." She grew up assimilated but went to Hebrew school and was *bat mitzvahed*. Kim admittedly wrestles with her "Jewish female identity," often playing astute devil's advocate. She is a corporate consultant with an activist mindset. Her partner is a white Jewish man, and she was a stepparent in her previous marriage.

Rani, 24 (Mizrahi/Ashkenazi, family from Iraq/Poland): Her Polish grandfather was in Auschwitz, and being the grandchild of survivors has been a "huge part" of her identity. Growing up Orthodox in Montreal, she would never use the term "assimilated" for her family. Although she was mostly raised with her mother's Ashkenazi family, Rani feels connected in her body to her father's Iraqi side and looks like them. Class issues were tough growing up, since after her parents' divorce she felt excluded by the affluent Jews around her. In her queer youth-culture community, Rani feels desirable as a Jew; her Otherness is seen as exotic but nonthreatening. Still, "nobody understands when I say *Bubbe* (grandmother) and *Zedde* (grandfather)." A social worker for people with disabilities, she brings a spirit both gutsy and out-of-the-box.

☙

Finally, my own journey is a work in progress. The point, I keep learning, is to face the complexities, not look the other way when a situation is confusing or painful or without clear answers. To nourish the positive spark, the soulful place, that is also our heritage. In activist Rabbi Abraham Joshua Heschel's words, "I did not ask for success; I asked for wonder."[11]

I don't make it to *shul* (synagogue) often, but one evening I was sponsoring the *kiddush*, the refreshments after *Shabbat*, in honor of my parents' (Dutch and Artie's) *yartzeits*, the anniversaries of their deaths. The words leapt out at me from the *siddur* (prayerbook): "And you shall love yourself, for you are a spark of the divine."[12] For me, the divine is *Shechina*, the feminine indwelling spirit, and also nature. To consider that these sparks shine through me, whether I acknowledge them or not…to just know that they are there.

Part of my wrestling: how to hold the suffering of so many in our world who are daily impoverished, ignored, brutalized — and to also hold the absolute validity of Jewish pain, whether directly from genocide or pogroms, or indirectly from self-disdain, *without exaggerating, without diminishing.* To bear both, while holding, too, the indomitable, irresistible life force, *l'chayim*, both Jewish and human.

Especially I question what it will take for us to transform self-blame and fear, to harness that energy for *tikkun olam*, to midwife a more compassionate, peace-filled, sustainable, and equitable world[13]…because uprooting internalized oppression can exponentially expand our sense of what is possible, profoundly empowering a practice of social justice. Bottom line: when I feel better about myself, I am more loving, thoughtful, and generous. I treat people better, my work is more positive; I make the world a tiny bit more just and kind.

♋

> dedicating these pages
> to those who resisted
> in whatever ways they did
> sneaking through holes in ghetto walls
> stealing food
> organizing
> leaping off trains
> burying what's precious
> encouraging others
> dynamite in their fingernails
> singing
> These are my people.

> —Penny Rosenwasser, Ph.D.
> Oakland, California, 2013

PART ONE

How Did Things Get So Hard?

1

Anti-Semitism 101

"There are times when I've heard someone say something anti-Semitic, and I felt my body go numb," Elly admitted. "I was terrified, unable to say anything—so I justified it to myself, 'It wasn't a big deal, it's not worth the effort.' Because I couldn't say, 'I'm overwhelmed and feel physically unable to respond.' That would be humiliating."

ANTI-JEWISH SLURS AND BEHAVIORS TODAY do not equal violent attacks, deportations, massive incarceration. Still they take a toll. Absorbing the toxicity feels awful, even though none of it is about who *we* really are. And once internalized, as feminist Sally Kempton put it, "It's hard to fight an enemy who has outposts in your head."[1]

Beneath the surface we might feel: afraid, discouraged, profoundly sad—all feelings passed through our families in response to ferocious anti-Semitic assaults over centuries. How to confront the harsh internal messages and heal the wounds? It helps to grasp what has happened to Jews, why we have the inner battles that we do. *"The most poignant evidence of anti-Jewish oppression,"* write professors Maurianne Adams and Katja Hahn D'errico, *"often lies in the personal pain and struggles that individual Jews experience in their daily lives"*[2]—so much of what this book is about.

How does anti-Semitism manifest? It differs over region, country, and decade, from swastikas on synagogues or school lockers to accusing Jews of "controlling the media"…from demeaning Jewish women to ignoring our holy days, all the way to (historical) genocide. It's insidious, sometimes complicated; it might not even look like it's there, when it's there.

The hard-core aspects, like racism in general, lie in seeing Jews as less than fully human. Here's what anti-Jewish prejudice looks like in the U.S. today:

- An eighth-grader in Orange County, California, is driven out of school when fellow students build an anti-Jewish hate-site against her online.
- An Arkansas Republican lawmaker refers to New York Senator Chuck Schumer as "that Jew." My San Francisco community college students confide how friends sneer that someone is "just like a Jew."
- A school district employee protesting at Occupy Los Angeles declares "The Zionist Jews who are running these big banks and our Federal Reserve…need to be run out of this country."[3]
- An eighty-eight-year-old, white Christian fanatic walks into the Holocaust Museum in tourist-packed Washington, D.C., and fires his shotgun, murdering the (African American, gentile) security guard who tried to open the door for him. A note in his car reads, "The Holocaust is a lie. Obama was created by Jews."[4]
- A Catholic employee in a women's studies department is stunned to learn that Jews did not kill Jesus.
- A high-profile Fox News commentator dramatically accuses Jewish philanthropist George Soros of orchestrating a coup to bring down the U.S. government, blaming him "for virtually every catastrophe of the past half-century."[5]
- Also: Philadelphia high-schoolers taunting a rival basketball team, "Warm up the ovens…We'll write you letters…in Auschwitz."[6] A CNN anchor implying that Jews run the media outlets.[7] Southern Baptist messianic churches (still) aggressively trying to convert Jews.[8] Stones thrown through the window of a school bus carrying Orthodox Jewish children, in Crown Heights, Brooklyn.[9] White supremacists in Florida arrested for planning to kill Jews, immigrants, people of color as part of a "race war."[10] In one month's time, three of my gentile friends casually referring to a "New York Jew." Or the isolation common to many marginalized groups: "On Passover, I sat…in the school cafeteria, carefully unwrapping my matzo and avoiding the stares."[11]

Although Austrian journalist Wilhelm Marr coined the term anti-Semitism in the 1870s to pointedly stigmatize Jews as racially inferior, "Semites" actually refers to Arabs as well. But for the purposes of this book, while anti-Arabism or racism describe the mistreatment of Arabs (or other people of color, where applicable), anti-Semitism—or anti-Jewish oppression or Jew-hatred—specifically refers to the denigrating, ignoring, exploiting, or violating of Jews, our cultures, our histories, and our religion: a systemic phenomenon of targeting us simply because we are Jews.

Jews are a multiracial, multiethnic people, and Jewish oppression has reflected that. We have been linked by religious rituals, languages, and shared history since the Hebrew tribes in Canaan thousands of years ago. After ancient Israel was destroyed by conquest, forcing most Jews into exile, some settled in countries that today are called (among others) Iraq, Yemen, or Iran, usually speaking Judeo-Arabic/Arabic or Judeo-Persian. These Jews, who never left the Middle East or North Africa, are *Mizrahim*. Other Jews, *Sephardim*, followed a diasporic path through the Iberian Peninsula, settling in Spain and Portugal; they were later expelled to Turkey, the Mediterranean, the Americas, and elsewhere, and they share the Ladino language. *Beita Yisrael* Jews lived in Ethiopia for centuries; and various other small but distinct Jewish ethnic groups prevail throughout Africa, in India, and beyond.

These pages focus on Ashkenazi Jews, whose exile led to Eastern and Central Europe, because anti-Semitism there laid the groundwork for most U.S. anti-Jewish hostility. The dominant culture of U.S. Jewry is Eurocentric, and Ashkenazim are roughly 80 percent of the thirteen to fifteen million (or more) Jews worldwide.[12] But while persecution has hounded Jews in most of the 120-plus countries where we now live—including Chile, Uganda, Finland—our histories differ widely.[13] We even lack one set of physical characteristics.[14] The Ashkenazi story is one of multiple Jewish narratives.

Our experiences are also interconnected. Life was precarious, from Europe to North Africa to the Middle East, where Jewish communities variously survived periods of comparative calm, interrupted by violence, destruction, loss, and/or forced exile or conversion. While especially "cruel under the Cross," Jewish life could be "harsh under the Crescent" as well.[15]

How anti-Semitism works
Stereotypes, scapegoats, Jews in middle roles

The origins of Ashkenazi anti-Jewish oppression are *theological* and *economic*; racial anti-Semitism came later. What makes the system work? Ruling elites created demonizing stereotypes of Jews, which then justified scapegoating us for any number of disasters, thereby absolving themselves of wrongdoing.[16] *The job of anti-Semitism is to set up Jewish buffers for the power elite, rendering the decision-makers invisible and so covering up the roots of injustice, while shifting responsibility to Jews.* So in many ways, anti-Semitism masks class power.

"CHRIST-KILLERS AND INFIDELS"

The first legendary stereotype, Jews as Christ-killers in league with secret "diabolical forces," marked the birth of theological Jew-hatred and kicked scapegoating into gear, arousing anti-Jewish resentment for millennia.[17] The Fourth Gospel of John made it official, charging Jews with "deicide." The only possibility of forgiveness? To accept Jesus.

When the Holy Roman Empire anointed Christianity as the state religion in the fourth century, Jews officially became (hated) outsiders, despite our having lived in Europe for over two thousand years. Visionary activist and intellectual Melanie Kaye/Kantrowitz names the marginalizing of anyone/thing not Christian as *Christianism*, another spin on Christian hegemony or dominance—a system of oppression advantaging those whom analyst and activist-author Paul Kivel calls "all Christians, all those raised Christian, and those passing as Christian."[18] This ideology is based on dualism: cosmic good versus evil.

"We must never forget," wrote Russian Tsar Alexander III, "that the Jews…crucified our Master and have shed his precious blood."[19] Enter the Christian Crusades, when mobs clutching crosses rampaged through thriving communities. Murdering tens of thousands of Jews on their way to attacking Muslims, they torched synagogues with Jews inside. Especially egged on through the centuries during Easter, writes Catholic ex-priest

James Carroll, crowds "poured out of churches in search of Jews to harass and kill."[20]

Once responsibility for crucifying Jesus had been diverted from the Romans, it became easy to fault Jews for succeeding tragedies. When Christian children died from uncertain causes, Jews were charged with sacrificing them to use their blood to make *matzoh* (unleavened bread). Such bizarre accusations birthed the blood libel/ritual murder myth.[21] Another far-fetched allegation: that Jews were responsible for the Bubonic Plague, which wiped out over one-third of Europe, including Jews.

Almost two centuries later, after founding Protestantism in reaction to Catholicism, theologian Martin Luther was enraged that "infidel" Jews refused to convert, fuming, "May we all be free of this insufferable burden, the Jews," and exhorting destruction of homes and synagogues.[22] The Second Vatican Council finally exonerated Jews for Jesus' death in 1965, but Pope John Paul II did not officially apologize until 2000. Yet the stereotype stuck: "the ultimate source of evil."

ECONOMIC SHOCK ABSORBERS

In a second trademark stereotype, European Christians targeted Jews as "too powerful," more powerful than we actually are. (See Chapter Three.) When the aristocracy needed our skills, they exploited Jews in middle roles, making them the public faces for actual decision-makers, so that Jews *looked* like the ones in control (often in some relationship to money). But we were simply the most visible, the first to be accused when catastrophe struck, conveniently available to absorb the brunt of mass outrage and violence.

Often denied access to land or to many trades, in the Middle Ages Jews turned to commerce, money lending (at interest), tax collecting, and eventually, banking: "odious" work that Christianity forbade its followers. These jobs situated Jews as a precapitalist middle class, leading to the stereotypes: misers, unscrupulous money lovers. Some Jews served the Polish, Russian, or French nobility doing such "dirty work"; others were court advisors. A clever strategy by the Christian elite: setting up Jews to rebel against when Christian peasants couldn't pay their taxes. Historian and poet Aurora Levins Morales dubs these buffer roles "shock absorbers"[23] for the real *responsables*.

The pattern unfolds: trading utility, sometimes sacrificing integrity, to secure communal protection. For Jews, becoming indispensable ensured security, at least for a while; and working with money became a survival tool, synonymous with safety.

∽

The compelling formula: once gentiles are convinced that Jews are satanic God-killers or exploitive power-mongers—conspiring towards "evil" ends—it's easy to hold us responsible when the economy nosedives or planes demolish the World Trade Center.[24] We also become guilty by deviating from Protestant behaviors. Jews are "different."

Meanwhile, who benefits? The top government and corporate echelon, majority Christian, that calls the shots and consolidates power and wealth. And who suffers? Everyone exploited by those decisions who could be joining together to create systems that benefit most people. As Levins Morales clarifies, "Stereotypes about rich, secretive, conspiring... Jews are used to persuade non-Jewish oppressed people that the cause of their oppression is Jewish greed...rather than an economic system that requires the majority to have too little so a minority can have too much."[25]

Cycles of persecution

Anti-Semitism is tricky because its brutality has been intermittent, running in cycles. In feudal times, Jews were conditionally invited to fill gaps in the labor force and offered protection in exchange. Decades of relative calm and acceptance followed, sometimes prosperity. But highly visible in middle roles, Jews were highly vulnerable. Periodically, after sudden crisis came attacks, often state-sanctioned rampages, *pogroms*. In 1348, nearly every Jewish community in Europe was assaulted: 200 were demolished.[26] In 17th century Poland alone, 100,000 Jews were massacred.[27]

Russian revolutionary Leon Trotsky described the 1905 pogroms:

A hundred of Russia's towns...were transformed into hells...The gang rushes through the town, drunk on vodka and the smell of blood...hounded by police and starvation, [the rioter] now feels himself an unlimited despot... he can throw an old woman out of a third-floor window...rape a little girl

while the entire crowd looks on, hammer a nail into a living human body...
He exterminates whole families, he pours petrol over a house, transforms it
into a mass of flames.[28]

Sephardic and Mizrahi oppression

Persecution also became forced conversion. During the Spanish
(Christian) Inquisition, Ferdinand and Isabella of Spain issued the
Edict of Expulsion in 1492, followed by an order of King Manuel I from
Portugal in 1497, condemning 200,000[29] Sephardic Jews to exile, while
pocketing their resources (funds which possibly funded Columbus'
voyage),[30] destroying a great Jewish civilization. Tens of thousands were
killed as they fled, thousands more tortured and burned at the stake after
pledging to convert — Conversos — but found (or assumed) to be secretly
practicing Judaism.[31]

Though forced to become Catholics, many Spanish and Portuguese
Jews did continue Jewish customs undercover. Over the generations, the
"secret" was often lost, and they grew up covertly lighting candles in the
cellar on Friday nights without knowing why. Today, conversos, or "crypto
[hidden] Jews," in the southwestern U.S. and Latin America have begun
telling the stories, finding community, reclaiming mixed heritage.

Jews living in Islamic lands, Mizrahim, were often treated as second-
class along with Christians, bearing the sub-status of *dhimmi*,[32] enduring conversion, clothing restrictions, bans on holding office, and taxes,
which also granted protection. Land was confiscated, property wrecked,
cultures devalued. On rare occasions, they were tortured, expelled, or
killed; in one example, in 1066 a mob in Granada massacred 4000 Jews.
But in Muslim lands overall, argues Iraqi international relations scholar
Avi Shlaim, the reality was complex. Being cast as second-class was the
rule, persecution the exception, alongside tolerance, multiculturalism,
and "creative coexistence."[33]

Still, in 1941, nearly 200 Baghdad Jews were murdered during the
holiday of *Shavuot*, in the *Farhud* pogrom. Recalling her mother's memories, therapist Rachel Wahba describes, "the screams, the screams...
When it was over my mother saw the Tigris River filled with pieces of
Jewish...lives."[34] After watching "mothers and daughters raped in front

of their families, babies pulled limb from limb," her mother fled Iraq.[35]

Also, during World War II, Libyan Jews were exterminated, and Algerian, Tunisian, and Moroccan Jews were deported to camps, even though Moroccan King Mohammed V managed to protect some. In the mid to late 1940s, anti-Jewish riots killed hundreds from Libya to Egypt, from Yemen to Iraq; and tens of thousands escaped Iran in the wake of the 1979 Islamic revolution.

Racially stigmatized bodies: a new(er) stereotype

Despite what St. Augustine preached, European Jews didn't have horns or tails. But in some ways we looked different from most Christians: our hair, noses, body shapes. Our skin color was sometimes dark, even swarthy, the legacy of our Middle Eastern origins—another reason, ostensibly, to see us as a people apart. Jews were Europe's "racialized Other."[36]

A portent of what would follow, the Spanish Inquisition deemed any converso who had one drop of Jewish blood to be impure, according to the *Limpieza de Sangre* (Christian blood purity standards). By the 1800s, *pseudo*-scientific racial determinism was sweeping through Europe, stamping Jews with a new stereotype: physically decadent, shifty bulging eyes, hooked noses, moist hands, and a "furtive nervous look."[37]

Anti-Semitism became racism, stigmatizing Jews not just as theologically guilty or economically exploitative, but as genetically inferior. Our bodies, supposedly scarred by God, reflected the sin within: "Being black, being Jewish, being diseased and being 'ugly.'"[38] This accusation conveniently justified the right-around-the-corner Nazi ideology, that Jews contaminate Aryan blood—an ideology that would wipe out well over one-third of the world's Jews,[39] two-thirds of all European Jews.[40]

The Shoah: persecution to genocide

November 9, 1938, *Kristallnacht* (Crystal Night—for the broken glass), the state-orchestrated riot in Germany and Austria that launched the most massive extermination in Jewish history: the Shoah, or Nazi Holocaust. For two days, gangs terrorized Jews, smashing windows, looting homes and businesses, burning synagogues, killing one hundred. The Nazis fined German Jews a billion marks to pay for the damage.[41]

∽

Krakow, September 2008 — a sparkling afternoon: I'm in Poland for the first time, for a workshop on healing from World War II. My friends and I arrived early to explore, to steep ourselves in context. With our young Polish (Christian) guide Eva, my group of four U.S. Jews — including the daughter of an Auschwitz survivor, and a rabbi whose great-grandparents were killed in Auschwitz-Birkenau — approaches the site where Jews were deported to the camps: the Umschlagplatz. A simple square of red bricks, the edge of the former ghetto, it lies just across the Vistula River, now surrounded by shops, flashing neon, honking horns.

This is a memorial to the 64,000 Jews who lived in Krakow before the war, Eva explains; 6000 survived. Now only 200 Jews are registered here. We draw closer, and I stop, stunned. Before me are sixty-four empty metal chairs, planted throughout the square–waiting for most of the 64,000 who never returned.

We learn about the Christian pharmacist whose office bordered the square. Persuading the Nazis to let him remain so that he (ostensibly) could treat typhus, he saved Jews by hiding them in his office.

What else stands out? The ghetto wall, partially constructed using Jewish tombstones: "You are living in a graveyard," the Nazis emphasized. "This is the end of the Jewish nation." (A nation which, Hitler proselytized, was conspiring to destroy Germany.) Yet we also hear about Poles who tossed food over the walls, to keep Jews from starving. In the Warsaw Ghetto, children escaped through holes in the walls and smuggled food back in — if they weren't discovered. There's a note about one guard who shot two young smugglers, then returned to eating his sandwich.

Now at the workshop, with me are seventy others: from Europe, including Russia and Latvia, as well as Israel, the U.S., and Australia. One-third of us are Jews. The Auschwitz-Birkenau Memorial staff say we are the only group that includes descendants of Shoah survivors and descendants of Nazis. Our guide Franz (another Polish Christian) tells us that over 200,000 children were murdered in the gas chambers, as soon as they arrived at Birkenau. "The Nazis working in the crematoria drank alcohol and used drugs to kill their conscience," he continues. "We call them monsters — but they were human and felt great shame. They had to numb that feeling."

On the trip, I am reading Daniel Mendelsohn's The Lost: A Search for Six of Six Million. *I learn that 1.5 million Jews were shot by mobile killing squads,* Einsatzkommandos: *in the forests of Ponar, the ditches of Babi Yar, the woods at Rumbula (throughout Russia, Poland, Ukraine). I read about mass graves in the Galicia forests, how, after hundreds were stripped and shot, "the earth continued to move for days...because not all of the victims were...dead when the grave was filled in."*[42]

I also read "The Germans and Ukrainians preyed especially on children. They took the children...and bashed their heads on...the sidewalks, whilst they laughed and tried to kill them with one blow."[43] *Yet I also learn from Mendelsohn that the up-close mass shootings of Jewish children, women, and the elderly in 1941 were traumatic for some soldiers. Deeply shaken, they had mental breakdowns. Mendelsohn says that this psychological effect on the young recruits was one factor leading to more impersonal modes of murder: gas chambers.*[44]

Later, in Warsaw, I meet Martin, a Polish Christian from Lublin, who tells me about the "Memory Stones," stolperstein, *in Berlin and Budapest: small brass stones, a name emblazoned on each—plus where they were born and where they were killed—placed in front of their homes.*

I also remember: somewhere between five and eleven million non-Jews were victims as well.[45] *And there have been other unimaginable genocides— Pol Pot's killing of two million Cambodians; Stalin's starvation of five to seven million Ukrainians; the Turks' slaughter of 1.5 million Armenians; also, the horrendous conditions of the Middle Passage. The U.S. ethnic cleansing of many millions of indigenous peoples.*

UNITED STATES ANTI-SEMITISM
The Christian myth planted in new soil

Although not what we're told in history class, the United States was founded on Euro-Christian values and norms, Protestantism being the nearly "universal creed."[46] Early settlers carried Christ-killing images from Europe, myths which seeped into the psyche of future generations.[47]

It's a potent concept still. According to 2011 U.S. polls, 31 percent still believed Jews killed God.[48] The United States remains predominantly

Christian, (77 percent, according to a 2012 Gallup poll), where *The Passion of the Christ* was a box office phenomenon—blaming Jews for the crucifixion, relying on the stereotypes: Jews as evil, über-powerful. Religious bigotry (including from Jews) slams Muslims as well, with attacks on mosques, Koran-burnings, street harassment, police surveillance, and hate-ads on subways (demonizing Muslims as "savages"[49]). When accusers falsely charged that President Obama is Muslim, their signs read: "This is a Christian country."

In fact, Christian values and institutions systematically dominate our lives, Paul Kivel points out, but often so invisibly that we see these as secular, not religious.[50] Still, the U.S. thankfully lacks a violent history of Jew hating, Euro style. Here, anti-Semitism shows up as stereotyping, racial stigmatizing, scapegoating...sometimes as indifference...and, occasionally, as assaulting or killing individual Jews.

Everything to do with race[51]

Even though Jews aren't a race, Kaye/Kantrowitz asserts, "We have been racially hated as if we were a race."[52] With religious anti-Jewishness, Jews get the chance to convert and save ourselves—but racial anti-Semitism sees us as inherently polluting. According to this mindset, the "real Americans" came from northwest Europe, Jews mongrelize white Christian purity.[53]

At the Nuremberg trials, for example, Nazi doctors "named American eugenicists [as] their ideological mentors;"[54] these eugenicists gave the Germans charts, photos, and data to support the "validity" of racist theories.[55] And although the G.I. Bill after World War II gave (white Ashkenazi) Jews institutional privilege, benefits usually denied to Negro veterans and women, white supremacists still condemn us as racially inferior. In 2009, when I was presenting at the White Privilege Conference in Memphis, a headline blasted across David Duke's website, describing our 1000-strong gathering: "Where Blacks, Jews, and other minorities gather to defame White people."

Stereotyping, U.S. style

In 1938, U.S. polls revealed that 60 percent saw Jews as greedy, dishonest, aggressive.[56] The Eurocentric meta-narrative still often views white Christian business leaders as thrifty and ambitious, with commercial smarts, while Jewish execs (also Korean and Arab) are seen as conniving and exploitative. Compared to white-middle-class-Protestant norms, Jews still look "different"—blameworthy.

The bottom line, once again? Stereotypes justify scapegoating, a sometime road to violence. The solution? To deconstruct the mythologies of Jews as power-mongers, God-killers, and racial misfits, instead focusing on the elite class behind noxious policies.

Jewish women

"Gentiles blame Jews, and Jews blame Jewish women."[57]
—*Riv-Ellen Prell*

Stereotypes about Jews running the banks, media, and movies are complicated, and Chapter Three explores those in depth. Less discussed is the antipathy and misogyny by Christians and Jews towards Jewish women. For Jewish men, this means deflecting anti-Semitism, plus projecting their self-hatred, onto Jewish women.

Nearly a century ago, young working-class Yiddish-speaking women of the 1920s were branded "Ghetto Girls" by newly middle-class Jews.[58] Vilified as vulgar, flamboyant, garish, these "girls" held down factory jobs and supported families, often struggling through night school.

After World War II, second-generation Jewish men (comedians and more) began ridiculing the "Jewish Mother," mocking the very nurturance that had helped them succeed.[59] Criticized for making "giving a poisoned act,"[60] she was denounced as suffocating and manipulative, also for her insatiable needs (read: strong, passionate, direct about what she wanted). "No one laughed at Jewish father jokes in the 1950s and 1960s because there were none," feminist anthropologist Riv-Ellen Prell noticed; instead, Dad was a "passive foil to the monster wife."[61] Jewish (and black) families were called "dysfunctional" in contrast again to the white Protestant middle-class ideal—stoic male patriarch, subservient wife. Feminist scholar Evelyn Torton Beck reminds us that all mothers worried about their children, only Jewish mothers were ridiculed for it.[62]

Add up anti-Semitism, misogyny, and mother-bashing and the Jewish Mother became a lightning rod for Jewish self-contempt. The feisty women who led kosher meat boycotts, rent strikes, and garment workers' protests were swept from memory.

Enter the 1970s and the crowning of the Jewish American Princess, the "J.A.P.": anti-Semitic when demeaned by Christians, sexist or self-hating from Jews. Despised as materialistic, loud, needy, the J.A.P. has been called withholding and repulsive; birthed during Second Wave feminism, she won't s**k up to men. Anti-J.A.P. slurs sometimes led to other slogans, "Give Hitler a second chance!"[63] At George Washington University, a newspaper editor wrote: "If you think your black Steve Madden flip-flops and Kate Spade purse give you that big-city money look all the guys drool over, you might be a JAP. If you whine in a painstakingly high pitch, that your daddy doesn't love you because he limited your credit card purchases to $500 this month, you might be a JAP."[64]

Her Third Wave West Coast counterpart, the "Valley Girl," has likewise been condemned as crass, money-grubbing.[65] In California, Urban Outfitters created the "Everybody Loves a Jewish Girl" T-shirt, sporting dollar signs and shopping symbols. Shirts flew off the shelves. When Jewish groups protested, the designer reluctantly removed the dollar signs.

These images have real-world consequences. Steven Steinberg stabbed his wife Elana to death (26 wounds) and pleaded "temporary insanity," since his wife's J.A.P. demands drove him "crazy."[66] When he was acquitted, jurors hugged him; apparently she deserved what she got. Kaye/Kantrowitz sums up the stereotype: "A sexist scapegoating of Jewish middle-class women for the crimes of capitalism."[67]

Jewish women fought back, and finally the Jewish establishment condemned the grotesque targeting.[68] Still, the stereotype lives on. *Heeb* magazine sardonically implored women to "liberate" their "inner JAP": to "straighten their hair, cut calories, and construct themselves as capitalist subjects."[69] The saucy models on display were glamorous and multiracial, portraying the J.A.P. as desirable just as she is mocked. Anti-Jewish, anti-woman images overall are still considered humorous, unobjectionable, charges Rachel Siegel. But Jewish men would be "up in arms" if ridiculed that way.[70]

Scapegoating: Jews' hidden vulnerability

Christian leaders sometimes continue to set up Jews (among others) as the source of troubles, attributing more power than we have. And the more visible we are, the more vulnerable to attack, whether as public officials, teachers, landlords, social workers, union organizers, administrators, community leaders—all middle managers—often taking the heat for the inaccessible school superintendent, corporate landowner, policy-setter. This "hidden vulnerability" in the middle- agent role, explains *Tikkun* editor and activist Rabbi Michael Lerner, is a key aspect of anti-Semitism.[71] "Visibly oppressed groups" are taught to see Jews rather than the Fortune 500 companies as impeding their progress.[72]

> With some exceptions, we're mostly not the corporate chiefs, we're the smaller business owners, the people that African-Americans have to pay rent to or get credit from. And that's where the anger is aimed. The Capital "E" Enemy is too large: the small "e" enemy is in your face every day. (Elly)

The past teems with examples. Judah Benjamin, a former U.S. senator and right-hand man to Confederacy President Jefferson Davis, studied at Yale, married a Catholic, even (problematically) owned slaves. Yet, as the war worsened, "many confederates attributed military losses" to Benjamin being Jewish.[73] And who was to blame for wartime military scandals and inflated prices? General Grant expelled the Jews from part of Tennessee (although President Lincoln cancelled the order), because among all those who traded with the enemy, Jews were the "most physically visible...their... accents and surnames invited special attention."[74] Scapegoating intensifies when strife is greatest.

In the early 1920s, Henry Ford's paper *The Dearborn Independent* published "The International Jew: The World's Problem," reproducing the core of the fraudulent *Protocols of the Elders of Zion*. The *Protocols*, a forged manifesto, were penned as imaginary proceedings of Jewish leaders plotting to control the world. Originally written by the tsar's police to discredit Jewish leaders of Russia's revolutionary movement, the *Protocols* were/are the conspiracy myth updated. For ninety-one weeks, Ford accused Jews of hijacking banks and media, and predicted a Jewish takeover of the country—massively increasing the paper's sales.

By 1933-1939, the United States was exploding with anti-Jewishness "more virulent and...vicious"[75] than before or since—the "High Tide"[76] of U.S. anti-Semitism—fed by the sagging economy. President Roosevelt's reforms were attacked as the "Jew Deal."[77] Michigan charismatic demagogue Father Charles Coughlin (who idolized Hitler) led the charge, blaming Jews as both capitalist bankers and Communists. Coughlin's forty-million-plus followers were mostly religious, poor, working class. In January 1940, the FBI shut down his Christian Front upon discovering the group arming itself, "planning to murder Jews, Communists, and a dozen Congressmen."[78]

But Jew-blaming was not limited to Coughlin and company. Even after the *L.A. Examiner* carried the 1938 headline "Nazis warn world [that] Jews will be wiped out unless evacuated by Democracies,"[79] nearly half of Americans polled that year blamed Jews for Hitler's policies.[80] Feminist author and activist Marge Piercy learned the A-word (anti-Semitism) early, growing up in 1940s Detroit. Beaten regularly at school, "I was a Jew, and thus an outsider. My mother was always saying *Don't tell anyone.* She was terrified that the Nazis would appear and carry us away to a concentration camp."[81]

In response to Hitler's slaughter, many terrified Jews sought a Jewish homeland (Zionism) and European survivors fled to Palestine. (Who else would let them in?) But when Jews founded Israel as a Jewish state in 1948, they drove hundreds of thousands of indigenous Palestinians from their homes, creating the Palestinian *Nakba* (catastrophe).[82] So *European anti-Semitism is one root cause of the Israel-Palestine tragedy.* Even though Great Britain, France, and the United States were also culpable, and Christian Zionists originated the Jewish-homeland-in-Palestine idea three centuries earlier,[83] Israel and Jews are usually held exclusively responsible.

And dragging up the "Jewish foreign agent" stereotype? During the 1950s "Red Scare," the House Un-American Activities Committee (HUAC), and Senator Joseph McCarthy, ruthlessly blacklisted Communists and leftists, ruining lives. Most visibly targeted among artists, actors, writers, and activists were Jews.[84]

Battered by centuries of blame and past persecution, Jews keep searching for security, sometimes desperately. In middle-agent roles we may compromise fairness, opting for what feels like safety; sometimes we *are* responsible for the wrongs we are accused of. Yet continuing the "dirty work" of our ancestors, we are also often installed in public positions to take the heat for policies made by (Christian) leaders who wield the most power. And just as white Jews are accused of capitalism's crimes, "young disenfranchised men of color" are blamed for "capitalism's fallout," when they are unable to find jobs or support families.[85] Kaye/Kantrowitz asks, "Do I need to point out who escapes all blame?"[86] "The problem is not relative Jewish success," she concludes. "The problem is a severe class system that distributes success so unequally."[87]

Keeping Jews out

In colonial times, Jews were often not allowed to vote or hold office, an experience shared by the Irish and Chinese in the 1800s. Then during the late 1800s, when 2.3 million Jews from Eastern Europe and Russia poured in, more visibility led to more bigotry. "One of the first immigrant groups to encroach on Brahmin terrain," Jews were undesirables, driving out "the old order...of inherited social distinction."[88] The white Christian elite scrambled to erect barriers, to keep Jews from infiltrating their prestigious schools, professions, neighborhoods ("No Jews or dogs allowed"). In the Chicago want ads, "'Gentile-only' was as common as 'whites only.'"[89] Columbia University denied aid if your name sounded Jewish, awarding scholarships only if your parents were born in the U.S, bending rules "to fill slots with under-qualified Christian students."[90]

By 1924, xenophobia led to U.S. immigration quotas severely restricting Jews and other Southern/Eastern Europeans (and completely barring Asians), while large groups from Ireland, Great Britain, and Germany were welcomed; the Chinese had been slammed with exclusionary bans since 1882. A congressional report called Jews "filthy, un-American."[91] Generally, Jews were targeted as radicals; many anarchists were deported.

The late African American history professor John Hope Franklin even said that anti-Semitism at Harvard in 1935 was worse than the racism.[92] In my own life, when my mother graduated from a small southern women's college in 1940 near the top of her class, she couldn't land a teaching job. Exasperated, she hid behind a door after a job interview, and confirmed her suspicions: no one wanted to hire a Jew. Finally, she was hired—on condition that she sponsor the Baptist youth group.

In 1939—as Jews in Germany were banished from schools, prohibited from practicing law, medicine, or commerce—66 percent of the U.S. population still opposed allowing 10,000 Jewish refugee children to immigrate.[93] By 1941, only a small number of European Jews had been allowed to squeeze through.

We'll never know the full cost of immigration quotas, the Jewish lives that could have been saved. U.S. complicity is glaring in failing to rescue Jews by adhering to rigid immigration restrictions.[94] Several Congress members fought the limitations, but most opposed easing quotas, and President Roosevelt (though next-to-God for Jews like my parents) was consumed with addressing unemployment and bank failures—and didn't want to alienate isolationist (and anti-Semitic) popular opinion.[95]

Another factor: U.S corporations, from Ford and General Motors (GM) to IBM, were raking in money from German partnerships and were loath to jeopardize profits by offending Hitler. Hitler and Henry Ford shared mutual admiration; the dictator hung Ford's photo on his wall and awarded him a prestigious medal, while Ford's subsidiary in Cologne exploited slave labor at Buchenwald camp to make armored Nazi vehicles.[96] U.S. G.I.s invading Europe would have been shocked to learn that their enemy was flying planes built by Opel, driving trucks made by Ford.[97]

GM exec James Mooney also earned a trophy for "service to the Reich." Hitler "would never have considered invading Poland," said Nazi arms chief Albert Speer, without GM's synthetic fuel technology.[98] U.S. automakers were indispensable, collaborating with Nazis to reap mega profits "at the expense of everything else."[99]

As IBM's alphabetizing machines helped organize the deporting of Polish Jews, their New York corporate headquarters directed the Dutch subsidiary in liquidating Holland's Jews. IBM punch cards coded concentration camp prisoners (such as "death by gas chamber").[100] This equipment was vital to the

Reich, and IBM President Thomas Watson "received a one-percent commission on all Nazi business profits...It was never about the antisemitisim...It was always about the money."[101]

According to Holocaust historian Michael Berenbaum, by August 1942 the U.S. knew of Hitler's Final Solution to exterminate Jews.[102] Even then Congress refused to swing open America's doors. The State Department tried to keep news of Hitler's plan from reaching Jewry leadership and signaled its consulates in neutral countries that it was "uninterested in information concerning the Jews."[103]

In 1943, Polish resistance fighter/secret courier Jan Karski, a Roman Catholic, raced to the U.S. to report the mass murder he had witnessed in camps and ghettos, desperately hoping to persuade government leaders to rescue Jews. Meeting with President Roosevelt, Supreme Court Justice Felix Frankfurter, and other leaders (and prominent Jews), Karski found Frankfurter "unable to believe" him and Roosevelt "noncommittal."[104] Apparently, he learned, nothing could interfere with the war strategy of defeating the Nazis as soon as possible (and thus saving the Jews).[105] Still, Karski publicized what he had seen, through hundreds of lectures, meetings, and publishing a Book-of-the-Month (in 2012 President Barack Obama posthumously awarded Karski a Presidential Medal of Freedom for his courage). Marge Piercy writes, "Mother told me about what was happening to the Jews in Europe—it is foolish to imagine people did not know. It was all over the Yiddish papers."[106]

Then in 1944, Treasury Secretary Henry Morgenthau received a memo on "the Acquiescence of This Government in the Murder of the Jews," via a government lawyer whose investigation unlocked a State Department cover-up of the Final Solution.[107] Influenced by pressure from Morgenthau, along with Karski's report and political repercussions if the facts got out,[108] Roosevelt finally set up a War Refugee Board, which saved about 200,000 Jews—partially through the heroism of Swedish diplomat Raoul Wallenberg, who personally rescued 20,000 and averted the massacre of 70,000 in the Budapest ghetto. But even by 1945, when the horrific conditions facing displaced Europeans were discovered, only 5 percent of those polled in the U.S. supported loosening immigration bans.[109] From Jewish *Forward* editor and author J. J. Goldberg: "Opposition to helping Jews was not merely widespread, it was *intense.*"[110]

Some Jews refer to U.S. complicity as the most recent abandonment in a continual historical trajectory; other historians chalk it up to "extensive bureaucratic indifference."[111] Not to mention some U.S. officials who sheltered Nazis postwar—information the Justice Department tried to hide.[112]

Why didn't the U.S. bomb railway lines to Auschwitz? The War Refugee Board and Jewish organizations pleaded with Roosevelt, while rumors flew about State Department anti-Semitism.[113] The War Department continued to insist such bombing would divert the military from "more important military targets"; yet the air force dropped a thousand bombs on a factory only five miles from the rail lines.[114] Then it said bombing Auschwitz might provoke a vindictive response. But how much more vindictive could the Nazis be?

Violence

Rule #1: Physical assaults usually focus on those most visible: those wearing religious clothing, for example, or people in Jewish places, like President of Marietta, Georgia's *B'nai B'rith* chapter and pencil factory owner Leo Frank—the only known U.S. victim of anti-Jewish lynching. Set up by false testimony, in 1913 Frank was convicted of raping and murdering (white Christian) thirteen-year-old worker Mary Phagan. Historian Leonard Dinnerstein speculates that the verdict stemmed from "resentment of educated Northern industrialists [Frank]...perceived to be wielding *too much power* in the South, threatening southern culture and morality."[115] (Italics added) After his death sentence was commuted to life imprisonment, the enraged community kidnapped Frank from jail and killed him, reinvigorating the Ku Klux Klan.

Three thousand terrified Jews fled Georgia, but the atrocity also spurred Jews to found the watchdog Anti-Defamation League. Reports from deathbed confessions later exposed the illustrious townfolk behind the lynching, self-named "The Knights of Mary Phagan": a judge, a financier, a sheriff, a mayor.[116] Not a hotheaded crime of passion, the attack was "coldly calculated...with military attention to detail."[117]

Forty years later, the United States executed two young Jewish Communists, Ethel and Julius Rosenberg: victims of Cold War hysteria, a government frame-up, and anti-Semitism.[118] Based on fabricated evidence and perjured testimony, they were convicted of conspiring to transmit classified atomic secrets to the Russians, secrets later found to be of dubious significance.[119] Their fate warned U.S. Jews, don't step out of line. Then a decade later, another horror (one of many in the civil rights struggle): three young civil rights workers were murdered in Mississippi in 1964 for registering black voters. Michael Schwerner and Andrew Goodman were white Jews, James Chaney an African American gentile.

Lefty bias

"Smash the Jewish state, smash the Jewish race" read a sign at a San Francisco antiwar rally. Referring to another anti-Semitic sign, Kaye/Kantrowitz asks:

> Do I groan when I see it, and hope we can keep it from the television cameras? Yes.
> Do I feel threatened or attacked? No.
> Do I understand if some other Jew feels threatened or attacked? Yes.
> Is it my job to police the signs? No.
> Is it my job to talk with the freaked-out Jew? Probably.
> Is it true that the Israeli government is committing hideous crimes? Yes.
> Is it true that Israel is targeted disproportionately? Yes.
> Is it true that Israel is paid disproportionately? Yes.[120]

Let's be clear: bigotry against Jews is far worse on the Right than the Left. And anti-Semitic ideas do not necessarily equate with real ill will against Jews. But progressives need to understand how anti-Semitism functions, so that it stops dividing us, because the bias, whether intended or unconscious, can feel painful, unnerving, debilitating. On the Left, anti-Jewish antipathy or ignorance shows itself as characterizing Jews only as oppressors, devaluing Jewish identity, discounting anti-Semitism as unimportant, holding the Jewish people responsible for U.S. Middle East (or other) policy. Equating Israel with all Jewish people. And also, castigating Israel for human-rights violations against Palestinians while ignoring other abusers or occupiers—the United States bombing Afghani and Pakistani civilians, India occupying Kashmir, Morocco occupying Western Sahara, China occupying Tibet—since no state is above conforming to human-rights standards.

Yet the United States sends the most aid to Israel by far, so it makes sense to question how those funds are spent. In *Reframing Anti-Semitism: Alternative Jewish Perspectives*, coeditor Henri Picciotto explains: "When the Israeli military kills children, demolishes houses, uproots olive trees, steals water, bombs apartment buildings, commits assassinations, impos-es...curfews, and humiliates an entire people, it is inevitable someone will speak out against it, and not only in the ways that we would."[121]

Meanwhile, we also see at peace demonstrations: equating the Star of David with the swastika. (Sometimes Jews themselves hold the upset-ting signs.) Atrocities by Nazis, and by the Israeli Defense Forces (IDF) and extremist settlers, were and are all horrific. But comparisons are inaccurate and not useful; there is no comparison between the IDF and mass genocide. Despite heartbreaking similarities in some of the brutality and policies,[122] the Nazis implemented a systematic ideological state deci-sion to exterminate every Jew. What the IDF, Israeli state, and settlers are doing deserves severe condemnation and resistance—but does not reflect a state plan to murder every Palestinian.

Let's pay attention, in Aurora Levins Morales' words, when: "Criticism of Israel does take on a special tone of hatred and contempt that draws on the same poisoned well as attacking Jewish slumlords as Jews, or singling out the Jewishness of one group of developers...while never mentioning the religion of the many Christian developers. Israel is a colonial country with a strong right wing nationalist ideology that does what such regimes do, and it's not any better or worse than other colonial regimes with right wing nationalist ideologies."[123]

The pervasiveness of some lefty bias can be unsettling. Award-winning investigative journalist/activist Naomi Klein writes that every time she logs on to certain (leftist) news sites, "I'm confronted with a string of Jew-ish conspiracy theories about 9/11 and excerpts from *The Protocols of the Elders of Zion*."[124] When progressives blame "the Jewish people" for

U.S Middle East policy—rather than taking on "the American government, the Christian Right, and the arms industry,"[125] along with the Israel Lobby—these accusations sometimes persuade well-intentioned but less-informed peace activists. And when no one condemns the scapegoating and the signs, it can drive Jews away and deplete the movement.

Then there's good old stereotyping, even by progressives, even in the women's movement. Consultant Evie Litwok explained years ago, "I'm perceived as intimidating and overbearing, in other words, *Jewish*...Well, my style is a result of my being the child of [Nazi Holocaust] survivors...I was brought up to take risks. That style is a threat to some women."[126] Same deal with feminist publisher Gloria Greenfield; when negotiating contracts, she was accused "of being a 'cheap Jew,'" even of "Jewing someone down."[127]

Also, some leftists expect prejudice towards Jews to look like racism against people of color, notes public school teacher Terry Fletcher. The gauge of anti-Jewish bias is not how poor Jews are, she points out, "but how confused society is about who really holds the power and... resources."[128] Some groups don't see whose foot is really on their necks, because anti-Semitism has convinced them "the Jews" are blocking their progress.

So when Jews bring up discrimination, or seek inclusion in multicultural studies programs or anthologies, we are sometimes accused of competing for "victim status," of "draining the movement." Gen-X activist writer April Rosenblum bemoans "the eye-rolls, insults or changes of subject when someone raises anti-Semitism...the refusals to include anti-Semitism on the list of oppressions a coalition stands against."[129] Or maybe: "We'll get it on the agenda *next* time." The resistance (also from other Jews) is to hearing the pain and invisibility that Jews may feel. It's easier to be a Jew on the Left, Rosenblum adds, "if you don't feel *so* Jewish."[130]

Gen-Y spoken-word artist Dyanna Loeb writes (excerpt):

> "when I say anti-semitism its
> quizzical eyes accusing me of lying
> insisting it doesn't exist

there is no space for me to claim it
on the rare occasions
I open my mouth and let genocide slip out
folks act like im complaining
exaggerating...”[131]

Recent times: the U.S....

Glancing back, anti-Semitism began diminishing after World War II ended, correlating with a booming postwar economy, and perhaps empathy with Jewish suffering. By the 1950s, restrictions and socio-economic barriers were falling, Jewish professionals were multiplying, doors to elite neighborhoods and social groups were easing open: white Jews were accruing white privilege (see Chapter Two). Shame about the Nazi Holocaust even led to fierce attacks against institutionalized bias targeting Jews, and anti-Semitism slipped beneath the surface. In 2004, an Office To Monitor and Combat Anti-Semitism was created in the State Department; and *in 2012 the Anti-Defamation League (ADL) concluded that only 15 percent of Americans, or roughly 35 million, held extremely anti-Semitic views,* a fairly consistent level for the previous decade.[132]

Notwithstanding: Fox pundit Glenn Beck’s vicious accusations against George Soros; the U.S. Holocaust Museum attack; a woman shot to death and three injured critically at Seattle’s Jewish Federation in 2006 (the shooter yelled, “I am a Muslim American angry at Israel!”); men caught trying to blow up the Bronx’s Riverdale Temple in 2009, and the Gospels read every Easter, still casting Jews as God-killers. “The vast majority [of Christian worshippers]...believe they are hearing a report of what actually happened.”[133] Plus, there’s ongoing vandalism of synagogues, campus *sukkahs*,[134] cemeteries and Holocaust memorials, also bullying at schools. And from some folks, just a “queasy feeling about Jews.”[135] Anti-Jewish attitudes and actions often amp up when the stress barometer peaks.

As shock absorbers for the power elite, Jews remain vulnerable as “visible and apparently responsible for policies we didn’t make, but sometimes represent,” to those who “encounter Jews with a little better economic situation as shopkeepers, teachers, social workers, or land-lords, but [who] don't directly encounter white Christian ruling and managerial class people."[136]

Still, anti-Jewish slurs are less tolerated than ever[137]—and there is no widely accepted U.S. political philosophy, or institutional power, that promotes anti-Jewish bigotry.[138] In modern times, says history professor David Biale, no other Diaspora community has encountered less prejudice.[139] U.S. anti-Semitism today does "not represent anything like the...obstacles and threats...that many disenfranchised and oppressed people face."[140]

...and beyond

Outside the U.S. though, blatant hostility simmers: in Europe, from violence against individuals to defacing sacred sites, sometimes spray-painting "Juden Raus" (Jews out). A 2008 Pew study reported that a "generally unfavourable view of Jews" was held by nearly half of Spaniards and by roughly one-third of Russians and Poles, along with one-quarter of Germans and one-fifth of the French.[141] (In all but Russia, anti-Muslim attitudes were even stronger.) In France, Spain, and Germany this broke down as 34 percent of conservatives and 28 percent of the Left.[142] Blatantly racist and anti-Semitic ultranationalist parties gained significantly in parliamentary elections, on the Euro Right in 2009, and continue to grow (correlating with more attacks on immigrants), while a 2012 ADL survey found increased anti-Jewish attitudes in Spain (53 percent) and Poland (48 percent), with high levels in Hungary (63 percent) as well.[143]

U.K. sociologist Frank Furedi speculated that in Europe, "the rise of overt anti-Semitism amongst some Muslim youth" gave "permission to others to express more traditional forms."[144] What most concerned Furedi is this new "culture of accommodation to anti-Semitism" by the Euro Left.[145] French Jewish establishment leader Roger Cukleman agreed: French anti-Semitism is no longer the extreme right's sole domain. Instead it is "something for those who feel excluded from society and...are looking for a scapegoat," often having to do with religion, race, and the old accusation of "Jews, power, and money."[146] Dyanna Loeb writes (excerpt):

"arsonists in Greece hurl bars of soap
leave sud streaks on singed synagogue walls
to remind us
that Nazis melted our remains into soap
and neo-Nazis still desecrate Jewish cemeteries
scrawling
      jews   get   out!
shattering our tombstones...
even in graves we take up
too
   much
      space..."[147]

And anti-Jewishness thrives in some segments of the Islamic world, often closely linked to rage at Israeli state policies. Iranian President Mahmoud Ahmadinejad organized a Nazi Holocaust denier's conference, while the Hamas covenant (Hamas, a nationalist and Islamist extremist movement, also the democratically elected Palestinian government of Gaza) condemns so-called Jewish control of world finances and media. The leader of Hezbollah, a major Lebanese nationalist political force, has also spouted anti-Semitism,[148] and caricatures of Jews are not uncommon in Arab press cartoons. In a 2008 terrorist attack in Mumbai, India, Pakistani Muslims targeted a Jewish center, murdering a rabbi and his pregnant wife (also killing 164 tourists in various locations). And extremist groups in many Arab countries distribute *The Protocols of the Elders of Zion*.

When anger at Israeli policies targets Jews

Like it or not, Israeli government abuses continually trigger underlying anti-Jewish animosity, anger that fails to distinguish between the acts of governments and the humanity of peoples: a pattern replicated since Israel declared statehood in 1948 and drove out most Palestinians, and again in 1967 when Israel began occupying the West Bank, Gaza, and East Jerusalem.

For example, anti-Semitic events escalated worldwide after Israel bombed Gazans for three weeks, starting in late December 2008, leaving nearly 1400 Palestinians dead, over half noncombatants.[149] Outrage at the deadly onslaught spewed onto Jewish communities. Vandals spray-painted the San Francisco Holocaust Memorial— "Israel, their blood is on your hands"[150]—while a slogan appeared in the Netherlands, "Hamas, Hamas, all Jews to the gas."[151] Yet prominent British Muslims signed a public letter condemning the Gaza-related attacks on Jews, arguing that their Jewish neighbors were not responsible for Israel's actions.[152]

After Venezuela expelled Israeli diplomats, in protest of the Gaza assault, vandals desecrated my friend Sydney's childhood synagogue in Caracas. They defaced sacred Torah scrolls, scrawling "Death to Cursed Israel" and "Jews get out." I e-mailed the Consulado General, asking President Chavez to condemn the anti-Semitism (he did) and urging that protest confront the Israeli and U.S. governments, not the Jewish people.[153]

And in 2012, a radical Islamist Algerian-French gunman murdered Rabbi Jonathan Sandler and his two young sons, also a young girl, at a Jewish school in Toulouse, France—after earlier killing soldiers of North African (Muslim) and Caribbean descent—to avenge the deaths of Palestinian children, and to protest French army actions in Afghanistan. Thousands marched in memory of the victims.[154]

An obvious strategy for diminishing anti-Jewish actions? Ending Israeli repression of Palestinians. But even before the Gaza attack, Furedi noticed from the Euro Left the "leap from criticizing Israel to targeting Jews"—a leap accompanied by "a slightly embarrassed 'see nothing, hear nothing' attitude," simply switching off "when it comes to confronting anti-Jewish comments."[155]

The "new anti-Semitism": muzzling debate, discrediting the message

It's also true that when Israel increases brutality against Palestinians, just as anti-Jewishness flares, international criticism of Israeli policies (not of Jews per se) amps up. The two dynamics are interrelated, sometimes blurry, but different. "Many countries deliberately single out Israel," Jewish Voice for Peace Deputy Director Cecilie Surasky points out, "while ignoring their own terrible human-rights records."[156]

That said, what has been called "new anti-Semitism" is actually, erroneously, *conflating any criticism of Israeli policies with anti-Jewish bigotry*—including branding critiques by Jews as "self-hating," all attempts to attack the messenger and discredit the message. Some Jewish establishment leaders stigmatize voices they see as airing "dirty laundry" partly because they fear public dialogue will increase anti-Jewishness. And it's true that bona fide bigots use solidarity with Palestinians to mask contempt of Jews. But attempts to crush debate only inflame animosity, from anti-Semites as well as from sincere peace advocates. Many dissenters against Israeli policies care deeply about Jews.

Manipulating the anti-Semitism slur to stifle dissent also serves other agendas: supporting U.S. strategic goals and arms sales, and Jewish organization-building. (See Chapter Ten.) We need to take back the fight against legitimate anti-Semitism, because if the accusation is abused, how do well-meaning allies know when it's the real thing?

The *Muzzlewatch* blog has documented attempts to silence debate on U.S.-Israeli policy by using the anti-Semitism charge. One prominent example (among far too many): in 2007, Jewish leaders in Minneapolis persuaded the University of St. Thomas to disinvite Nobel Peace Prize-winner Archbishop Desmond Tutu from speaking, erroneously accusing him of comparing Israeli atrocities to the Nazis.[157] After activists campaigned to clear Tutu's name, the university re-invited him. Two years later, when the ADL again tried the demonizing, both Michigan State and the University of North Carolina insisted "Tutu is our man."[158] "It is not with rancor that we criticize the Israeli government," explained Tutu in 2010, "but with hope…that a better future can be made for… Israelis and Palestinians…in which both the violence of the occupier and the resulting violent resistance of the occupied come to an end, and where one people need not rule over another, engendering suffering, humiliation, and retaliation."[159]

And in a troubling legislative example: In 2012, the California Assembly passed (nonbinding) H.R. 35, "ostensibly aimed at protecting Jewish students from experiencing anti-Semitism on campus," while in actuality conflating "principled criticism of Israeli policy with anti-Semitism, raising concerns about free speech rights and academic freedom"—a motion strongly condemned by the University of California Student Association, representing students at ten U.C. campuses.[160]

Attacking Judge Goldstone and the U.N. report

Israeli *Haaretz* journalist Gideon Levy refers to "the anti-Semitism weapon"[161] used to try to discredit the Goldstone Report, the meticulous study by the United Nations Fact Finding Mission on the Gaza Conflict, headed by highly reputed (Zionist) international jurist Richard Goldstone. Although focusing on "Israel's excessive and indiscriminate uses of force" against civilians, the watershed report concludes that "both Israel and Hamas seem responsible for...war crimes, if not crimes against humanity."[162] It mandates either to conduct independent investigations or else to face the International Criminal Court. Backing key points of the study have been human-rights groups like Amnesty International and the Israeli *B'Tselem*,[163] plus the European Parliament, the U.N. General Assembly, and various rabbis.[164] In 2010, an Israeli Defense Forces report confirmed key findings of the Goldstone study, including the use of white phosphorous on civilians.[165]

But the U.S. Rabbinical Assembly of the Conservative movement, Nobel Peace Prize-winner Elie Wiesel,[166] professor Alan Dershowitz,[167] and other Israel Lobby bedfellows blasted the entire report (and often Goldstone) as anti-Semitic and anti-Israel, saying the study blames Israel "disproportionately": in effect attacking the messenger while dismissing the message. A member of *B'nai Brith*'s legal counsel compared the report to "anti-Semitism by gangs in the street."[168]

Joining the charge, Obama's administration called the study "flawed"[169] and lobbied furiously to bury it,[170] shielding Israel from accountability, because Israel is a key U.S. ally. Congress overwhelmingly passed a nonbinding resolution to quash the report. But "How can we ever expect there to be peace in the Middle East," Congress member Dennis Kucinich asked, "if we tacitly approve of violations of international law and...human rights...if we close our eyes to the heartbreak of people on both sides by white-washing a legitimate investigation?"[171]

U.N. Special Rapporteur on Palestinian human rights Richard Falk argued that the report "was eminently mindful of Israel's arguments relating to security,"[172] while Letty Cottin Pogrebin decried the character assassination campaign against Goldstone.[173] When Rabbi Michael Lerner announced a special award to Goldstone for his courageous efforts, Lerner's home was vandalized, his support likened to terrorism.[174] Who is Judge Richard Goldstone? A prosecutor of war crimes tribunals in Yugoslavia and Rwanda, a member of the board of governors of Jerusalem's Hebrew University. A "lover of Israel and its true friend," says his daughter: "All he wants is an Israel that is more just."[175]

Postscript: after the vitriol nearly disallowed Goldstone from attending his grandson's *bar mitzvah* in South Africa, he backtracked, writing that he had since become convinced that Gaza "civilians were not intentionally targeted [by Israel] as a matter of policy."[176] Yet his partial retraction failed to challenge most of the report's key allegations, including the "intentional policy…of attacking the civilian infrastructure, the electricity, the food, the people…to punish them for electing Hamas."[177]

From attempted silencing to blacklisting

Another example of manipulating anti-Semitism charges, in an attempt to squelch debate about Israeli government actions: in July 2009, the San Francisco Jewish Film Festival screened the documentary *Rachel* (by award-winning French-Israeli filmmaker Simone Bitton), about young U.S. activist Rachel Corrie, crushed to death in 2003 by a U.S.-made Israeli bulldozer while defending a Palestinian home from demolition. The film draws no conclusion but explores the driver's culpability.[178] Organizational sponsors for the film were Jewish Voice for Peace (JVP) and the (Quaker) American Friends Service Committee (AFSC).

The festival routinely shows anti-occupation films as well as Israel-positive ones: its mission is to "catalyze conversation, however uncomfortable it may be."[179] Yet two prestigious Jewish foundations and festival funders attacked the festival for showing *Rachel* and for inviting Corrie's mother, Cindy, to speak after the film; they threatened to pull funds and branded both JVP and AFSC (whose regional Middle East codirector was a rabbi) "virulently anti-Semitic."[180] After a firestorm of protest, the Festival scheduled a right-wing activist to speak as a "balance" to Cindy Corrie, and the film played to a packed house.

But in an effort to prevent future open debate, conservative funders pressured the San Francisco Jewish Community Federation (JCF, which raises and allocates dollars to Jewish groups) to institute "litmus test" funding guidelines: blacklisting those they deemed as "undermining the legitimacy of Israel" and denying support to those who *associate* with banned groups (by cosponsoring events, etc.). One of many resulting casualties: the San Francisco Bureau of Jewish Education was successfully pressured to cancel an event, "Reclaiming Jewish Activism: Re-discovering Voices of our Ancestors," because of prospective panelist Rae Abileah's affiliation with "an organization that opposes occupation profiteering and supports the boycott of products made in illegal Israeli settlements."[181] Yet Abileah, of Israeli descent, was not officially representing Code Pink, but was excited to speak about her great-uncle, a spiritual Israeli Zionist nominated for various peace awards.

The guidelines set a dangerous precedent, withholding money to clamp down public disagreement about Israeli policies, even though the JCF professes a commitment to pluralism. Applying the guidelines to Jewish studies programs, Hebrew literature professor Chana Kronfeld assessed, "All the major Israeli writers would probably be banned."[182] "The notion that we are better off hearing only the opinions that make us comfortable," said Rabbi Lavey Derby, "denies us the opportunity of greater growth."[183]

∽

When efforts to muzzle crucial dialogue lump together authentic human-rights advocates with anti-Semites, actual Jew-bashing is trivialized. And the climate of intimidation can frighten others from speaking out. "A line in the sand is there, and if you step across it, you will be crushed," admitted a progressive Jewish director.[184] The Jewish establishment is clearly beleaguered, unable to tolerate the open discussion and sharp debate that is a cornerstone of our tradition. Supreme Court Justice Louis Brandeis opined years ago, "The remedy...is more speech, not enforced silence."[185] As if heeding Brandeis' words, young Israeli army refusers touring the United States in 2009 welcomed dissent. Speaking to overflow audiences, the women facilitated respectful discussions, to educate, not intimidate. They later wrote: "There is an openness...that is refreshing, even on a tension-ridden campus, even in a synagogue."[186]

Anti-Semitism in the Occupy movement?

And true enough, a few signs and/or protestors at New York, D.C., and L.A. Occupy actions insisted "Jews [or Zionists] control Wall Street." Upsetting? Absolutely. In response, ex-Chabadnik Kobi Skolnick explained, in New York other protestors wrote on a larger placard: "This sign sucks, and...is not representative here"[187]; and even the ADL said the bigoted signs don't represent the larger Occupy movement.[188] When cars were torched and "f**k the Jews" scrawled in a Brooklyn neighborhood,[189] Occupy Wall Street (OWS) condemned the anti-Semitism and joined a protest rally.[190] A gentile activist colleague who researches anti-Jewish prejudice wrote me that anti-Semitism was simply "not accepted" among the majority of the "OWS crowd."[191]

Yet right-wingers try to undermine the Occupy movement by leveling what prominent Jewish politicos, labor leaders, and activist groups condemn as "false charges of anti-Semitism"[192]—referring to charges lambasting Occupy arguments that the military-industrial complex drains the U.S. economy by supporting war and occupation, including the Israeli occupation of Palestine.[193] Describing similar attacks, policy analyst M. J. Rosenberg points out that in accusing OWS of bigotry, extremists like the Emergency Committee for Israel handily exploit anti-Semitism. Such extremists try to "break the backs of popular movements that threaten the power of the...1 percent"—this time using "Israel and Jews...to direct money and votes toward Republicans," and so "promoting its billionaire donors' economic interests."[194]

Undeniably, sparked by the Arab Spring, the Occupy movement has shaken up the national dialogue, insistently injecting economic justice into the agenda—in what riveting civil rights activist/scholar Dr. Cornel West names "a magnificent moment of democratic awakening."[195]

Not just anti-Semitism: "Tools of Fear"[196]

Certainly, "the legacy of persecution against Jews runs deep," and this prejudice remains real, assert Rabbis Alissa Wise and Brant Rosen.[197] Like all oppression, "accusations of anti-Semitism should not be taken lightly. Nor should they be issued carelessly."[198]

In the still-early years of the twenty-first century, a key challenge for many groups is the right-wing tidal wave. Violent rhetoric has created a hate climate: casting President Obama as Hitler, inflaming racial divisions, demonizing a centrist agenda. Fueled by feelings of white dispossession ("we want our country back!")—plus (legitimate) worries about jobs and foreclosures—in the line of fire are immigrants, Muslims and people of color, also abortionists, queers, women, and sometimes Jews.

"The white supremacist crowd is up in arms, literally," noted *New York Times* columnist Bob Herbert, because "in addition to the presence of Mr. Obama in the White House, racism and anti-Semitism are no longer tolerated as overt factors in American life…[But] the social fabric is extremely delicate and fragile. Forces bent on destruction …can tear it to pieces…We need to be vigilant."[199]

Insurgents range from tea-partyers to neo-Nazis, skinheads to minutemen, and Holocaust deniers. "With a wink and a nod," wrote political analyst Chip Berlet, "the apocalyptic Christian right" is networking with "resurgent armed militias…Scratch the surface and you find people peddling bogus conspiracy theories about liberal secular humanists, collectivist labor bosses, Muslim terrorists, Jewish cabals, homosexual child molesters, and murderous abortionists."[200] Arizona, then Alabama and others, raised the bar, racially profiling anyone brown-looking (stopped by police) for possible deportation if they can't prove citizenship, also banning ethnic studies programs, though millions march in protest.[201]

And feeding the extremism? The conservative media, which influences millions, and the right-leaning Republican Party, both of which Nobel laureate economist Paul Krugman said provide "a platform for conspiracy theories and apocalyptic rhetoric."[202]

Harking back to the beginning of this chapter: it's the combo of "demagogic demonization" (stereotyping) plus massive scapegoating, "tools of fear" as described by Berlet, that has proved so dangerous in the past.[203] Outrageous allegations trigger mobilized resentment into violence.[204] As moral people, we need to stand up for whoever is being vilified. Jews are no longer "a people apart," and we are not the key targets this time around. We have to fight the backlash, all of us together.

2

Insider/Outsider:
Jews, Race, and Privilege

"When Jews perceive themselves as vulnerable, they compare themselves to the dominant cultural community, who have...discriminated against them. When other minority groups look at [white] Jews, however...Jews look settled and safe."[1]

—Cheryl Greenberg

"I came here and it was...'You're Egyptian-Iraqi? You don't know bagels and cream cheese? Then you can't be Jewish.'"[2]

—Rachel Wahba

[As a gentile African American] "I always expect Jews to be my allies. It's a surprise to me when they aren't. I never expect gentile white people to be my allies, it's a surprise to me when they are."[3]

—Akaya Windwood

As U.S. JEWS, WE EMBODY THE FLUIDITY OF RACE AND ETHNICITY, and the interplay between privilege (unearned advantage) and vulnerability. On a skin color spectrum we vary from pale to olive, brown, and black. For light-skinned Ashkenazim, "We are the closest of the coloreds to white, or the closest of the whites to colored."[4] Our privilege shifts: we are given racial advantage, we marginalize other Jews, we are targets, we are racist ourselves. Sometimes we are allies across racial and ethnic lines.

We are also dark-skinned Ashkenazi Jews of color, Mizrahi, Sephardic, multiethnic, and multiracial. And more.

"Jews complicate things":[5]
slices from a racial continuum

Forced to wander from our Middle Eastern roots, beginning in 70 C E, Jews dispersed worldwide. Some intermarried, some were raped, some non-Jews converted. Today our racial and ethnic categories vary, depending on where our geographic journeys took us, our current class status, our generation…and how we self-identify. "Jews," points out Lewis Ricardo Gordon of Temple University's Institute for the Study of Race and Social Thought, "are among the most racially diverse people on the globe."[6]

Ever notice how a "white" Ashkenazi Jew from the Bronx gains "color" in Indiana or Arkansas? In a strictly black/white binary, some white Ashkenazi Jews blur boundaries, spilling over edges, even feeling erased when called white. Meanwhile, Jews of color (a term some do not relate to)—of Middle Eastern, African, Latino, Native American, Asian/Pacific Islander, Portuguese, or Spanish descent, and/or from multiethnic backgrounds[7]—defy rigid racial classifications. Those who do not present as "white" may not be recognized as Jews.

Egyptian-Iraqi refugee Rachel Wahba was born in India, grew up in Japan. Ridiculed there as "crumbo" (literally: blackie), she remembers thinking at age eight, "I will sell my soul to be white."[8] But as a 1960s teenager, after finally gaining entry to the States, to her amazement her peers ogled, "Wow, where'd you get your tan?"[9] Third Wave feminist writer Ophira Edut says that her dark-skinned Iranian-American Sephardic father saw himself as white: "Jews can and do swing both ways," she concludes.[10]

Loolwa Khazzoom, a founder of the Jewish multicultural movement who was raised in 1970s California, identifies as a light-skinned woman of color. "In the non-Jewish people of color world, I am accepted if I am Iraqi, but don't say I am an Iraqi Jew. As soon as I add the Jew, I get shit."[11] That comment resonates with educator Shoshana Simons, who is of mixed Ashkenazi-Sephardi Turkish heritage. Her keen sense of being *Jewish* supersedes social constructions of ethnicity and race. "That hyper-awareness of difference: 'Yes, *but*' I'm always a Jew."[12] When she first visited

Istanbul to reconnect with her roots: "I felt like I 'belonged' in how I looked. And I felt like an outsider as a Jew. The fact is, to be a Diaspora Jew [in the U.S.] is my identity, outside of being Sephardi. I say that not to wipe out the real material effects of racial and social oppression, but as a baseline for alliances across our early 21st century differences."[13]

On a racial continuum, for some white-ish Ashkenazi women it's tricky to slot ourselves. Growing up in 1940s Detroit, Marge Piercy remembers "I was not white and I was not Black, but something in between. Jews...were kept out of most neighborhoods...as were the Blacks."[14] Karen Brodkin, a child of the 1950s, wrote the groundbreaking book *How the Jews Became White Folks and What That Says About Race in America*. The women in her Brooklyn/suburban family "felt different...in relation to 'the blond people'" but "in relation to African Americans, we experienced ourselves as mainstream and white."[15] And 1960s Freedom Rider Ellen Broms was arrested with others when they sat down in a Houston coffee shop. Charged with unlawful assembly, at the jail Broms declined to state her race; so she was booked as "Negro," classified "High Yellow," and put in the "tank" for black women—because of her complexion and dark hair.[16]

ELLY: CLAIMING THE IDENTITY— "WHITE JEW"

In our Jewish women's group, we posed more questions about our racial identity and privilege than we answered. Growing up in a 1960s Chicago working-class neighborhood, a landscape shell-shocked from the Nazi Shoah, Elly is quick-witted, brimming with insight. "To not call myself white would be to minimize that which is in my bones." She paused. "It's like *breathing*, how much I take for granted my privilege: the safety I *do* feel, not being bombarded 24/7 by racism."[17]

Ardently she claims the identity "white Jew: separate from white non-Jew, separate from non-Jew of color. I can go out of my way to understand racial injustice, but it still won't be in my pores. The world is designed for us; that's the norm." Her eyes flew around the table. "I'm not aware of what it's like to try and get a job, or a house, or a bank loan, if you're not white." She believes, she said, that there is conscious intent to teach racial superiority to folks with white skin, "and that does not make any of us bad."

Commanding our attention, Elly juxtaposed the tension of white privilege and anti-Semitism, the "amazing pull to rule out one or the other, as if they were contradictory realities. Like now I am either a privileged white person, or I am a targeted Jew. How do I acknowledge that both can be true at the same time?"

DEENA: "I'M OFF-WHITE"

Soft-spoken, with a keen intelligence and quick laugh, Deena is multiracial, multicultural. Her Iraqi father grew up in India before immigrating to the United States; her mother is a white Ashkenazi baby-boomer from the Midwest. She experienced moving in and out of whiteness in her Los Angeles hometown. When a close Christian friend literally shut her out on Christmas, the exclusion stung. Even worse was being ridiculed in junior high as a "big-nosed Jew." She recoiled from the hostility.

From childhood, Deena's alliance with African Americans was unquestioned, a lesson from her grandfather. During a 1960s race riot, his was the only white-owned neighborhood store left unscathed; "black brother" was written on his door.

But when Deena tried to integrate her Arab-Jewish culture into her beloved Zionist youth group, her Mizrahi side was ignored. After she ululated, someone cried "*Intifada!*"[18] "That's Iraqi-Jewish," Deena told them. "No," they insisted, "that's Palestinian." "No. The way I'm doing it is Iraqi-Jewish," she explained patiently. "They couldn't accept the idea," she told our group, "that you can be Arab *and* Jewish."

Upon visiting Israel, she found another version of bias. When her Iraqi uncle tried to rent in one neighborhood, he was told: "Those apartments are reserved for western immigrants." Read: *Ashkenazi*. When she told the story to her Israeli Ashkenazi peers, they scolded "You're American, don't even comment." She frowned, "They want me to just be Ashkenazi."

How to fit in, with all of herself? Sighing, Deena admitted that with only one other Middle Eastern Jew in our group, part of her story never emerged; there just weren't many occasions to hear someone reflect back, "Yeah, that was my experience, too." Raised in mostly Ashkenazi environments, but with a vibrant Iraqi-Indian Jewish culture as well, and with olive skin, she felt: "I'm off-white."

RANI: "LIGHTER IS BETTER"

Rani's parents divorced when she was three. Her Mizrahi father grew up in Baghdad; her Polish maternal grandfather survived Auschwitz. In her early twenties, with dark curls growing out after shaving her head, Rani is sometimes provocative, often hilarious, always self-confident and thoughtful. There's a rebellious compelling air about her. Having recently moved to San Francisco from Montreal, "I've started feeling like Jews are Other. Not quite people of color, but not the dominant white thing."

She told us that her mother's Ashkenazi family, with whom she mostly lived, hates her father's side, "because they're Iraqi Jews. The ultimate insult was that I was 'just like the Iraqis.'" In that world, she stands out because she's darker. But when she spent summers with her father's family, they berated her the same way: "You're too polite, in a chicken kind of way. You're just like the Ashkenazis."

Rani's Mizrahi family instructs, "You're an Iraqi Jew, because that's where we were born. But you're not an Iraqi, you're a *Jew*; Arabs are one people and Jews are another." She said that they don't consider themselves, or Arabs, to be people of color. "I think internationally there is this belief: 'lighter is better.'"

Illustrating her point, she told us about her last visit to her Ashkenazi family in Florida. "I asked them, 'Do you think Jewish people are white?' 'Of course!' 'Really, what about Jews from Iraq?' I asked. 'No, they're dark,' they told me. 'Well, am I white?' I asked. 'Uh, no,' they replied. 'Are you white?' I questioned. 'Yes,' they said. There was just silence at the table," Rani murmured. "And they changed the subject."

Jewish multiculturalism/
challenging the notion: Jew = white and Ashkenazi

Chinese-American Jew Linda C. Jum wrote: "When I attend a Jewish event, people...often feel entitled to ask, 'So how are you Jewish?' My response depends on how cranky I might be that day, and will range from using this as a teachable moment to snapping back, 'You go first: How are *you* Jewish?'"[19]

Collectively, Jewish identity is rooted in Africa and West Asia (the Middle East). The first Jews arriving in the United States were Portuguese Sephardim escaping persecution in Brazil, where they fled from the Inquisition.[20] Yet Middle Eastern/American biracial Jew Loolwa Khazzoom explains that most U.S. Ashkenazi organizations, synagogues, and media convey that only Jews from Eastern/Central Europe (80-90 percent of U.S. Jews)[21] are the "normal"[22] ones—so "anything billed as 'Jewish'" actually just reflects *Ashkenazi* identity—and if it doesn't, "it must not be valid."[23] (Italics added) This attitude is known as Ashkenazi centrism, aka racism. In contrast, Jews whose heritage is Asian, African, Latin American, Middle Eastern, Southern European, or Native American are often discounted as exotic curiosities. "How many of us," asks Khazzoom, "visualize Moses, an African man, as...dark-skinned?"[24]

Put another way by Melanie Kaye/Kantrowitz, white Ashkenazi author of *The Colors of Jews*: "The number of Jews of color"—roughly one in five U.S. Jews[25]— "is large enough that Jewish whiteness should never be assumed."[26] At least 200,000 people in the United States are "both Jewish and of African descent";[27] some African Americans belong to Hebrew Israelite congregations founded over a century ago.[28] Given that the white Ashkenazi community has not extended the warmest welcome, who knows how many Jews of color may choose not to identify themselves to white Jews?

Moroccan writer and poet Ruth Knafo Setton says that when her family first came to the States, her father met the synagogue board of directors. Shocked to learn that Jews lived in Morocco, they suggested he return to Africa: "There's nothing for your kind here."[29] That same day, Setton tells us, "My teacher...asked me loudly, in front of the class, 'Is it true you eat people in Morocco?'"[30] While Miriam Ventura, editor of New York City's *Tora Tropical*, the Jewish Spanish-language newspaper, reports that people would call and ask "how Dominicans or Cubans could be Jews?"[31]

African American educator Yavilah McCoy also tells excruciating stories. In her Hasidic New York elementary school, "They would make us hold hands on trips, and kids would cry rather than touch my hand. They were afraid I would turn them black..."[32] McCoy was in tears when she left her own children in Jewish day school. "It would make it easier to just 'BE' as a Jewish person of color if 'black' and 'Jewish' identity were not… assumed to be mutually exclusive."[33]

"I was made to feel like a visitor in the synagogue," confided B., of Ethiopian Jewish mixed heritage. To enroll her child in the Hebrew Academy, she had to bring documents confirming her Jewishness. While in her white northern California neighborhood, "I've been called 'kike' as well as the 'N' word." "Are you the Sammy Davis Jr. kind of Jew?" someone asked. Rap star Aubrey "Drake" Graham said he was called *schvartze* more than once as a boy in his Toronto Jewish day school.[34] And my colleague tells how her black daughter was mistaken for the "coat-check girl" at a synagogue event.

Rachel Wahba identifies as a Mizrahi-Sephardi, Middle Eastern-North African Arab Jew. After immigrating to the States she found herself having to explain "Yes, I was a Jew, even though my parents were from Egypt and Iraq. *Even though?*"[35] When her Ashkenazi roommate's mother heard about Rachel's background, she warned her daughter, "Watch out, those people can be very dirty."[36] And in her Jewish Spirituality class, Rachel remembered the teacher explaining that Jewish mysticism began with the Ba'al Shem Tov in Eastern Europe. "I waited for her to talk about the Sephardi mystics, who far predated the Ba'al Shem Tov," Rachel sighed.[37] "Not only did she not mention them…she seemed completely uninterested."[38]

The white Ashkenazi exclusion of U.S. Jews of color is what folks of color from various backgrounds endure daily: their experiences disbelieved or trivialized, their cultures disregarded, their histories erased. Why is Yiddish credited as "more Jewish" than Ladino or Judeo-Arabic? Or why is Wahba's traditional Yom Kippur break fast meal of *ba'aba* filled with mashed dates, *ka'ak* with coriander, and cheese *sambousak* not seen as Jewish as matzoh ball soup? "When we ignore, devalue, or cut off branches from our collective Jewish tree," points out Khazzoom, "we amputate a vital part of ourselves."[39] She adds (elsewhere), "Since European Jews come from non-European Jews," their oppression of non-Europeans "is… like hating your ancestors."[40]

I remember Orthodox Passover seders at Loolwa's house, racing at midnight through Berkeley streets, swatting Pharaoh and his soldiers with cattails—for me, an exhilarating new Mizrahi custom. As a child I had no idea there were Jews who didn't know blintzes and challah. Only decades later, when I taught a class about racism, and A. told me she was a Middle Eastern Jew, did I realize I'd been missing out. After investigating, listening, I started noticing Jews from India and Venezuela and Lebanon. They'd been in my life all along, but my Ashkenazi blinders had blotted out their backgrounds. My Jewish world is richer now, and more complicated, in a wonderful way.

Khazzoom took on her pioneering work as a child. In Jewish school, teachers said her Iraqi traditions were "not really Jewish," because Jewish = Ashkenazi.[41] Keep your "ethnic" identity to yourself, they warned, if you want to be accepted.[42] But after her parents switched her to public school, she persevered, founding the Student Organization for Jews from Iran and Arab Countries, later incorporated into the Jewish Federation. In her twenties, in a group less dominated by Ashkenazim, she felt mirrored by Mizrahi and Sephardic women for the first time. "I put my weapons down..." she remembers.[43] "Everything about me was seen...appreciated and loved."[44]

Khazzoom points out changing Jewish ethnic demographics in Los Angeles, one of the largest metropolitan U.S. Jewish populations, where Persian-American Jews have reached a critical mass in Jewish schools and synagogues.[45] "As long as the power structure...is maintained," she argues, "multiculturalism is a comfortable ideal."[46] But what happens, she asks, when Jews of color and white Jews become equal in number?

Embarrassed, I feel my disorientation as Loolwa describes this shift. At the same time, I'm excited. Like the nervousness I sometimes feel in a room of people of color. Stay with the discomfort, admit my inner qualms about sharing power/losing control, acknowledge my sense of entitlement. Not my fault, but nothing to be complacent about.

(Also: as Ashkenazim, are we unconsciously afraid that by connecting with Mizrahi/Sephardic Jews, and other Jews of color, that we ourselves will slip back into being seen as nonwhite? And lose the privileges our parents/ grandparents/great-grandparents made such sacrifices for?)

"The crux of diversity work," writes Khazzoom, "lies in letting go of a...comfortable diversity that maintains the status quo...[Let's] do what it takes to welcome all Jews as equal partners at the collective table." [47]

How did white U.S. Ashkenazi Jews *become* white?

"I've learned a tremendous amount," admits Paul Golin of the Jewish Outreach Institute, not only about "Ashkenazi privilege in the Jewish world," but about "what it means to have white privilege...in America."[48] So time now for a bit of context-widening, to dip back into history and understand how white U.S. Jews gained our advantages in the first place.

Jews get a leg up, Blacks don't

Good timing, good fortune, and light-skinned privilege helped Ashkenazi Jews begin to escape their less-than-white status. In nineteenth century Europe, Jews were considered threats to the white race but "became" lighter-skinned upon reaching North American shores.[49] Then by the very late 1800s, xenophobia zeroed in on the majority of immigrants from Southern/Eastern Europe, Jews and Catholics, so the census and popular culture branded these newcomers "less than fully white."[50] Not just that: Karen Brodkin argues that the "degraded forms of work" these immigrants did, although vital to the economy, apparently "confirmed the...racial inferiority of the workers who did it."[51] "Scientific" racism stigmatized the Jews even further, as inherently diseased.

But immigrant Jews arrived with a wide array of industrial and occupational skills most needed by burgeoning U.S. industry, especially the garment industry, which hired them by the tens of thousands—experience other groups of arriving peasants and farmers lacked.[52] Two-thirds of turn-of-the-century Jewish immigrants were skilled tailors, seamstresses, capmakers, furriers, and more.[53] Jews also entered with a higher literacy rate than most immigrants, so they learned English quickly, opening up opportunity.[54]

"It would be difficult to exaggerate the significance" of the garment industry, argues sociologist Stephen Steinberg, "for the economic adjustment of Jewish immigrants."[55] But the Jews' good fortune partially came at the expense of southern black sharecroppers and tenant farmers, whose sweat built the industry that gave many immigrant Jews an early chance to succeed.

Enter the Great Compromise of 1877, reinforced by southern Jim Crow segregation laws, trophies of white supremacy. With southern planters needing the recently emancipated workers to stay south of the Mason-Dixon Line, to pick cotton for little pay and enable hefty profits—cotton crucial to the *national* economy—northern industrialists agreed not to recruit southern black labor, effectively trapping workers in continued backbreaking lives of poverty.[56]

Jews (and others) who arrived between 1880 and 1924 benefitted from these "color line" practices that kept black workers harvesting southern cotton, practices that almost completely barred blacks from northern industry ("until the supply of [Northern] white labor had been exhausted."[57]) By 1900, nearly half of New York City's industrial workforce was Eastern European Jews, mostly in textiles.[58] As the industry mushroomed, most textile jobs were "deskilled" into mass production assembly lines, work that southern blacks presumably could have qualified for.[59] Urban Studies professor Henry Louis Taylor brings home the painful truth: "The process of keeping blacks from competing with whites in the labor market is the foundation upon which American racism is built."[60]

Despite sweatshop wages, over time garment workers' earnings accumulated and Jewish children could remain in school, no longer needing to quit early to contribute to family income. Jewish "greenhorns" (new immigrants) flocked to New York City College, benefitting from the free admissions policy of the 1930s and '40s, and thousands earned college degrees at night. It was only when people of color enrolled in droves in the 1960s that City College began charging tuition.[61]

Steinberg points out that for Jews, "economic mobility occurred *first*," which *then* opened up educational opportunity and the chance for upward mobility and security.[62] (Italics added) So while Jewish values of education and learning (values shared by Chinese and Japanese immigrants) helped Jews succeed, what was crucial was arriving at the right time, with the "fortuitous match" between their skills and industry needs, to land those jobs in the first place.[63] Then economic gain paved the way for education.

And as Jews were given a leg up, institutional racism kept black workers picking southern cotton to supply the textile industry—limiting them from competing for northern industrial jobs, anchoring them as the U.S. underclass condemned to poverty for generations. "Major economic interests were served," Steinberg emphasizes, "by the deployment of blacks to southern agriculture and [lighter-skinned] immigrants to northern industry."[64] Concludes Brodkin, "This construction of race almost is the American construction of class."[65]

Compared to nonimmigrant whites, however, Jews lacked many options. Despite their skills, Jews were frozen out of WASP bastions like crafts unions "where whiteness was a...prerequisite for membership."[66] On the upside for social change: in response to grueling sweatshop conditions, many Jews joined socialist and communist movements and began leading groundbreaking labor struggles on New York City's Lower East Side.

The G.I. Bill: class whitens

Another fortuitous turning point for U.S. Jews, along with other less-than-fully-white Mediterranean immigrants, was the post-World War II G.I. Bill of Rights. Dubbed "the most massive affirmative action program" in U.S. history, the 1944 Serviceman's Readjustment Act disproportionately benefitted Euro-descended males, redrew racial lines, and expanded the notion of whiteness.[67]

Specifically, the G.I. Bill gave sixteen million veterans priority in landing jobs, financial support to look for work, home loans and cheap mortgages, business start-up loans, and scholarships for college and technical schools. These advantages catapulted overwhelming numbers into the middle class, effectively whitening them. Since half of all eligible Jewish men served in the War, this was an enormous boost for Jewish families.[68] Economically motivated, the G.I. Bill was designed to develop labor force skills needed for the world's strongest postwar economy. Jews were needed as managers, technicians, and various professionals. "Class whitens," concludes Kaye/Kantrowitz.[69]

A letter from my father, October 29, 1947, referred to the Arlington, Virginia, apartment complex where my parents hoped to rent a one-bedroom. He wrote my mother, "The new owners of the apartments will assert the right to exercise choice of tenants. Under the contract they must give preference to veterans." Lucky for me, both my parents were vets, and so this modest but semi-suburban setting, with stubby grass and weeping willows, became my first home. Question: Would they have given the apartment to my mother, who had served as a WAVE in the navy, on her own?

In practice, G.I. benefits excluded most women and African American vets.[70] Since black G.I.'s served under white (sometimes racist) officers, disproportionate numbers were dishonorably discharged, disqualifying them for veteran's benefits.[71] And few African Americans were counselors at the U.S. Employment Service, hampering black veterans' chances of finding good jobs.[72] Black vets were also unwelcome in white universities (which began lifting quotas against Jews), and by 1947 crowded black colleges could only accommodate 20,000 of the 35,000 applying.[73]

In segregationist covenants, banks often refused to lend money in "redlined" neighborhoods, even though such covenants were outlawed in 1948, nor would the Federal Housing Administration insure mortgages there.[74] Disdained as slums, these communities had low property values and were considered bad investments, which kept many black vets from accessing funds to repair or buy homes in the only places they were allowed to live. And while nearly all suburban developers refused to sell to African Americans, many Christians were becoming more tolerant of whitened Jews, so housing development restrictions were gradually lifted for them.

So much for Horatio Alger: Ashkenazi Jews did not pull ourselves up by our bootstraps. Our families worked hard, like many other families. But we were awarded racial privileges, allowing us to benefit from postwar government programs that simultaneously discriminated against the women and African Americans among us. Brodkin names these "racially skewed gains,"[75] which advanced large numbers of Jews into the middle class, privileges passed on to children like me as inheritance: houses, savings, health care pensions, and investments accumulated through higher education and good jobs. So, as (white) Ashkenazi Jews *became* white and middle-class, we helped construct American whiteness.

Meanwhile, were Jews whose families didn't climb the ladder still considered less-than-white? Working-class Ashkenazi peace educator Laura Rifkin says on the Lower East Side she was often mistaken for

Puerto Rican. She adds that the upwardly mobile ascent came at a painful price: separation from working-class Jews. Assimilated middle-class Jews conveyed, "We were too Jewish, too dark, too dirty—too second-class."[76]

In other places, too, the new Jewish whiteness didn't reach. Dyanna Loeb writes about her baby-boomer dad growing up in white suburbs (excerpt):

> "folks in my father's midwest hometown
> still couldn't accept him
> Jewish
> was a dirty word."[77]

The deal we struck: white privilege

Munching on pita bread one Sunday afternoon during our group conversation, Deena's eyes lit up. "White privilege was the *compromise*, the deal we struck as Jews in America: 'You'll allow us to become white, to be free, to live and get rich,'" she laughed nervously. "And in exchange, we won't talk about racism or anti-Semitism. So it's not just a choice of white privilege. It's also about agreeing to ignore injustice."

The conditions for whiteness—whose benefits included upward mobility, security, and increased tolerance from a Christian society—meant submerging Jewishness and accepting a racial hierarchy, sacrificing relationships with people of color in order to feel safer. The problem with whiteness was, is, its institutionalized subordination of people of color.

In our group, Amy told us about her Florida grandparents, who bought the deal. They said black people were "several rungs lower on the ladder" than Jews and didn't hide their drive to cling to middle-class (Christian) whites, to share status, and safety. Even so, their deal-making failed to protect their son, Amy's dad. Teaching at a university notorious for anti-Semitism, he was run out of Canada by the Mounties, the equivalent of COINTELPRO,[78] for being a Marxist New York Jew. "Get out right away!" an ally warned him. Amy's voice rose, then fell. "It was an ugly story he never referred to."

Those who most visibly colluded with this unwritten arrangement were a group of high-profile, mostly male, mostly conservative intellectuals, raised working class, whose writing suggests that they felt like underdogs. They translated their new acceptance and privileges as earned entitlement, believing other minorities should follow their lead—ignoring the backbreaking labor by enslaved Africans, and Mexican, Chinese, and Native American workers who built this country. The intellectuals invented a Jewish "patriarchal whiteness," creating their worth in contrast to blackness.[79] Probably best known is neocon Norman Podhoretz. Unitarian minister and television producer Thandeka summarizes Podhoretz's memoir, *Making It*: "...the American social contract he...faced as a lower-class Jewish student from Brooklyn, the child of immigrants, who wanted the class privileges and securities of goyish American high culture...demanded that he become a 'facsimile WASP.'"[80]

Shedding ethnic Jewishness, Podhoretz secured entry to an Ivy League school despite its Jewish quota. After becoming editor of the influential *Commentary* (published by the American Jewish Committee), he abandoned the Left, believing the sixties movements threatened his hard-won establishment credentials. Gradually, he transformed the journal to a neocon bastion that attacked welfare and affirmative action, arguing that "cutting benefits to our nation's most needy will actually make them better off."[81]

Tracing Podhoretz's fear as a Jewish boy attacked by Negro children, Thandeka theorizes that Podhoretz projected onto black people his own self-contempt at conforming to a WASP social contract: a contract dictated by a ruling class who allowed in acceptable Jewish voices, like his, while targeting less cooperative ones, like playwright Arthur Miller.[82] Although Podhoretz "made it," as a Jew into the prestige-and-power arena, he knew he was swimming in the waters of a world that scorned his Jewishness— "the stuff of Jewish self-hatred" suggests Thandeka.[83]

Once more, Aurora Levins Morales lays out the "deal" made in response to anti-Semitism's aim: "...to create a vulnerable buffer group that can be bribed with some privileges into managing the exploitation of... urban people of color...and often becoming one of the...faces of oppression...implementing policies that serve others...Jews are by no means the majority in...these roles, but it's been a widespread defensive strategy, in response to the instability of Jewish life, to seek upward mobility...as a safety net against persecution."[84]

Visible perks, hidden worries: conditional whiteness?

Challenging the blended-together "melting pot" story, the cultural pluralism of early-twentieth-century progressives valorized ethnic differences, including Jewishness. But in the late 1960s, (mostly working-class) communities of color and feminists heralded multiculturalism and identity politics, centering race, power, and privilege—and drawing a new line between insider and outsider. Freshly defined as Euro-Americans, white Ashkenazi Jews became lumped in with our former persecutors.

Over the last decades, white Ashkenazi Jews have been allowed to continue moving to society's inside, but our positionality remains complex. For example, argues Paul Kivel (author of *Uprooting Racism*), although our advantages are undeniable, "In fundamental ways white Jews are not fully accepted as white."[85] Because some still see our Eastern Euro roots as racially tainted. Some stereotype us as too powerful, "dangerous" to white society (see Chapter Three). And because we reject Jesus as God.

No wonder our whiteness, including our benefits, sometimes feels precarious in this society laced with Christian dominance—in a time when tea partyers talk "Christian values" and sow seeds of fear, not to mention anti-immigrant chants at white extremist rallies: "No ['N' word], No Jews, Mexicans must go too!"[86] The difference between white and Christian privilege is real, as is the difference between white privilege and racism.

Relative economic well-being does not necessarily equal full security. Our experiences differ, depending on our skin shade, our gender, where we call home, whom we love, our years on this earth, the jobs our parents had, our disabilities, the effect of assimilation—plus past trauma and/or present discrimination. Just as "some Jews have taken on racist ideas," points out Aurora Levins Morales, "many Ashkenazi Jews experience themselves as 'off-white'...in a *conditional* state of privilege."[87]

The common thread of Jewish vulnerability is fear, a terror so deep that, when activated, it feels like reality. In some of our psyches, recent genocide overrides current advantage, recalling the historic cycle: privilege one day, persecution the next—and how Jews have been used as buffers, middle agents, by ruling elites. Fear can unconsciously steer us into opting for security over integrity, separating us from allies of color.

When criticized for such compromises, we may become rigid, afraid that catastrophe looms around the corner. So while white Jews often look like insiders, after factoring in religious/cultural/psychological factors in this Christian-drenched country, many still feel as if we straddle the margins. As recently as 1987, a Supreme Court ruling allowed Arabs and Jews to "use civil rights laws to gain redress for discrimination against them...*on the grounds that they are not racial whites.*"[88] (Italics added)

Kaye/Kantrowitz suggests that post-9/11, Jews who are visibly white, male, straight, and comfortable economically "are definitely insiders—though history teaches us that this could shift at any moment."[89] The insider privileges so many of us have remain real: we don't have to sweat being deported as "alien," having our families ripped apart; or being shot by cops because of our skin color (and our youth); or being railroaded into prison while white-collar offenders elude jail time. A Latina colleague points out to me, "Swastikas are also directed at people of color. When I see them, I feel fear, like they're gonna do something to me. You have white privilege, I don't."

Yet again the tough question: how do we factor in the less visible, the fallout from mass murder not *that* long ago? A Gen-X friend shudders remembering the bomb threat to her Jewish kindergarten in Atlanta. Another recalls an antiracism training for white folks: "I asked the Jews in the room to stand up. Later two young women told me they froze and couldn't stand. Until that moment, they thought they were unaffected by anti-Semitism." Lurking just below the surface, these harsh insecurities remain part of the white-Jewish-privilege equation, no matter how much structural advantage we have. At the same time, we need to acknowledge our privilege—advantages we rarely consider, because having white privilege means not having to think about it, that's how privilege works—and our responsibility for acting justly, as Jewish ethical tradition directs, using our "middle roles" to fight racism. For many Jews, our vulnerability and our advantages exist simultaneously.

In our group, Jessie knows that she passes as white, but she feels very Other around WASPs. When some learn she is Jewish, "anti-Semitic things pop from their mouths. Then I don't feel white at all." The stepchild of a survivor whose family was killed in the ovens, Jesse grew up working class in 1950s Sacramento. She grimaces, "So what am I? In the Pale in Russia, and in Nazi Germany, it was clear what Jews were." Searching our faces, she insists, "Who killed us for centuries? White Europeans!"

Emily confides that people have always asked: "What *are* you?" Dubbed "brillo head" by peers in her black/Italian/Jewish, 1960s, New York City (NYC) neighborhood, she acknowledges the benefits she had. "But I didn't fit into the white Christian community," she shrugs. "I felt closer to black folks. But I'm not black." One summer in rural Michigan, on her way to a lesbian festival, she ran out of gas. "As a Jewish dyke I was scared for my life! Put me in East Oakland and I'll be fine. But here I stand out, and I don't feel safe."

Complicated intersections

"I would say that white privilege is a constant," Elly suggested, "a constant that sometimes coexists with anti-Semitism. It doesn't save you from anti-Semitism, sexism, homophobia, whatever else."

"Because if you're Jewish and the Ku Klux Klan is coming after you, white privilege is not in that picture frame," Judith declared.

"But white privilege is relevant there," Elly insisted, "because they'll come after you differently than if you were black."

"I'm not positive I disagree," Rani interjected, "but I think a hate crime is a hate crime. If you're coming after me because I'm black, or if you're coming after me because I'm a chick who likes other chicks, there's really no difference. You're coming after me—know what I mean? We should just say there's no language for it," she concluded. "There's no language that describes our Otherness."

Abrasions and alliances: racism and anti-Semitism

The juxtaposition of (white) Jewish privilege, versus our fears, sets up a minefield for our relationships with gentile people of color. Like some other marginalized groups, Jews have been oppressed, and sometimes we are oppressors. And as Paul Kivel points out, "White Christian leaders like nothing better than to see [other] groups taking potshots at each other," while the media zooms in on these tensions.[90]

Especially: because of the ghastly structural exclusion of systemic racism, there is a "fundamental asymmetry in the relationship of Blacks to [white] Jews," writes Michael Lerner.[91] We can't minimize that legacy, and we can't duck accountability for our personal racism: what we say, how we act, who we leave out.[92] In our often mid-level roles as managers, social workers, and teachers—or as peers—despite our efforts at respectful interaction, we can end up controlling, patronizing, condescending...being unconscious.

Not that long ago, for example, I remember leading a project in grad school with T., a gentile African American colleague. In a (magnanimous) sincere effort to shift the power imbalance of white privilege, I suggested the black students present first. T. swiftly stopped me. "Penny, don't you see what you're doing? We can decide for ourselves when we'll present; we'll let you know."

Sometimes we feel like whatever it is that *we* need to do is The Most Important, and it Needs to Happen Immediately, In Just The Way We Think It Should Happen (as in "Don't you see that I am *right?*"). We don't consider how it feels to be on the receiving end of these behaviors.

So here we are as Jews, hauling our baggage of anxiety—which shows up as worry, urgency, hypervigilance—in response to historical horrors. But to less fortunate folks of color, we look downright "cozy with power."[93] How do we keep this almost unbearable tension between "Jewish self-perception of vulnerability" and the "external perception of Jewish [class] security" from getting in the way of our working, loving, and being together?[94]

At a conference about anti-Semitism on the Left, I am facilitating a workshop for gentiles and Jews. An African American gentile, S., sits beside me. In a room of fifty-plus, I ask the Jews: "Stand up if you have ever been the target of violence because you are a Jew?" Twelve rise, then sit down. "Stand up if you have ever had dreams or waking nightmares about being in prison or a concentration camp?" Sixteen stand, and then sit. Finally: "Stand up if you often imagine dying a violent death." Nearly every Jew—over half the room—rises. There is a tangible hush. Later, at lunch, S. confides: "That exercise brought me to tears. I saw Jewish pain for the first time."[95]

And we gained a new ally...But from our end as Jews, do we notice when we allow our fear to divert agendas from racial injustice to Jewish concerns? Or when we use anti-Semitism from gentile people of color to excuse us from taking right action?

When unawareness, or even antagonism, shows itself in our movement-building work, what keeps us from jumping ship? How do we hang with each other, sorting through misunderstanding and hurt to create relationships that are real? After a confrontation between (presumably white) Jewish women and (presumably gentile) women of color, activist women of color leaders Cherie Moraga, Julia Perez, Barbara Smith, and Beverly Smith urged them *all*: "Be accountable for our ignorance... Refuse to give up on each other."[96]

Abrasions...

Not uncommonly, Jews have been louder about Minister Louis Farrakhan's anti-Semitism, or a biased remark from Reverend Jeremiah Wright, than about hate speech from white extremists like David Duke or Fred Phelps,[97] even though the Christian Right is far more wealthy and powerful than Farrakhan's Nation of Islam.[98] And speaking of Islam, U.S. Jews often pile our fear onto Muslims and Arabs, feelings sometimes orchestrated by Jewish and Christian leaders to support their own agendas, leading to signs at Jewish establishment rallies, "Islam = Cult of Hate," or malicious ads on San Francisco buses demonizing Arabs and Muslims.

Or Jewish insensitivity may play out as a "What's Good for the Jews?" perspective, forgetting Rabbi Hillel's famous instruction, "That which is hateful unto yourself, do not do unto others."[99] In one example of such institutional Jewish racism: the Los Angeles-based Simon Wiesenthal Center—which confronts anti-Semitism and teaches lessons of the Holocaust—working with the Israeli government, has dug up hundreds of Muslim Palestinian graves (including those of saints and scholars) from the 800-year-old Jerusalem *Ma'man Allah* (Mamilla) cemetery, in order to construct a "Museum of Tolerance" atop part of the graveyard.[100] Urging the center to build elsewhere, the U.S. Central Conference of American (Reform) Rabbis explains that in Jewish tradition, "cemeteries are sacred ground...we must oppose the removal of another people's sacred burial ground."[101] Also fighting the project: Americans for Peace Now, the Center for Constitutional Rights, over eighty respected archeologists, Israelis, and

Palestinians.[102] Would the Wiesenthal Center build such a museum atop a white Jewish gravesite?

And a nightmarish example of a successful plan to divert the agenda from racism to right-wing Jewish priorities: the April 2009 U.N. Durban Review Conference on Racism (in Geneva, Switzerland) known as "Durban II." Calling it a well-organized disinformation campaign, Cecilie Surasky reported that the experience felt like "a slow-motion train wreck."[103] She described "several hundred...privileged white...Ashkenazi Jewish youth and many [U.S. Jewish and Israel advocacy NGO] groups disrupting, taking up space" on a world stage—in nonstop panels, press conferences, and pro-tests—in effect derailing attempts of the Global South and others from strategizing about slavery, trafficking, poverty, and reparations.[104] Even the Jewish Telegraph Agency admitted, "This time...the Jews actually did conspire, albeit openly, to sabotage the conference."[105]

Their rationale? That the first U.N. conference on racism, in Durban, South Africa in 2001, was an anti-Jewish anti-Israel "diplomatic pogrom," and they wanted to prevent a repeat performance.[106] The reality? Complex. At the Durban NGO Forum *preceding* the U.N. conference, various street protests targeted Israeli anti-Palestinian policies. Some demonstrators sensationalized their outrage, wearing despicable "Hitler didn't finish the job" buttons, or posting ugly fliers caricaturing money-hungry Jews with big noses: clearly frightening.[107] And the final (controversial) NGO declaration challenged discriminatory policies of Israel's Zionist govern-ment, naming "the practices of Zionism as racist practices which propagate the racial domination of one group over another"[108]—resulting in U.N. condemnation of the manifesto.[109] (The NGO document also condemned anti-Semitism and Holocaust denial and acknowledged Jewish suffering.)

Although these actions usurped attention, the U.N. conference itself focused "overwhelmingly about Africa, the ongoing legacy of slavery, and the huge unpaid debts that the rich owe the poor."[110] *The official U.N. Durban I Declaration (approved by 189 countries)* read: "the Holocaust must never be forgotten," recognizing "with deep con-cern the increase in anti-Semitism and Islamophobia."[111] It affirmed "the right to security for all States in the region, including Israel," while

also expressing regard for "the Palestinian people under foreign occupation," supporting their self-determination and right to an independent state,
calling for a "peace...in which all peoples shall co-exist and enjoy equality, justice...and security."[112] Is this Jew-hatred? Shimon Peres, then Israel's
foreign minister, called the document "an accomplishment of the first
order for Israel."[113]

What the obstructing groups at the Geneva U.N. conference (which
omitted an NGO Forum) really wanted, says Surasky, was to focus on
abuses by Islamic states—and divert scrutiny of "Israeli-only" roads in
the Occupied Territories, and of Jewish National Fund involvement in
reserving (sometimes confiscating) nearly all of Israel's land exclusively
for Jews.[114] Discussion of these practices, they warned, would threaten
Israel's existence. They also successfully lobbied the U.N. to bar Palestinians from participating on any panels.[115]

And true to form, Iran President Mahmoud Ahmadinejad called Israel
"the most cruel and repressive regime," fifty European Union delegates
walked out in protest, and Secretary-General Ban Ki-moon denounced
the bigotry.[116] But as Naomi Klein pointed out in *Harper's*, most Western
governments were glad to collude with the derailment (by boycotting the
conference, at the behest of Jewish groups) "if it meant getting out of
having to discuss...race-relations commitments" they had made at
Durban I.[117] In historic style, these countries conveniently used the
Jews to benefit their own interests.

The effect of the Jewish actions? Fueling anti-Semitism by their
demonizing of Arabs and Muslims (and the U.N.). "They torpedoed the
whole idea of a world conference on racism," Surasky sighed to me in a
phone call afterwards. "It was the most extraordinary example of white
privilege." An African American delegate agreed: "What this is really
about is whose issues trump."[118] Naomi Klein concludes: "For many civil
rights leaders at the conference, it seemed that Jews—more than any sector of
society—should have been their natural allies in the reparations call. Instead,
it was large Jewish organizations and the state of Israel...that successfully
undermined the one international forum in which reparations for slavery
were on the agenda."[119]

⧼∽

Of course, anti-Semitism by gentile peoples of color is also part of the equation, with special attention landing on African Americans. Cornel West describes black anti-Semitism as "xenophobia from below" lacking "the same institutional power of those racisms that afflict their victims from above" yet deserving "the same moral condemnation."[120]

What girds this bias? Among several factors, West calls out the obvious: Jewish racism. In reaction, blacks can vent their outrage about *all* white racism onto Jews, since white anti-Semitism condones such a response. Another reason: African Americans have had higher expectations of Jews, due to a common, though distinct, legacy of suffering. And then, the age-old fallback: since Jews are sometimes the visible middle-agent face of the decision-makers, Jews are easy to blame. The 2009 documentary *Defamation* illustrates one example, when African Americans in Crown Heights (Brooklyn) explain to Israeli filmmaker Yoav Shamir that Jews are "part of the money control system"—adding that their (Jewishly visible) Chasidic neighbors are treated better by the cops, neighbors who "never took the time to get to know us."

Definitely problematic is the Jewish establishment defense of Israeli policies that brutalize Palestinians, whose struggle many people of color relate to. Also, Jews colluding with a racial hierarchy—conservative Jewish men opposing affirmative action, for example (a reaction to previous anti-Jewish quotas)—has felt like betrayal. Not to mention that many of those from a Protestant black culture have "inherited...Christian anti-Semitic narratives of Jews as Christ-killers."[121] Finally, West names the dynamic "underdog resentment" of "another underdog who has made it."[122] Upsetting? Yes. Understandable? Well, yes.

In our group, Deena reflected on her experience as a biracial Jew working with youth of color: "The difference between anti-Semitism and racism in my generation is you can go in and out of experiencing anti-Semitism, which I did. But racism is much more constant."

When her gentile African American partner was anti-Semitic, Elly grappled with her disappointment and pain. "How do I keep from becoming a victim, and feeling 'You are the oppressor'—as if she were a white person being anti-Semitic?" Her eyes blazed. "I maintain white privilege in her face at the same time she is being anti-Semitic to me. Both are true in the same moment. Boy oh boy! Sometimes, it's just overwhelming," she laughed rue-fully. "If I'm not saying ten different 'yes/buts' or 'and/alsos' at the same time, I feel like I'm not doing justice in addressing the complexities."

"Anti-Semitism has never been as strong among blacks," argues historian Marshall Stevenson, "as among the mutual enemies of blacks and Jews."[123] Of a similar mind, feminist trailblazer Barbara Smith wrote to Jews and African Americans: "We are certainly damaged people. The question is...do we use that...first-hand knowledge of oppression...to do what work we can together? Or do we use it to destroy?"[124]

Alliances: fighting shoulder to shoulder

When my anthropologist friend Misha moved to Oklahoma, she wrote me about the excellent Jewish museum in Tulsa. "The first thing you see when you walk into their Holocaust exhibit," she said, "is a KKK robe and hood, where they make the connection with the Tulsa race riots of 1921."

The connections are there, just waiting for us to notice. The first U.S. newspaper to call for boycotting German products, in response to Nazism, was *The Pittsburgh Courier*, an African American paper;[125] and national black leaders Paul Robeson, A. Phillip Randolph, James Bald-win, and Ossie Davis all spoke out against anti-Semitism.[126] Meanwhile, vast numbers of Jews fought hard with blacks against Jim Crow laws and lynchings. More than one of my black friends has told me that their par-ents instructed, "If you're in trouble, ask a Jew for help."

When Rose Schneiderman led the International Ladies Garment Workers Union, she ensured that their meetings were held in English, not Yiddish, so that black women could take part.[127] The Emma Laza-rus Federation of Jewish Women's Clubs, founded in 1944, specifically focused on antiracist activism (as well as on combatting anti-Semitism).

And Esther Brown, a Kansas Jew, hated the inferior education that her housekeeper's children were getting, so she initiated the groundbreaking Brown vs. Topeka Board of Education lawsuit, leading to the Supreme Court's 1954 decision outlawing segregated schools—undeterred by a cross-burning on her lawn or her husband losing his job.[128]

As Martin Luther King Jr. entered the hall of the (Conservative movement's) Rabbinical Assembly, 1000 rabbis greeted him, singing "We Shall Overcome" in Hebrew.[129] And at San Francisco State University, when a Malcolm X mural was painted with dollar signs next to Jewish stars, African American professor Lois Lyles painted STOP on the mural and was subsequently arrested. "Attributing anti-Semitism to Malcolm defamed his memory," Lyles explained.[130]

When Adrienne Rich, Audre Lorde, and Alice Walker were all nominated for the 1974 National Book Award, they together assumed, as Walker later described, "that under a system which favored white people" the award would go to Rich.[131] Added Walker, Rich "was a great poet, but it would go to her also because she was a white person. And to her immense credit, she had no desire to be honored as we would be dishonored."[132] They agreed to only accept the award "in the name of all women"[133]—so when Rich was named winner, jointly with Allen Ginsburg, Lorde joined her onstage (Walker didn't attend); Rich read the statement the three women had prepared together, declaring "we will share this prize among us..."[134]

"My parents were excellent allies to each other," writes Caribbean Jew Aurora Levins Morales, who "loved watching my parents twirl around the kitchen dancing...my [Puerto Rican-American Catholic] mother singing *Tumbalalaika* in Yiddish and my [white Ashkenazi] father...composing silly rhymes in his accented Spanish."[135] And a Japanese-American family who were interned during World War II at a camp at Heart Mountain, Wyoming, told how their Jewish landlords safeguarded their property, mailing care packages until they were released.[136]

In July 2010, special U.S. envoy to combat anti-Semitism, Hannah Rosenthal, was at a conference in Kazakhstan, along with U.S. special representative to Muslim communities, Farah Anwar Pandith. To spice up their presentations, they exchanged prepared speeches: Pandith condemned anti-Semitism, while Rosenthal blasted Islamophobia. "It wasn't just a gimmick," wrote Israeli historian Tom Segev.[137] "Rosenthal believes that Jews cannot fight anti-Semitism by themselves and Muslims cannot fight the hatred they experience by themselves: There is need for a joint war against racism..."[138]

"Solidarity Sunday": that's what Pastor J. Alfred Smith, Jr., called it, pastor of Allen Temple Baptist Church, the largest African-American church in Oakland. Even two days earlier I'd had no idea I would be there today with about thirty other Jews and "spiritual progressives." We'd all responded to Rabbi Michael Lerner's spontaneous invitation (he first checked it out with church leaders) to show Jewish support after the heart-breaking/enraging July 2013 verdict exonerating George Zimmerman for the murder of 17-year-old unarmed (and black) Trayvon Martin—who as the pastor put it, was "just on his way home." Especially, Rabbi Lerner invited us to express solidarity to African Americans who might not be the same folks as those at the street protests: that's what most hooked me. To let them know they're not alone.

The church had saved us pews up front, and early on church leaders invited the congregation to welcome us. I was overcome by how many folks came over to shake our hands, look in our eyes, and thank us for being there. I've rarely felt so welcome, anywhere. When Pastor Smith said a prayer in Hebrew in appreciation of our presence, I was glad that I'd remembered to wear my kippah, from the Jewish Quarter of Krakow, Poland. And I loved gazing up to see the stained glass window-art with likenesses of Miriam Makeba, Frederick Douglass, Marian Anderson, Martin Luther King.

Pastor Emeritus J. Alfred Smith, Sr.'s riveting sermon drew on the scripture, "The foundations of law and order have been destroyed, what can the righteous do?" He reminded us "Slavery was legal, segregation was legal;" he preached that "Stand your ground"[139] had become state-sanctioned, corporate-sanctioned, and socially acceptable. He recalled NAACP leader Ben Jealous' words, that we must move "from Anger to Action." Pastor Smith invoked, "We are a proud people. We are a dignified people." But when he asked all the young black men to come stand on the altar – beautiful young black boys and men – that's when the tears came.[140] I recognized their vulnerability in a whole new way after the Zimmerman verdict, a verdict which to me sent a dangerous green light for other vigilante actions.

When Pastor Smith called Rabbi Lerner up to join him – calling him "friend" because of their long relationship – Michael passionately spoke of us being there that morning as Jews "standing here with you, caring about *you." Thanking Michael, Smith told folks about the death threats against Rabbi Lerner "for saying God doesn't just love Jewish people, God loves Palestinian people too." The room erupted in applause.*

The experience was extraordinary: to feel seen and appreciated as Jews, to feel connected to this community in such a powerful way...As we all sang together "We Shall Overcome," for the first time in a long time, I really believed it.

∽

How to move forward? We have been taught racism; we can unlearn it...noticing our privilege, and those who don't have it, recognizing who was given perks along the way, and why. Cutting ourselves slack in the places we get frightened, holding ourselves to standards of integrity. Also, in Shoshana Simons' words, using our shared Diaspora ethnically-diverse Jewishness as a baseline for alliance building. Speaking out against injustice—period—including the discounting of Jewish minorities. Decentering Ashkenazi. Taking leadership from the marginalized, valuing all voices as equally precious, sharing power...and backing up our words with action.

3

Let's Talk About "Jewish Power": Rethinking Stereotypes

"There is something...all too familiar about Gentiles in powerful positions maintaining that it is not they who are responsible for their actions but a cabal of rich and influential Jews manipulating events behind the scenes."[1]

—*Stephen Zunes*

GIVEN OUR HISTORY, what a *bracha* (blessing) that Jews overall are prospering in this country, are affluent, educated, accomplished. Hardly anything is off-limits to white U.S. Jews today (at least to most of the assimilated middle/upper-class, straight men)—amazing good fortune, given that when roughly two million-plus immigrated here just over a century ago, we came fleeing poverty and pogroms.

Yet there's a gap between our actual success—structural advantage,[2] and some policy-setting clout—and the exaggerated ideas of overarching "Jewish power," beliefs that can morph into conspiracy theories. Although some are well-entrenched in the halls of power, Jews do not have as much systemic influence as undercurrents of anti-Semitism sometimes attribute to us.

The "insidiously powerful" stereotype certainly feels demonizing, but most damaging is how the accusation masks the complex system that sets policy and controls resources: the corporate/military/government mostly-Christian-and-white-male power elite. The disinformation, spread by extremists but also sprinkled throughout mainstream and otherwise-progressive pockets, is that (conspiratorial) Jews run the banks, the media,

Hollywood, the government…that whenever Jews are in influential positions, they serve "Jewish interests," which are antithetical to everyone else's…and that the "Jewish Lobby" (the Israel Lobby) controls U.S. foreign policy in the Middle East.

The reality is complicated and bears repeating. It's a combination of: potent stereotypes still alive-and-kicking, overall white Jewish success plus some weighty structural influence, the sometimes exaggeration of that power, and how Jew-blaming can be used to disguise class power. Jews are roughly 1.7 percent of the U.S. population,[3] and we have disproportionate influence in some areas of the power elite. Still, predominantly white Christian men call the shots, whether out front or behind the scenes.

Letty Cottin Pogrebin nails it: the accusation "'Jewish power' re-casts the Christian majority as pawns, and helps justify" anti-Jewish bigotry.[4] Not to mention how these stereotypes are piercing for some of us as Jewish women. We recoil in response, feeling that we have done something wrong. But when we tone down our leadership, to avoid being derided as too pushy or powerful, we weaken the impact of our activism.

The power elite: the ruling class, the managerial class

Who are the power elite? An overwhelmingly white, male, and Christian slice of the ruling and managerial classes. According to Paul Kivel, author of *You Call This a Democracy?*, the ruling class is the richest and most powerful in our society, comprising about 1 percent of the population. It controls who gets resources, who benefits from social policies, who is marginalized. Operating chiefly through business, government, and the courts, the ruling class decides who can access political power. It owns the dominant share of stocks and bonds, private land, buildings, and other assets.

There is "a higher percentage of Jews in the U.S. ruling class [structural power] than their representation in the general population," Kivel explains, but "despite the stereotypes, *they still constitute a small part of that class*."[5] (Italics added) Most Jews are not ruling class. Put another way (by Kivel): "The largest concentration of people in the ruling class by far are Christian, not Jewish—and even the wealthiest Jews have often been excluded from top levels of decision making."[6]

The managerial class, the next 19 percent according to Kivel, works for the ruling class—managerial because of its wealth, income, and access to resources. Its members are corporate managers, politicians, lawyers, foundation and business directors, architects, doctors, elite university professors... also sometimes independent large farmers, major nonprofit directors, top-level administrators, consultants. Holding prestigious positions in our most influential institutions, they benefit from the power elite's policies. Mostly they are white Christian, although "significant minorities" are Jews, people of color, recent immigrants, others.[7] Together, the ruling class and the managerial class comprise the Owning Class, or the top 20 percent.[8] In 2007, this 20 percent owned 85 percent of privately held U.S. wealth.[9]

The power elite, a tiny cadre of these ruling and managerial classes, determines how the society runs.[10] In 1956, sociologist C. Wright Mills documented how World War II solidified this trinity of U.S. corporate/military/government elites, "in a centralized power structure working in unison."[11] Both "non-elected" and "self-selected," they are also "self-perpetuating."[12]

It is the power elite's decisions—as leaders in business, politics, the military, philanthropy, religion, and culture—*that affect the rest of us every day*, decisions made to benefit the owning class. This elite controls banking, insurance, and industrial assets; television networks; and the largest news-media companies. These leaders head the defense, oil, and computer industries; lead the top investment firms; and dominate the key law practices and cultural/civic groups. They also hold the highest positions in the government and military, and control most assets of private universities and foundations. And they circulate between all of these. Some of them are Jews; a few are Muslim, Buddhist, Hindu. Most are Christian. *Regardless of where they come from, they favor narrow class interests.*[13] Their culture of power is Christian, white, male.[14]

Now let's return to the stereotypes and explore the realities.

"Jewish money"

"Money, when Jews wanted it, had it, or lent it to others, seemed to take on a peculiar nastiness; Jews and money had some...unspeakable relation."

—*Adrienne Rich, "Split at the Root: An essay on Jewish identity"*

Take "Jewish money," for example. Riv-Ellen Prell points out that from 1938 to 1945, almost 45 percent of the U.S. population imagined Jews had "too much power" in commerce, business, finance.[15] The actuality, in terms of systemic power? In New York, some Jews owned many factories, and throughout the country Jews owned various stores, large and small. Yet through the 1930s, *Fortune* magazine reported that the majority of U.S. Jews were poor or hovering on the brink. Although Jews "had to endure accusations that they controlled the banks and monopolized economic opportunity," *Fortune* concluded, there was "no basis" for these charges.[16]

And while Jewish executives amassed influence in textiles, film, and broadcasting, Jews were nearly nonexistent in insurance, finance, automobiles, steel, railroads, or utilities, at least through 1950.[17] "No industry," confirms Leonard Dinnerstein, was "more antisemitic than commercial banking."[18] This policy didn't end until 1980, when banks, needing to compete internationally, began hiring Jews, Italians, and others, a shift heralded by a *New York Times* article, "No Longer a WASP Preserve."[19]

In 1941, American hero Charles Lindbergh proclaimed that the great danger of Jews "lies in their large ownership...in our motion pictures, our press, our radio, and our government."[20] To their credit, most newspapers, church, and political leaders shouted him down. But think about it: *If Jews had had real power then, wouldn't they have been able to persuade Roosevelt to bomb the rail lines to Auschwitz, or open up America's doors, before millions were slaughtered?*

Moving ahead, the landscape shifted dramatically: as anti-Semitism decreased, Jews gained privilege (social advantage). By 1962, those believing Jews had "too much power" dropped to 17 percent.[21] Psychologist Richard Zweigenhaft and sociologist William Domhoff found that by 2004, Jews had secured 11.1 percent of U.S. corporate board seats (disproportionate to our 2.3 percent of the population then), indicating a foothold in structural power.[22] *And 88.9 percent of these seats were held by gentiles.*

Indicators of more widespread Jewish success, accompanied by increased visibility: the 2000-2001 National Jewish Population Study showed that over 60 percent of working Jews now had jobs in the three highest status categories—professional/technical, management, and business—compared to 46 percent of non-Jews. Relative to a $42,000 median income for all U.S. households, the Jewish median household income rose to $54,000. By 2007, a Pew survey showed 46 percent of Jews with incomes of $100,000-plus—compared to 43 percent of Hindus, 21 percent from "mainline churches," 19 percent of Catholics, 16 percent of Muslims, and 8 percent from "historically black churches" in the same income range.[23]

On the other end, a minority of Jews were and are struggling to keep their heads above water. *Forward* journalist Nathaniel Popper pointed to a 2004 study showing 14 percent of Jews as low-income (roughly one million): mostly old people (many Nazi Holocaust survivors), single parents (usually women), Orthodox Jews, and Russian immigrants[24]—while the national low-income rate hovered at 20 percent.[25] In 2011, my social worker friend Sarah recounted painful stories of her Jewish clients in L.A., each one elderly and penniless. The "all Jews are rich" stereotype renders poor and working-class Jews invisible, leading some to believe that they've done something "wrong": when one of my twenty-something working-class friends requested financial aid at her private college, the officer replied, "I've never met a Jew who needed more money."

The current reality: (white) Jews are usually considered the most affluent white U.S. ethnic group; some are rich, about one-sixth are poor. But more important? Although Jews are disproportionately well off, Jews do not "control" the economy.

Jewish structural power in finance, on Wall Street

When the global economy began crashing in 2008, bringing millions to their knees, Jew-blaming predictably resurfaced. But the rancor has often been anecdotal, via innuendo, or on Internet sites, usually from the Right (including speeches by Nation of Islam leader Louis Farrakhan), atypically from the Left (a few protestors at Occupy demos: "The Jews Control Wall Street"). Although the impact on Jews is personally offensive, it rarely turns violent as in times past. Most significant: historian Jerry Muller, who wrote *Capitalism and the Jews*, says there has been "no

[U.S.] wave of public sentiment"[26] holding Jews responsible for the financial meltdown, a welcome sign of declining anti-Semitism.

Jews began gaining national policy-making power in finance, from government to Wall Street, in the 1980s. To name a few: Nobel Prize-winner and Reagan economics advisor Milton Friedman, Federal Reserve Board Chairs Alan Greenspan and Ben Bernanke, Treasury Secretary and then key Obama economic advisor Lawrence Summers. They all played a part, along with a plethora of Christian leaders (including former Presidents Bill Clinton and George W. Bush, then Barack Obama), some more so than others, in bringing on the catastrophic recession.

Jewish-founded Wall Street investment firm Goldman Sachs had a leading role in the meltdown—with plenty of company. (Execs from Goldman "bragged about profiting from the collapse of the housing market"[27] and, in a landmark settlement, agreed to pay $550 million to settle charges of defrauding investors.) The complexity, true of marginalized groups overall, is that some Jews clearly collude in oppressive influential roles, continuing to serve power elite interests as well as themselves—while those Jews, at the same time, can be targeted by prejudice.[28]

When Bernard Madoff stole $50 billion from investors, foundations, and banks, primarily from other Jews, he became a convenient lightning rod for blaming Jewish people for the behavior of a few. Though the crime failed to ignite high-impact anti-Semitism, bigotry showed up on the Internet, including mainstream comment sections: "Ho hum, another Crooked Wall Street Jew. Find a Jew who isn't Crooked. Now that would be a story," or "Jews have only one god—money." And the blame was conveyed stereotypically: The "Bernie Madoff doll," which debuted at New York City's 2009 Toy Fair, was dressed as the devil, complete with a hammer for hitting him.[29] The toymaker admitted the $99.95 gift was "tasteless." Have Christian financial criminals been portrayed in this way?[30]

Meanwhile, other influential Jews bird-dogged the government to rein in Wall Street, as Muller points out, from Nobel Prize-winning economist Paul Krugman to Vermont independent Senator Bernie Sanders.

"We had a systemic breakdown," concludes Les Leopold, author of *The Looting of America*, "because nearly all of our policy makers, academics, politicians, and pundits promoted and clung to a failed ideology of self-correcting financial markets...There are plenty of croupiers of all races, religions and creeds who walked off with big bucks while doing their part to crash the system...This is not about good guys and bad guys. Rather it's all about a very flawed financial *system*."[31] (Italics added)

Not to mention (from *Time* magazine): "The financial wreckage littering our world is the creation, almost exclusively, of men."[32] Men (mostly) created the mess, but women leaders are challenging the status quo, "telling Wall Street how to clean up its act."[33]

While the policy-setting power elite for this country remain overwhelmingly Christian, in 2011 nearly a fifth of Americans still believed it was "probably true" that "Jews have too much control/influence on Wall Street"[34] (a vast/welcome decline from 1945). But as racial justice educator and author Tim Wise argues:

> If media or financial wrongdoing is Jewish inspired, since Jews are prominent in media and finance, should the depredations of white Christian-dominated industries (like the tobacco or automobile industries) be viewed as examples of white Christian malfeasance? After all, 400,000 people per year die because of smoking-related illnesses, and tobacco companies withheld information on the cancerous properties of their products. Likewise, should executives at Ford and Firestone be thought of as specifically white Christian criminals, due to...disclosures that defective tires were installed on SUV's, resulting in the deaths of over 150 people worldwide?...Why is it suddenly relevant when the executives in question are Jewish?[35]

Paul Kivel agrees, pointing out that "Blaming Jewish bankers or African-American women on welfare are parallel strategies to divert our attention from the corporate elite that make the economic decisions that affect our lives."[36] We're talking class disparities. "Whenever the stereotypes of Jewish money or power go unchallenged," Kivel continues, "the injustice of our economic system is strengthened and racism is continued...These strategies give the majority of white people the mistaken impression that they are controlled by Jews and in competition with people of color—squeezed on both sides."[37]

Jews and the media

What gives any credence to the "Jews controlling the media" stereo-type? J. J. Goldberg's (admittedly dated) 1996 data pointed to Jews comprising about one-fourth of the elite producers, writers, and editors, a clearly dispro-portionate influence.[38] Yet it means that 75 percent would be non-Jews. Jewish *prominence* in journalism is distinct from *control* by "Jewish interests."

Also to the point, the media industry transforms by the minute. From constantly shifting corporate entities to Internet innovations, pinpointing influence is complicated. Nevertheless, let's examine a few mega-giants. Among the top media conglomerates—Disney, News Corporation (Rupert Murdoch), Time Warner, General Electric, CBS, and Viacom—each own dozens of companies, from sports teams to theme parks, retail outlets to magazines, extending their reach to HBO, Fox network, more.[39] They rake in billions.

Not just that. They also share revolving-door board members with oil companies and banks, technology and pharmaceuticals, investment and health care: interlocking directorates. Together, they own the vast major-ity of U.S. media holdings, and they are primarily loyal to their advertisers, the government, and each other.[40] "The watchdogs of acceptable ideo-logical messages," they control news and information, they fund conserva-tive think tanks.[41] And they are closely linked with Washington's foreign policy establishment.[42]

In their 2009 article "Inside the Military-Industrial-Media Complex," sociologist Peter Phillips and historian Mickey Huff, who direct Project Censored, reported that: "Only 118 people comprise the membership on the boards of directors of the ten big media giants. These 118 individuals in turn sit on the corporate boards of 288 national and international corpora-tions. Four of the top 10 media corporations share board director positions with the major defense contractors."[43]

"There is no evidence that Jews have...overriding influence in this sphere," Paul Kivel points out.[44] Big media represents corporate class interests, not Jewish ones. Most telling, explains Kivel, "We *are en-couraged to see Jews more visibly than white Christians"*—like Warren Buffet, Bill Gates, the Koch Brothers, William Randolph Hearst,

Arianna Huffington, Donald Trump — so that our attention focuses less on the Christian white leadership of corporations and government.[45] (Italics added)

What about Hollywood?

Jewish immigrant entrepreneurs moved west to create the "Hollywood dream factory" because so many other doors slammed in their faces — like the Producer's Trust that Thomas Edison organized in New York to keep "outsiders" (guess who?) out of the movie industry.[46] With U.S. Jewish life precarious in the early 1900s, as an insurance policy of sorts, Jewish moviemakers succeeded by offering a predominantly Christian audience an idealized version of itself.[47]

J. J. Goldberg's 1996 stats reported that most Hollywood senior executives were Jews, as well as many writers and producers. And Hollywood remains Jewish terrain. *Los Angeles Times* columnist Joel Stein jokes, "Hollywood: If you enjoy TV and movies, then you probably like Jews after all."[48] Is that "Jewish power"? One fantasy is that Jews work in cahoots, with evil intent. If there were a disproportionate representation of Baptist bosses in the steel and auto industries, for example, would we call that "Baptist power"? Jews are hardly the only execs: on its "cinema power" list, the 2009 *Hollywood Reporter* rated (Christian) Rupert Murdoch number one; Steven Spielberg came in third.[49]

Most significantly, as with the media, the movie studios are smaller components of their parent companies' predominantly Christian-owned corporate empires: (as of 2012) Murdoch's News Corp owns 20th Century Fox, weapons manufacturer General Electric (and Comcast) own NBC Universal, Paramount is a subsidiary of Viacom. The decisions of these conglomerates are influenced by box office appeal, plus close ties with the arms industry and dependence on the U.S. government for tax breaks.[50]

Movie deals skew towards vetoing films deemed counter to company interests, while endorsing films that promote corporate values. For example, the Motion Picture Association of America was set up to enforce Christian morality and most of its directors have been staunch conservatives; Walt Disney, a known anti-Semite, unabashedly promoted conservative Christian values. So in truth, the visible Jewish Hollywood executives are often mid-level corporate managers, public faces of the buck-stops-here mostly Christian decision-makers. Again, Jewish prominence does not = Jewish control. It's big business we need to target, whoever they are: not Jews, as Jews.

The trouble with Jewish success

One "problem," it seems, that motivates anti-Semitic stereotypes, is Jewish accomplishment. The more successful we are, the more visible; and the more visible, the more susceptible to blame. No wonder some of us fear a spotlight on Jews, wondering when it will twist into a laser.

Policy analyst and historian Stephen Zunes suggests that a look at elite power brokers—like the National Association of Manufacturers, the Trilateral Commission, the Business Roundtable, U.S. cabinet officials, or university trustees—reveals who is usually "overrepresented" given their comprising 1.5 percent of the population: Episcopalians. The son of an Episcopal priest, Zunes says that when it comes to the "ultimate decision makers," most are not Jews, and many are Episcopalian.[51]

When *Vanity Fair* paraded its 2007 top 100 "New Establishment" leaders, mostly in finance and the media, more than half were Jews, an extraordinary indicator of acceptance, success, and influence—although two gentiles led the list: Rupert Murdoch and Apple cofounder (the late) Steve Jobs. But why the focus on media and finance, both arenas where Jews are disproportionately represented? What about leaders in automobiles, aerospace, steel? Would so many on the list have been Jews? And by which standards were the "winners" selected? It's worth remembering that in old Europe, Jews became traders and tax collectors because Christians considered it usury to handle money. For them, this was "dirty work"; for Jews it was survival.

According to research primarily by the Jewish Telegraph Agency's chief philanthropy correspondent, roughly one-third of the 2009 Forbes 400 richest Americans were Jewish (not the top two)[52]—likely the ruling class of the U.S. Jewish community, those with the most money.[53] The Forbes list, clearly one significant measure of wealth (ranging from Google to real estate, hedge funds to hotels, oil and gas to the Philadelphia Eagles), doesn't convey the broader distribution of wealth in this country.[54] How many of the three million-something in the U.S. ruling class (the top 1 percent) are Jews? "The concentration of power, wealth, and privilege under Christian hegemony," Kivel points out, "accumulates to the ruling class and the predominantly white male Christian power elite that serve its interests."[55]

A 2010 anti-Semitic reaction to Jewish success: tea-party icon Glenn Beck's mini-documentary, which cast successful philanthropist/investor (and Holocaust survivor) George Soros as a string-pulling "puppet master." This was Beck's attempt to explain "things...happening in this country that don't make sense" (part of the attraction of conspiracy ideas).[56] When Soros was born, Beck insists, "Little did the world know then, economies would collapse, currencies would become worthless, elections would be stolen, regimes would fall. And one billionaire would find himself coincidentally at the center of it all."[57]

Despite what journalist Jonathan Schell called Beck's "crackpot vision of a grand conspiracy," Schell warned in *The Nation*: "Beck's undoubted centrality in the present moment requires that he be taken seriously [because]...His smears mark the first time in recent memory that a major network has leveled anti-Semitic charges in a calculated campaign ...Political fantasies based on conspiracy theories are dangerous. Beware gifted hysterics who make things up. That usually ends badly."[58]

Other than misleading people about who the actual policy-setters are, a searing impact of "Jewish power" stereotypes on us as Jews can be psychological: Jewish feminists may sit on our strength for fear of being targeted, paralyzing our effectiveness. "I know what anti-Semitism can...do, when we internalize it,"Melanie Kaye/Kantrowitz says.[59] "Anti-Semitism humiliates, isolates, and silences us; mutes our loud proud Jewish energy. How can we fight injustice powerfully if we fear our power?"[60]

Courageously, young Jews *are* stirring things up. Journalist Kiera Feldman describes a spirited "mic check" protest at a Jewish establishment event, calling for: "a redistribution of power/in the *Jewish* community...Throughout history/Jews have been persecuted/as scapegoats for powerful bankers./These memories/give us responsibility/to speak out/against corporate exploitation/and human-rights violations."[61] (Italics added)

This brings back in focus the larger issue, pointed out by Paul Krugman, that "extreme concentration of income is incompatible with real democracy. Can anyone...deny that our political system is being warped by the influence of big money" [whether from gentile or Jew]?[62] Exactly why thousands of protests against global/corporate greed have ricocheted from Madrid to Moscow, from Athens to Santiago.

Jewish political power

The movement of Jews into the U.S. political elite, points out David Biale, signifies "one of the most radical social transformations in Jewish history."[63] In 2010, Jews became one-third of the Supreme Court. In 2013, Jews were 6 percent of the houses of Congress, and several Jews have been among President Obama's key advisers—all indicators of some influence...yet still overwhelmingly a minority swimming in a hegemonically Christian sea.

Jewish voters turn out in numbers, are concentrated in decisive states, and are often campaign donors, so candidates avoid antagonizing them.[64] Political philosopher Michael Walzer believes that Jews contribute massively to political campaigns partly to continue the tradition of "protection money," an antidote to not-that-long-ago persecution.[65] Although Jews have undeniable privileges, many still have big-time fears.

The majority of U.S. Jews lean liberal, sending the Democrats hefty hunks of their campaign funds (roughly 60 percent),[66] though giving sizable sums to Republicans as well[67]—like far-right billionaire Sheldon Adelson, who spent nearly $150 million trying to defeat President Obama in 2012, to reinforce congressional support of hawkish Israeli policies, also to defeat Obama's "socialist-style" economics.[68] (While the gentile Republican-affiliated Koch brothers and company intended "to spend...something like $400 million" before the 2012 election."[69]) Most crucial: as the Jewish *Forward* points out, it was the Supreme Court's 2010 *Citizens United* "disastrous decision" that structurally opened the floodgates for unlimited financial influence on political campaigns, by individuals and corporations, Jews and non-Jews.[70]

Two overlapping charges refer to foreign policy accusations: that Jews were responsible for the U.S. occupation of Iraq and that Jews control U.S. Middle East policy via the Israel Lobby. (Read: the "Jewish Lobby.")

Just ask Hollywood star Mel Gibson: when arrested for drunk driving, Gibson belligerently accosted the Jewish policeman, "F***ing Jews, Jews are responsible for the wars in the world."[71]

The reality, again, is complicated. The well-organized Jewish establishment wields influence with a heavy hand, leaving what J. J. Goldberg calls "a big footprint on the national stage"[72]—while also inflating its power-image to achieve its agenda. But it is one among various power brokers, or factors, helping shape foreign policy: from the Christian Right, to arms dealers and the U.S. military, to multinational oil companies (and government efforts to control access to oil), to Arab world uprisings.

Who really "made" Bush and Cheney invade Iraq?

Jewish Americans opposed the Iraq war more than any other religious group, including early on, when most Americans supported it. So who lobbied hard to invade Iraq? The neocons, both Jews and non-Jews, including evangelical Christians…also the Israel Lobby, military contractors, various Republicans, and oil interests.[73] And Saudi Arabia, just to name a few. It's a both/and: *both* Jewish neocons *and* others, with *all* the neoconservatives playing a key role. And although neocons like Martin Peretz and William Kristol cast themselves as spokespeople for all Jews, analyst Glenn Greenwald points out this was far from true.[74] Illustrating the complex landscape, Stephen Zunes says that think tanks supporting U.S. militarism often include a "disproportionate number of Jews in influential positions"—while on their boards sit Christians representing weapons manufacturers like Lockheed Martin, Northrop Grumman, and Boeing.[75]

During George W. Bush's in-your-face-Christian presidency, Jewish conservatives were among the *visible* faces of aggressive U.S. foreign policies, policies framed by Christians and Jews alike. While President Bush, Vice President Cheney, Secretary of State Rice, and other top decision-makers shared priorities with the neocons, it was Bush and his administration that called the shots. And all these players pushed policies consistent with previous U.S. imperial designs.[76]

In 1991, after the first U.S. invasion of Iraq, the neocons' Defense Guidance Plan (a Pentagon document) heralded U.S. hegemony: "In the Middle East and Southwest Asia, our overall objective is to remain the predominant outside power...and preserve U.S....access to the region's oil."[77] Although annulled by Clinton's White House, Dick Cheney later integrated the plan into Bush's 2002 strategy. Even by 1997, Cheney, Rumsfeld, Paul Wolfowitz, Lewis (Scooter) Libby, and other hawks (Jews and gentiles) had birthed the Project for a New American Century (PNAC), focused on overthrowing Saddam Hussein and installing the United States as sole superpower. Many also backed Israel's hawkish policies, seeing Israel as a tool of U.S. empire; and some were partly motivated by concern for Israel's security.

Meanwhile, the Israel Lobby drummed up support for this decision that Bush and Cheney were already making.[78] The American Israel Public Affairs Committee (AIPAC) gladly took credit for successfully lobbying Congress. Human-rights expert Ian Buruma runs down the chorus behind the invasion:

> What we see...is not a Jewish conspiracy, but a peculiar alliance of evangelical Christians, foreign policy hard-liners, lobbyists for the Israel government and neoconservatives, a number of whom happen to be Jewish... But the Jews among them—Perle, Wolfowitz, William Kristol...are more likely to speak about freedom and democracy than about Halakha [Jewish law]. What unites this...is a shared vision of American destiny and the conviction that American force and a tough Israeli line on the Arabs are the best ways to make the United States strong, Israel safe and the world a better place.[79]

The Israel Lobby

WHO IS IT?

In addition to AIPAC—the 100,000-member Jewishly visible lobby leader—the Israel Lobby includes a loose amalgamation of groups: advocacy organizations, political action committees, think tanks, watchdog groups, and individuals who share a common (conservative) cause but differ in approach and agenda.[80] Much of its less-visible clout comes from the Christian Right and the weapons industry. It is among Washington's most powerful and effective lobbies.[81]

The overall goal? In their landmark essay (and book on the subject) "The Israel Lobby," political scientist John Mearsheimer and international affairs expert Stephen Walt explain the Lobby's aim: "To steer US foreign policy in a pro-Israel direction," which also means "controlling the [Israel-

Palestine] debate" to guarantee U.S. support for Israel.[82] Despite the Lobby's seeming vice-grip on Capitol Hill, U.S. Middle East strategy has continued to align with most U.S. strategy worldwide—policies that support military occupations and dictatorships, exploit area resources, use double standards regarding human rights, and opt for bombs (or sanctions) over diplomacy— challenging the claim that "Jewish power" is to blame for skewing U.S. policies against U.S. interests.[83]

Crucially, much of the right-wing, pro-Israel advocacy comes from Christian Zionists and the Christian Right, who provide mega-funding and mobilizing. Policy specialist Walter Russell Mead corroborates that "Widespread *gentile* support for Israel is one of the most potent political forces in U.S. foreign policy,"[84] while Israeli Prime Minister Netanyahu proclaims, "We have no greater friends and allies than right-wing American Christians."[85] (Italics added)

Take, for example, televangelist Pastor John Hagee. His Christians United for Israel (CUFI) group of Christian Zionists sends millions of dollars yearly to Israel (much of it to settlements), claims over a million members,[86] and beats drums for war with Iran. Hagee preached that God orchestrated the Nazi Holocaust so that Jews would flee to Israel and fulfill biblical prophecy. Christian Zionism depends on a "Jewish return to Zion," where, incidentally, "Armageddon will see the Jews all converted or destroyed."[87] But such ravings haven't cut ties between Hagee and AIPAC or the Conference of Presidents of Major American Jewish Organizations.[88] Christian power in pro-Israel advocacy is usually underestimated, and Jewish influence can be exaggerated, "an indication," argues Paul Kivel, "of the invisibility of Christian dominance and the...existence of anti-Semitism."[89]

Specifically, what does the Lobby do? AIPAC and other organizations try to shape policy by emphasizing to legislators the U.S.-Israel alliance (via news analysis, also free trips to Israel—for nearly one-fifth of the House of Representatives in summer 2011 alone).[90] They also influence funding to Congresspeople and have directed funds to political opponents if Congress members don't heed their bidding; while their Christian Zionist cohorts fund candidates directly. In my rabbi's Yom Kippur sermon about Israel-Palestine, he told us that AIPAC sends "weekly advice to rabbis on how to use the weekly *dvar Torah* [commentary on the Torah] to work in a plug for AIPAC's policies, as if these policies were required by the text of the *Torah*."[91]

How powerful is it?

"The influence of the Israel lobby," argue political analysts Mitchell Plitnick and Chris Toensing, "should neither be underestimated nor overstated."[92] Mearsheimer and Walt charge that the Lobby is so powerful it has influenced the United States to act against its own best interests. Noted *New York Times* columnist Thomas Friedman referred to the twenty-nine standing ovations Congress gave Netanyahu when he spoke in May 2011: "That ovation was bought and paid for by the Israel Lobby."[93] Yet worldrenowned intellectual and dissident Noam Chomsky argues that the idea of an all-powerful "Jewish Lobby," "leaves the U.S. government untouched [blameless] on its high pinnacle of nobility"—later adding, "If the U.S. military and business lobbies wanted to, they could put an end to AIPAC's influence in five minutes."[94]

Policy analyst Phyllis Bennis similarly explains the Israel Lobby has appeared more powerful than it is, because it has often supported "traditional definitions of U.S. national interest as defined by the Pentagon, the White House, and the State Department,[95] interests consistent with foreign policy since the Cold War, in Southeast Asia, Africa, Latin America, and the Middle East. Practically regardless of who they are, *groups overall are most influential*, suggests Kivel, *"where their interests align with the power elite and the ruling class."*[96]

Arab Politics professor Joseph Massad nearly lost his job at Columbia University due to Lobby pressure; yet he wrote that the Lobby may be responsible for "the details and intensity but not the direction, content, or impact" of U.S. foreign policy.[97] "Is the pro-Israel Lobby extremely powerful in the United States? As someone who has been facing...their power for the last three years...and their attempts to get me fired, I answer with a resounding yes. Are they primarily responsible for U.S. policies towards the Palestinians and the Arab world? Absolutely not."[98]

One of the most potent forces behind pro-Israel policies is the weapons industry. Since 75 percent of the $3 billion in annual aid to Israel ends up, by law, in the pockets of U.S. arms manufacturers,[99] why wouldn't they push Congress to keep the aid coming, to press for policies requiring more F-16 fighter jets and Blackhawk helicopters? In 2006, weapons dealers sent $7 million or more per election cycle to congressional campaigns—twice as much as (other) pro-Israel organizations did.[100] Lockheed Martin, the largest U.S. defense contractor has, along with Boeing, GE, Northrup Grumman, and Raytheon, outspent AIPAC in lobbying.[101] Meanwhile, munitions factories provide jobs and revenue in many congressional districts, hard for Congress members to ignore.[102]

So how powerful is the Israel Lobby really? On the influence side, it is more effective and substantial than other foreign policy lobbies; and such advocacy is part of how U.S politics work. It has skillfully stifled public debate about Israel-Palestine (misnaming it "new anti-Semitism," see Chapter One), though that power is sometimes-waning. And AIPAC unquestionably fosters an intimidating climate, as do other lobbies— for example, sending a 2009 warning to Obama to "work closely and privately with Israel," signed by the vast majority of the House and the Senate.[103]

Yet sometimes AIPAC's power is overblown. Where it has brought pressure, many congressional votes have been nonbinding, and attempts at binding legislation have often failed.[104] Although the Lobby claims to unseat Congress members who oppose Israeli policies, most House members who have resisted AIPAC have won reelection.[105] (And most congressional reps already supported Israel.) In terms of the Lobby's influence on Jews, prior to the 2012 elections, only 4 percent of Jewish registered voters said Israel would be a key decisive issue in their vote.[106]

Part of AIPAC's sway has sometimes been in telling the U.S. government, especially George W. Bush, what it wanted to hear.[107] But it's also true that Obama's strategy, while often consistent with U.S. policy since Israel was founded (before AIPAC's rise)—as in Obama's 2012 election year "unshakeable" commitment to Israel—has responded to Lobby pressure. (Not to mention that in 2008 AIPAC's president was a major Obama fundraiser.)[108] One striking example: when military chiefs blamed "Israeli intransigence" for jeopardizing the security of U.S. troops in Afghanistan, Iraq, and Pakistan in 2010, Obama's administration sharply criticized Israeli settlement building, despite AIPAC and company backing Israel. Nearly half of U.S. voters supported Obama's stand.[109] Yet the next year, the United

States backtracked, blocking a key U.N. resolution against settlements: a turnaround from longtime U.S. policy, and a move many analysts saw as bowing to AIPAC.[110]

FROM INSIDE THE JEWISH WORLD:
CHALLENGES TO THE RIGHT-WING LOBBY

Much of AIPAC's success has come from lack of opposition in Washington, but its right-wing bent is increasingly out of sync with growing numbers of U.S. Jews. The tide is shifting. Lobby newcomer J Street, a Jewish moderate-to-liberal D.C.-based group, over 180,000-online-supporters strong, is directly countering AIPAC.

Strategizing to "rock the status quo"[111] with a more enlightened pro-Israel mindset, J Street's "No. 1 agenda item" has been to back Obama in Congress.[112] It is bent on transforming mainstream terrain: to break AIPAC's iron fist and challenge hard-line Israeli policies...to open up debate about Israel/Palestine within the Jewish community, making room to "hug and wrestle with Israel at the very same time."[113] Clustering with other "pro-peace, pro-Israel" lobby groups, J Street stands out as mostly staffed by younger leaders, signaling a new style, while drawing a multigenerational constituency.

An important mainstream "rupture...in the supposed American Jewish consensus over Israel/Palestine,"[114] J Street promotes "a Palestinian state alongside...Israel with recognized borders," and a "resolution that meets the core interests of both parties,"[115] a plan close to President Clinton's in 2000. Strategically, it leans towards diplomacy over military force, pressing for a strong U.S. role in a peace process. Key is focusing on Israel's well-being and preserving Israel as a national Jewish homeland. Nearly 150 congressional reps joined the host committee of J Streets' 2009 founding conference (though over half of Congress packed AIPAC's conference that year; and Obama himself spoke at AIPAC's 2012 meeting).

J Street usually frames the conversation as (the age-old) "Is it good for the Jews?" Deepening the dialogue, Jewish Voice for Peace is a non-Lobby, grassroots AIPAC-challenger, with 130,000 online supporters, which instead foregrounds human rights and international law, asking "Is it good for Israelis *and* for Palestinians?" Joining "Occupy AIPAC" 2012, JVP activists rallied with hundreds more in week-long actions decrying AIPAC practices, including its fear-mongering push for war with Iran (an aggression shared by gentile Republican presidential hopefuls and Capitol Hill hawks).

⁂

When my friend Liat was invited to a Bay Area retreat for young (lefty) activist leaders, she e-mailed afterwards: not only wasn't anti-Semitism acknowledged along with the other "isms," but some gentiles blamed all Jews for Israeli government policies—even though our Jewish organization was visibly fighting those policies. They also accused Jews of initiating war on Iraq and of controlling the media. When Liat called out their (possibly unaware) bias, they denied it. Even among activists, old stereotypes die hard.

Anti-Semitism has laid the groundwork for attacking Jews as "too powerful"; yet untangling prejudice from actual Jewish influence can be complicated. Attributing disproportionate power to the Israel Lobby—a neoconservative interest lobby, actually made up of Jewish *and* Christian organizations—is not inherently anti-Jewish, since the Lobby's influence is immense. And AIPAC intentionally overstates its power, exploiting the stereotype to manipulate support for an invincible militaristic Israel: a goal challenged by U.S. human-rights activists, Jewish and gentile.

But given the complexities of how policy is formulated and implemented, blaming Jews for controlling U.S. foreign policy is inaccurate, offensive, and too close for comfort to the tired "Jewish power" stereotypes. Why is it that only when it comes to the Middle East, some people believe that U.S. policy is based on "Jewish interests"?[116] As a peace activist colleague charges, "It gives U.S. imperialism a free pass."

Absolutely, many white U.S. Jews are fortunate to lead lives of advantage, while a select cadre wields exceptional power in certain elite spheres. But when anti-Semitism exaggerates that influence, including when prominence is conflated with intent to control, it obscures the overwhelmingly Christian culture of class power that persistently impacts our lives.

PART TWO

Wrestling with the Voices

4

The Trickster in Our Heads:
Internalized Jewish Oppression

"The true focus of revolutionary change is never merely the oppressive situations which we seek to escape, but that piece of the oppressor which is planted deep within each of us."[1]

—*Audre Lorde*

IF A MIRACLE HAPPENED, AND SUDDENLY THERE WERE NO MORE RACISM, sexism, or classism; heterosexism/transphobia, ableism or ageism; or anti-Jewish bigotry—how long would it take targeted groups in the United States to free ourselves from *internalized oppression?* In our intersecting and hyphenated Jewish women's (also trans, genderqueer) identities, we have somehow, unwillingly, ingested that something is very wrong with who we are.

Remember Sally Kempton's words (Chapter One) about how tricky it is to fight an enemy with outposts in our heads? This enemy is the voice of internalized oppression, what the late Brazilian educator Paulo Freire called internalizing the consciousness of the oppressor.[2] Dominant groups spread their seemingly unquestionable view of reality—white Christian gendered norms—so successfully that their perspective can become widely accepted as common sense, often even by us as Jewish women.

How does the process play out? Strike One for Jews is the anti-Semitism—the stereotyping, scapegoating, violence, and past persecution—which *implants, constructs*, the insidious messages in us. Messages that tell Jewish women that we are (for starters) "pushy/loud/politico/power trippy/cheap/dominating/garish/sexy/emotional/always screaming/bossy/ scary temper/difficult style/(and, of course) Jewish mother/(and) Jewish princess."[3] Part of the hurtful dynamic, explains social justice educator Julian Weissglass, involves some gentiles projecting onto Jews "the anger and hate that they themselves have experienced," possibly from child-hood abuse, religious indoctrination, poverty, and/or racism.[4]

Strike Two is *believing* that this antagonism is based on reality: unwill-ingly seeing ourselves through the eyes of the dominant culture, accept-ing that perspective as accurate. Sometimes just looking at other Jews' stricken or enraged or terrified faces, says coalition-building leader Cherie Brown, confirms how badly they (we) have been hurt, how much we have believed such messages.[5]

Strike Three? Since internalized anti-Semitism includes all the effects on us of dehumanization, Strike Three is the *devastating feelings and be-haviors passed down through our families* for generations, in response to historic persecution.[6] Pre-Nazi Holocaust. Pre-Cossack. The transmission of Jewish fear, grief, and helplessness. Discouragement. Humiliation. Self-loathing. Just because many of us have privilege today doesn't wipe out or invalidate these emotions. Again, we can see each other's pain in how we each navigate the world.

The way through is to examine the messages installed in our heads, the (often-defensive) behaviors that get triggered when someone blames or excludes, frightens or abandons us. Mostly, these feelings are responses to g*d-awful things that happened a long time ago, a legacy of powerless-ness passed through our families and communities. But it's time: to begin releasing, or resisting, the emotions—with support—until we can see our lives in a new (real) light, so we can heal…to cultivate self-love as an ongo-ing process.[7] Diversity educator Yeshi Sherover Neumann points out, we have to face all these feelings—and have "the courage not to act on them."[8]

Voices of the trickster

"I think that Jews are not okay. We're weird and we're bad. This culture makes us feel that way, and that comes from Christian theology: that Jews were the devil's representatives on earth and Jews are evil. I get enraged but I also start taking it in—which is where the self-hatred comes in. That's why you have to be vigilant and constantly work at countering it. And part of me, I'm shocked, says 'Are they right? Is this true?' Of course it's not true. But you get to the point where you're thinking, 'How do I counter the constant onslaught of that kind of thing?'"—*Jessie*

How to recognize the enemy inside our heads? Aurora Levins Morales told me one day, "Anytime you cast doubt on the usefulness, brilliance, and power of your thoughts, chances are it's him again":[9] "You're disgusting." "You're ugly!" "Who do you think you are, anyway?" "And, *it's all your fault!*" No way. Because "living in a society that maps oppression onto us, it is impossible not to internalize it."[10]

The voices may tell us that it's shameful to be Jewish. That the only ones we can trust are Jews. That other Jews are yucky. That it's dangerous to be visible. That no one wants us. That we have to appear tough, at all costs. That we are too much, or not enough. That the whole world is against us, and our suffering differs from everyone else's. That we are the Lone Ranger, all alone.

Or the voices may sound like spoken-word artist Vanessa Hidary: "I've been swayed to believe that being Jewish is not too cool, not too sexy."[11] Or the late Marek Edelman, a courageous leader of the Warsaw Ghetto Uprising, who at twenty years old trudged daily past Nazi posters caricaturing Jewish faces to look like rats. He then saw his own as "repugnant, sinister...Whereas everybody else...had fair faces. They were handsome, relaxed...because they were aware of their...beauty."[12]

Loolwa Khazzoom says some Mizrahi, Sephardi, Ethiopian Jews (learn to) feel embarrassment, even contempt, for their heritages—in response to mainstream Jewish racism.[13] And a phone-banker in an electoral campaign hid her real name because she couldn't bear "turning off" any voters by being identifiably Jewish. When I shared these stories with J., she replied, "I work in a Jewish institution. If you need more examples, I've got plenty!"

Has Jewish self-hatred always existed? At least since Jews were maligned as God-killers, with the accompanying barrage of demonization.[14] Measured by white Christian scales, we were different = inferior = bad. Internalized anti-Semitism has also been a by-product of assimilation, of losing that deep sense of connection to our people.

Of course we don't all have the same inner voices, and these toxins aren't reserved just for Jews. Yet psychologist Melissa Schwartz says that Jewish women consistently bring into therapy issues of grief, loss, pressure to conform to dominant Christian culture—and chronic terror.[15] The deep-down fear of annihilation. We feel like we have to prove our "right to exist, over and over again."[16]

Physician and activist Alice Rothchild noticed early on, with empathy, the internalized trauma of Nazi Holocaust survivors: "...whether it was my red-faced Hebrew school principal screaming uncontrollably at a group of unruly students or the vulnerable rabbi's wife who always overdressed her children as if she could not protect them from some fierce internal cold."[17]

I know my own "enemy" is lurking when my buttons are pushed by other Jewish women, especially if they're "bossy," "needy," "loud." With characteristic compassion, Yeshi Neumann explains that many of these ("irritating") coping behaviors were developed in reaction to anti-Jewishness. Especially, she says, notice whatever bugs us about other Jews; that's a big clue about our own internalized anti-Semitism.

Most compelling of all is what I consistently hear from amazing and accomplished Jewish women, eyes clouded with pain—in fact, from women, period: *"There's something wrong with me."* This is the heart of women's internalized oppression. Again, for me, it can show up as "What's holding you back? Look how much better you have it than most people in the world. You should be out there really changing things. What's WRONG with you?"

Melanie Kaye/Kantrowitz shares the secret (internalized) fears some of us have: "Maybe we really are...rich and greedy, taking over, too loud, too pushy, snatching up more than our share, ugly and parasitical, Jewish American Princesses, Jewish landlords, Jewish bosses, emphasis on Jewish. Maybe we really deserve to be hated."[18]

Different battles, familiar voices

Even though marginalized groups each have their own distinct experiences, we sometimes share soul-crushing inner diatribes and learned helplessness. Isolation is a grim by-product of mistreatment, so why not support each other in uprooting the internalized voices? Various messages of internalized sexism, racism, ageism, ableism, and heterosexism/homophobia intersect with Jewish ones.[19] Some examples:

In our group, Jessie confided, gazing at the floor, "Being Jewish is not my biggest issue. I'll do anything to avoid people knowing that I'm disabled. When I had to use a cane, it was hell. I felt so stigmatized."

As a body/voice instructor, Emily noticed how internalized sexism "is a common theme for women, how we contract our voices and submit our bodies. It's hard for us to fill out our space. And because it's familiar, we sometimes think we're comfortable that way." Kim refined the analysis. "In the process work I've done, some gentiles have shared about not being able to 'break out of the sexism cage.' I think Jewish women push the cage bars more, but then we feel we're 'too much.' Non-Jewish white women are more stuck in those cages and don't even know how to break out."

Self-proclaimed "feminist hothead" writer Kay Leigh Hagan sees codependency, a struggle for many Jewish women, as code for internalized sexism: a patriarchal bullhorn clamped inside our heads, training us into subordination and "giving." Feeling unlovable, involuntarily we comply—believing our self-worth is pinned to caretaking. Then we're (understandably) resentful when our own needs are ignored. "What would happen at those 12-step meetings," Hagan asks, eyes twinkling, "if instead of women saying 'I'm codependent,' they said, 'I'm oppressed!'"[20]

Elly likened her constant turmoil about whether or not to show her Jewishness, to her choice/effort not to "pass" as heterosexual. She can pass, and…"It's painful. People don't necessarily know I'm a lesbian because I'm a femme. They need to expand their interpretation of what a lesbian is. When someone looks at my wedding ring and makes assumptions, based on how they perceive me, I have to let them know, 'Excuse me! Hello! My husband is a woman!'"

And in her keynote at the National Women's Studies Association (NWSA) Conference, activist scholar Bette Tallen noted that over half the organizational members at the time (2000) were lesbians, a group "peculiarly silent on our own behalf."[21] They failed to center lesbian issues in their academic work or on NWSA's agenda. "What is the source of this silence?" Tallen challenged, then replied: "Our fear of losing our place at the table...We are talking about internalized oppression."[22]

Back in 1941, social psychologist Kurt Lewin proposed that Jewish self-hatred was paralleled by self-hatred among "American Negroes."[23] More recently Suzanne Lipsky wrote (an apt description of internalized oppression overall): "I can be sure that anytime I feel intolerant of, irritated by, impatient with, embarrassed by, ashamed of, 'not as black as,' 'blacker than,' better than, not as good as, fearful of, not safe with, isolated from, mistrustful of, not cared about by, unable to support, or not supported by another black person, some pattern of internalized racism is at work."[24]

The late Chicana feminist leader and scholar Gloria Anzaldua confided, "We, Chicanos...hate ourselves...We suspect that there is something 'wrong' with us, something fundamentally 'wrong.'"[25] And my colleague who was viciously targeted in school after 9/11 admitted, "I say that I am Middle Eastern. I can't say 'Arab.' The racial slurs are embedded in me; I'm afraid that they're true." Yet change is possible: during 2011 victory celebrations in Cairo's Tahrir Square, after President Mubarak was ousted, how moving to see activists proclaim with jubilant faces, "Finally, I am proud to be Egyptian."

Psychodynamics at work

How does the toxicity worm its way inside? Crucially: the internalization process is involuntary and subtle. We're bombarded daily by messages of bias and exclusion, from TV, the Internet, radio; by movies and magazines, song lyrics and cultural practices, in school and synagogue, and of course, in our families. The process is complex, since power is dynamic and relational, not just imposed from above but instead circulating "within a web of relationships in which we all participate."[26] The mistreatment itself is part of "the everyday practices of a well-intentioned... society."[27] Such socialization constructs how we should be, what to think, and who should be demeaned: a brainwashing virtually "woven into every structural thread of the fabric of our culture."[28]

We resist the relentless onslaught, but it grinds us down. Diversity educators Hugh Vazquez and Isoke Femi explain, "Through no fault of our own, we begin to wear the scars and misconceptions about ourselves like an ill-fitting garment."[29] As youngsters, when we're constantly shushed into silencing the outrage, fright, disappointment, and pain that come up when injustice slams us in the face, these repressed feelings lock into place deep inside. They rigidify into voices thundering in our ears. And they sometimes spew out onto someone else—onto someone like us.

The good news

Since the debilitating inner accusations have become our own, *we can change them.* But they are so embedded, it takes ongoing intention and patience to disentangle their roots. The final chapters of this book suggest how. "Sometimes it is necessary," writes poet Galway Kinnell, "to reteach a thing its loveliness."[30]

What's key is remembering that these internalized voices and feelings are not personal pathologies. Instead, despite diverse backgrounds, many of us share a common experience of systemic bias and hurt—and it can help just to feel heard. As Elly realized after listening to so many Jewish women's stories, "Oh, *you* feel like that too? So I have these responses because I'm *Jewish.* Like it's not so much my *fault!*"

Next up: the complex variations of internalized anti-Semitism waiting to be exposed and disempowered—because understanding the ways we've been hurt can help us heal. When we truly like who we are, we like and treat others better as well. Healthy self-reflection, as opposed to self-blame, moves us forward.

Ushering in the rest of this book is the stirring call of my talented/ outrageous performer friend "Bitch." Picture her at the opening of the Michigan Womyn's Music Festival, perched on scaffolding high above our heads, furiously playing her violin:

> "Something's rumbling–can you feel it? Look around and you'll see the rebels of our time. The women who have come to this world scarred or shining, battered or bold, fiery and fierce or frantic and frail...We've fought through years or tears or society's fears. We've opened our hearts even though hearts break...We are warriors of the world just by bodies female...We are choosing to acknowledge that our pain holds hands with our power, that our scars are as colorful as stars, that our bodies are birthing places of revolution and that revolution starts here."[31]

5

Suckled on Worry

"Something. Bad. Can. Always. Happen."[1]
— *Rabbi Susan Schnur*

How many of us clench with defensiveness and fear—automatically, unconsciously—when we are disagreed with, criticized, excluded? Maybe simply when we show our Jewish-women selves, speak our minds? We may feel a deep need for self-protection (including from other Jews).

For example: at a workshop about race, a white Jewish woman brought up anti-Semitism and asked all the Jews to stand up. "I was physically in agony," Elly groaned. "I *hated* her. I thought, 'We're here to deal with *real* issues like racism. And besides, if I stand up and am seen, they'll kill us!'"

Although we're often unaware that fear is running us, when we scratch the surface of our Jewish stories, Kim observed, "what we notice is fear for our safety." Fallout from centuries of persecution. For Elly, whose childhood was imprinted with "visions of flames" from Nazi Holocaust stories, "*Jewish* survival issues feel deeper than survival issues as a woman. *Much* deeper. When I read in the paper about a woman being raped, I'm horrified. But I don't feel threatened. Yet when I read about a synagogue being firebombed, I feel 'Oh my God, it's starting up, they're gonna get us.' It's something about the *intention* to 'get' *all Jews*."

Anxiety, urgency, hypervigilance: "be careful!"

Mostly our fear shows up as Worry—and big-time distrust (of almost anyone), waiting for the next shoe to drop. Our necks ache from glancing over our shoulders. Geri told us about an evening of Jewish comedy where a hilarious group of gay men performed their version of Bobby McFerrin's song, "Don't Worry, Be Happy." Only their remake was "Don't Be Happy—Worry!" My friend's five-year-old (gentile) daughter complained after only one morning at Jewish day camp, "Mom, I don't want to go back there, all they do is worry!" *Lilith* editor Rabbi Susan Schnur, posits that many Jewish women practically "vibrate with anxiety."[2] "After generations of its being an adaptive survival skill," she writes, "worrying has become hardwired into our Jewish genes."[3]

We may act ultra-confident, competitive, even arrogant, to hide the frightened child inside. Absently twirling a finger through her curls, Emily confides: "The kind of survivor I learned to be was, 'You tough it out.' But when you're being tough, people can't get close. You're so scared you're gonna be hurt, you don't let anybody in, and I think a lot of that has to do with Jewish oppression. You feel like you don't have the luxury of being soft, you're fighting on the front lines."

And why wouldn't we worry?

Remember the history. Rabbi Michael Lerner characterized Europeans from the 11th to the 20th centuries as "a surrounding population that might at any moment explode in irrational violence"[4] against Jews—including pre-Holocaust—from pogroms back to the Inquisition and the Crusades. U.S. bigotry is not comparable to European anti-Semitism; but even by 1944, when word was leaking out in the U.S. press about genocide, 43 percent of those surveyed in the U.S. said they would "support a campaign against Jews."[5] Forty-two percent reported not wanting Jews to move into their neighborhoods, second only to "Negroes."[6] So why wouldn't we feel shaky now and then?

Despite current advantages, psychologist Melissa Schwartz believes it would be "unique to be a Jew in this day and age and not have some fear around getting killed."[7] Put differently, in ways that few of us realize, "The unconscious collective memory of the Holocaust invades every part of our daily lives as Jews."[8] A Jewish leader confided, "People have asked me my whole life, 'Why are you so insecure? You're so successful, so strong!' But not long ago I found out how many of my cousins, aunts, and uncles were killed in the Holocaust. No one told me, but somehow I guess I just knew." A friend described to me the "loose noose" theory, that deep inside some Jews feel as if we have a loose noose around our necks, not knowing if that noose will ever be tightened: living in constant fear that danger is just around the corner, even if it's not immediate.

Though hostility has plummeted since the 1940s, some still simmers, erupting into violent attacks on Jewish day schools and community centers, holocaust museums and synagogues. Living in the Castro, a visibly gay San Francisco neighborhood, Geri remembers spending "a million years imagining they'll try to come get us. It's about being a Jew or being queer. I think I need to be strong and smart, and I'll die on the barricades. Fear is a huge motivator for my activism, I feel I have no choice."

Compounding our anxiety is the way Jews are ostracized for how we may show worry, behaviors simply different from the Christian norm. We're ridiculed as "neurotic," when a little patience and understanding would go a long way. A Gen-Y friend notices the differences when she's with (presumably white) non-Jews who "seem far less fearful when we go hiking, camping, traveling. They don't see danger around every corner. Sometimes they seem naïve, like they cannot fathom how bad things can get."

"What if I relax?" Emily asked, hunched over on the couch. "If I'm not looking over my shoulder, or ahead of me, will that put my survival at stake?"

"Right, Jews got killed when they weren't hypervigilant," Kim added, clutching her arms. "If we stop being on guard..." Her voice trailed off.

"Not in India," Deena pointed out, where her father grew up, where the miniscule Jewish communities were mostly free from attack.

But we knew that Jews were also killed when they *were* vigilant. In the Pale of Russia, for example—where the tsar forced Jews to live in the 1800s, including much of present-day Lithuania, Belarus, Poland, Bessarabia, Ukraine, and parts of western Russia —Jews learned to listen for warning signs. The thundering hooves of Cossacks or the shouts of a mob sent them racing for their lives.

Kim described day-to-day hypervigilance as anticipating someone's need before they have a chance to feel it. "Like, 'Don't forget to bring your sweater.'"

"It's watching constantly," Elly chimed in, wiping her glasses. "What would happen if she forgot her sweater? That would be a terrible thing!" Hypervigilance translates, too, as keeping passports updated and cash on hand in case we need to beat a hasty retreat. Or stashing away food. Or, in the backs of our minds, remembering places to hide. To manage the anxiety inside, some of us compulsively overeat, one way we self-medicate.

"Working in a Jewish organization, I can say hypervigilance is definitely a Jewish thing," Judith testified. Nazi Holocaust scholar and psychologist Barbara Hammer characterizes the Anti-Defamation League as just such a fear-based Jewish group, eyes peeled for any perceived harmful intent towards Jews. It sometimes requires negotiating a foray of locked doors to enter such high-profile Jewish establishments.

Yet this vigilance can serve us as well: as social workers, project managers, event planners. "I'm very good at managing other people's lives for them," Elly joked, as morning light streamed through the window: "If we take care of other people and make them happy, will we be allowed to live?"

"That we're continually strategizing shows how deep this issue goes for us," Kim sighed. "As if there is a *Plan* that will make us secure."

Underneath lies the need to control our environment, to do everything right, so that we won't be blamed. "It's about 'If everything is in place, and everyone does exactly what they're supposed to, then *maybe* we'll be safe,'" Elly proposed, pulling down the shade. "If I can control my environment, and your environment, then maybe I'll be okay. And when someone says 'Back off,' I know I'm doing anxiety management," she laughed.

"Feeling responsible for the entire universe?" Kim asked.

"It's just that life as we know it will come to an end if the water spills on the floor. And it will be my fault," Elly replied.

"Nothing bad should happen while you're on watch," offered Amy.

Elly laughed again. "And I'm always on watch!"

Who wouldn't feel a little bit urgent? In Yiddish it's *shpilkos*: above all, don't slow down! "If you want to live, keep moving forward," a Nazi death march survivor advised his son. While a Gen-Y friend confides, "I was SO rushed as a kid. It was always 'hurry up!' And never rest." A compulsion to get things done, *now.*

Diversity educator Cherie Brown lovingly characterizes Jews as a "panicked people,"[9] frantically overworking, trying to be smarter and "better," to prove our worth...so we won't be wiped out next time around. Brown tells a story that elicits knowing laughter from other Jews: When Protestants are afraid, they become stoic, frozen. When Jews are scared, we dash out and start five new organizations.[10]

Avoiding visibility

Our worry might manifest as the low Jewish profile we learn to keep, avoiding visibility to deter rejection or anti-Semitic jabs. Jewish leadership can be strikingly noticeable in a Christian environment (Read: vulnerable). "The more I openly express...my Jewish identity," says teacher Terry Fletcher, "the more I experience...a backlash."[11] Writer Bernice Mennis described her immigrant working-class parents trembling at "doing anything big," afraid it "would place them in danger."[12] And an Occupy Boston activist confides, it's "still sometimes scary to be a public Jew."

A colleague reveals that his parents, who lost most of their families to the Shoah, gave him a *Chai* ("Life") necklace at age fifteen, with the caveat, "Keep it on UNDER your shirt." And Cherie Brown tells of her friend who wouldn't nail a *mezuzah* to her door, because she feared being targeted.[13] She "was working hard to make the world...safe...for everyone. But she couldn't speak up to make it safe for...her family as Jews."[14]

One of my students, R., told our class that "in nineteen years of [her own] teaching, I...never told my students that I was Jewish...because I'm afraid someone will harm me—even though there is little overt anti-Semitism in San Francisco." But soon after our class, one of R.'s students invited her to dinner; and when he said something anti-Semitic, R. told him she was Jewish (for the first time ever).[15] He was embarrassed, she reported, but nothing else happened. "Maybe it's just not the big deal I feared it was."

Melissa Schwartz's Jewish clients also admit they fear harm if they draw too much attention, look too good, act too powerfully: "If I do, they'll envy...and...hate me and...I'll be killed."[16] Tragically, once in a long while it happens. In 2009, a male stalker wrote in his journal, "I think it's okay to kill Jews," and gunned down a Jewish coed he had followed from Virginia to Connecticut.[17] The worry we feel is scarcely our fault. Fear is a no-brainer reaction to past danger and to the rare present-day attack as well.

Transmitting trauma

"The internalized terror of the Holocaust generation...[was] passed on to a new generation, shaping their personal lives, their politics, and most important, their ability as Jews to see the present as a fresh new moment filled with possibility."[18] —*Cherie Brown*

Post-traumatic Stress Disorder (PTSD) was initially applied to Vietnam War vets, and then to Nazi Holocaust survivors. In her groundbreaking volume, *Trauma and Recovery*, psychiatry professor Judith Herman explains that with psychological trauma, the common denominator is intense fear, loss of control, helplessness, and feeling threat of annihilation. The late somatic psychotherapist Maryanna Eckberg, along with Barbara Hammer, added symptoms: psychic numbing, shame, resentment, alienation, flashbacks, and repeated attempts to make meaning of the experience.[19]

Hammer believes that Ashkenazi Jews are a "traumatized group" who experience elements of PTSD interwoven with cultural patterns and family dynamics.[20] When trauma isn't healed, Eckberg argued, it lives inside the person as if happening right now: imagining a death camp "shower" while bathing, or a bombing raid when plaster falls from the ceiling (see Chapter Fourteen). Daniel Mendelsohn recalls the son of a survivor describing his mother: "'Something in her had been broken,' and when he said this I had thought, The ones who were killed were not the only ones who'd been lost."[21]

These feelings and behaviors are often passed through generations. Irena Klepfisz, a feminist writer and Yiddish professor, survived the Warsaw Ghetto Uprising as a child, but her father perished while helping lead that resistance. She felt the war herself and then relived it through her survivor mother. "My first conscious feeling about being Jewish was that it was dangerous, something to be hidden...As a child, I was old with terror and the...haphazardness of survival."[22]

Polish feminist poet and scholar Bozena Umiñska hosted me in Warsaw. She felt literally enslaved by the terror her mother endured fleeing the Nazis. Both her parents' families were wiped out, most shot by firing squads. And Auschwitz survivor Gloria escaped death at age fourteen by leaping off a truck bound for the gas chambers; she said she took courses in child psychology so that she wouldn't pass on to her children the horror of her captivity.

Physician and author Gabor Maté was an infant when the Nazis marched into Budapest. When his mother called the pediatrician because of his continual crying, the doctor replied that all his Jewish babies were crying. "Now infants don't know anything about...Hitler," Maté said, "they're picking up on the stresses of their parents."[23] Later, studying stress in Shoah survivors' children, he found "the greater the degree of PTSD of the parent, the higher the stress hormone level of the child."[24] Maté learned to soothe his own anxiety by nonstop work, getting "lots of respect and people wanting me. If you get the impression early in life that the world doesn't want you, then you're going to make yourself wanted and indispensable."[25]

Many Jewish children get the message early that the world isn't safe. In her poem "Growing Up Haunted," Marge Piercy writes, "Fear was the underside of every leaf/we turned, the knowledge that our/cousins, our other selves, had been/starved and butchered to ghosts."[26] Writer and activist Sandy Butler also learned young that there was "something dangerous about being Jewish, but...except for muttered conversations abruptly ended when I entered the room about the 'camps,' I didn't know what it was."[27]

"Even when the descendants live under very improved conditions," educator Julian Weissglass points out, "the effect of the...violence persists."[28] Cherie Brown tells of leading a class in 2010 for twenty-five young U.S. and British Jews about healing from the Nazi Holocaust. "I was surprised to discover," she said, "that thirteen-, twenty- and twenty-five-year-old Jews, if listened to attentively, have just as much unhealed terror from the Holocaust as do many of their elders."[29]

Some survivors' descendants carry a dead weight inside. For others, it's anger. Witness the words of Nina Rachel, whose mother, Evelyn Torton Beck, escaped the Shoah:

> "Growing up in fear
> I learned anger
> Knowing even before knowing
> that I was not
> supposed to be
> Should be dead
> Should be grateful...
> And if they called out
> "kike" or "big-nosed hairy-legs Jews"
> I would not run
> also
> did not fight
> But died a thousand tiny deaths in places still
> frozen inside."[30]

"Auschwitz...was always in my house as I grew up," Liat Weingart, grandchild of survivors, confides. "No one talked about it. But you could feel it."[31] Another third-generation survivor, P., says her dad remembers his father waking up screaming. When liberated from the camps, her grandfather weighed eighty-four pounds; thirty years later he committed suicide. "We have a crazy anxiety disorder in our family," P. says. "My father keeps everything in and then explodes, yelling and throwing things. Sometimes," she admits, "I just want to stand in the room myself and scream."

A baby-boomer colleague, Charna, who lost many older relatives in the Shoah writes, "I just sense that our generation, the freest group of Jews ever in history, still carries a shadow over us...a shadow...so intensely frightening, that we understand [it] intellectually but rarely really feel [it]. And that might be a key to...healing."

Acting in spite of the fear

When Jessie was eight years old, a Catholic boy beat her up for being Jewish. "That stayed with me, it was traumatic." Yet even though she is still taunted ("Jews are disgusting," "Hitler should have finished the job"), she insists on wearing her Jewish star.

The John Birch Society threatened my friend's father in 1970s San Jose, California, warning "We don't want any kikes on the school board." The German neighbor next door hung Hitler's picture over the bed. Still, my friend's father ran for election—and won.

Israeli-Canadian Jewish activist Neta Golan has walked through blockades of Israeli tanks to bring milk powder to Palestinian infants under siege. When I asked wasn't she scared, "Of course!" she laughed. "You feel the fear. But you don't let that stop you from doing what's right." Thirty-something schoolteacher Shira Katz agrees: "My dad's a Holocaust survivor, so Jewish fear is part of who I am. I have to...act in spite of it."[32] In Hebron, on the West Bank, Katz and her group helped Palestinians build a fence to protect them from Jewish Israeli settlers—and then were beaten by the settlers. "It's like a dance," Katz said, "having the fear and having the convictions. If I had let my fear...stop me...look what I would have lost: connections with Palestinians, a deep sense of working for what's right...Moving through the fear has enriched my life."[33] Isn't it, then, about building from our dreams—not from our fears?[34]

Combatting her trepidation, Emily "came out" as a Jew onstage in Germany, performing a concert for 2,000 people. "It was the scariest thing I've ever done. My grandparents could not fathom that I would go. But I couldn't be a Jew in Germany and not come out." Though her father instilled his own lack of safety in her, "The work I am doing is breaking that down."

6

"Hello Assimilation, Goodbye Persecution"

"Hello, assimilation; good-bye persecution, McCarthyism, immigrant poverty, Holocaust. Who wouldn't want to drop twenty pounds, change his name to Blair and move to Connecticut?"[1]

—*Ophira Edut*

"THE PUSH FOR ASSIMILATION COMES *FROM* SOMEWHERE," Elly insisted. "A craving to survive."

"In the face of overwhelming evidence that it has not necessarily protected us," sighed Kim, "like during Nazi Germany." Assimilation as a response to past anti-Semitism: a strategy for safety, acceptance. After hearing hours of women's stories at a workshop, "What I heard was how many Jews will do anything to be safe: however they want us to be, we'll accommodate and shape ourselves," Deena noticed. "I don't even know what I've done to be safe."

Stating the obvious, in the United States this strategy has meant shedding (at least some) Jewishness and adopting white Christian middle-class values, appearance, language. But "not going towards non-Jewish," suggested Elly, "as much as going away from Jewish"—to escape the stigma and sometimes-high price paid for being a Jew. The result? Ethnic and cultural near-erasure. Americanization.

Yet isn't this process also a natural, even inevitable, adaptation to a new land, new cultures?

After the massive turn-of-the-century Jewish immigration wave, in just one or two generations many of our ancestors escaped tenements and sweatshops for middle-class offices, suburban green lawns, and incomes. But as they (at least partially) said goodbye to Jewish cultures and religion in response to anti-Semitism, they disconnected from juicy Jewish identities — reinforcing vulnerability to internalizing prejudice, fueling self-hatred. As assimilation has delivered indisputable benefits, it has also sapped a precious Jewish*ness* from many of our lives.

"Bleaching out the Jew"—Americanization

After eons of longing to reach these shores, Rachel Wahba was ecstatic. On arrival, though, she was stunned to discover that some of her new Ashkenazi friends shrank from her own proudly-Jewish (Mizrahi) identity. "They were busy being Los Angeles teenagers, bleaching out the Jew in them, being cool. It was as if I were exposing something they were trying to assimilate out of."[2]

They were following rules directed to Irena Klepfisz a decade earlier in the 1950s, on the opposite coast: "Change your name. Americanize. Forget the past. Forget your people."[3] Chief indoctrinators were free public schools; the City College of New York required immigrants' children—Jews, Chinese, Italian, and Spanish-speakers, more—to take speech classes, to "erase all traces of who we were and where we came from."[4] At least to blur the identity a bit. Maybe to be a Public Jew, but acceptable to the conservative Christian power elite, like Senator Joseph Lieberman. Otherwise, to keep mum about *Jewish* issues, except for unconditionally supporting Israel, which was compatible with U.S. policy. The rest of the instructions? Steer clear of "stereotypical Jews." Get socialized into Christian values. Lay low about bigotry, hope it will go away.

As a result, writes Matthew Nemiroff Lyons: "Americanization reinforced the psychology of oppression that Jews had long carried...many learned to be ashamed of their backgrounds, and to internalize Jewish stereotypes and attitudes of self-hatred, fear, power-lessness, arrogance and mistrust. *The process left a legacy of cultural invisibility and loss with which many Jews continue to struggle today.*"[5] (Italics added)

Take Judith, for example, who describes her Cincinnati family as very assimilated. When she saw Mandy Patinkin on a television talk show teaching his son Hebrew, she freaked: "That's too Jewish. You can't *do* that!" After Patinkin sang in Yiddish from his Broadway show, "What are you wasting your time for?" she protested. "That's not legitimate." Or my friend T., who like so many others, was embarrassed by his animated Yiddish-speaking immigrant grandparents, also by Oberlin classmates unabashedly handing out Purim packages in the student union.

To be fair, some religious Jews relinquished tradition because of economic necessity, working on *Shabbat* to put food on the table.[6] Still, the next steps became easier: shaving beards, shortening names, removing *kippahs*…lessening bigotry, but at a cost.

The ultimate goal in Americanizing, for Jews, was Acceptance from a society that denigrated Jewishness—propelled by the dream: upward mobility might protect us.

Craving to survive: upward mobility

"It's like one word: nicemiddleclassJewishfamily. Is there any other kind?"[7]

Jews scrambled into the middle class the minute the floodgates opened, fervently hoping financial security could keep persecution at bay. Geri told us her first-generation East Coast father "walks around with unbelievable fear. His family was so poor, he's the only one who 'made it.' He knows what he has to lose, and it has to do with being Jewish." And Deena verified, "This Materialism Thing goes across Mizrahi, Sephardic, and Ashkenazi communities." In the West, Kim described her Denver community as "very loving, and very materially oriented, post-Holocaust: people concerned about survival."

Case in point: the Hollywood moguls. After escaping the tsar's pogroms and childhood poverty, "They felt driven to be seen as American, in order to feel safe," Elly explained. No wonder Hollywood has been called "a dream dreamt by Jews fleeing a nightmare."[8] Ambitiously vaulting themselves into prosperity, most of these men weren't at ease being Jews (although Carl Laemmle sponsored Jewish refugees escaping Germany;

and Warner Brothers produced more than one anti-Nazi film, despite attacks from isolationist critics).[9] "Most felt pushed to divorce their Jewish wives and marry *shiksas* [non-Jews]," Elly continued, "raising children oblivious to their Jewishness."

It's tricky untangling assimilation, internalized anti-Semitism, and middle-class aspirations. Most German Jews immigrated in the early 1800s and acculturated successfully, even prospering. But when Jews from Eastern Europe's working classes surged into the States decades later, the middle-class Germans feared the newcomers' *Yiddish-keit* (visible Jewishness) would prove "objectionable to our fellow citizens," so "all of us will suffer"[10]—jeopardizing the Germans' "carefully cultivated status."[11] They strategized to "reshape" the greenhorns through Americanization agencies; their settlement houses taught not just hygiene and English, but patriotism, sometimes visibly shaming those caught speaking Yiddish.[12]

Such was their horizontal hostility.[13] German American Jews even tried safeguarding their privilege by backing the early 1900s immigration quotas against Jews fleeing southeastern Europe. But although one German paper, the *Hebrew Standard*, boasted that Americanized German Jews seemed "closer to the Christian sentiment" around them "than to the Judaism of these miserable darkened Hebrews,"[14] the Germans' fear proved true: as Jewish numbers mushroomed, *all* Jews became stigmatized as aliens.

Socialization into Christian middle class-ness for young women translated into the R word, Respectability: modest dress, punctuality, modulated tones. Good manners equaled good Americans. "The assimilation of Jews in Western societies," explained the late historian Paula Hyman, is indistinguishable from "the middle-class context in which these processes were embedded."[15] The late Adrienne Rich, award-winning feminist poet and writer, remembered her (southern) father's instructions "to assimilate with a world which might see us as too flamboyant."[16] While traveling or out to eat, "the Rich women were always tuned down to some WASP level [that] my father believed...would protect us all."[17] And a twenty-something middle-class friend writes: "I'm much quieter than my ancestors. I'm polite in ways they were not. In a sense, I'm smaller, I take up less space."

Who wouldn't make a few trade-offs to escape perilous jobs, teeming tenements, harsh poverty? Yet some did resist the Dream. Recalling her Lower East Side working-class childhood, Laura Rifkin's voice trembles: "We represent so often everything they [middle-class Jews] are afraid of in themselves. We did not pass. We did not renounce our culture. We were not all striving to be Americans...[or] centered around surviving through renouncing our identity. We did not all have money."[18] Growing up with "roots intact," Rifkin cherishes her "Jewish soul wisdom."[19]

Complexity prevails. Elly's Chicago working-class family did focus on becoming "successful." "I'm one of the Jews with a BMW," she grinned. "And my goal is to get a newer model."

"Keep your Jewish self hidden"

One of assimilation's fierce messages is voluntary Jewish silence: downplaying Jewishness, not drawing attention to it. Suffering silently in response to hostility, rather than speaking out and risking attack, because of the legacy clutching our psyches. Early/mid-twentieth century Jewish establishment leadership advised: *Don't be a shande far di goyim. Don't embarrass us in front of gentiles.* Especially, please, "remain invisible...so that we will not have to be subordinated by violent means."[20] April Rosenblum argues: "The vulnerability of their brethren in Europe had a concrete impact on how Jews in the U.S. carried themselves in their daily lives, regardless of how safe their U.S. surroundings might have seemed...The 1950s...provided the most vulnerable psychological moment...for American Jews...Political events warned...that if they were really glad to be in America, they would do well to keep a low profile and conform as much as possible."[21]

"When I don't say something," Judith admitted, "it's because I'm fearful." She paused. "Part of that is because I'm assimilated, I just want things to be nice, I don't want to make waves. But at the same time," she looked up, eyes dancing, "my whole life is about making waves!"

Emily told us that her working-class, urban, East Coast parents (in the 1950s) "stayed really Jewish—but both became alcoholics. That's how they navigated anti-Semitism." Absentmindedly clenching her fists, she said: "Without a doubt, their alcoholism is about their assimilation, and ways they couldn't deal with who they were as Jews. It was 'Keep yourself hidden and inebriated so you don't have feelings and can block out anything negative coming at you.' Most of the decisions my parents made were around fear. They raised us to have strength around our Judaism — like 'We're Jews, and here's what we do.' We didn't do Christmas. But there was this flip side: 'Keep yourself hidden.'"

Hidden even as in Jewishly disappearing. Helen Fremont describes being raised Catholic in the 1950s Midwest suburbs, only discovering decades later her parents' Jewishness. Her mother taught her to say the sign of the cross in six languages. "What I didn't understand was that my mother was equipping me with the means of survival: proof of my Catholicism to anyone in a dozen countries."[22] In 1996, I remember teaching an antiracism class for young white activists; five of the twenty reported discovering only recently that they were Jews.

Jewish communal responses

Back in 19th-century Europe, assimilation was the official response of Jewish leaders to *emancipation*, the process that granted citizenship, civic and social equality to western/central European Jews. Finally! *For the first time*, Ashkenazim could mix into society, with one caveat — to "become like their fellow countrymen."[23] They could practice Judaism but were expected to adopt each country's language, dress, and culture, obliterating "aspects of Jewish life that had preserved Jewish communal identity."[24] Kaye/Kantrowitz refers to the high "psychic cost" for Jews in the Weimar Republic, who, in response, committed suicide almost twice as often as Protestants, almost four times as often as Catholics.[25] In the Islamic world, Jews were not as encouraged to assimilate, but they were allowed more cultural interaction with gentiles.[26]

Carrying this strategy to the States, from the early 1900s until the 1940s, most key Jewish establishment communities decided to keep quiet, or their challenges were discreet, hoping discrimination would wither away.[27] They wanted to show they were "good Americans," lest they threaten tenuous security. The assumption of many leaders was revealing: "successful completion of...assimilation would eliminate the last vestiges of social prejudice against Jews."[28] Period.

In examples typical of the times, when Henry Ford reprinted the fraudulent *Protocols of the Elders of Zion* in the 1920s, American Jewish Committee President and prominent spokesperson for Jewish rights Louis Marshall protested. But he stopped after Detroit Jews, fearing retaliation, demanded he back off [29] (although many Jews did boycott Ford cars). And when the Women's Division of the American Jewish Congress, with others, organized the 1933-41 boycott of German goods, the American Jewish Committee refused endorsement: "Shhh, you'll make it worse."[30]

President Roosevelt was about to name Felix Frankfurter to the Supreme Court, when two politically influential Jews—Treasury Secretary Henry Morgenthau and *New York Times* publisher Arthur Sulzberger—urged him not to. Since Louis Brandeis was already a justice, they feared "a second Jew would play into the hands of anti-Semites."[31] Thankfully, Roosevelt persevered. Most revealing of internalized anti-Semitism and most painful: even during the Nazi Holocaust—although the AJ Congress organized anti-Hitler protests and tried to rally support for rescuing Jews—most Jewish groups recoiled from battling quotas barring refugees, fearing a Jewish influx would provoke more backlash.

A decade later, the ADL and the L.A. Jewish Community Relations Committee even cooperated with the HUAC/McCarthy witch hunts, insisting "most Jews were not Communists."[32] Ironically, although Jewish Communists militantly fought Nazism, their Jewishness was (somewhat) undercover, since they valorized class, not ethnicity.[33]

Yet the secular Workmen's Circle/Arbeter Ring charted a middle path, rooted in Yiddish-keit while helping communities assimilate. Their mission was (still is) fostering Jewish identity as well as socioeconomic justice; they fought overcrowded housing and exploitative labor practices, later working to rescue European Jews. Also pushing back, the American Jewish Congress mobilized a 1943 protest of 70,000 people at Madison Square Garden in NYC, demanding the United States act to save Jews. And when Harvard instituted anti-Jewish quotas, Harry Starr of the student-run Menorah Society organized a coalition of Jews-plus-allies, to force abandonment of the quotas (although these were replaced by "geographic diversity" policies which effectively cut back Jewish admissions).[34]

Prominent among communal cultural responses, the radio hit "The Goldbergs," in the 1930s-'40s, showcased liberal Jewish family challenges of assimilating, while holding on to some Old Country values. Who were the Goldbergs? Proudly American. Gertrude Berg, the Oprah of her day, created and played Molly Goldberg; writing the scripts, she offered hope during a fearful time.[35] The show morphed into a successful TV sitcom in 1949, and Berg won the first Emmy for Best Actress.

Back in Hollywood, Jewish moguls tried bribing Darryl Zanuck, gentile producer of *The Gentleman's Agreement*, not to release the film, fearing repercussions since it exposed anti-Semitism.[36] Their efforts failed, and the movie won the 1947 Oscar for Best Picture.

Although most of the era's major musical theater writers and composers were Jews (or born of Jewish parents)—from Richard Rodgers and Oscar Hammerstein to Leonard Bernstein and Irving Berlin—none risked writing a Broadway musical about their cultural roots until *Fiddler on the Roof* in 1964, the phenomenal hit based on *Tevye the Dairyman* by Yiddish storyteller Sholem Aleichem. [37] Paula Hyman points out that "Like most ethnic writers in America, immigrant and second generation Jewish writers expressed profound ambivalence about their culture of origin or the culture of their parents...they focused on assimilation rather than on cultural transmission...yet *the burden [of their traditions]could not be cast off without doing psychological harm to the self*.[38] (Italics added)

As (some) men often cast off this "burden," Hyman argues, showing the complexity of the assimilation picture, they left to women any responsibility for teaching children customs and rituals, to instill some sense of Jewishness. Also, adds Hyman, "The very strength of the Jewish mother" signaled "the incomplete Americanization of her family,"[39] since middle-class Protestant norms prescribed a docile wife/dominant husband.

Incorporating the highly developed skill of "living with uncertainty,"[40] part of the communal strategy was accommodation—enrolling at less-elite quota-free schools, starting up their own businesses, working for other Jews. And some groups, cautiously, did mobilize to challenge barriers and stereotypes, eventually winning legal protection through antidiscrimination laws. Predictably, they chose spokespeople amenable to the Christian power elite.

But as U.S. anti-Semitism peaked in the 1940s, and in response to the Nazi Holocaust itself, more Jews who had tried patriotism, silence, and accommodation shrugged off discretion, rolled up their sleeves and fought back. Postwar, the organized Jewish community launched comprehensive antibias campaigns in schools, housing, and workplaces—also helping refugees and building positive images of Jews—eventually forging coalitions with black groups, trade unions, liberal churches, others. The 1940s and '50s actually marked a "heyday of Black-Jewish political cooperation."[41] A 1957 suburban Chicago survey showcased the growing visibility strategy: in response to "What are the components of a good Jew?" the second-ranked answer was "To accept one's Jewishness and not try to hide it."[42] After 1967, new peace-and-justice groups challenged Jewish political conservatism and Zionism, misogyny, and homophobia, insisting on the legitimacy of "radical *Jewish* voices," reenergizing a longtime tradition.[43]

Yet despite the rise of noticeable Jewish resistance, many southern Jews kept low profiles, still frightened of retaliation, given the 1913 resurgence of the Ku Klux Klan. When northern Jews surged south to join the 1950s-'60s Civil Rights Movement, many southern Jews feared their businesses would be torched; and, in fact, various southern Jewish community centers, temples and rabbi's homes were bombed in the '50s. Then during 1964's Freedom Summer, (white) Jewish activists Michael Schwerner and Andrew Goodman were murdered in Mississippi, with black gentile James Chaney, for registering black voters."

Assimilation: not monolithic

Although most (non-Orthodox) U.S. Jews have jumped on the assimilation bandwagon, we've done it in complicated, hardly uniform ways. Some fairly readily discarded Jewishness, along with the hardships of being poor, demonized, ostracized. Some continued raising (radical) Jewish voices, from inspiring/unstoppable early 1900s labor organizers, like the charismatic "Bread and Roses" Rose Schneiderman (also a suffragist), to feminist/anarchist/anticapitalist birth-control-advocate-and-more Emma Goldman. Many remain staunchly visible, challenging bias. Others opt for muting public identity while hanging on to Jewishness, such as Riv-Ellen Prell's family in the 1950s-'60s: "We would maintain our difference, but not too much."[44] Still others have felt ambivalent. *There are as many different ways to be Jewish as there are Jews.*

Take secular Jews, for example: nonreligious Jews who foreground ethnic/cultural Jewishness. Secular *not* another meaning for assimilated.

And admittedly a charged issue, intermarriage is sometimes called "radical assimilation"—but it can also "welcome in" gentiles to Jewishness.[45] Various sources say about half of Jews are marrying Jews (a heterosexual count only), and one-third to one-fourth of these mixed families are raising Jewish children.[46] Post-genocide, many Jewish women feel pressure to bring Jewish babies into the world, navigating the message "We can't let our people die."

Exemplifying complexities in our group across the spectrum: "I would never use the term 'assimilated' for any member of my family," Rani scoffed. "My grandparents were very Jewish, *Iraqi*-Jewish." Deena grew up devotedly secular, loving her vibrant cultural Jewishness as well as her socialist Zionist youth group. Judith was the first *bat mitzvah* in her family in 100 years—and her Midwestern household celebrated Christmas. And Emily is now visibly active in her synagogue; but in her twenties, "if people asked if I were Jewish, I told them, 'No, my parents were, but I'm not.'"

In Elly's Ashkenazi working-class Chicago family, "we absolutely did not assimilate. Yet my parents also believed, 'This was America, the melting pot.'" She grinned, "But my God, we kept kosher, we observed every goddamn Jewish holiday, went to Hebrew school. We couldn't have been more different!"

Many feel the confusing mix of Jewishness and reactions to assimilation, compounded by internalized anti-Semitism. Jessie, for example, is adamant: "No Christmas tree. No!" She is drawn to Judaism's beauty—but shrinks from Jews: "Get 'em away!" She shrugged, "It's a tug of war, the conflict I have."

Especially for Elly, this tug is wrenching. "Going to synagogue feels like going home," she says, gripping her elbows. "But part of it feels like 'Get me out of here!' On one hand, just loving it and feeling like I wanted a neon sign: I could never look Jewish enough! And I like how I connect with other Jews, I hunger for it. On the other hand, I feel repulsion, disliking the qualities in myself and other Jews that I identify with being Jewish. And similarly with Jewish religion and culture, feeling drawn towards and repelled by. So I yearn—and I'm very uncomfortable at the same time. And I'm ashamed for feeling that way."

Cultural loss

For some of us, an overwhelming by-product of assimilation is the loss of deep connection to our people, to where we come from.

The catharsis hits during my grad school cohort, after six months of a deep experiential group process about racism, with our white and black "teams." In the middle of an exercise one spring morning, my Israeli Jewish classmate Anna blurts out her grief about assimilating into white U.S. culture—whereas "In Israel, on Yom Kippur," she says, "no one drives their cars. Everyone hangs out in the street together. There is such a feeling of being connected." Inexplicably—despite my upset with Israeli government policies—something breaks inside me.

"By not speaking Yiddish here, I look white," Anna continues. My heart leaps. Granddaddy! I hear his soft Yiddish-inflected voice, feel his starched white shirt against my cheek, smell his sweet pipe tobacco. A sense of loss surges through my belly. Then anger starts to engulf me: upset at my white team members for allowing the Jews in our group to be erased, at myself for my acquiescence.

Our months of work together are hitting me now in a new way. Soon I'm shaking with grief, stunned, feeling the impact of the loss of deep connection to my heritage. My parents chose to raise me assimilated so I could pass and fit in, in ways they never could—but even though I did the whole Jewish Sunday School thing, my JewishNESS got stuffed. I suddenly understand why I've often felt so empty: the deal was no good, the bargain failed—the trade of my Jewish birthright for the privileges whiteness could offer.

As a result of my parents' efforts to help me blend in as "American"... born soon after the Nazi Holocaust...I lost my sense of belonging to my past and my people.

I'm in Anna's arms sobbing, pain swallows me whole. Assimilation used to be an intellectual construct. Now I feel it in my bones. Anna frames it: "The privilege on the one hand, the selling out on the other."

Later, at lunch with my (gentile) African American classmates, the print dances on the menu, lights shimmer, the air pulsates. Colette tells me this can happen after deep intense work, that the body changes on a cellular level. Earthlyn asks, "From where you are now, where can you go? Because, like me with slavery, we can't erase what happened." Now I understand how my assimilation as a Jew, the disregard of where I came from, fed by white privilege, let me disassociate and cut off. Let me look away from the trauma to my people. Also let me numb my grief about white people's enslavement of blacks. Such is the bounty of assimilation...

And why the breakthrough now? Our process together as black and white teams pierced denial, cracked me open...leading me back to my most Jewish self.

Sickness of the soul: self-hatred, grief, and shame

The message that the world conveyed to Jews:

"There is something so wrong with you that you do not deserve to exist."[47]
—*Rabbi Michael Lerner*

"The persecution of Jews over the centuries," explains Rabbi Robert Marx, "has produced an intensity of self-hatred that is searing."[48] Likewise, adds Hebrew literature professor Gilead Moragh, "The Nazi project of total Jewish degradation was so effective that many of its victims came to believe that...Jewish sub-humanity was actually true."[49] No wonder some of us are having a hard time.

Like a one-two punch, assimilation reinforces the damage done by anti-Semitism, robbing us of our rich heritage, shoving Jews into WASP conformity, inviting us to loathe who we really are. Assimilation amputates roots that can nourish, that can connect us to one another; without these, it's no surprise that waves of shame, grief, self-disgust might engulf us. And the feelings can pass from parents to children to grandchildren. Philosopher Martin Buber and psychologist Bruno Bettelheim nailed it, characterizing self-hatred as the psychopathology of assimilation.[50]

"Many young Jews I know in L.A.," Deena confided, "won't identify as Jews because of self-hatred or shame, because of assimilation." Shame about being Jewish, about being different. Shame as in ferocious,[51] as in transforming "other's contempt into self-contempt."[52] As in "sickness of the soul."[53]

Jewish women, especially, have been left with such self-loathing that it can be tough trusting anyone's love.[54] Gender-bender writer Jyl Lyn Felman exposes her despair, blunted only by antidepressants: her "terror of unproductivity" and fear of not living up to her potential, the "generations of...grief" handed down through her family, with utter isolation at the core: "I am afraid to ask for help."[55]

Because we blame ourselves, it bears repeating: none of these feelings are our fault. Even though we feel alone with our heartbreak, these are battles that many of us share, battles we can win. Subvert the shame, drain the grief, overturn the self-hatred. Since shame can result from what we believe others think about us, let's shift focus—let's instead practice reclaiming our exquisite, glittering, imperfect, outrageous, interconnected, Jewish selves.

Discounting Jewishness

As I mentioned in the Introduction, as a hippie radical in my twenties, I was on the streets protesting all the time, for every issue. But if you had asked me, I would have replied, "Why would anyone march for a Jewish issue? That would be the last thing in the world I would march for!"

Reclaiming our self-love includes valuing where we come from and who we are, contradicting shame that can be assimilation's shadow. When we believe anti-Jewish prejudice is not important, it's a baby step to believing deep down that we don't matter either. Disdaining Jewishness is often the lesson of a Christian-centric society; it's what assimilation teaches.

As progressives, the dynamic affects us in a particular way. We come to believe: how could Jewish issues possibly matter, compared to sexual slavery, homelessness, hunger, global warming, AIDS, racism, queer-bashing, military occupations?

Judith speaks the small voice lurking inside: "Part of me still says 'Why are you talking about anti-Semitism? It's no big deal, everybody has problems!' It feels like whining, complaining. I know that's probably part of the whole thing, but I can't even say 'internalized Jewish oppression'; it makes my skin crawl!" We asked Judith how it would be if anti-Jewishness did deserve some attention. "But it doesn't!" she laughed.

Yet only recently, Judith discovered that the five-year age difference between the first two and the last three siblings in her dad's family was because of the Nazi Holocaust. "Jews didn't know what was going to happen," her uncle mentioned casually. "So why bring in more kids when you didn't know?"

"I was *stunned*," she exclaimed. "That was never talked about in my family. It's 'We're Jewish—and we're just like everyone else. Except we're Jewish.'"

Growing up assimilated, we may learn not only to blind ourselves to anti-Jewish bias, but to discount Jewishness as significant. Consider, for example, the white Jewish teacher who fought for an ethnic studies department, but who was unsure if it was legitimate to teach Jewish literature as part of the department's offerings.[56] "I don't remember a single conversation in which we discussed the fact that so many of us were Jewish," Mark Rudd wrote of his coconspirators in the 1968 Students for a Democratic Society strike at Columbia University.[57] "Being radicals, we thought we could escape our Jewishness."[58] Some young white Jewish civil rights workers felt the same.[59] Michael Lerner underscores, "It is easier to function as a Jew on the left to the degree to which you already reject your Jewishness."[60]

If we do screw up the courage to raise Jewish issues, in nearly any context, we can be patronized, ignored, even attacked; rarely are we given the progressive stamp of approval, so we doubt the validity of our own experience. Who wouldn't decide to chuck it and focus elsewhere? Mistreating Jews matters as much as mistreating children, or women, or animals, or anyone else. There is room on a progressive agenda for it all—and some issues may be more desperate/salient at one moment or another, may need more of our attention. But we are *all* worth fighting for. And we can do it best together, in alliance, across differences.

Another glaring reason we may downplay Jewishness or Jewish issues is because of how the anti-Semitism charge is abused (see Chapter One), leaving some lefties skeptical of *any* accusation of anti-Semitism. Depending on how we've been affected by assimilation and internalized oppression, it can feel easier to ignore Jewish issues altogether, to clarify that we don't support bogus bigotry charges. But it's possible to support fair treatment for Jews *and* for all people; one does not cancel out the other. We can keep our minds open and our thinking both critical and flexible.

Or our disparaging of Jewishness may relate to heartache about Israeli Jewish mistreatment of Palestinians, so (it feels like) we can't bear to feel anything positive about Jews—because it hurts so much to face that some of our people are doing these misdeeds, are supporting this behavior. *Even though Jews are no worse, no better, than any other peoples.* In fact, other power elites, and regular people, are committing atrocities around the world all the time. Not to excuse; just to notice and factor in.

Our anguish and grief distort our perspective, so we can't distinguish the inherent goodness of Jewish people, like all people, from sometimes-misguided/fear-driven U.S. Jewish establishment *behavior* or from Israeli government *policies*—policies funded by U.S. taxes and supported by U.S. diplomacy. We can end up disdaining anything Jewish. Out of shame, or outrage, we might deprive others of knowing we are Jews, possibly increasing their own isolation. But as activists, when we opt for invisibility, we also hide the Jewish prophetic tradition of *tikkun olam*, of changing the world— Jewish radicalism. Whereas when we are loudly and proudly visible Jews, whatever that means to us, we are also more credible when we expose the misuse of anti-Semitism. And we tend to feel better about ourselves.

Again, none of the discounting or disdaining is our fault; it's all internalized anti-Semitism. We can change it.

Taking charge...

So, assimilation as a somewhat mixed blessing? On one side of the ledger: loss of culture, disconnection from heritage, hiding, passivity, self-hatred, shame. On the other, (at least conditional) security, acceptance, sometimes prosperity, integration into an exciting multicultural/multiracial world—and then, countering assimilation by reclaiming the best of our magnificent cultures.

L.A. *Times* journalists Alan Abrahamson and Judy Pasternak concluded that assimilation has been definitively good for the Jews: "After centuries of persecution…murders…poverty and exile, Jews in America have found themselves in a land that offers freedom, wealth, and security—all on a scale no previous Jewish community ever experienced in 4000 years of tribal history."[61]

Sound convincing? Dyanna Loeb tells another story (excerpt):

> "people try to change me. it's murder.
> asking me to cut my roots I refuse
> to bleed sap
> or memory loss
> my people fought for too long to be forgot."[62]

Rather than assimilation (or nationalism), suggests Melanie Kaye/Kantrowitz, let's try a new twenty-first century *Diasporism*,[63] in which we value/show ourselves in our full and diverse Jewishness, bent on human rights and solidarity, right here and now—roots and all.

7

"There Is a 'Real' Jewish Woman and I Am Not Her": Too Much/Not Enough

"If I become 'too Jewish,' it could cost me my job...whereas someone else is looked at as 'just having a bad day.' I see how they act when they talk about 'those annoying Jews,' and I don't want to be there."

—Deena

Whether we grew up in working-class ethnically mixed communities on Chicago's South Side, L.A. Jewish enclaves, or Protestant suburbs of northern Virginia, many Jewish women have been made to feel that we're *Too Much, Not Enough*, or *All of the Above*—compared to assumptions about who a Jewish woman should be. "When people say 'you don't look Jewish,'" a twenty-something friend confides, "they mean it as a compliment. It's definitely not cool to be a Jew."

TOO MUCH-NESS

Let's be clear: For Jewish women, "too much" is code for "too Jewish"— or "not Christian/WASP enough." One implies the other. And anti-Jewish bias piled onto misogyny is doubly disparaging.

This terrain is a central enemy stronghold in our heads. The specific messages? We're too intense, too needy, too hairy, too dark. Too materialistic, too large, too exuberant. Too difficult, too opinionated. Or too powerful, too whiny, and, of course, too pushy. And a few extras for Mizrahi women: too irrational or too primitive, too sexually overactive—or too repressed.[1] We're made to feel that by showing our full Jewish selves we'll be unwanted, abandoned.

"If I'm too Jewish," Deena murmured, eyes brimming, "then I won't be accepted. If I speak too loudly, I'll be the aggressive Jew. Then I'll be difficult, then they won't be able to tolerate me. Then they'll leave me." At one group meeting, Judith's vulnerability drew us in, inviting deep connection. But afterwards, she said, her internal demon scorned her for opening so fully: "For feeling too much, for wanting too much. That *I'm* too much."

Reminding us that we didn't create these messages, feminist playwright and activist Eve Ensler refers to how the dominant culture tries to subdue the "too-ness" of girls in general. "Get used to it!" she urges girls to say, "This is who I am."[2]

Curator/author Norman Kleeblatt's confrontational (NYC) art exhibit and anthology, *Too Jewish*, brings the issue front-and-center. On her framed linen hand towels (part of the book/exhibit), artist Elaine Reichek embroidered "**J.E.W.**"—provoking nervousness from Jews and gentiles alike.[3] On another she embroidered: "If you think you can be a little bit Jewish, you think you can be a little bit pregnant."[4]

Cringing

Not only do we disparage ourselves, but the voice inside tells us to hang back from other Jews who are "too much"—so that we won't be stigmatized the way they are. We end up shoving distaste onto each other. "I look at her and cringe," Elly admitted. "Cringe comes from embarrassment, shame, a sick feeling. It's 'Uch! I'm not *that*, don't think of us like *that!*' When my clients complain," she added, "it makes my skin crawl, because of the whiny Jew it evokes for me." She blushed. "I just want to slap 'em!"

Deena loves Judaism and identifies with individuals. But "I can't be as loud or as powerful as I want to be, I'm afraid I'll be demonized"—for being "'too much.'" On her Iraqi father's side, "Jewish women were celebrated: no stereotypes of 'brash' or 'pushy.'" But her Midwestern Ashkenazi mom taught her to be "refined in a restaurant, quiet." Now in her twenties, Deena is desperate to be Cool, definitely not "too nerdy."

Different generation, related issue: the late feminist theorist/activist Andrea Dworkin confided, "I keep quiet at meetings more than I should because I don't like feeling singled out as the Jew with the words."[5] Speaking of meetings: Elly Bulkin says that when there's more than token Jewish visibility, it's sometimes seen as a bid for "Jewish control."[6] Just speaking up can engender being seen as that "unpleasant/ obnoxious Jew." Not *being* an unpleasant person, but being *perceived* that way: and then believing that's who we are. When J. challenged a speaker spewing anti-Semitic ideas, and then wasn't supported by those around her, she felt, she said, "like a pushy, self-absorbed, whiny, victim-y Jew."

And what about those Jewish women who do "make it harder for the rest of us"? Kim heard a woman rabbi on the radio advocating gay marriage, pitted against an evangelical minister. "'Thank God she's out there,' I felt. 'She's so strong and articulate.' But I also thought, 'She's too aggressive, interrupting him constantly. She's just adding to the stereotype!' On the one hand, I was so proud; I'm *kvelling*, 'Look at what we do!' But then, 'Oh my god, why do we have to do it that way?'"

Bringing it all home, Melanie Kaye/Kantrowitz crystallizes our challenge: "Stereotypes of Jewish women combine with prejudice against powerful women, pressuring us to cloak our strength lest we be seen as pushy; hide our desire, lest we be deemed oversexed...mute our feelings, lest we be judged overemotional...Jewish women are asked to sit on ourselves, lest we seem...too powerful...[and] depending on the extent of our assimilation and our feelings about our own Jewishness, [we] may respond negatively to strength in other Jewish women...Loving ourselves insufficiently, trafficking too much in other people's conception of us, we fear our own strength...The task of self-love is endless."[7]

I remember when my gutsy (also less assimilated working-class) friend Mel and I organized an unlearning anti-Semitism workshop for our staff colleagues at the Michigan Womyn's Music Festival. While xeroxing handouts beforehand, Mel yelled across the courtyard, "Penny, how many more copies of the Jewish Liberation piece do we need?" Right there in the sweet summer morning, surrounded by women who were family, I shrank into my Doc Martins, muscles tightening, blood draining from my face. "Ohmygoddess, are they rolling their eyes about 'those loud pushy Jews'?" I worried. "We should be quieter!" Then Melanie Kaye/Kantrowitz's words floated before me. "Someone will always call us pushy. Isn't it time to really push?"[8] I breathed again. Yep, it's time.

"Too Jewish"—according to whom?

"We Jewesses get the message early: It's better to be Barbie than Barbra Streisand."[9] — *Ophira Edut*

Remember: Christian hegemony (the rewarding of things Christian, usually white) can cast Jewishness as undesirable, sometimes evil. Assimilation backs up the message, nudging us to replicate the WASP norm. When we misstep, even when we don't, our inner trickster may sneer at how disgusting/deviant we are: what we've ingested from prejudice and historic oppression. Worse yet, we think we're somehow to blame.

The *coup de grâce*? Our behavior supposedly "justifies" any mistreatment: "She's so bossy [maybe more direct about what she thinks than her Protestant counterpart], why would we hire someone like *that*?" Often we sweat to trim pounds, bleach hair, alter names and noses, trying to disguise ourselves. So that we will fit in, be loved. (No wonder savvy activists advise our allies: "When it comes to telling Jews that we're liked and wanted and totally good-looking, you really can't overdo it."[10])

Turning WASP values on their head, writer Rhonda Lieberman fantasizes a Jewish Barbie parody in Kleeblatt's *Too Jewish* collection. Asks Lieberman, *What if Barbie's Jewish roots started showing?* — referring to Barbie's creator, Ruth Handler, daughter of Polish Jews, married to the Jewish cofounder of Mattel toys. What if the slim-hipped, gentile-looking doll became "Nose-Bob Barb (with pre-op detachable beak)"?[11]

Lieberman's tongue-in-cheek stereotype is born in a parallel universe to (Christian) Barbie. "*Everyone* thinks I'm annoying," Jewish Barbie moans, flaunting qualities Barbie repressed: brunette or frosted hair, noticeable thighs, incessant whining.[12] Her body size? "She's *too thin* — you'll love her!...I can't get a *latke* into that girl."[13] So Jewish Barbie hangs out at the college eating disorders clinic. She's the "Hebrew Vogue" zine cover girl, wins a *Manischewitz* grant in Post-Colonialism Studies, and makes her summer camp debut in *"Katz,"* about Jewish cats working in the garment district (before the Anglicized version became a hit). But cruelly, Barbie refuses to acknowledge her Other, leaving Jewish Barbie to wail, "I'm *not* evil!"[14] "Too Jewish" on parade.

Switching gears, remembering our history: in Nazi-occupied Warsaw, any Jew was "too Jewish." Hiding Jewishness was a survival strategy. Allies from the Polish Underground instructed women escaping the Ghetto "how to appear Aryan and not attract notice."[15] Jews learned to restrain gestures, and to style hair without frizz or curls; surgeons reshaped Jewish noses.

Not life-threatening like in Europe, but in the 1940s U.S. many Jews felt the need for restraint. Marge Piercy remembers her father's Christian family who were "casually and relentlessly anti-Semitic."[16] "If my mother or I ever laughed, or raised our voices, or used our hands in talking,...a look...would pass between them that would silence us, as if we had been pushed under a glass bell."[17]

In safer times like these, the antidote is valuing who we are, just as we are. Kim noticed, sometimes when Jewish women are disagreeing, or just schmoozing, "Protestants perceive us as 'difficult and controlling.' But we're just sharing our thoughts."

"That's nothing," Rani laughed. "I was just visiting my family, and was on the phone with my (WASP) girlfriend. She heard my family in the background and asked 'Oh my god, why are they screaming at each other?' Rani grinned. 'They're talking, that's the way they talk. And this isn't even the Iraqi side,' she chuckled, who are *louder.*"

"Which ethnic looks are okay?"

Our bodies, ourselves

But possibly most insidious? The (perceived) Too Much-ness of Jewish women's bodies. Bellies, breasts, and hips, Too Large. Voices, Too Loud. Hair, Too Frizzy, or showing up in Too Many Places. All measured against pearly skin, wispy blonde hair, sky-blue eyes, svelte bodies: the White Anglo-Saxon Protestant Ideal. (And need we say it? Some Jews look like this too.)

Body image as another site where degradation of women and of Jews merge into a toxic soup that far too many of us absorb—trying to control bodies out of control, to contain our Jewishness "so that it conforms to whiteness."[18]

Speaking to the excruciating struggle for women overall, feminist trailblazer Gloria Steinem reiterates in *Revolution from Within* how U.S., white, patriarchal culture promotes thinness "and impossible standards of appearance for women instead of individuality and health."[19] While Letty Cottin Pogrebin reveals, "the average American woman wears a size 12...supermodels wear size zero."[20] Clearly pinpointing internalized sexism, in *The Beauty Myth*, author Naomi Wolf explains "while women unrealistically distort [describe] their bodies negatively, men distort theirs positively."[21] Rabbi Harold Kushner injects the role of capitalism. "Entire industries—fashion, cosmetics, perfume, low-calorie foods, bestselling diet books, plastic surgery, weight loss clinics—have been built on the foundation of women's feeling ashamed of their appearance, to the point where one could speculate that *if all the women in America were to wake up one morning feeling good about themselves, the American economy would collapse.*[22] (Italics added)

"In a male-superior culture," Steinem concludes, "women...rarely [see themselves as] okay no matter how they look, and thus feel constantly in need of 'fixing.'"[23]

Jewish women get a double-dose of the crushing messages, as women *and* as Jews, including from Jewish men. Ophira Edut cites personal ads from men seeking slender Jewish women who are "not Jewish-looking."[24] A millennial friend sends me a YouTube video she found, "Sh*t Christians say to Jews," all apparently actual comments: "You're like really pretty for a Jew" (also, "Adam Sandler is super cute for a Jew").[25]

Like Jewish Barbie, disproportionate percentages of Jewish women battle eating disorders, attributable to poor self-image, trauma (including sexual abuse), assimilation, feeling powerless.[26] From years of clinical practice, Melissa Schwartz has learned that eating disorders often result from rejecting the *zaftig* (full-figured), robust, hard-working body many Jewish women inherit. Edut recalls her family simultaneously urging her to eat, while (taking the bait from WASP-land) ridiculing her "extra body baggage."[27] Mixed messages pummeled Rani as well: "Pretty common in the Jewish experience is 'Eat more, eat more!' I landed in Florida at 7:30 a.m. and first thing they offered me was chocolate chip cookies. Of course what came fifteen minutes after that: 'You've gained a lot of weight, why do you eat so much?' Followed by 'Why don't you have another bite?'"

For Judith, the trouble started when she was sexually molested as a child. Getting along with others became harder, she admits, and she gained weight: "Being 'too heavy' or 'too loud' became part of my identity." Meanwhile, "every kid in school" used Jessie as a punching bag: a chubby, shy, too-Jewish tomboy. And Amy shudders recalling a childhood trip to Copenhagen, where she felt her whole body was "disgustingly dark and hairy and Jewish."

Deena yearns for a movement that affirms "Jewish noses and big hairy stomachs are beautiful!" A still-hurtful memory: when a seventh-grade teacher complained that her voice sounded "like nails on a chalkboard. He would go like this [cringing] whenever I spoke. So I just stopped talking in class." The offending teacher? A Jew.

Sighing, Emily brushes the curls off her forehead. "It's painful to hear how ashamed we feel because we have the bodies we do. We make people's nonacceptance of us as Jewish women *our* problem—instead of the other way around."

Hair!

A twenty-something friend confides: "When I style my hair to be straight, I get 75 percent more comments 'You're so pretty!' than when I let it be its naturally curly self."

Chin digging into her hand, Deena posed the question: "What ethnic looks are okay? My Eastern European and Arab blood make me hairier than others. That's not considered attractive, I'm not seen as a darker version of Barbie." When body hair issues surfaced with her partner, she says, "I was afraid he would think I'm nasty." She even worried that we would be disgusted at her "hairy stuff."

Rani, too, was chagrined. In Israel, she had a shaved head, "but I didn't shave my armpits or legs. When they saw my legs, people looked at me with horror. They stopped walking, their jaws dropped. I was shocked! I thought they were going to give me grief about my head being shaved. I think it's very specific to *female* Jewish oppression."

Then while visiting her Ashkenazi family in Florida, even though Rani waxed her legs beforehand, "They didn't appreciate it. I still had some weird 'hair places' and didn't look normal enough." As self-assured as she seemed, Rani admitted later, "When I wear shorts, I feel ashamed. I hate it when people stare at me. I look at girls with their skirts and pretty legs, and I wish I could feel okay with not looking like that."

And Dyanna Loeb confided about her affluent Bay Area public school (excerpt),

> "Every popular girl had yellow hair
> hanging limp…
> so the boy from 7th grade used to call me *hebrew slave*
> girls on the playground scoffed at my curls
> asking me
> 'have you ever seen a hairbrush
> and a mirror?'
> so I tug hot irons thru my locks
> wishing my waves light and lifeless."[28]

In the *Too Jewish* collection, artist Beverly Naidus also shared embarrassment at her "dark, hairy-arm-pitted body."[29] Captioning her visual art "What Kinda Name Is That?" and evoking a deadly comparison, she wrote: "She comes home from summer camp ashamed of her curly hair. All the hip campers had long, straight hair…She buys a hair straightening product and suffers through the stench and sting of it…Her next effort is wrapping her hair in curlers the size of orange juice cans. Bobbie pins become embedded in her scalp as she struggles to sleep. Finally, her cousin teaches her how to iron her hair. The smell of it burning reminds her of something so horrible, it is unspeakable."[30]

Flashpoint: the Jewish nose

"A nose job breaks the nose, bruises the face and eye area like a grotesque beating. It hurts. It takes weeks to heal."[31]

—*Melanie Kaye/Kantrowitz*

European Christians believed marks of sin, or virtue, could be read on the body. In the 1800s, they attacked the Jewish nose as a sign of depravity, another justification for anti-Semitism: "Jewish noses cannot be reformed."[32] Today these testimonials say it all.

"I had a nose job in eighth grade," Deena confided, "after I got targeted for having a big nose. Seventh grade was hellish. One friend wrote me an anti-Semitic note and stuck it in my locker, saying she no longer wanted to be my friend. My mom said 'Never let racism or anti-Semitism go unchecked,' so I told people about it. But nobody stood up for me, even though privately they said, 'That sucks, she's a bitch.' It was really isolating. One guy walked by me and turned his head in disgust. I felt ugly and horrible, and I lost myself that year. Even after the nose job, a Jewish boy called me 'big nose.'"

And Aishe Berger writes, from "Nose is a country...I am the second generation":

> "The little Yeshiva boys yelled
> that I took all their air up
> when I walked down the hall
> Then the boys at camp said
> they'd kiss me if they could
> ever find my lips
> My dermatologist pierces
> my ears
> when I'm ten and advises me
> to wear big earrings
> it will distract people away from my face."[33]

NOT ENOUGH

"There is a 'real' Jewish woman—and I am not her!" —*Deena*

Ever feel that gnawing inside, "I'm not doing enough"? Or "I'm not Jewish enough"? Underneath, in words we can barely face, feeling simply "not worthy enough"? Unproductive, inadequate. Unwanted.

My worth is what I do

"Having grown up fat and Jewish, I knew somehow intrinsically I was not acceptable or lovable. That I had to do or give, in order to be valued: in relationship, in my job, in the world. And I have to keep doing in order to sustain. I have a lot of grief about that." —*Elly*

"If I've accomplished something, it doesn't mean that I can stop moving," Deena sighed. "As Jews, we have to keep on the go, so we always have something 'to show,' to make ourselves valid. As an excuse for being present."

"Hmm, that smacks of Holocaust mentality," Rani mused, the grandchild of Shoah survivors.

"Or even before that," Elly added, leaning back into the couch. "Surviving shtetls, pogroms. Because my worth is so exclusively what I do, especially for others, rather than just who I am. The minute I am no longer needed, I am no longer wanted. My utility is all that matters. The association I just had, in terms of survival and the Holocaust, was if you fell off in terms of work, you were dead."

In *The Lost*, Daniel Mendelssohn tells stories he heard in Ukraine, formerly Galicia, Poland: hundreds of Jews herded from factories where they were producing war-goods, "led to the town square and...sorted near the town hall. *The most talented...were released and the rest...were killed...* The...pavements...literally splashed in blood."[34] (Italics added)

I think back to the *umshlakplatz* in the Krakow ghetto. Our guide Eva told us how that December of 1942, the Nazis selected the "useful"—the strong—into Section A, relegating the "useless"—the old, the disabled, the children—into Section B. Many were executed on the spot. And my colleague tells a story of her Aunt Hannah in Auschwitz: When Hannah's niece Rivka, age thirteen, was in line for the gas chambers, Hannah informed the guard, "Rivka is a good worker."

"Is she a relative?" the guard asked.

"No," Hannah lied. "Just a good worker." Rivka's life was spared.

"Not Jewish in the right way"

"I don't have shame about *being* a Jew," Elly clarified. "I'm ashamed that I'm not Jewish in the 'right way.'" Even though she made it through ten years of Hebrew school, she felt ignorant. Illegitimate. When Deena went to an Orthodox service at a Berkeley synagogue that was "very open," still she "didn't feel knowledgeable enough." She frowned. "Even though people were very accepting, I didn't feel accepted." And a Gen-Y friend admits: "I was a leader at Jewish summer camp for eight years. But outside of camp, I never feel confident enough to lead one single prayer. People would be shocked to know this: like, I'm supposed to be the super-strong confident one. I even get nervous lighting the candles, like I'm not going to do it right."

A Jewish mover-and-shaker in her community tells a story about honoring her father's *yarzheit* (anniversary of a death):

> We were in a circle, and the most traditionally knowledgeable people were conferring about what we should do. I knew it wasn't quite right, but I was deferring to them because of "not feeling Jewish enough." Then K. stepped in and asked me, "What do you want to do?" And I realized, "Right, this is my dad's yarzheit, I get to decide." I realized that I wanted to talk about him, have us all say the mourner's kaddish [prayer for the dead] and sing a song. So we did and it felt good—but it was interesting that someone I had just met had to step in and break up some of our group dynamics about who "knows" the most.

As an aside: when men are hotly debating a million topics, why is it that many Jewish women feel we need to achieve some level of intellectual accomplishment before we can say what *we* think?[35]

Judith's story has a different twist. Her mother converted to Judaism and is not ethnically Jewish in the way Judith's father is, so some don't consider Judith a "real Jew"—even though her father was president of their Cincinnati congregation. She frowned, kicking off her sandals. "I still don't get it that my mom's Jewish, even though she converted and raised me as a Jew. Am I 'Jewish enough'?"

Jessie admitted she had felt worthless much of her life, because she'd gotten the message, "if you were a Jew who wasn't a high achiever, you weren't good enough to be a real Jew." And Elly fears that she doesn't "look Jewish enough": "As a child, I was embarrassed that I didn't have curly hair, dark skin, or a classically Jewish nose." Even today, she admits, "I'm afraid that just by looking at me, no one knows I'm a Jew."

And what does "Jewish enough" mean, anyway? "The notion of someone 'looking Jewish,'" says Rabbi Steven Kushner, reflects "an ethnocentric [white] Ashkenazi world-view" that many Jews are just becoming aware of.[36] Rabbi and cantor Angela Warnick Buchdahl has an Ashkenazi father, a Korean Buddhist mother. "It was a 'stab in my heart,'" she admits, when as a child, Jews told her she couldn't be Jewish since her mother wasn't a Jew (forget the fact that her mom learned Hebrew and was in the synagogue sisterhood).[37] When Angela led college Hillel services, "I would be chanting in Hebrew and wearing a *talit* (prayer shawl), and afterwards people would still say, 'Are you Jewish?'...They couldn't suspend their stereotypes enough to see me."[38]

It's worth repeating: there are as many different ways to be Jewish as there are Jews. Yet in a U.C. Berkeley class on Jewish identity, remembers organizer Michael Taller, students were asked to list the qualities of a "good Jew." They were then asked did they see themselves as "good Jews"? None raised their hands, including Jewish leaders. Taller later spoke to his Hillel congregants: "For those of you who join us only on these holidays...your celebration of Judaism is legitimate. You are not required to do or be anything specific in order to be part of the Jewish community... You are not a bad or inadequate Jew, regardless of what you or anyone else may feel...You belong because you are."[39]

Intersections—and antidotes

Jews are hardly the only ones who feel "too much" compared to the dominant culture, or "not enough" compared to others in our constituency. In her dissertation about healing from internalized racism, Taj Johns writes about loved ones "who feel they have our best interests at heart" accusing each other, "Why you gotta be so Black?"[40] And I think of Mexican-heritage friends who feel they are "not Chicana enough" because they don't speak Spanish. Banding together, we can share camaraderie, gain perspective.

"Things are connecting for me," Judith announced. "I'm seeing how much of this internalized stuff I have to wade through. With all our talk about 'Am I Jewish enough, am I too Jewish?' my feelings about 'Am I lesbian enough? Am I too lesbian?' are coming up big-time! Because even though I 'came out' during my job interview, and I have my girlfriend's picture on my desk, among lesbians I still don't feel 'lesbian enough.'"

With a little determination and support, we can uproot or transform the stings we've internalized, and give ourselves validation instead. As Kim encouraged, "I find myself wanting to tell you how wonderful you are. But it isn't from me that you really need it. It's from inside of you." Practice, practice. Also, we can stand up for each other. When people sneered "Well, she's Jewish!" behind her coworker's back, Jessie stared at them matter-of-factly: "Do you know that I am Jewish too?"

Finally, an irresistible trick for our toolkit, the power of reframing—including the "too loud and pushy" stereotype. "Gentile women have accused me, 'Why are you arguing?'" Emily winked, "'I'm just passionate, I told them!"

]

8

Push/Push/Push for Perfection

"I don't look at what I've achieved, or where I've learned or grown; I still look at where the gaps are, and I kick myself for it."

—*Elly*

"THIS NEED FOR PERFECTION DRIVES ME ALL THE TIME," said Elly. "It's so unspoken that I don't even recognize it." Because just maybe, if we do everything right, we will be wanted, we won't be criticized or blamed. The strategy often learned from our families? Drive ourselves relentlessly. Focus on mistakes, not successes, so that we don't mess up again. Critique ourselves harshly, so that we get Better. And pass the blame along so that other Jews will shape up as well.

The ultimate goal? To Achieve and Accomplish as much as we can. Convinced that our self-worth depends on this, to compulsively Do. Written in invisible ink: prove once again that we're useful, that it's worthwhile keeping us around.

High expectations—and self-blame

"How big is our expectation to be perfect, to have all the right answers?" Elly mused, absently smoothing her dress.

"I beat myself up all the time," Judith replied. "'You're not good enough: be better!'"

"And if something's not working right," Elly shot back, "it's my fault, and I need to fix it!"

Jessie winced, "When I read the notes from our last meeting together,

147

I thought, 'You idiot, you sound ridiculous!' I felt so embarrassed." Yet everyone else recalled how eloquent Jessie's words had been.

"Being so tight with what we're expecting of ourselves relates to avoiding rejection," Kim suggested. "As Jews, trying to prove 'We really are good!'–so that people will believe it."

Not so far-fetched really. A baby-boomer friend told me how neighbors she had known as a child in Indiana felt her head looking for horns, believing the myth that Jews were the devil. I remember my southern-raised mother admitting that she felt she had to work twice as hard, as a Jew, to be seen as "measuring up"—and she was proud that she did. Bigoted pundit Ann Coulter actually declared that Jews should be "perfected" into Christians.[1]

"I don't necessarily expect anyone else to be perfect," Elly sighed, "but I damn well better be!"

Deena felt the pressure most at her job. "Gentiles in my workplace feel safe dumping their frustration onto other people," she told us. "But if someone's venting at me, I don't lash back. I find ways to challenge that are creative, that 'go from the side.' Because I can't screw up; if I piss them off, it's permanent. There's more slack for other people than for me." She paused. "Or maybe that's just my fear talking."

"What I hear you describing," Emily reflected, "is that risk factor that Jews sometimes feel, that survival's at stake. It's beyond just 'I made a mistake.'"

✼

Meanwhile, as Judith bent over the table, meticulously organizing lists of logistics for our next meetings, Emily laughed. "I really want to acknowledge you for doing that perfectly—ten hours later, still trying to get it right!" When Judith finally put it aside to eat lunch, Kim chided her with a grin, hands on hips: "Quitting so soon? What kind of Jew are you anyway?"

The flip side of blaming ourselves

As hard as we are on ourselves, we often shift the blame to each other. To deflect the occasional zaps we feel? Maybe to subconsciously "help" other Jews "improve," so that nothing bad will happen to any of us? Perhaps to fault in them what we feel ashamed of in ourselves? Historian Sander

Gilman speculates, "By creating the image of a Jew...who embodied all the negative qualities feared within oneself, one could distance the specter of self-hatred."[2] Reminds me of the HBO series *The L Word*, which I loved; but the one truly unlikable character, Jenny, was also the Jewish one (by turns disingenuous, cloying, dishonest, victim-y, ruthless). Interestingly, several of the scriptwriters and creators were Jewish women.

Kim confided, "I just felt really attacked by a Jewish woman, and I was furious with her. But then I saw in her a critical voice just like my own, both of us blaming ourselves deep down. I could see her struggling the same way I am."

For some of us, blame from other Jews feels the most devastating. My psyche still reels from the attack e-mails on my Jewish activist Listserve a few years back. My heart pounded with anxiety as I logged on, wondering what assault would be leveled at me (or my friends) that day? And then I found myself falling into the same punching-bag mindset. Feh!

And how many of us grew up in families where criticism flowed like our mother's milk? In fact, that's where we learned to do it so well. Sometimes the attacks were (confusingly) meant to be construed as love, often showing up as disappointment. More than once I've heard, "They were so crushed when I wasn't perfect." "We may have gotten the message of perfection," Rabbi Harold Kushner suggests, "from parents who genuinely loved us and wanted the best for us, and acted out that concern by correcting our every trivial mistake and constantly urging us to do better."[3] Continuing the same pattern thrust onto them. Friends tell me a version of this pattern runs in the black community as well, a legacy from the brutality of slavery: parents hard on their kids (then and now) so that they would "shape up" and be less victimized by the Master.

"You make it harder for the rest of us"

In his *Washington Post* column, journalist Gene Weingarten wrote to his mother in heaven, after Al Gore chose Orthodox Jew Joe Lieberman as his vice presidential running-mate: "Always you worried when a Jewish person got too prominent...You were afraid this person might mess up—a shame...a shanda for the goyim, you called it...and when he did, all the non-Jews...would point and say, 'SEE? See how bad Jews are?' When Son of Sam turned out to be some schlemiel named Berkowitz, it nearly broke you...If you weren't already dead for Lewinsky, it would have killed you."[4]

Many Jews learn the same message from prejudice: *any* of us who mess up reflect on all Jews. And then what could come down? Amy chuckled, "When my grandparents watched the news and somebody did some god-awful thing, they'd say: 'Thank God he wasn't a Jew.'"

"I find myself doing that now," Kim admitted. (Question: did Christians worry that because Timothy McVeigh bombed the Oklahoma City Federal Building, killing 168 people, that this reflected on all white Christians?)

Sighing, Jessie told us about a Jewish administrator at her school, someone she described as hypercritical, snobbish, bigoted. "Why do you have to be one of the higher-ups at the school and feed into all the stereotypes?" she wailed. "I wince every time I look at you. You make it harder for the rest of us."

As executive director of her synagogue, Judith said she has to act in a certain way when she communicates to the outside world—even if she is just calling the phone company—"because they're gonna think 'This is true about *all* Jews.'" And when Amy wears her *kippah* in public, "I monitor my behavior closely, because with my *yarmulke* on, I'm seen as the representational Jew, I can't afford to deviate."

Elly mused, "If a woman does something, I don't think 'Now they're gonna think badly about women.' But I do about Jews." Still, the reality is, one of us does not stand in for the rest. The real *tsuris* (trouble) is anti-Semitism.

We need to remember...

Jews are not the only marginalized group that internalizes oppression and constantly pummels ourselves, as a corrective strategy, to do everything right. "I was working with a gentile Japanese American client," Amy told us. "And the same phrases about perfection that we used, word for word, were coming out of her mouth. She could have been one of us sitting in the room!"

"Perfectionism thrives on comparison and competition," notes writer Julia Cameron.[5] "It doesn't know how to say, 'Good try,' or 'Job well done.'

The critic does not believe in creative glee...The larger our perfectionism looms, the smaller our talent seems to become. It is our perfectionism that needs to be miniaturized."[6] She adds, "When I become too serious, my pets come to the rescue...Tugging at their leashes, [my dogs]...chase squirrels they will never catch, and they do so with enthusiasm."[7]

So how can we get it that we don't have to drive ourselves so desperately to achieve perfection, that our survival is no longer at stake? That being a little "broken" is only human; that it doesn't help to beat ourselves up, or to project that brokenness onto others. That we can make mistakes without withdrawing from each other. And that when someone criticizes us, it's not about our worthiness—because we are valuable just as we are. In fact, when we turn the tables, when we acknowledge and appreciate ourselves and each other, it can build community, even movements. My friend Bola's parents taught her, "You can catch more flies with honey..."

In *How Good Do We Have to Be?* Rabbi Harold Kushner points to studies showing that "athletes who obsess over their mistakes...do much worse than athletes who say to themselves, 'That wasn't very good; the next one will be better.'"[8] They refuse to let one play define their self-worth. "The question," he continues "is not whether or not...we will get some important things wrong from time to time and feel terrible about it...The question is, how shall we deal with...our sense of inadequacy?[9] It ought to be with a sense of relief...that we come to the conclusion that we...never will be perfect[10]...When you do wrong, realize that that was not the essential you. It was because the challenge of being human is so great that no one gets it right every time."[11]

Kushner quotes physician Rachel Ramen: "I am not perfect, but I am enough. Knowing that...allows healing to happen."[12]

9

"Where Do I Belong?"

"To be Jewish in America meant being an outsider."[1]
— Dr. Alice Rothchild

EVEN THOUGH THESE DAYS MANY WHITE U.S. JEWS have insider privileges, sometimes we still feel we don't belong—anywhere. Sometimes we're made to feel that way. Understandably, we might be hauling around old feelings of isolation, after being abandoned in Nazi Germany, and after widespread bigotry in this country not so far back. Before that, Ashkenazi Jews were shut into European ghettos for centuries, while the welcome mat was not always warmly extended to Jews in Islamic countries either.

Then again, we might feel we simply don't fit with other Jews. Or specifically with Jews who are middle-class, Ashkenazi, or heterosexual, who are observant or older, who are mainstream or male.

So it's complicated. Again, the Jewish feeling of not belonging might be a sensibility passed through our families after being ostracized in Europe, elsewhere. It can be a response to marginalization/exclusion even today in a Christian-centric land, or by other Jews. Or it can connect to feeling somehow inferior, not a legitimate group member—"not Jewish enough," as described earlier. Or any combination of these…feeling Different, Other, Alone.

Where do I fit with other Jews?

When I asked Jewish friends, "Who ever felt you didn't belong in a group of Jews?" all hands shot up. (Common internalized oppression for *any* targeted group, including women, trans/genderqueer folks, constituencies of color, especially if you're mixed.)

Comparing her family to generalizations about U.S. Jews, Emily chuckled. "The stereotypes are: Jews don't drink, they don't beat their kids, they're not physical, and they're not in the military. What's my family? My mother was a phys. ed. teacher; my father went through the military to put himself through college. They're both alcoholics. And they beat their kids. So where does that leave me? I'm Jewish—but where do I fit with other Jews?"

Deena questioned whether she belonged, since she didn't know everything about Jewish rituals. On High Holy Day services she performed her "First Official Jewish Thing Ever," by opening the Ark (where the holy Torah scrolls are kept), "like it was a statement, 'I'm part of these people.'" But after she stumbled, not knowing that "after you open it, you have to close it," she concluded, "I'm not part of these people after all." Then as Mizrahi/Ashkenazi she felt, "Sometimes I belong. Sometimes I don't. And then I do. And then I don't."

Sometimes we feel we don't belong in Jewish communities because of Ashkenazi centrism/racism. Tunisian Jew Caroline Smadja, a writer and intercultural trainer, was raised mostly in France surrounded by Tunisian Jews, with a brief sojourn in Jerusalem. Living in the United States for twenty years gave her "a sense of home I thought was unattainable."[2] But she found that "...as a group, American Jews have an ethnocentric view that ignores the very existence of people like me. They assume all Jews originate from Eastern Europe; they think of Yiddish as the only Jewish language besides Hebrew; and they presume that all worthwhile Jewish leaders, artists, and thinkers are Ashkenazi.

"Every time I have tried to take part in American Jewish communities," she explained, "I have been faced, once again, with the feeling of being different, not fitting in. Lost among people who delight in matzo ball soup and can barely locate Tunisia on a world map, I have yet to find a place where I can be myself without feeling invisible, dismissed, or treated like a rare, exotic species. As a result, I am still haunted by the need to belong[3]...for a community to call my own."[4]

Class dominance, too, rears its imperious head. "If you're not middle class," Rachel Wahba declares, "you don't exist in the Jewish community."[5] When Emily felt ignored by other Jews at a workshop, it kicked up working-class pain from her childhood, when she "didn't have the right clothes, or the right ideas, or the right looks. I *hated* it. I was scared as hell of other Jews, I knew how to protect myself better with non-Jews." One of Elly's biggest wounds as working class was being made to feel "You don't fit, you don't belong" by middle-class peers in Hebrew school. "I grew up angry at the Jewish world we lived in," she said, eyes blazing, "for making me feel so Different. So Less Than. I resented it like hell. I didn't have a context to understand it was the world I lived in that said it wasn't okay to be a Jew."

The spiritual leader of the largest Lesbian/Gay/Bisexual/Transgender/Queer, and Questioning (LGBTQ) synagogue worldwide (NYC), Rabbi Sharon Kleinbaum (named one of *Newsweek*'s 50 most influential U.S. rabbis) makes a plea for opening up the Jewish community tent, explaining: "As Jews with varied and violent histories of persecution, we have a hard time trusting others, let alone each other. As queer and trans Jews, as Jews of color, as working-class Jews, we have often had experience within Jewish communities that amplify that distrust, pushing us out of communities and into isolation. Too many Jewish communities across the country are moving further to the right...and those of us on the left are feeling the danger of this shift. We feel the tent curtains...squeezing us out of *where we know we belong*."[6] (Italics added)

Imploring those who have managed to stay inside "to remain accountable to those who have not been welcomed in," Kleinbaum urges our communities to "stretch the tent curtains wider."[7]

Not belonging—in WASP land, or anywhere

How many of us feel that we don't belong, period? A sense of homelessness, Judith called it.

"My whole life has been about 'I don't fit in,' and a lot of it is from being Jewish," Emily confided. Whether as the only Jew on her (white, gentile) childhood swim team, or the only non-African American at citywide track meets,[8] "No one was very welcoming. It was more like 'Sorry, door's closed.' So it's been hard to find my way." Tears welled up in her eyes. "As a kid I would have given my life to belong or feel wanted. So I've gotten really good at going into any group—it could be 'Jewish single moms of adopted babies from China,'" she half smiled—"and I will find the ways that I don't belong. It's a feeling I need to keep chiseling away at." Gazing at a photo of herself as a little girl, she sighed. "I really love that picture. There's a look in my eyes that's so poignant, trying to connect. I just want those deep roots."

Then there's the overwhelming Christianism in the air, especially thick during Christmas and Easter, times when Jessie wants to "leave the planet." She rolls her eyes. "All the questions I get asked: 'What are you doing for Christmas?' 'I don't celebrate Christmas.' 'You *don't*?' 'No. I'm Jewish.' 'OHHHHHH.'"

"Oh God," Jessie moaned "how many times do I have to go through this? I totally leave my body. One person asked, 'If you don't go to other people's houses and exchange gifts, what do you people *do* for two weeks?' I was so taken aback. I said, 'We live. What do you think we do?' 'But how can you survive without Christmas?'"

By this time, Jessie was laughing hysterically. "We've done it for 5000 years, you idiot. We're doing just fine!"

Moving on...

For many Jews, why is feeling that we don't belong so acute? "It's connected to anti-Semitism," speculated Deena. "Deep down, it feels like what's at stake for belonging, or not belonging, could be our *lives*."

"It does feel like that for me," Judith jumped in. "Definitely that intense." Related, but also different—for some of us what's most overwhelming may be the wall of aloneness, transmitted through our families for generations in response to all that has happened.

Yet the U.S. landscape has changed for us, is changing still. No reason to keep scanning the horizon for the next attack, the next hate-filled look. We can decide to grow roots, to create a new language of belonging. Right here.

"Home, I have learned, is where we sit down and decide to build it," writes Kyla Wazan Tompkins, a scholar and Moroccan/Canadian Jew, calling this decision "the most profound lesson of the Diaspora."[9] Where we resolve to reach through our alienation, our covered-over but deep-down isolation, to notice how we belong to each other. Casting no one out of the circle, we can also each nestle into our own juicy Jewish (and ally) constellation of resonance and support.

"Weave real connections," writes Marge Piercy.[10] Connections with Jews across ethnicities and race, across class and gender identities. Connections with non-Jews. Creating our own communities, helping us belong wherever we go. "For every gardener knows," Piercy continues, "that after the digging, after the planting/after the long season of tending and growth, the harvest comes."[11] Part of the growth and tending, for ourselves, is giving "difference" a positive spin: splashy, engaging, with stories to tell.

Noticing how we actually belong already, in our Jewishly-different (also similar) ways, in a U.S. society growing more multicultural by the minute — a land beset with white Christian norms, but one that (twice) elected a biracial African American president with a Muslim father, a place transforming every day…a place that is now our well-deserved home.

10

Taking Egypt Out of the Jews

"It was not only necessary to take the Jews out of Egypt; it was also necessary
to take Egypt out of the Jews."

— *Passover Haggadah*

WE ARE A MAGNIFICENT PEOPLE—as are other peoples. Despite sometimes-
catastrophic hardship and trauma, we have contributed gloriously to our
world. Spanning diverse cultures, Jews are known for our humor and
resilience, our vitality, intelligence, and warmth. And thankfully, Jewish
survival is not at risk now. Then why, ask scholars David Biale, Michael
Galchinsky, and Susannah Heschel, is Jewish identity today still "founded so centrally...on a history of victimization"?[1] Is this who we *want* to
be, as Jews?

Why is it that, deep inside, many of us still feel beleaguered and powerless, the slaves of Pharaoh, and so behave as if we are still victims? Over generations, we have internalized what has happened to our people, and the
terror, grief, and pain live inside us still. Sometimes these erupt when we
feel threatened: whether we are truly endangered, or more often, when
fear has warped our thinking.

We may sink into "Look what's been done to us!," ignoring Jewish
resistance, even blaming ourselves or each other for the mistreatment—
forgetting that Jewish identity is more than the Shoah or Israel, or suffering. We might wear victimhood like a badge, using past persecution to let
us off the hook for our actions now.

Purging behaviors and beliefs that we adopted in response to centuries of demonization is a tall order. And true enough, individual Jews are occasionally violently assaulted, even killed, just for being Jewish. But this is the exception. As a once multiply victimized people, if we don't work through the inherited wounds, we can become victimizers and perpetuate the damage. Child psychologist/sociologist Alice Miller's exemplary work describes a related pattern: how "the devastating effects of the traumatization of children take their toll on society, leading to inconceivable violence...and...repetition" of abuse in the next generation.[2]

The anxiety passed through our families is usually greater than the current reality warrants. Sometimes confusing past with present, our fear ripples out onto those who were *not* the ones who shipped us to camps, or shot us in shtetls or torched us in medieval synagogues. This is not our fault, but it's simply not acceptable. We can do better. And as horrendous as Jews' experience was, it didn't catapult us into exalted status. We are not the only peoples who have suffered, who feel vulnerable.

Whether we lapse into personal helplessness, victimize family members, or project our terror onto other peoples, even harming them—we need to recover from our trauma. To (compassionately) face our feelings, work through them, heal. To see that we are just as valuable, and usually, just as wanted, as every other people. No more, no less.

To join with millions of Jews worldwide who are ignoring the voice that whispers we are victims, who resist manipulation by our communal and national leaders, Christian and Jewish, to serve their agendas. To end our cycle of isolated suffering. Instead to ensure human rights, and practice the empathy, solidarity, and joy that is also our heritage.

Litany of suffering

"But what is Jewish identity if it's not suffering?" Kim asked. "Seriously," she grinned: "The presumption is we're gonna be victims unless we keep our eye out for 'What's good for the Jews.'"

"For many Ashkenazim, we just assume bad things will happen," Amy replied glumly.

"I'm thinking of my friends," Kim continued, "who went to Jewish Renewal *Yom Kippur* services [the Day of Atonement, the holiest religious day for Jews]. They complained that it was 'too joyful!' It wasn't painful enough."

"But I went to that same service," Emily protested, flinging her arms. "And I *loved* it. There was gorgeous music. And it embraced different aspects of the holiday, not just Jews wearing the badge of victim. That's our history, but how do we move on? Is that what I want to pass on to my daughter? To me, it's not disowning my Jewishness or what the wounds have been, but it's also figuring out how to walk better in the world without victimization and shame.

Absently twirling her hair, Elly described learning that she came from "a people of victimhood—almost as if we hoarded it." She absorbed the teaching not only from her family, "but also from Hebrew school: it was a litany of victimization, almost a pride in being victims. Even more than 'see what we've survived.'"

As if Jews were "the only true victims," wrote Silva Tennenbaum, who fled Hitler in 1938.[3] How might it shift our isolation to let ourselves feel connected to other Nazi victims: the Roma (Gypsies), commies, gays, trade unionists, and the physically/mentally disabled, more? As if no other people have endured horrific holocausts—different, but genocides just the same—in Armenia, Cambodia, Rwanda, Bosnia?

Elly continued, "It's almost like we think being victims makes us purer, like we're operating from some high moral code. As if we're better people because we've been hit by oppression rather than being oppressors. But it's not true! Look at the Jews in power in Israel. It doesn't matter that it's the same generation that survived Nazism. They turn around and do some of the same kind of genocidal behavior. I think we've brought suffering almost to a point of holiness—and it justifies everything. Then you don't have to take responsibility for the power and privilege you have."

Ariana Melamed, columnist for Israel's daily, *Yediot Acharonot*, admits the same. "We are victims so we are allowed:…When the IDF showers Gazan civilians with molten lead, questions must not be asked in wartime and mistakes must not be admitted to…[But] being relatives and children of victims does not justify our own injustices...[or free us] of the lesson that is as important as sovereignty and power: the duty to create a moral society that is sensitive to injustice."[4]

From the receiving end of this dynamic, African American literary giant James Baldwin wrote, "It is galling to be told by a Jew whom you know to be exploiting you that he cannot possibly be doing what you know he is doing, because he is a Jew."[5]

And it's also true that anti-Semitism (and sometimes, attacks on Jews) exists. Referring to both ends of the spectrum, Elly confides: "In my own healing process, I've come to loathe victimization because I've carried so much of it. I've also gone to the other extreme of 'Huh! Anti-Semitism is nothing in America compared to the real oppression of racism. Anti-Semitism is like a toothache.' So it's been a process of validating for myself, 'Wait a minute, anti-Semitism doesn't have to be the same as racism to be important.' In fact, it minimizes both to compare, even though sometimes they almost beg for comparison."

Martyrdom: "I'll just sit over here and bleed"

Then there's the dynamic of blaming ourselves—or being blamed by others. Jessie told us she was admonished, "What's wrong with your people? Bad things don't happen to people unless they bring it on themselves." "What IS wrong with us?" Jessie thought. "Why were we hated for so long by so many?" As if Jews deserved the abuse.

Or maybe we just feel hopeless, our families having transferred the message: life is hard, there's nothing you can do about it. Like in Emily's working-class home: "If we were sick, we were told 'You're not dying, it's not the Holocaust, so get over it.' Because 'with what we've been through, you just go on.' I wish we had been told, 'Be strong and courageous and have faith.' Instead we got, 'Drag yourself through the mud and the muck.'"

After such grim messages (reinforced by sexism, constructing women to take care of everyone but ourselves) it's not such a stretch to a martyr-mentality: "My pain doesn't matter," Amy grinned, "I don't want to burden you."

"Don't mind me, I'll sit in the dark," shouted Geri.

"It's not important," chimed in Elly, "I'll just sit over here and bleed."

Brushing away tears of laughter, Rani gasped, "My mother said that soooo many times when I was a kid. I thought she made it up!"

Fear bigger than the situation warrants

When trauma lives in us, it keeps getting recharged. Elly realized the effect of seeing Auschwitz tattoos throughout her childhood. "I have *huge* fear. And it's bigger than the situation warrants. But what I'm responding to has been passed through generations; it's *their* words I use, not my own. I've internalized the anti-Semitism. We need to remember this as part of our history, *not* live it like it's present time."

"It's true," Emily mused, stretching. "There's a way that Jews feel things as life-threatening, when they usually aren't. Something has been transmitted, nonverbally, verbally. We pop out of the womb," she cupped her hands, "and we get that message right off, that it's not safe."

Amy spoke up. "But I've been discovering, the more I confront my anxiety, and my desire to hide, the more powerful I feel." She was just back from a San Francisco rally supporting activist journalist Mumia Abu-Jamal, who was on death row for thirty years, fighting for his life. Wearing her yarmulke in public, she worried she would be pelted with derisive comments, or worse. "Not only did no one spit on me or hit me, several people wished me 'Good Shabbos.'" Her eyes glowed. "I'm learning that my fear is much larger than the reality."

Another compelling example is the mainstream U.S. Jewish response to Louis Farrakhan. "If we hadn't such a sense of victimization," Elly noticed, "we wouldn't be so scared of him. Where we need to put our anger is not on him, he's been scapegoated in a certain way." She continued,

> If we look at this only through the filter of Jewish history, we look through a filter of "victim," rather than focusing on our experience as U.S. Jews *today*. We hear virulent anti-Semitism, and we become emotionally triggered, without acknowledging the context. We go into gut-level survival mode, of "I get to destroy you because I'm terrified, and don't hold me accountable, because I had to survive the Holocaust, etc." We go there without realizing, "Wait a minute, I'm not in Nazi Germany. I'm not in an Eastern European pogrom. I'm a white Jew, middle to upper-middle class, in America. No one's gonna kill me today

or tomorrow. In fact, that's not Hitler speaking, that's an African American person in America, with their history.

"Sure, Farrakhan has said some vitriolic things," Elly acknowledged— and then offered a non-victimized perspective.

He has also taken affirmative healing stands about economic recovery for his people. Did you know that, statistically, money changes hands twelve times before it leaves the U.S. Jewish community? Money changes hands one time before it leaves the African American community.[6] He is speaking from pain and anger, and he is identifying an enemy that the African American experience resonates with. Some Jewish landlords and storeowners have been other than kind and helpful, you know? I think rather than for us to act victimized, we could take responsibility. If there were not a grain of truth, his words wouldn't resonate so deeply.

All eyes on her, Elly shifted in her chair. "No, Farrakhan is not prioritizing Jewish concerns," she said.

If we want to build an alliance, then we have to step out of our "Is it good for the Jews?" perspective. There's no room for movement there. We need to talk with him, instead of "Let's blast him out of the water," using every tool we have as white Jews to do that. "And gee, why is he angry, why isn't he listening to us?" Being in dialogue means our being willing to listen, too. If Jews didn't wear victimization as a badge, I think our reaction to Farrakhan would be different. To me, our work as Jews is to get out from under that way of thinking.

The tension was palpable. Taking a deep breath, Kim jumped in. "Maybe the question is also what do we do with the *intensity* of our fear, which could have something to do with inherited patterns? If someone in a workshop says something anti-Semitic, and I confront them, and they yell and put me down, how real is the damaging effect versus how I perceive it? To me, I've just died in the "workshop holocaust," but really, somebody just got angry at me.

Okay—so what about the Holocaust?

The legacy of the Shoah is laced throughout this book. As survivors of a hunted people, devastated by attempted annihilation less than seventy years ago, how do we fully face what happened—"un-numb" from it—without becoming immobilized?[7] Without letting it fuel misguided action?

The collective unconscious memory of the Nazi Holocaust invades our lives and leaves its mark in ways most of us don't even realize.[8] Some families had to welcome babies into a world that had just killed two-thirds of Europe's Jews.

Yet escaping the Warsaw Ghetto as a child, Irena Klepfisz aptly points out how unhealed horror confuses many Jews into placing the Holocaust "at the center of our Jewishness," committing to "a lifetime of mourning"—rather than engaging with the present.[9] Instead, she urges, we need to recontextualize the Shoah, to move "toward a Jewish future that is *informed, but not defined*" by it."[10] (Italics added)

Israeli political psychologist Daniel Bar Tal agrees. "If we are defined by...our victimhood," he asks, how can we ever "think clearly about the problem of Israel-Palestine and the problem of anti-Semitism?"[11] As Elly questioned earlier, how do we get out from under that way of thinking? Not to mention that an obsessive focus on the Shoah adds to the invisibility of non-European Jewish histories.

The word "Holocaust" was not commonly used before the 1960s.[12] Nazi executioner Adolf Eichmann's 1961 trial galvanized U.S. Jewish attention, but it was Israel's Six-Day War in 1967, with Egypt, Jordan, and Syria that opened "a floodgate of associations" with a genocide most Jews had avoided confronting.[13] The associations made, fear mounted that the new Jewish state could be destroyed[14]—paradoxically, just as Jews were gaining influence in U.S. institutions. In 1978, the TV miniseries *Holocaust* hit the airwaves.

J. J. Goldberg argues that it was the Six-Day War, and the accompanying unexamined Holocaust memories, that created the opening for militant U.S. Jewish leaders to take control of our institutions, pounding home the chilling narrative: *We must never again let down our guard*, a sea change from a tolerance-and-social-justice stance to a defensive bunkermentality. The mantra was manipulated by passionate leaders driven by this circling-the-wagons mindset, as well as by "guilt over past Jewish timidity, and by suspicion of Gentiles, liberalism, and coalition politics."[15] Goldberg dubs them "the New Jews of 1967": the Zionists, the Orthodox, and the neoconservatives (many formerly Marxists).[16] *It was the manipulation of Holocaust trauma*, charges historian Norman Finkelstein, the child of concentration camp survivors, *that led to Israel becoming the "new religion" of U.S. Jews.*[17] At the same time, the 1967 War elevated Israel into becoming a U.S. strategic asset in the Middle East.[18]

The first Jewish Israeli leader to emerge from, and to focus on, the Nazi Holocaust experience was Menachem Begin, elected prime minister in 1977. With Begin, David Biale writes, "the experience of the Holocaust survivors became the ethos of the state...Israel became the embodiment of persecuted and desperate Jewry. The Jew remained a victim, but now a victim with an army."[19]

Israel and Zionism: response to anti-Semitism

For those grabbing the reins of the U.S. Jewish establishment, the rigid, anxiety-driven narrative wrung from genocide birthed a defensive Zionism, a militant ideology of survival, partly reacting to the myth of Diaspora Jews as historically impotent.[20]

Founded in the late 1800s as a utopian solution to European anti-Semitism, Zionism first emerged as a form of ethnic Jewish nationalism and self-determination (surrounded by Euro nationalisms), bent on founding a safe haven for Jews. Early Zionist supporters of the *Brit Shalom* Movement—philosopher Martin Buber and Rabbi Judah Magnes among them—advocated for one binational state for Jews and Arabs, with equal rights for all.[21] Rejecting nationalistic domination, Buber insisted "In this land...there is room both for us and for its present inhabitants [Palestinians]. Our return to the Land of Israel...will not be achieved at the expense of other people's rights."[22]

But abetted by the terror of the Shoah, hard-line groups won control, believing "Jews had been victims in the past because they did not make survival their cardinal commandment."[23] Zionism became the "irrefutable answer to Jewish powerlessness during the Holocaust."[24] Revisionist Zionism's right-wing leader, Ze'ev Jabotinsky, even seized upon Arab resistance to Jewish settlement in Palestine as an opportunity "to refute the legacy of Jewish passivity by making armed self-defense a necessity."[25]

When the Jewish state was founded in 1948, sanctioned by the U.N., Jews achieved their homeland, and a state privileging only Jews.[26] "One of the defining problems of Zionism," says U.K. English professor Jacqueline Rose, is that "it imported into the Middle East a Central European concept of nationhood," a mini-Europe "founded on ethnicity and blood."[27] But the colonial/expansionist brand of Zionism, which still dominates Israel today—crushing Palestinians and taking their land to build lush Jewish-only settlement-suburbs that control nearly half of the (Palestinian) West Bank—remains a consistently contested strategy.[28]

Meanwhile, Israeli Zionism's defiant ideology determined to "return" Jews to active agents of history, so the new Zionist man was born—and "man" he definitely was—who would "never again" endure humiliation or near-annihilation. This emerging warrior breed towered over the supposedly weak/shameful/inferior shtetl-born Holocaust victim. The "new [Israeli] Jew" was tough and self-sufficient, brimming with machismo, brute strength, military swagger. Yet "the Jew-as-pathetic-victim stereotype," Sander Gilman warned, "ignores the courageous resistance of Jews throughout history."[29] And must refuting alleged passivity inherently lead to victimizing others?

When abused becomes abuser

My friends who work on restorative justice remind me: *Hurt people hurt people.*[30]

People "who have been oppressed," Cherie Brown explains, "often internalize the behaviors of the oppressor and act them out unintentionally against their own people."[31] Applying it specifically to Jews, "The hostility and brutality leveled at Jews, *when left unhealed,* can be internalized and then Jews may become hostile, hypercritical, or even brutal to one another. This cycle of repeating the initial mistreatment is one of the most insidious results of oppression."[32] (Italics added)

Also, Brown adds, because of not having healed from the Shoah and earlier, it has been almost impossible for Jews "to see ourselves both as victims and in the oppressor role with regard to another people."[33] The Israeli group Rabbis for Human Rights echoes this: "Our experience as victims blinds us to the possibility that we can be both victims and victimizers at the same time."[34] Other groups have experienced the same—emancipated slaves who became slaveholders, escapees from religious persecution in England who became witch-burners in New England. Victimizers, in fact, often continue to feel like victims themselves inside.

The key to reversing internalized victimization? Authentically grappling with, and then moving through whatever terrible thing was done to us, even if the damage was indirect. Otherwise we can become abusers to Jews and to others as well.

Recycling the hurt: incest and domestic abuse

Typical of how "hurt people hurt people" Gloria Steinem notices, "Our children are the only people on whom we can safely take revenge for what was done to us," because they have so little agency.[35] In one of many such stories, performance artist Ursula Katan's Jewish family lit candles on Friday nights, gave money to plant trees in Israel, and sent her to Hebrew school and camp. But in *To Open My Mouth and Speak What I Know*, she confides being molested not only by her "heroic" Holocaust survivor grandfather, who lost most of his family, but also by his son—her father, who also "bears the emotional scars of the camps," whose "sweaty hands advanced heavily up my thigh while the rabbi droned on" during Friday morning prayers.[36] Was her grandfather a victim of incest or abuse, she wonders? "Or was his behavior [at least partly] caused by...five years in a... concentration camp and five years more in a displaced person's camp?"[37]

"We Jews often look to our victim status," Katan points out, "yet we never acknowledge our role as perpetrator...our own country's oppression of the Palestinian people."[38] We need to break the protective silence, she says, including admitting Jewish family abuse, in order to "heal both from the violence we have suffered and the violence we have perpetrated."[39] Otherwise, "we risk becoming the monsters we have fought."[40]

Making the link with other domestic abuse, anti-Semitism, and anti-Arabism, peace activist Tema Okun writes, "We are like the child who has been abused and grows up to recycle the abuse on a less powerful woman or child...I've sat across the table from devout Jews screaming at me that all Arabs do is breed suicide bombers, without seeing that their screaming hatred of Palestinians is the flip side of our experience."[41]

Confusing past with present: Israel/Palestine

"The 2000-year trauma of the blood libel, the Inquisition, the pogroms, Auschwitz and Chelmno and the Gulag Archipelago, have produced a distorted vision, where every shriek of pain directed at Israel can sound like the rumble beginning in the massed crowds at Nuremberg."[42]

—Israeli Haaretz journalist Gideon Levy

As two millennial peace activists put it, "No one is really done dealing with this trauma [the Shoah], and that makes it hard to understand the present without being overwhelmed by the past."[43] The perception gap between present reality and the feeling of Jewish vulnerability has been described as running "like a crack through the...[U.S.] Jewish community."[44] For some of us, trapped in our history, an anti-Semitic act can feel symptomatic "of a smoldering global epidemic of Jew-hatred," making it "impossible for Israel to over-react to any act of Palestinian hostility."[45] Legitimate critiques of Israeli policy can activate fear stuck just below the surface, that maybe it's starting, again.

Describing how this "Holocaust syndrome" plays out in Israel, Maryanna Eckberg explains, "When an entire population is traumatized," it's not surprising "for the trauma to be enacted on a societal level in the form of violence."[46] Founded mostly by Jews fleeing the Nazis—scarcely any other country would let Jews in—Israel is a very frightened society, using force "because Hitler caused us deep psychic damage."[47]

Feeling abandoned by most of the world, many Israeli Jews see their country as fragile and small, surrounded by club-wielding giants. "The history of Jewish persecution," testifies Jessica Montell, who leads Israeli human-rights group *B'Tselem*, "influences Israeli reactions to modern-day security threats, even when the resulting self-perception of Jews as defenseless victims clashes markedly with Israel's military might."[48] Professor James Berger cuts to the chase: "In the Middle East, Israel is fighting not just the Palestinians, but the Nazis and centuries of haters of Jews."[49]

Projecting onto Others

"Many years back, historian Isaac Deutscher compared European Jews 'to a man standing on the roof of his burning house. He jumped off to save himself and landed on a neighbor whose bones he broke. Instead, however, of apologizing, helping the neighbor up, calling the doctor, and paying for the damage, he began cursing the neighbor for being under him when he jumped and punishing him for lashing out in pain.'"[50]

—*Retold by Talmudic scholar Daniel Boyarin.*

When we confuse past and present, it's easy to project our upset onto whomever we have been taught to fear or despise—often not the source of our mistreatment. U.S. Jews have projected our anxiety, Sander Gilman suggests, onto those "perceived as lower in the estimation of the privileged group."[51] Today, says Cherie Brown, this "dangerous part of our internalized oppression" often "lends itself to being acted out on the Palestinians."[52] (Also, for Euro-descended white Jews and white gentiles, learning racist messages has made Palestinians easy targets.)

In a striking example, Palestinian psychiatrist/peace activist Eyad Sarraj describes former Israeli Prime Minister Ariel Sharon: "who has a deep trauma buried into his unconscious level, as a Jew from the generation of victims of persecution. Victims who have not dealt with their victimization become both narcissistic and paranoid...*They export their victimization onto others.* The sad thing is that the worst kind of people [are]...the people who have been victims and then suddenly become powerful."[53] (Italics added)

New York Times columnist Roger Cohen reiterates, "Past persecution of the Jews cannot be a license to subjugate another people, the Palestinians."[54] Which is also not to disregard that Jewish Israeli and Palestinian peoples have distinct narratives—including Palestinians with Israeli citizenship, treated as second-class inside Israel—narratives manipulated by leaders worldwide, Jewish and gentile.

Visiting Israel as a young girl, Alice Rothchild heard one story. Only years later did she learn the Palestinian story, "interwoven with our own."[55] "Despite my...sensitivity for victims all over the world, I never asked what happened to the Arabs in those white stone houses...A decade after the worst genocide the world had ever experienced, I had never heard of the expulsion and flight of 750,000 Palestinians...of the destruction of hundreds of Arab villages, of the victims that were created, in significant part, by my own people's victimization[56]...I now understand that buried in the wounds of my...people's near annihilation and the subsequent victories of war, another people's story was lost."[57]

Yet whenever a Jewish or a Muslim mother loses her child to violence from Israeli or Palestinian fighters, their loss and grief are the same.

The current conflict is not intractable. And the U.S. government has hardly helped Jews examine the situation dispassionately and clearly. Barely a century old,[58] the struggle manifests now as an Israeli military occupation of the West Bank, including Palestinian East Jerusalem and Gaza. Although this occupation sets up separate and unequal systems for Israelis and Palestinians, and it violates international laws created after World War II to redress Nazi atrocities, our government persists in funding it.[59] Israeli activist publisher Yael Lerer points out, "Israel could not continue the occupation" without U.S. and European Union support.[60]

Still, as U.S. Jews, it's up to us to stop projecting our past trauma onto Palestinians. It's not our fault we were hurt, but it's not the Palestinians' fault either. "Like many Jews, I feel sorry I didn't kill Hitler with my bare hands,"[61] wrote Israeli author Amos Oz. "But...tens of thousands of dead Arabs will not heal that wound...Hitler...is not hiding in Nabatiyah, in Sidon, or in Beirut."[62] When our fear justifies Israeli actions as "self-defense," activist/author Anna Baltzer clarifies: "There is nothing defensive about denying Palestinians water. There is nothing defensive about preventing people from having materials to build their homes."[63] Avraham Shalom, from Israel's *Shin Bet* (secret service) acknowledged, "We must once and for all admit there is another side...that it is suffering, and that we are behaving disgracefully—this entire behavior is the result of the occupation."[64]

We need to reach out for help to those who are allies to both peoples, who can be truly even-handed brokers, to reach a fair solution: equal rights for all, the core of international law.

U.S. Holocaust survivor and scholar Annette Herskovitz gets bundles of mail from Jewish organizations "calling on memory: 'We must never forget.'" But, she cautions, "Israel's leaders have forgotten the one important thing there was to remember: never dehumanize/demonize another people."[65] "The true lesson of the Nazi genocide," she concludes, is that "we are fully human only when we are able to see the world from the perspective of others and behave with compassion."[66]

To finally lift the burden of misery and dread, we have to examine the pain. "People who discover their past with the help of their feelings," writes Alice Miller, "who learn...to look for...*real causes*...will no longer be compelled to displace their hatred onto innocents."[67] Deeply submerged shame can be part of the picture: from being humiliated, from not responding differently. But "shame swept under the carpet," suggests Jacqueline Rose, "breeds violence like nothing else."[68] The antidote? Exposing the shame to daylight, and then excavating it. "The message of Torah," says Rabbi Michael Lerner, "is that the chain of pain can be broken, that we do not have to pass on to others what was done to us."[69]

"Let Gaza live"

In facing what Jewish internalized victimization, manipulated by our leaders, can lead to, we need look no further than the December 2008-January 2009 Israeli invasion of Gaza. Using U.S.-made Apache helicopters, fighter jets, and gunships, as well as white phosphorous[70]—which sears through flesh, reaching 1500°, and is illegal to use on civilians—the Israeli Defense Forces (IDF), one of the world's strongest militaries, killed nearly 1400 Palestinians. Over half were civilians, at least 318 children.[71] More than one hundred Palestinians were killed for every one Israeli killed.

Thousands more were wounded in the three-week nearly nonstop bombardment of this 25-by-5-mile sandy strip of land, home to one and a half million people. One ton of explosives was used for every Gazan child, woman, or man. The reason for the onslaught? "To teach the people of Gaza a lesson for their support of Hamas," concluded U.N. official Richard Falk, even though punishing an entire population, or collective punishment, is also illegal.[72] The IDF even ordered people from their homes to supposed safe havens, like U.N. schools — and then bombed these.

In one example: *Haaretz* journalist Amira Hass reported that the IDF killed twenty-one of Salah Samouni's relatives, when the army shelled the house where the IDF had sent the family a day earlier, after clearly seeing "the faces of the children and the older women."[73] "I found my mother sitting by the hall with her head tilted downward...the right half of her face was gone," said Samouni.[74] [The day before] "the officer...verified that we were all civilians...why did they then shell us?"[75] Soldiers prevented the Red Cross from reaching the wounded for three days.

Amnesty International reported that soldiers commanded some families out of their homes and then executed them, including babies. People were shot waving white flags.[76]

The U.S. Jewish establishment claimed most of the Gazans killed were terrorists: "When Israel kills innocent civilians, it's by accident."[77] Roger Cohen replied in the *New York Times*, "Israel has the right to hit back at Hamas when attacked — but not to blow Gaza to pieces."[78] All this, following a strangling Israeli siege (also maintained by Mubarak's Egypt) that barred desperately needed food, medicine, and building materials from entering Gaza, leaving hundreds of thousands in ever more grinding poverty, malnutrition, and disease.

"No argument has any force," said former Knesset member Uri Avnery, "next to...a wounded little [Palestinian] girl lying on the floor, twisting with pain and crying out: 'Mama! Mama!'"[79] Even two years later, children's charity director Munir Barakat reported that the assault still constantly occupied the children's minds;[80] in 2010, two-thirds of Gazans still suffered from PTSD.[81] "Painful as it is...to admit," Rabbi Brant Rosen wrote in the *Chicago Tribune*, "Israel's behavior in Gaza has consistently betrayed our...Jewish ethical legacy."[82]

The thirteen Israelis who died were mostly hit by friendly fire; a few were killed by small Qassam rockets that Hamas shot into the Israeli border town of Sderot. It was frightening there as well: a woman running for shelter fell and was killed by a rocket. Young children could not remember a time without sirens signaling fifteen seconds to reach cover. These children, too, wet beds from fear.

Most Jewish Israelis supported the attack, a marker of unhealed trauma from the past, along with racist propaganda. High-schoolers shouted "Death to the Arabs!" saying this helps them prepare for the army.[83] A friend in Tel Aviv e-mailed in despair about her beloved Israeli mother-in-law—who months before had screamed at Jewish settler children when they stoned Palestinians—"who I know to be a...compassionate person." But who justified the Gaza assault, saying "They deserve it." To my friend, "This was the ultimate painful example of the spell the Israeli people fall under during their wars."

When questioned about the deaths of Palestinian children, the Gaza commander replied, "We have a choice, to fight the terrorists or to face being consumed by the flames again," invoking the Holocaust to justify state violence.[84] Later, Daniel Bar Tal asked Jewish Israelis how they felt about the conflict with Arabs overall. His findings: a "sense of victimization, a siege mentality, blind patriotism, belligerence," insensitivity to Palestinian suffering, and especially: a belief that "the whole world is against us."[85]

In the *Jerusalem Post*, Larry Derfner reported, "The Israeli notion of a fair deal: We're entitled to do whatever the hell we want to the Palestinians because, by definition, whatever we do to them is self-defense. They, however, are not entitled to lift a finger against us because, by definition, whatever they do to us is terrorism."[86]

"The truth," says Anna Baltzer, "is that everyday people of any background in any place are capable of unthinkable crimes."[87] Lest we forget: U.S. soldiers massacred 500 Vietnamese civilians in Mai Lai, and before that, thousands of indigenous Americans. Baltzer continues, "Germans were not born Nazis. Palestinians were not born suicide bombers. When you give 18-year-old boys big guns and tanks and send them into an area full of people they [have been taught to] fear... the result is predictable. It doesn't matter where you come from."[88]

Yet also during the Gaza onslaught, the Israeli peace movement (including Arab Israelis) resisted every day: ten thousand waved peace signs in Tel Aviv within hours of the attack; a few refused to serve in the army, others staged die-ins at air force bases. Jewish and Arab Israeli students unfurled their banner "We Refuse to be Enemies," while Holocaust survivors protested by the prime minister's home. Even in Sderot, 500 citizens called for a cease-fire.[89]

Efraim Halevy, a former national security advisor, exposed state policy when he said, "If Israel's goal were to remove the threat of rockets for...southern Israel, opening the border crossing [lifting the siege] would have ensured such quiet for a generation."[90]

Postscript: In November 2012, Israel launched a new eight-day bombing assault on Gaza, killing 167 Palestinians,[91] more than half civilians (including thirty-three children),[92] with over 1000 injured.[93] Jamal Dalou lost his wife, his sister, two daughters, and four grandchildren when their home was bombed.[94] Six Israelis (four civilians) were killed by Palestinian rockets; others were wounded by a bus bomb in Tel Aviv. All those killed had faces, names, families, dreams.

The IDF used U.S.-made Apache helicopters and F-16 warplanes,[95] and Congress passed resolutions unequivocally backing Israel.[96] President Obama fully supported the assault (although he helped pressure Israel to accept the Egyptian-brokered cease-fire). Once again, the military power was asymmetrical;[97] and while most Israelis had bomb shelters to run to, Gazans had nowhere safe to hide.[98] Some Israeli voices along the Gaza border petitioned Netanyahu: "Stop playing with our lives" and instead talk to Hamas, "to work for a long-term agreement" so that citizens on both sides can live normal lives.[99] U.N. human-rights official Richard Falk explained, "The rocket fire [from Gaza] has to stop...but it has to stop in the context of a ceasefire, of ending the blockade, of returning to a condition where diplomacy and law and morality are respected."[100]

The Gaza Freedom Flotilla: In one among many efforts to break the siege, in May 2010 a convoy of 700 activists, artists, and officials from dozens of countries sailed to bring 10,000 tons of badly needed supplies to Gaza—from wheelchairs to building materials (to rebuild 15,000 homes destroyed in the Israeli assault). When the flotilla was eighty miles away, around 4:30 a.m., one hundred Israeli commandos attacked the lead ship,[101] the Turkish *Mavi Marmara*. Although reports conflict about what happened when the soldiers illegally boarded the boat in international waters—rather than towing the convoy to shore—the commandos fired stun grenades, tear gas, and rubber-cased steel bullets,[102] killing nine activists (eight from Turkey and a 19-year-old Turkish American). One journalist "was shot directly through the forehead. The bullet...blew away the back third of his skull"; his colleague cradled him as he died.[103] On a nearby boat, activists were beaten but not killed: "We kept repeating...we were unarmed civilians," said leader Huwaida Araf, but "they did not lift the masks off their faces...they were carrying M-16s."[104]

Israel maintained that the *Mavi Marmara* carried supplies to build bunkers for firing rockets into Israel and was "too large to stop by non-violent means."[105] Insisted Netanyahu, "We will never apologize for defending ourselves" (although later he did apologize to Turkey)[106]—despite the fact that European authorities had thoroughly inspected all the boats beforehand, assuring no weapons onboard.[107] Analyst Phyllis Bennis argued, "No amount of Israeli spin can make us believe that an attack by heavily armed commandos, jumping onto the decks of an unarmed civilian ship in international waters, has anything to do with self-defense...*Israel has apparently decided that it's better to be perceived as savage than as weak*."[108] (Italics added)

When Israeli spokespeople called the flotilla a deliberate provocation, trying to break the Gaza siege, Professor Stephen Zunes (among others) contextualized the convoy as part of a "longstanding tradition of strategic nonviolent direct action...The four African American students who sat at the Woolworth's lunch counter in Greensboro in 1960...weren't just interested in a cup of coffee."[109]

The response worldwide? Protest and condemnation by thousands (including rabbis) of Israel's attack.[110] A call to lift the blockade by all U.N. Security Council members *except* the U.S.: while President Obama expressed "deep regret," all but a few Congress members backed Israel. Yet "There can be no excuse for the way that Israel completely mishandled the incident" wrote the *New York Times*: "The blockade is unjust and against Israel's long-term security."[111]

And in Israel? Overwhelming defense of the government, with parades celebrating the commandos' heroism—although 6000 in Tel Aviv protested with banners, "The government is drowning us all."[112]

Israel eventually eased the blockade and let more foodstuffs through, but still limits imports, exports, and mobility, controlling airspace and sea.[113] The virtual imprisonment of Gaza remains, the U.N. reporting that Gaza won't be "livable" by 2020, unless thousands of homes are built and sources of clean drinking water created.[114] Meanwhile, the U.N. Human Rights Council endorsed (opposed only by the U.S.) the findings of international jurists that accused Israeli forces of "willful killing" and torture in the flotilla raid;[115] and the Israeli State Comptroller noted "significant deficiencies" in Netanyahu's decision making regarding the attack.[116]

Writing in *Haaretz*, Orthodox rabbi and former American Jewish Congress director Henry Siegman broke from the U.S. Jewish establishment consensus:

> Even the most objectionable Israeli policies do not begin to compare with Hitler's Germany. But the essential moral issues are the same. How would Jews have reacted to their tormentors had they been consigned to the kind of existence Israel has imposed on Gaza's population? Would they not have seen human-rights activists prepared to risk their lives to call their plight to the world's attention as heroic, even if they had beaten up commandos trying to prevent their effort? Did Jews admire British commandos who boarded and diverted ships carrying illegal Jewish immigrants to Palestine in the aftermath of World War II...?...The significance of the Gaza Flotilla incident lies...in the larger questions raised about our common human condition by Israel's occupation policies and its devastation of Gaza's civilian population.[117]

In September 2010, ten Jews from the United States, Europe, and Israel sailed towards Gaza carrying toys, schoolbooks, and prosthetic limbs, to show the Gaza siege as "un-Jewish" and immoral.[118] The IDF was brutal in taking over the ship, but no one was killed. Reported passenger Reuben Moscowitz: "I as a Holocaust survivor cannot live with the fact that...Israel is imprisoning an entire people behind fences."[119]

Journalist Sandy Tolan calls Israel's responses "the politics of trauma... The Jewish state appears so trapped by the wounds of its...terrible history that it keeps repeating its...mistakes of excessive force, even though it knows these will only isolate it...further."[120]

Using Jewish victimhood: how we get stuck

Yet Jews weren't born afraid. Distorted perspectives were influenced by those who use our insecurity and grief for profit and power. But it's changeable.

Some Jews grew up being taught to dislike, even fear, other groups: maybe gentiles, Muslims, black folks—to see Arabs as Nazis. The narrative goes something like this: terrible things happened to us, we need to be vigilant, defended at every turn; it's better to attack other people than to be attacked ourselves. Suffering becomes our identity, rather than a devastating part of our history.

Doctors have identified a "stress hormone" in our bodies, cortisol, which can cloud rationality.[121] (Personally, I've noticed that when I'm really scared, upset, I can't think. I feel frozen, confused, off-kilter. Sometimes numb. I might overeat, or drive through a red light.) This inability to reason, along with numbness, may be most dangerous, since these block us from remembering that someone different from ourselves is still a human being. When we are most terrified, with muddled thinking, we are most vulnerable to sacrificing integrity.

Trauma is described as an "uncompleted biological response to threat, which leaves the system in a...high level of arousal, with thwarted movements of defense frozen in time."[122] Meaning, as the body tenses, ready to flee or fight, energy becomes rigidly stuck in place in the nervous system if we can't follow through. So "traumatized people are not suffering from a disease, instead they are stuck in a perpetually aroused state," feeling as if danger could loom any second.[123] (See Chapter Fourteen.)

Symptoms of unhealed trauma? Despair, overidentifying with the dead, using physical/verbal violence as a way to control. Viewing any conflict as possible annihilation. And trauma can be reactivated: by a piercing siren, a verbal attack, a defaced synagogue. But when our minds and hearts are immobilized, we can't accurately gauge whether something is dangerous in the present or not. We react first, think later.

Such powerful emotions can be passed down, passed on. "When we are collectively triggered," Rabbi Lynn Gottlieb explains, "conflict escalates and reason descends because we need our adrenaline to act in survival mode...[As our] heart rate and breathing go up, our intelligence goes down...Fear paralyzes our ability to learn, grow and heal. And we need to heal...That is why our sages counseled healing from love."[124]

One common response to terror is overwhelming grief. If we can't bear that, we may try denial. Rabbi Arthur Waskow, one of the first U.S. rabbis to call for justice for Jews and Palestinians, says we block out information when it feels too hard to face: "We need to open...to knowledge that is painful...in order to...reaffirm Jewish values."[125]

Manipulating fear

"It's the fear we're raised with: so much fear, bordering on paranoia. It helps to justify everything."[126]

—Maya Wind, 19-year-old Israeli army refuser

Often, we are indoctrinated as part of a specific game plan, our victimization is manipulated to achieve an organizational goal or political agenda. Example: "Holocaust memories are still very acute in Israel," says New York Times reporter Stephen Kinzer. "The political parties play on this."[127]

An Israeli American friend, Amir, e-mailed me his son Noam's "homework" in a Tel Aviv kindergarten—Noam, whom I cradled in my arms when he was one day old. It's a series of images, to be matched with identical images elsewhere on the page. The images are almost all military pictures: a warship, a jet fighter, a tank, a man in uniform. The message is clear, "The army and weapons are big in our lives, it's good to be a soldier." With the subtext: "We need them to protect us, there's something to be afraid of."[128]

In Israel, compulsory army service is key to social acceptance, career opportunities. Yet former recruit Inbal Michelzon, who initially wanted to serve her country, soon learned "the rules of the game. You need to make it hard for the Arabs...because they are the enemy."[129] "At the end," she said, "it felt like the army betrayed me—they used me. I couldn't recognize myself. What we call protecting our country is destroying lives."[130] Another soldier, Amit, revealed, "Going from a place where I was sure that we are the scapegoat, the miserable ones being killed, I saw a reality that, most of the time, was the opposite."[131]

❧

Several Israeli friends tell me of their high school trips to death camps. The teens are given no tools for processing the terror that comes up, no help releasing the pain. Often, it just stays stuck inside, ready to be ignited. Ten years later R. still shudders from the experience: "They deliberately introduce us to the camps in a traumatic way. It's like planting a button [or trigger] in us." Adds a former Israeli civics teacher, "The...trips to Poland could have been an occasion to reach broader humanistic understanding, but they end up being all about, 'Then we were weak and now we are strong. We won't give them another chance to kill us.'"[132]

In his documentary *Defamation*, award-winning Israeli filmmaker Yoav Shamir tracks one of these trips to the camps; he says Israel sends more than 30,000 youth each year. A student reports afterwards, "Everyone knows that Jews are hated. We were raised that way." Israel also sends army officers on these trips. "We live with the feeling that death is always with us," one officer confides.

"The Holocaust has been appropriated" by Israel's government and education system, charges Yonatan Shapira, to keep "Jews and Israelis in a state of frightened victims that worship militarism."[133] Shapira, an Israeli Air Force captain who organized pilots to refuse missions in the Palestinian territories (that targeted civilians or served occupation), points out a premier lesson from the Holocaust: "resistance to...racism."[134]

❧

Emblazoned in my memory, I can see them still, Israeli children dressed in full army regalia, parading around that giant Teddy stadium near Jerusalem, just at dusk: the Maccabiah Games, the Jewish Olympics! The tune they march to is familiar, I absently hum along...and then aghast, I realize it's a song I love singing on Shabbat. "Hine ma tov uma nayim, How good it is to gather here together." But now it is used as a military march in a ritual of fierce patriotism.

Then, in this vast arena of thousands, the huge screen shows the history of Jewish martyrs: Munich,[135] before, since. The bold Israeli activists next to me, who have chained themselves to Palestinians' olive trees to keep soldiers from uprooting them, are moved to tears. I'm witnessing the Israeli propaganda machine up close and personal, just a taste of what my friends have been raised with. So compelling—I feel the pull. Around us people are waving the miniature flags we were given upon entering the stadium.

I begin to understand what happens when you are surrounded by this your whole life. Of course you believe it: that you are a victim, alone, that the rest of the world is against you. That "never again" will we let something terrible happen. I see how pain over time can be forged into a weapon.

Soon after, I return to the States, and within weeks the World Trade Center is attacked. What I hear from President Bush is strikingly reminiscent of how it felt being at the Maccabia that day, "You're either with us— or against us." Within weeks the Patriot Act is pushed through Congress, shrinking civil liberties. Ironically, only one Senator dared vote against it: Russell Feingold, a Jew.

When we are afraid, we are most vulnerable to laying aside our moral compass, especially if we are made to feel that our lives are at stake. Some leaders manipulate Holocaust wounds until Jews believe catastrophe could happen any minute. No wonder so many people support disproportionate force when told they are under attack, even from groups whose weapons are negligible.

And true enough, the democratically elected (Islamic fundamentalist) government in Gaza, Hamas, includes threats to Israel's existence in its charter. Yet the Israeli government supported Hamas in the late 1980s, to destabilize the (secular) nationalist Palestine Liberation Organization (PLO).[136] And Hamas has offered truces, even saying it would "allow the Palestinian Authority to negotiate...a two-state solution."[137] Plus, the Palestinian Authority, the ruling Fatah Party, and the PLO have repeated their recognition of Israel's right to exist "as an independent viable state in peace and security."[138] A just peace and equal rights for both peoples in the region—within Israel's reach, with serious pressure from even-handed brokers, plus international assistance—would nip Palestinian violence in the bud.

Years ago in Deheisheh refugee camp, my host Wafa smoothed the folds of her dress, then looked up at me: "We don't want to push the Jews into the sea," she sighed. "All we want is food on the table, no tanks in the street, a safe place for our children to play. A chance for them to have a future."[139]

The day after Seth Freedman patrolled Aida refugee camp in Bethlehem with his army unit, he returned for a visit—this time, in jeans and a T-shirt. "The fear instilled in me by the army all but dissipated once I was simply a tourist strolling through the town. Conversely, the more weaponry and protective gear I carried, the more terrifying the place became...Fear of extermination is the ace in the Jewish pack of emotions..."[140]

"Endless war": who benefits?

So who benefits from keeping a population on perpetual high-alert? Obviously, fear is a terrific motivator for maintaining a world-class military— which means power, control, status. And of course, protection. But ripe for the challenge, the Israeli feminist group New Profile confronts Israeli militarism and the mantra of security/self-defense. Supporting refusal of army service, they write, "*While taught to believe* that the country is faced by threats beyond its control, we now realize that the words 'national security' have often masked *calculated decisions to choose military action for the achievement of political goals*"[141]—that it is these decisions which maintain a state of war, more so than external forces. (Italics added)

And not just political aims: War feeds the economy as well. "The state of constant [global] fear," charges Naomi Klein, "creates a bottomless global demand for devices that watch, listen, contain and target 'suspects.'"[142] She dubs fear "the ultimate renewable resource."[143]

In her groundbreaking book *The Shock Doctrine*, Klein explores the intersections of the Israeli military and security industries, which have their genesis in the occupation of Palestinians. After the dotcom crash, Israel transformed its high-tech economy into a homeland security industry, to exploit its status as a "fortressed state, surrounded by...enemies."[144] By

2006, it had become the world's fourth largest arms dealer, exporting $3.4 billion in products to security industries worldwide. Products like surveillance gear (at Israeli checkpoints on Palestinian roads); high-tech fences (such as the giant Separation Wall that confiscates Palestinian farmland); and remote control weapons (like "Spot and Shoot" machine guns mounted on watch towers but operated far away, usually by women[145]): a "kind of twenty-four-hour-a-day showroom" displaying "how to enjoy relative safety amid constant war...Israel has learned to turn endless war into a brand asset."[146]

Klein argues, "The high-tech security economy created a powerful appetite inside Israel's wealthy and most powerful sectors for abandoning peace in favor of fighting a continual...War on Terror."[147] The post-9/11 rise of Tel Aviv's stock exchange to record levels confirmed the investment in ongoing violence.[148] *Fortune* magazine quoted a prominent Israeli investment banker: "It's security that matters more than peace."[149]

But the grassroots Israeli Coalition of Women for Peace also stepped to the plate. Their "Who Profits?" economic activism project exposes (commercial) local and corporate complicity in "the Israeli Occupation Industry," and how such interests influence political decision making.[150] Corporations range from firms raking in profits by supplying equipment to the army—Caterpillar weaponized D9 bulldozers that demolish Palestinian homes, Northrop Grumman parts for Apache helicopters and F-16 aircraft used against civilians, Motorola Solutions surveillance systems around settlements, Hewlett-Packard technology for checkpoints,[151] Elbit electronic fences and drones—to companies building settlements. Some firms are based in (or have facilities in) settlements—from Soda Stream carbonation systems to Ahava, which turns Dead Sea minerals into cosmetics—and also export wine, fruit, and flowers.

So if war is turning such a profit, for the security/military industries, and also serving political goals, why end it? Keep feeding the fear, keep the war drums beating and the income flowing. And blame the violence on Palestinians.

Supporting U.S. strategic goals

From the U.S. end, it holds true as well: *playing on Jewish fear builds support for a militarized Israel—which translates to selling U.S. arms, profit-*

ing U.S. corporations, securing U.S. dominance and access to Middle East resources. With our legacy of worry, compounded by indoctrination, it's understandable why (problematically) so many Jews favor pumping billions into the Israeli military, as a backup plan. But power brokers of all stripes, including Christian Zionists, drive the strategy. (See Chapter Three.)

After noticing Israeli prowess in the 1967 War, U.S. policymakers conveniently "discovered" Israel as a military ally[152] and promoted the new state to U.S. surrogate,[153] also advantaging U.S. oil interests. "The Holocaust was 'remembered,'" convincing gentile and Jew alike that "because the Jews were victims of the unspeakable, it's our duty to arm Israel to the teeth."[154] Massive shipments of U.S. aid poured in, increasing with Israeli war victories. The United States now sends Israel over $3.1 billion yearly in military aid ($8 million per day)—even though U.S. laws say it's illegal to assist countries who consistently violate human rights and who use U.S.-bought weapons (including tear gas) against civilians.[155]

Crucially, since most U.S. aid must be spent with military contractors, the fruits of this policy subsidize domestic arms-makers.[156] A few examples: a 2007 U.S. deal transferred $1.3 billion in Raytheon missiles to Israel;[157] in 2008, Boeing received $77 million to transfer 1000 bombs;[158] and President Obama recommitted to maintaining Israel's "Qualitative Military Edge"[159] (while the United States also made over-the-top arms sales to Saudi Arabia, seen as "a huge gift to the weapons industry"[160]). In 2011, the United States agreed to stockpile $1 billion in U.S. arms in Israel, a stash Israel can access in case of emergency,[161] and 2012 saw 3500 U.S. troops and 1000 Israeli soldiers conducting "Austere Challenge," three weeks of "their largest-ever" joint military drills.[162] All this, on top of thirty billion *extra* in military aid to Israel over ten years, promised by President George W. Bush, continued by President Obama. "The unchanging collaboration" of the military, industrial, and intelligence alliances, argues Phyllis Bennis, makes "the political efforts of the pro-Israel and arms manufacturing lobbies, and...Congress, much more lucrative."[163]

The relationship serves other U.S. affinities too. In Israel, the United States conveniently has a (mostly) Eurocentric proxy to counter oil-rich

Arab and Iranian regional power. Plus, the alliance is responsive to pressure from the domestic Israel Lobby while assuaging U.S. guilt about past anti-Semitism.

The U.S. use of Israel is not new. Stephen Zunes points out, "Just as ruling elites of medieval Europe...used some...of the Jewish community as money-lenders and tax collectors in order to maintain their power and set up this vulnerable minority as scapegoats, so the United States is...using the world's only Jewish state to advance its hegemonic agenda in the Middle East, thereby contributing to the...rise of...anti-Jewish [and anti-U.S.] sentiments in the Islamic world."[164]

Bottom line, the United States wants a peace process, but one that advantages U.S. imperial interests: control of the region, stability, and access to Persian Gulf oil. For example, when the 2011 Egyptian popular revolution unseated President Hosni Mubarak, Obama said, "This is the power of human dignity"—while supporting repressive Arab regimes (all U.S. allies) in Saudi Arabia, Yemen, and Bahrain, home to the U.S. 5th fleet.

Since Israel is the supreme Middle East ally, the United States shields Israel from accountability/responsibility, just as it uses her: speaking of Israeli security needs, while ignoring the same needs of Palestinians;[165] condemning Palestinian rocket fire, with no word about Israeli assassinations of Palestinians or imprisonment of Palestinian children; claiming to support a Palestinian state, while opposing the Palestinian Authority's U.N. bid to upgrade to a nonmember observer state (which the General Assembly passed overwhelmingly anyway[166]—and when Israel reacted by announcing new settlement building that would split the West Bank in half, the United States blocked a Security Council resolution condemning the expansion[167]). The United States also stopped its funding for the U.N. cultural agency, UNESCO, after a vote granted Palestinians full UNESCO membership.[168]

U.S. policymakers and pundits often play on stereotypical fears about Arab and Islamic people—ignoring the moral force of Palestinian nonviolent resistance and Israeli peace activism. Meanwhile, Israel amps up attacks on civil liberties of such human-rights groups and activists—also "branding" Israel a tolerant/eco-conscious/gay-friendly safe haven, to divert attention from policies of occupation, seen as "greenwashing" and "pinkwashing."[169] Referring to pinkwashing, queer activist Wendy Elisheva Somerson writes, "We reject any rainbow that is used to cover up...human-rights abuses."[170]

Since Israel is already the strongest regional state, with its "formidable nuclear deterrent," *New York Times* writer Roger Cohen argues that "room exists for America to...apply pressure" rather than simply signing over a blank check.[171] That "things change through negotiation."[172]

Haaretz columnist Gideon Levy goes further: "As long as Israel feels...that America's automatic [Security Council] veto will save it from condemnations and sanctions, that it will receive massive aid unconditionally, and that it can continue waging punitive, lethal campaigns without a word from Washington,...it will continue in its ways...The United States has engendered this situation, which endangers the entire Mideast and Israel itself. That is why...Washington needs to finally say no to Israel and the occupation. An unambiguous, presidential no."[173]

Points well-taken, including acknowledging that when Israeli (U.S.-backed) policies in Israel and Palestine provoke global outrage, this fuels the increased targeting of Jews. "If Israel [and the United States] were truly concerned about Jews worldwide," points out Antony Lerman, former director of the Institute for Jewish Policy Research, they "would think long and hard about the implications of this reality."[174]

As U.S. Jews (and gentiles), it's high time we insist our government do the right thing: pressure Israel to end the occupation, including the Gaza siege,[175] by withdrawing U.S. support for the occupation...also pressure Israel to recognize the full rights of Palestinians living in Israel[176]—and so end Israel's isolation in the world. No more arms sold in our name, weapons that end up killing civilians. No more exploiting our victimhood to justify policies that cause suffering for Palestinians, and ultimately for Israelis, too. Instead, let's remember, from our tradition: "Choose life"— and justice—"that you and your children"—*all* our children—"may live" (Deuteronomy).

The role of institutional U.S. Jewry

Next up, the role the U.S. Jewish establishment plays in projecting and manipulating fear: from the Jewish part of the Israel Lobby, federations, service agencies, and philanthropies, to synagogues and community centers. By the late 1960s, institutional Jewry was on board with bunker-mentality Israeli policies; today most remain loyal to the Israeli right wing.

"For several decades, the Jewish establishment has asked American Jews to check their liberalism at Zionism's door," explains former *New Republic* editor and observant Jew Peter Beinart, in his landmark article, "The Failure of the American Jewish Establishment"—because "security justifies everything."[177] So watchdog groups organizationally fixate on Jews as victims, making it challenging to see the past as only *part* of our experience, not our defining identity. They saturate our psyches with communal defensiveness— so feeling powerless, we may count on them to "protect" us. Older Jewish communal leaders especially reveal anxiety-driven mindsets: the ADL and the Zionist Organization of America are led by two men, one born in 1940 Poland and another born to Holocaust survivors in a displaced persons camp, both with lives deeply tied to the near annihilation of European Jewry.

Meanwhile, AIPAC conferences are drenched in fear.[178] You can draw a direct line, observes peace activist Glen Hauer, from attempted genocide to "the desperate fury with which the Jewish establishment responds to challenges. As long as the Shoah is not fully faced and healed from," he suggests, "Jews are vulnerable to acting quite irrationally."[179]

But the times, they are a-changing. Even though these leaders (whom we don't elect)[180] claim to represent us, former Knesset Deputy Speaker Naomi Chazan points out "the bulk of American Jewry" no longer unequivocally supports Israeli government actions.[181] Not just that: Peter Beinart shines a light on studies of many young Jews who want to openly discuss flaws in Israeli positions, who "desperately want peace."[182] "The only kind of Zionism they found attractive...recognized Palestinians as deserving of dignity and capable of peace, and they were quite willing to condemn an Israeli government that did not share those beliefs...The only kind of Zionism they found attractive was the kind that the American Jewish establishment has been working against for most of their lives."[183]

Beinart's 2012 book, *The Crisis of Zionism*, boldly expands these ideas, drawing more young, and older, Jews to him, while bringing a hailstorm of attack from his (threatened) Jewish establishment fellows. His earlier article concludes: "Yes, Israel faces threats from Hezbollah and Hamas. Yes, Israelis understandably worry about a nuclear Iran. But the dilemmas you face when you possess dozens or hundreds of nuclear weapons, and your adversary...may acquire one, are not the dilemmas of the Warsaw Ghetto."[184]

We also need to remember: these organizations are "built on a foundation of money (lots of it)," points out Professor Joel Beinin, former president of the Middle East Studies Association.[185] To keep funds coming in, they rely on "the two main pillars of American Jewish identity—Holocaust commemoration and unquestioning 'support for Israel.' Taking away one of these pillars," Beinin charges, "would be an institutional disaster," vastly reducing the enormous gifts they depend on to survive.[186] Writ large: it serves them to keep us afraid.

So when we speak out against Israeli abuses, institutional leaders say "Keep quiet, now is not the time," partly because challenging Israeli policies can decimate their income. "Public criticism is frowned upon," admits Daniel Sokatch, former director of the Progressive Jewish Alliance, in the *Jewish Journal*.[187] "And outright disagreement with Israeli policy can open you up to charges of self-hatred and race traitorism. The idea that there might be more than one way to...support Israel is not reflected in the public posture of the American Jewish mainstream...We need to embrace the notion that *tokheha*, loving rebuke, is both profoundly patriotic and profoundly Jewish."[188]

Jews resisting victimization

From Maia Ettinger, whose mother escaped the Warsaw Ghetto as a child: "My mother believed passionately in a homeland for the Jews...But she despised the infliction of harm upon the vulnerable, and she refused to make an exception for her own people[189]...My mother accommodated contradictions, not out of a lack of rigor, but out of courage. Out of the ability to see things as they are: complicated, charged, and messy. And demanding of us that we not surrender empathy, even in the face of offense and fear."[190]

A reminder: we are a magnificent people. As our fears are used to serve other agendas, we are resisting in increasing numbers. We have always resisted—and we also need to be accountable for where we have missed the mark. Not all of us are guilty, Rabbi Abraham Joshua Heschel reminded us, but all of us are responsible.

In the United States, the largest rabbinical association, the Central Conference of Rabbis, nearly 2000 Reform theologians, supported the call for an Israeli settlement freeze. To lift the Israeli blockade, over seventy rabbis initiated a one-day-a-month Jewish Fast for Gaza, *Ta'anit Tzedek*, a "collective act of conscience"; wrote Rabbi Haim Beliak, "We don't seek to deny the suffering of Israelis by our gesture," but "this fast is an offering of solidarity...a reminder of Palestinian humanity."[191]

During the Gaza invasion, national Jewish peace organizations (Americans for Peace Now, Brit Tzedek v Shalom, Israel Policy Forum, Jewish Voice for Peace) called for a cease-fire and humanitarian aid to Gaza, some breaking for the first time with establishment groups. JVP's petition read: "We are the women, men, and children who are suffering... in Gaza and Israel and we are the people who seek to heal their suffering. We are mothers of soldiers and children of refuseniks." Jews held rallies from Philadelphia to Seattle; nine hundred New York City Jews, including Shoah survivors, held a twenty-four-hour vigil, crying "Not in Our Name." In Los Angeles, Toronto, and San Francisco, protesting Jews shut down Israeli consulates.

Heartsick from the Gaza onslaught, many Jewish activists began responding to the 2005 call of Palestinian civil society to participate in nonviolent resistance strategies to end the occupation and Israel's mistreatment of Palestinians—including boycotts, including divestment from companies that profit from occupation.[192] Israelis formed their own Boycott from Within.

Nearly sixty leading Israeli actors/playwrights publicly refused to work in Israeli settlements because settlements violate international law, and "the moment we perform there, we are giving legitimization to this settlement's existence."[193] They were not only supported by Israeli luminaries Amos Oz and David Grossman, followed by 150 mainstream Israeli intellectuals—but by over 200 Broadway/Hollywood (and U.K.) pros, and more...including Jewish "stars" Theodore Bikel (Tevye in

Fiddler on the Roof), composer Stephen Sondheim, renowned architect Frank Gehry, playwrights Tony Kushner and Eve Ensler, maestro Daniel Barenboim, producer Hal Prince, and actors Ed Asner, Mandy Patinkin, and Wallace Shawn.[194] As a teen, Bikel fled Vienna for Palestine after the Nazi takeover, and he's a Zionist; "There's an umbilical cord that ties me to Israel," he said, "but I have to act according to my conscience."[195]

These actions are about targeting injustice—Israel's occupation—and pressuring Israel to abide by international law. "When I critique... the U.S. occupation of Iraq or Afghanistan," says Rae Abileah, a CODE-PINK Women for Peace activist of Israeli descent, "I am not anti-American or unpatriotic. Passing a bill to divest from U.S. corporations who are profiteering from an illegal occupation is not anti-Israeli. It is in the best interest of Israel to end the occupation."[196] And Rabbi Rebecca Alpert points out, "Having long decried the violent means that some Palestinians have used to call attention to their plight, we in the American Jewish community cannot now turn our backs on a Palestinian movement that uses nonviolence to work for peace. Rather we must do everything in our power to raise Jewish voices, rabbinic voices, and proclaim our solidarity with them."[197]

And yes, these tactics can contribute to some Jews feeling "under siege" once again, but we can't give in to those feelings. We can't wait to act until we've healed all our wounds. Despite countless diplomatic efforts and activist campaigns (from lobbying and education to demonstrations and civil disobedience), the peace process has only slid backwards since the 1993 Oslo Accords.[198] Palestinians and Israelis need a just peace now, and hopefully these campaigns will boost that process by bringing economic and ethical pressure to change behavior—like the boycotts of Montgomery, Alabama, buses or California table grapes—raising public awareness, highlighting moral issues, showing the connections to U.S. policies. This is what the U.S. civil rights and women's and gay liberation movements were all about as well: nonviolently ending injustice.

In writing to encourage divestment from companies profiting from the occupation, noting what a difference such action made in freeing

South Africa from apartheid, Archbishop Desmond Tutu wrote: "These are among the hardest words I have ever written…I am enormously concerned that raising this issue will cause heartache to some in the Jewish community…But I cannot ignore the Palestinian suffering I have witnessed, nor the voices of those courageous Jews troubled by Israel's discriminatory course… My voice will always be raised…against the anti-Semitism that all sensible people…detest. But this cannot be an excuse for…standing aside as successive Israeli governments colonize the West Bank…"[199]

The vibrant worldwide *Jewish* movement for human rights is snowballing, battling racism, anti-Semitism, and Islamophobia; advocating for self-determination, security, resources, and equality for Israelis *and* Palestinians. Witness peace activist Ethan Heitner, who hung a banner over the Bronx Expressway, explaining, "We know from our own history what being sealed behind barbed wire and checkpoints is like… We know that 'Never Again' means not anyone, not anywhere—or it means nothing at all."[200]

"Justice shall you pursue"

"…how the impotent fury of victimization can become 'constructive rage' for the mending of the world…To acknowledge the devastating nature of the wounds, and then to direct the rage of the traumatized… into an assertion of humanity, into the deliberate decision that the cycle stops with us."[201]

—*Aurora Levins Morales*

"My mother and her sister had just been liberated from the concentration camp by the Russian army," begins political scientist Sara Roy:[202]

After having captured all the Nazi officials and guards who ran the camp, the Russian soldiers told the Jewish survivors that they could do whatever they wanted to their German persecutors. Many survivors, themselves emaciated and barely alive, immediately fell on the Germans, ravaging them. My mother and my aunt, just yards from the terrible scene unfolding in front of them, fell into each other's arms weeping…My aunt…said to my mother, "We cannot do this. Our father and mother would say this is wrong. Even now, even after everything we have endured, we must seek justice, not revenge. There is no other way." My mother, still crying, kissed her sister and the two of them, still one, turned and walked away.[203]

As U.S. Jews, how do we learn to see past our grief and rage to the humanity of others? To not bow to urges to attack or defend—instead, to look within, face our anxieties head-on, and find the courage to keep from acting on them?

When my friend Julia Caplan and I led an activist training about anti-Semitism, Julia said, "More Jews will work for justice in Israel and Palestine, once they know that their allies are as committed to fighting anti-Semitism as they are to ending the occupation."[204] To know that we won't be abandoned. And to relinquish the attitude that we are the only ones who have ever been victimized. In fact, to use our understanding of Jewish fear to inform our activism, in fighting all injustice.

Weeks after the Gaza invasion, villagers from the West Bank town of Ni'lin did an extraordinary thing: they created an exhibit to honor International Holocaust Remembrance Day. Despite the fact that the Israeli Separation Wall cuts them off from nearly half of their water and farmland, they wanted to extend sympathy to Jews. "We want peace for the people of Israel and...Palestine...This is our way to express this message."[205] If they can recognize Jewish suffering, how can we not respond in kind?

David Grossman understands suffering all too well, having lost his son in the 2006 Israeli attacks on Lebanon. Still, he implored then-Prime Minister Ehud Olmert, "Appeal to the Palestinian people. Speak to their deepest wound, acknowledge their unending suffering...Hearts will open a little to each other, and that opening has great power...Look at them, just once, not through a rifle's sights and not through a road block. You will see a people no less tortured than we are..."[206]

In a Yom Kippur *midrash* (teaching), Rabbi Lynn Gottlieb honored survivors of incest, torture, and the Shoah, who "turned their wounds into blessings. Although they never stopped acknowledging what happened," they "refused to be defeated by fear. Instead, they turned toward regeneration and life."[207] "...To create a world free of violence," she continued, "we must turn away from fear-driven behavior toward acts of renewal, alliance building, and love."[208]

Isn't it time to begin?

Above: Memorial in Warsaw, Poland's Okopowa Street Jewish Cemetery to Jewish children killed in the Shoah, including those who died in the Warsaw Ghetto of hunger and disease.

Left: Warsaw memorial to pediatrician Janusz Korczak, who founded two Warsaw orphanages. When the children were captured, he was offered escape, but refused. Instead he accompanied 200 children to the Treblinka gas chambers so they wouldn't be alone, carrying some in his arms and singing to give them courage.

PENNY ROSENWASSER

PENNY ROSENWASSER

Above: The Umschlagplatz of the Krakow Jewish Ghetto, the site where Jews were deported to the camps. These sixty-four empty metal chairs memorialize 64,000 Krakow Jews — chairs waiting for those who never returned (approximately 6,000 survived).

Left: Warsaw memorial to the Warsaw Ghetto Uprising. Beginning April 19, 1943, over 700 young men and women held off the Nazis for three weeks, in the first open urban European revolt. Their battle shook the world's conscience.

Top: The Jewish Historical Museum in Warsaw, 2008.
Bottom: Jude Raus: "Jews Get Out!" Graffiti on a street in downtown Warsaw, September 2008. A few thousand Jews now live in Warsaw, out of a population of 375,000 in 1939.

Above: Bay Area Women in Black marching in San Francisco in 2003 against the U.S. war in Iraq and the Israeli occupation of the West Bank, Gaza, and East Jerusalem. Israeli women started Women in Black in 1988, as a feminist nonviolent call to end the Israeli occupation, after the beginning of the first Palestinian intifada. (L-r.: Penny Rosenwasser, Donna Korones, Debbie Hoffmann, Adria Blum. Photo slightly altered from original.)

Right: Rahel Smith at a Jewish vigil protesting the Israeli bombing of Gaza in 2008-9, in front of the Israeli consulate in San Francisco. (Sign reads: "As a Jew i...Am proud to be Jewish. Have lived in Israel. Want Gaza killing to end.")

Right: Penny Rosenwasser leads Kaddish for Rachel Corrie, on the anniversary of her death, at a 2005 civil disobedience action by Jewish Voice for Peace against the Caterpillar Corporation in northern California. Rachel Corrie was a 23-year-old U.S. college student from Seattle; on March 16, 2003, she was run over by an Israeli-operated Caterpillar bulldozer while she was protecting a Palestinian home in Gaza from being demolished. The protest called on CAT to stop selling weaponized bull-dozers to Israel. (Seated l-r: Rebecca Vilkomerson, Wendy Kaufmyn, Seth Schneider.)

Below: Talia Cooper in front of the Sukkah she helped create, and slept in, at Occupy Oakland, fall 2011. Talia directs Jewish Youth for Community Action and is active with Kehilla Synagogue.

LIAT WEINGART

PENNY ROSENWASSER

PART THREE

Creating a Future

11

On the Front Lines:
An Activist's Vignettes

"You are not required to finish the job, but neither are you free to desist from embarking on it."

—*Rabbi Tarfon* (Pirkei Avot 2:21)

NOTHING HAS TAUGHT ME MORE *about the complexity of being a Jew, of being a human being, than my work for a just peace for Palestine and Israel. Sprawled in the summer grass, watching a play—the enactment of a Jewish nurse's letter home, about caring for Palestinian children dying after the (1982) massacre at Sabra and Shatila refugee camps[1]—I break down. Tears streaming, I wonder: how do I stretch enough to keep feeling joy in my Jewishness, while also facing the Israeli army's inhumanity towards Palestinians? Not cancelling out either one?*

I first ventured to Israel/Palestine in 1989, out of a burning need to witness, listen, understand. I fell in love with the ancient terraced land, the golden afternoon light, the vast expanses of stone and sky. I prayed for peace at the Western Wall, rode a burro in the Judean desert, and bobbed in the Dead Sea. At Jerusalem's Shoah Museum, Yad Vashem, I absorbed the horror of Nazi atrocities, while searching the faces of the barely-adult Jewish resistance fighters. What gave them their courage, grit, dignity? Could I find that in myself, if the time came?

Only days later, I ran from the clubs, water cannons and tear gas of barely-adult Israeli soldiers who attacked our exuberant 20,000-strong

(nonviolent) human chain for peace—of Israelis, Palestinians, internation-
als—around Jerusalem's Old City walls. I saw Palestinian men beaten,
Palestinian women's eyes streaming from tear gas; my friend Sarah was
knocked to the ground by a rearing police horse; an Italian activist lost
her eye in the assaults. I was horrified, disbelieving what I was experienc-
ing from "my people." Desperately wanting to distance myself from "those
Jews," I struggled to stay connected to a positive sense of Jewishness, while
squarely facing Israeli state brutality.

Seven trips later, and ever since, negotiating the intersections—current
Israeli extremism and injustices, along with my people's history of persecu-
tion, while proudly claiming my (renegade) Jewishness—remains a daunt-
ing, intriguing challenge. On various days I feel grief stricken/enraged/
torn/guilty/energized. One of the great gifts though is having Jews beside
me who share my turmoil, who remind me I am not alone.

༄

From that first 1989 journey, I felt bonds of kinship with Palestinian
women—Suha, Jamila, Rana, Maysoon, Amal, Majda, Nabila—inspired
by their fight for national self-determination and social equality, their vital-
ity, warmth, and smarts. Many opened their homes and their hearts to me.

And I reveled, tapping into the feisty, earnest, committed spirits of
Israeli Jewish women activists—Haya, Tikva, Ruth, Yvonne, Roni—who
organized peace conferences, led solidarity marches, stood vigil with
Women in Black,[2] holding Hebrew-and-Arabic signs: "End the Occupa-
tion." At the 5000-strong "Women Go for Peace" march, Haya said, eyes
sparkling, "We want the situation to change; we are into ACTION."

When I asked a thirteen-year-old how her parents felt about her being
there, she beamed, "They're proud of me." Another protestor confided: "I
would go crazy if I didn't do something." All despite slurs of "traitor" and
"whore," while ducking tomatoes and enduring bomb threats.

I also met Hava, a seventy-year-old Nazi Holocaust survivor who sup-
ported Palestinian women political prisoners. And Veronika, a musicologist
at Hebrew University, Orthodox, who organized Israeli/Palestinian dia-
logue groups, to share fears, and to show Israelis "they can spend a night
in a Palestinian village and come back alive." When I asked if she was

202

optimistic or pessimistic, she replied, "Neither, I'm working. Because if I meet somebody or something I don't like, I think maybe I can change it. You know," she added, "I'm aware of the fact that the same person who can break the arms of a Palestinian can turn around and be a very compassionate doctor...There is such complexity to the situation."[3]

They all told me how so many Jewish Israeli homes reverberated with violence, the by-product of being an occupying army. "Nearly half of the women killed in domestic violence in Israel during...[recent] years were murdered by soldiers," reports Haifa Feminist Center Isha L'Isha (Women to Women).[4]

And Palestinian Israeli Nabila explained to me, "I'm not ready to be dominated—not by a Jew, not by a man, not by a woman. I want to be fully a partner."[5] When I interviewed Rihab, whose Palestinian husband died in an Israeli prison, she gazed into my Jewish eyes: "We are the same; we have the same hearts."[6]

∽

(December 1989) My very first trip, and after my arrival, I spend a day with Hadijah, a twenty-something Palestinian activist, dressed in T-shirt and jeans. As we wind through the Ramallah hills in a battered VW, visiting health clinics, I ask her goal for the (first) intifada, although I already—I think—know her answer: a Palestinian state next to Israel. Instead, she replies calmly: "To throw all the Jews into the sea." Inside I panic. Thank g-d I haven't yet told her I'm Jewish. And then I remember my spiritual mentors reminding me to keep an open heart. I breathe, we keep talking. And that's how I learn that Hadijah's mother's legs were blown off by an Israeli explosive; she grew up with a mother both disabled and bitter. As hard as Hadijah's words are to hear, I grasp why she feels as she does. There are so many ways to respond to injustice. In Hadijah's shoes, might I feel the same?

Same trip, two weeks later: I'm going to Gaza for the first time, crammed into a Palestinian servis (taxi). No one speaks English. When we reach the Eretz checkpoint into Gaza, the Israeli guards let us through but not our driver. Out of the car, I wonder what to do. A woman from the taxi approaches me, wearing the traditional head covering and dress; she motions me to follow. Reaching the highway, she sticks out her thumb. A tractor-trailer pulls *over, she speaks to the driver; I climb in, he takes me where I need to go. I encounter such kindness again and again.*

Now I'm with a family in Jabalia refugee camp, huddling around a space heater, watching a Chanukah service on Israeli TV: that's all there is to watch. When I ask my host Jamal about his life, he replies: "I want to talk about solutions, not casualties." Hearing Israeli soldiers shouting outside, as they enforce the curfew, we shudder with fear. Later, I write in my journal, "When I get into my 'us and them' mentality, I have to remember that the 'them' is also part of me."

(The fear is also palpable for Haya, an "out" lesbian leader of the Israeli peace movement, when Iraqi scud missiles hit Tel Aviv the following winter, during the Gulf War. I read Haya's letter on my radio show. From her hiding place in her tiny bathroom, she writes, "I never remember myself this frightened...it is like a punch in the stomach...my mouth so dry with fear.")

Christmas Eve: Led by women and girls clutching candles and olive branches, we march through the Bethlehem hills down to Shepherd's Field, for mass with Archbishop Tutu. As we sing and chant slogans for peace, I think of Alice Walker's words: "I fall in love with the beauty of people in struggle. The beauty of resistance, especially when it is nonviolent...It is comparable to a sunrise."[7]

∞

(December 1991) I am leading my second women's peace delegation to Israel/Palestine. We've spent the day in the Palestinian slum of the Israeli city Lod, overrun with rats, sewage, poverty. It's painful to stomach. Similar to my Oakland, California, transplanted-hometown, tax revenues and services are distributed unequally to the Ashkenazi communities and to the neighborhoods of color.[8]

On the bus ride back to Jerusalem, our Palestinian guide tells a "joke" over the microphone, which ends with an Arab man complaining to Hitler: "You didn't finish the job, of killing all the Jews." My coleader Sarah and I move as one unit to our guide. We calmly explain that we understand why she might feel that way, but that many of us are Jewish, and some have lost family in the Holocaust. That we abhor the Israeli government's treatment of Palestinians, that we are trying to change these policies. And that her "joke" is wrenching to hear, because Hitler murdered over one-third of the world's Jews. (Stunned at our response, she apologizes and doesn't say another word.)

That experience shone a light on the intensity of doing this solidarity work, while belonging to a historically oppressed people—while also being connected to the group occupying those we are offering solidarity to (some of whom have anti-Jewish ideas). Afterwards, in our cramped Palestinian hotel room, we celebrate Shabbat with challah, wine, and singing, and a rose given to us by a man at the Women in Black vigil.

∾

(Spring 1992) Back in the U.S.A., touring with my book of interviews of Israeli and Palestinian peace activists, I'm speaking in Storrs, Connecticut, at the university. The sponsoring group was forced to call campus security to "protect" me from angry Jewish hecklers. One man jumps up, thrusts his finger at me, and yells, "Do you cry when Jewish children die?" It jolts me back to the moment when, in tears, I heard that Iraqi missiles had attacked Israel; I was about to leave for our nightly antiwar candlelight vigil when the news broke. "I did cry when Tel Aviv was hit," I say quietly. "While there's a huge imbalance in who is being killed, I care about them all."

Still on tour, I am now in Iowa, showing slides of Israel and Palestine. C. is president of the campus Zionist group, here because her religion professor assigned her class to come. Later the teacher sends me C.'s paper, which reads: "I spent at least two of my four undergraduate years waging a propaganda war against a group of people I had never actually spoken to, or really even listened to. I spoke to a Palestinian man for the first time today. Our conversation was brief, but it meant everything in the world. I wonder if it meant anything to him."

She continued, that sitting on her left "was a Jordanian student who had a constant stream of tears running down his face" throughout the slide-show, revealing:

A truly tragic sadness...I was able to feel it with him for the first time tonight. I am not sure why tonight was different from any other night (a familiar question within my tradition) that I have watched a film of this nature, but it was. I suppose something just needs to click inside a person before they are able to see beyond their loyalties. I hope this is just the beginning for me [of]...realizing that the Palestinians, by virtue of being human, are entitled to as much as any other group. And I especially hope that others can bring themselves to transcend their sacred bonds, before they are faced with tragedies of their own.

∽

(May 1998) *"Justice for Palestine, self-determination! U.S., Israel, end the occupation!" Hundreds of us—Jews, Arabs, other lefties—chant energetically, walking a picket line outside the St. Francis Hotel in San Francisco this spring afternoon. Inside, a huge banquet celebrates Israel's fiftieth birthday. Outside we are commemorating fifty years of Palestinian resistance.*

I'm grateful there was a place for some Jews to escape the Shoah, since the U.S. wouldn't let most Jews in. But I'm heartsick that the Israeli state drove out most Palestinians (just as I'm living in California on stolen indigenous land). I'm also angry, discouraged—and fervent. I carry the only sign that shows a Jewish Israeli; it's a poster of an Israeli woman and a Palestinian woman together, holding their flags for peace.

Meanwhile: my grad school dissertation committee just met, giving me the go-ahead to start my research. I'm excited to plunge into reading about Jewish history and oppression. And I remember what Melanie (Kaye/Kantrowitz) suggested, that I pay attention to the positionality of Jews who do Middle East peace work. What is my positionality right now? I'm sure some Jews are baffled that I could write about internalized Jewish oppression, while also standing here at this demo, shouting into a bullhorn. But it all connects, inside me. I can care about, and love, both peoples.

On the picket line, several of us (women) realize we want to do something more. Surreptitiously we slip into the hotel's side entrance and upstairs to Israel's fiftieth birthday party, in none other than the Colonial (!) Ballroom. We dash into the crowded banquet, shouting "Justice for Palestine! Justice for Palestine!" As heads turn, men race out from the shadows, and we bolt. Running down the stairs, I realize Gloria (the only person of color among us) is not behind me...Gloria, who returned yesterday from leading eighty Americans to Iraq to deliver three million dollars' worth of humanitarian aid.

I charge back up the stairs and try to pull one man (presumably the Mossad, Israeli secret police) off Gloria; he is pinning her to the ground.

Suddenly, three men tackle me. I calmly resist, telling them to leave me alone. This is the roughest I've seen them. It feels the way I remember them in Jerusalem, shooting water cannons at us with green water (to mark us for easier arrest later), at our Hands Around Jerusalem event.

They're after us as if we are truly dangerous. Then I remember Rabbi Jane's words at my dissertation meeting, about the difference between myth and history: "The Israelis' intense nationalism is a response to the myth that Jews never fought back." Wow. For the first time I have some inkling about their reaction: what if we did have a bomb? It's happened before. But now, how do we break through this fear and hostility?

Another man rushes up, shouting at me in an Israeli accent, "You're trespassing." I reply that we have freedom of speech. "But you disrupted our event," he argues.

"And Israel has been disrupting Palestinian lives for fifty years," I retort (proud to have thought of such a clever reply). They handcuff us briefly, and then we are released.

Now it's three days later, and I'm meeting with the Jewish women I've recruited for my dissertation research, to spend ten months exploring our internalized anti-Semitism. This is our orientation meeting, and it's a great group. I'm ecstatic.

I feel passionately about it all. I desperately want justice for Palestinians: for those who have taken care of me, as a U.S. Jew, in their refugee camps and villages, who've shared their lives, their labenah (yogurt) and hummus—and for those I've never met. I also want healing for my people, for Jews everywhere.

Who ARE my people? Those on the picket line? Those in the ballroom? The police shooting the water cannon? The women in the inquiry group? All of the above? And what is my part in moving us all forward?

৵

(Fall 2000) The Second Intifada. I am with other progressive Jews, meeting with a rabbi from the Jewish Community Relations Council (which represents area groups and synagogues). I say that muting Jewish dissent against Israeli state policies does not serve us as Jews—that history shows that silence in response to injustice never serves us.

On June 8, 2001, I colead a 500-strong Jewish peace vigil in San Francisco, one of many organized by women worldwide that day. When it's my turn at the mic, I say:

We are here today because we want to do the right thing. Some of us have lost family in the Nazi Holocaust. Some of us may have lost friends in the intifada. What is important is that we are here together.

Anti-Semitism is wrong—but criticizing Israel does not have to be anti-Semitic. Jews have suffered horribly from 2,000 years of exile, murder, rape, isolation, and humiliation—and the memory of this suffering should link us to the plight of anyone who is oppressed. If we are fearful for Israel's security, it is not our fault that we have this deep fear. But we cannot use our suffering as a reason to hurt another people who want self-determination just as we did. Palestinians are scared too, they have their own history of oppression. As Jews, we recognize our kinship with Jews in Israel, and we stand with the Israeli peace movement. As human beings, we recognize our kinship with the Palestinian people.[9]

For those of us who are Jewish, let's also remember that when we stand up against occupation, as visible Jews, it allows others who may have been holding back for fear of being called anti-Semitic, or self-hating, to stand against occupation as well—to not stay silent.

∞

(June/July 2001) Back in Israel-Palestine, some snapshots:

In Tel Aviv, my friend's young son Ilan screams when his parents leave to go to the movies. He's terrified they will be killed by a bomb, or return without a leg or an arm. His father sighs, "Whenever I see ten people in a group, I think 'This is a good target.'"

I join Rabbi Arik Ascherman's solidarity visit to the South Hebron hills, where the army has demolished the cave dwellings and wells of over 500 Palestinians (water being especially crucial here), punishment for a settler who was killed.[10] Arik explains that the Israeli government wants this land for the nearby Sussya Jewish settlement. The Palestinian shepherds and farmers are now forced to live in flimsy tents, with little protection from the relentless sun. I spend hours with Ahlem, Abed, Aslam, Suhair, and Haya, all under ten years old. We communicate with our eyes, we hold on to each other as they lead me around their arid hilltop home. Over my protests, they fill my water bottle from their one remaining well and bring me fresh cucumbers from their fields. Saying goodbye, we cling together.

In Al-Amari refugee camp, I witness soldiers barging into homes, rounding up hundreds of Palestinian men and boys, holding them all day in a field, handcuffed. "You're scaring women and children. Do you ever think about what you're doing?" my friend asks one young soldier. He looks down. "I think about it all the time," he murmurs.

Under a blazing sun, I negotiate for hours with Moshe, an Israeli soldier, to let my group of international activists cross a checkpoint into Nablus; we want to join a nonviolent peace march there. He looks at me intently. "I want to help, I believe in what you are doing," he says quietly. Finally, he gets word from his commander and waves us through. As I walk by, Moshe crosses the road to shake my hand. "Good luck," he smiles.

In Gaza City, our host, Ali, proudly introduces my group on the dusty street: "These are Jews, and they are standing with us for peace." He beams. In Rafah Camp, Ali shows us where twenty homes were just demolished by Israeli bulldozers, leaving over one hundred people without shelter in the night. In a house left standing—the wall of the children's bedroom bears fist-sized artillery holes—I meet Deeah, two years old, with bright brown eyes, wearing pajamas with elephants on them. His mother tells me that he is so frightened from the constant shelling, he still doesn't speak. He cries most of the time.

Manal, twenty-seven, also shows me around Gaza. She has nightmares from being beaten by Israeli guards when she was a political prisoner. But she keeps me laughing for three hours in the boiling sun as we wait in an endless line of cars to get through the checkpoint. When we part, she slips the bracelet off her wrist. Pressing it into my hand, "Please don't forget me," she whispers.

Also in Gaza, I see scrawled on a Khan Younis camp wall: "If you destroy our houses, you will not destroy our souls." Then there is Bedouin farmer-poet Suliman, who dug a deep hole in the ground inside his small tent, so that he can sleep there without being shot by soldiers who have taken over his house next door. He writes verses: to give himself hope that someday he will get his land back—to remember who he is.

And I meet fifteen-year-old Moussa, who quit school to support five brothers and sisters after his father was killed. When I left Jerusalem, an Israeli Jewish friend gave me cash she had on hand—forty dollars—asking that I give it to a Palestinian who needed it. When I give Moussa the money, with my friend's words that it is not charity, but solidarity, his eyes fill with tears.

༄

(July 2001) Dripping with sweat, I stand with tough Jewish Israeli women as they monitor soldiers at checkpoints: Machsom Watch. *By their presence, they hope to diminish human-rights abuses against Palestinians trying to pass through on their way home, or to school or work, maybe to the clinic. One of the coordinators, Adi, twenty-eight, emigrated from St. Petersburg to escape anti-Semitism.* "When we are here, they let people through faster," *she says.* "Once we leave, they make people wait hours." *She adds,* "When you get involved, you feel less afraid."

"How did you feel when the Russian teens were bombed at the Tel Aviv disco?" *I ask. Adi pauses.* "It was hard."

My friend Terry brought me to Machsom Watch *today. Her stomach doesn't calm down until she returns to West Jerusalem, she tells me.* "But I want to be able to look my children in the eyes, without shame," *she says* "and tell them that injustice was committed in my name, and I did my best to stop it."[11]

My greatest hope is with the women, Palestinian and Israeli, with whom I share coffee, stories, dreams. Terry directs the Israeli women's peace group, Bat Shalom, *whose Palestinian partner is the* Jerusalem Center for Women. Speaking of both groups, "We are learning to shift our positions," *she explains,* "finding ourselves moving towards each other, without tearing out our roots in the process. Even when we are women whose very existence and narrative contradicts each other, we will talk; we will not shoot."[12]

On the plane back to the States, I sit next to Inbal, a sixteen-year-old Israeli who plans to do army service, but not in the Territories. When the school principal spoke to her class, about the importance of serving in the army to defend their community, Inbal walked out—"because the principal was presenting her point of view as if it were the only way to think."

At home I work with women, too, Bay Area Women in Black. *We create community events that weave Jewish rituals, poetry, music, and the-*

ater throughout our peace work, complete with huge black papier-mâché' women puppets, which we mount on our shoulders. We wear black to sym- bolize mourning for all victims of war; the puppets have black veils. Our signs read: "Mothers are grieving in Afghanistan.and New York, in Israel and Palestine." With our fliers and our theater, we want to offer informa- tion, perspective, compassion. Yet we struggle: sometimes criticizing and mistrusting each other, thrusting onto one another how we have been mis- treated by anti-Semitism (and sexism)…also jumping into frenzied activity to drown our grief and outrage.

Still, a supporter says that our rituals create what he calls a new Jewish peace liturgy. From one of our handouts: "Only words will succeed where bombs and rockets now fall. Words offered with care, face to face, across a table…with respect and a sense of hope…to strengthen our resolve for a dif- ferent future."

At one action, we try to join a Jewish Federation rally supporting Israel's right to security. We believe that security for Israelis will come when there is security and a home for Palestinians as well; our banner reads "For the Love of Israel, the Occupation must end." But afraid for our safety, the police separate us from the rally itself. Fenced off, we can only stand behind the large crowd. But during our interview with network TV, the rally sings an Israeli peace song, dear to us all: Od Yavo Shalom Aleinu. We join in, swaying together, crying. Baffled, the reporter asks how we can sing the same song as "those on the other side." "We both want peace," we explain. "Our groups differ in what that means, and how we can make it happen. We would like to work together."[13]

∽

(August 2001) I publish an Op-Ed in the San Francisco Chronicle about my most recent trip to Israel/Palestine. There are many heartwarming phone messages in response, only one naysayer, in a thick Yiddish accent: "Have you ever heard of the Holocaust? Too bad they missed you."

(April 2002) When the Israeli army invades Jenin refugee camp, in two days we organize a Jewish Voice for Peace civil disobedience action and public protest at San Francisco's Israeli Consulate. Hundreds gather for the demo, the mood is outraged but also upbeat, warm, connected—and visibly Jewish.

We alternate anti-occupation chants with Israeli peace songs, connecting to Jewish social justice tradition. Our T-shirts and banners read: "Jews to Bush and Sharon: End the Occupation! Security for Israel requires Justice for Palestinians." As the police arrest us—after we shut down the consulate, then block the street—Henri cries, "We call on all Jews, speak up in your synagogues! Every Jew who is holding back for fear of hurting Israel IS hurting Israel."

As we are led to the paddy-wagon, I remember the "thank you" in people's eyes. I realize how important it is, in heart-wrenching times, to create moments where we can feel our power, make a difference, feel connected to each other, in our mutual hunger for justice. Activism as therapy.

⚯

(March 2004) With dozens of JVP colleagues, we spill into the crowded California office of a Caterpillar dealership—builders of the bulldozer that crushed twenty-three-year-old Rachel Corrie to death, while she was trying to protect a Palestinian home. We ask them to tell headquarters to take responsibility and stop selling these weaponized D-9 tractors to the Israeli military. Then we quietly light candles, while I drape my prayer shawl around my shoulders and lead kaddish for Rachel; it is the first anniversary of her death. The company officials gaze at us, speechless.

⚯

(December 2008-January 2009) I have just begun writing the first chapter of this book, about injustices against my people. A friend calls, frantically, to say that Israel is bombing Gaza. Dozens of kids killed walking home from school, as well as women shopping in the market at midday. Five girls from one family blown up, their mother cannot even recognize the charred bodies of Jawaher, Dina, Sahar, Ikram, and Tahrir.

And then next door, I hear my neighbor Richard, a cantor, practicing: his voice soars with Sephardic melodies. The music opens me, I'm raw with love for my heritage, and, again, feel heartbreak over what my people are doing.

Another phone call: now an Israeli has been killed in Sderot from a quassam rocket. I fire off e-mails to Bush and Obama, I call the White House and the State Department. Do I keep writing, to meet my timeline? Or do I get on the phone, organize?

I organize, like so many Jews and others around me. Ours is (again) a visibly Jewish protest outside the Israeli consulate. My rabbi even publicizes it on the synagogue Listserve. No media shows up, but about 200 Jews are glad to be there with each other, in solidarity with Palestinians; for some, this is the only action where they feel safe enough to come. Calling for a cease-fire, an end to killing civilians on both sides, we wave to cars that slow down to read our banner: "850,000 children in Gaza with no place to hide: Jewish Voice for Peace." My favorite sign, scrawled by my friend Rahel: "I am proud to be a Jew, I lived in Israel, Stop the killing in Gaza."

In fact, her sign brings my tears. The Gaza assault has shaken me to the core, more than ever before. Had I really still believed, deep inside, that Jews were somehow "better" than this? Yet I also need to grasp: we are not worse...

৵৹

Years ago, I spoke at a San Francisco activist conference, Waging Peace. "If I am not working to actively create new visions for peace and justice," I said, "I feel like I will explode with outrage. Or sink into despair, which is easy for many of us as Jews to fall into, given our history."

I quoted from the late African American, lesbian "Warrior Poet"[14] Audre Lorde, who found that "Battling despair does not mean closing my eyes to the enormity of the tasks of effecting change...It means teaching, surviving, and fighting with the most important resource I have, myself, and taking joy in that battle. It means, for me, recognizing the enemy outside, and the enemy within, *and knowing that my work is part of a continuum of women's work, of reclaiming this earth and our power, and knowing that this work did not begin with my birth nor will it end with my death...*"[15] *(Non-italics added)*

I ended by describing our women's peace delegation protest at the U.S. consulate in Jerusalem, December 1990, against the upcoming Gulf War. As we shouted "No Blood for Oil," the police warned us to stop chanting. So we started singing...

]

Cracking the Code of
Our Conditioning

"Since the voices in our heads are our own, we can change them."[1]
—*Kay Leigh Hagan*

WE ARE WHOLE ALREADY, ALWAYS HAVE BEEN. We just need to remember to act based on that reality.

Restorative strategies can give us a hand with cracking the massive "code of our conditioning" that tells us otherwise, so we can change our inner world while confronting the outer one.[2] Support is crucial in helping shift perspective: communities of healing, cultures of resistance, sanctuaries to remind us how valued, brilliant, and lovable we are. Where we can cry in each other's arms, learn, create meaning, *together*—reframing messages, imagining possibilities. Reclaiming power, recovering joy.

We're talking an intentional recovery process, because lifelong wounds and inherited trauma won't vanish on their own. And working through emotional pain is not all that we're after. Eyes on the prize, we also lighten our loads by channeling rage into changing systems that perpetuate unfairness, helping Jewish and other communities heal as well—linking personal healing with social justice. "There are never any guarantees," says magnificent freedom fighter/intellectual Angela Davis, "but it is important to act as if it were possible to radically change the world."[3]

Communities of healing, cultures of resistance

"In the same way that women who participated in consciousness-raising groups in…the women's movement listened to each other's stories and came to understand that what…appeared to be an individual struggle was in fact a political issue connected to…sexism and internalized sexism, so too can Jews, through telling their life stories…and releasing the grief and terror…, come to understand that our difficulties are not our isolated problems but…are a result of a history of anti-Semitism and internalized oppression."[4] —*Cherie Brown*

Let's be clear. Support groups are not relics from the 1970s women's movement. They still work—truth-telling, vulnerability, intimacy; feeling validated, cared for; educating ourselves; finding commonality; celebrating difference…building Jewish women's (also trans/genderqueer) community.

In our group, as we poured out stories, Amy sensed "electricity in the air." "They're fascinating, just because they're *Jewish* stories," Judith mused, buttering her toast. "Hearing them helps me know better who I am."

"I felt very heard," Geri told us, "and I've never had that experience on this material before."

"Which is why we're here," Emily chimed in. "To say these things that we haven't been able to acknowledge, out loud, in a group of Jewish women. To give ourselves breathing room."

Despite differences, our sharing exposed a communal experience of internalized anti-Semitism, insights crystallized from breaking isolation, both a relief and eye-opening. *For the first time* we realized that our feelings were fallout from anti-Semitism —so "not so much my fault!"

Since community is inherent in Jewish traditions, it makes sense that's how we can heal, creating refuge and safety together, contradicting the harshness of historic anti-Semitism. Creating, in Emily's words, "a place with other Jewish women where I can be all of me: the coarse parts, the insightful parts, the parts that bug other people. Things that in other situations are 'x'ed out: around class, heritage, my family's history, being a lesbian. It feels like 'Bring your whole self in and we'll be with you.' It's been painful feeling that I haven't belonged with Jews. So to feel like there's a place for me in this group, it's a major shift! Even broken, I got to bring all of me there."

When Amy risked being Jewishly visible, "It helped a lot knowing that you all were behind me."

Facilitating our process of opening to each other? Giving attention, care. Active listening can ease nearly any dilemma. And who says interrupting is a must-do for Jews? Ever try just being heard, until you blurted out your whole heart, with no one else butting in with advice or commentary? When we get things off our chest, it often clears up our thinking — and we have more room to do the same for others.

And sure, sometimes groups are uncomfortable, confusing, chaotic. Learning *is* that way: discomfort can be key for catalytic growth. Transformative learning theory calls these tough periods "disorienting dilemmas": times of big change or crisis—from a new environment, loss, or rejection, to an earthshaking insight or heartbreak—when everything we thought we knew is shaken up. Forced to question what was once a given, we scramble to ground ourselves, realign. Our groups can be havens, fertile pastures, for learning about our Jewish lives, shepherding us to nourishing new perspectives.

Also helpful? Therapy with those who grasp the systemic character of what we're grappling with, in response to prejudice and past intolerance/genocide. Gloria Steinem suggests an "empathetic guide," perhaps "a personal commitment to a trusted process," as "necessary before the unconscious that has protected us all these years will make the journey home."[5]

Changing our lens

> "Learning makes healing. And when you heal, you behave differently in the world, because you feel differently about yourself. That's what healing is all about." —*Jessie*

It's no surprise that anti-Jewishness is often invisible; we've been taught not to notice it. Jessie often heard: "Prejudice? Ridiculous! All Jews are rich and powerful, and have everything!" But pooling knowledge, grasping how often-underlying anti-Semitism (intersecting with gender, race, class, disability, and/or sexuality bias) affected our lives, gave us "flashes of 'Oh yeah, of course!'"—changing the lenses we looked through, "so the world makes sense in a new way."

"The more we discuss anti-Semitism," Amy realized, "I get how it plays out in my job, or with my friends, even in my activism. And then how I've internalized it. And just like being around folks who are confronting racism helps me do that more, when we talk about anti-Jewishness, it gives me strength to interrupt that as well, including in myself. The more I do it, the easier it gets."

We were realizing the "problem" was not really with us at all. "Those 'ah-ha's' are so valuable," Elly laughed. "Now I see *why* I'm feeling this way, how this piece is connected to that, so I can move through the world as a whole person." Our stories *are* important enough to pay attention to.

Meanwhile: valuing every voice, in a process feminist, democratic, and emergent; sharing leadership and power. Exploring, disagreeing, melting down. In sync with Jewish mystical tradition, "God did not give us absolute truth: we talk to make meaning."

Key to our learning? Inventing actions to test new ideas, then sharing what we discovered: action/reflection. Sometimes we tried out ideas together right in the moment, and then generated theories, distilling new meaning about internalized oppression.[6] Emily remembered one gloomy morning. "We'd all sunk into the couch, hit with the knowledge of how we each had been affected by anti-Semitism. But there was something compelling about having it be tangible. And we had come to it as a group!" She laughed, pouring her tea. "I don't know that one person could have done what we did. Our new awareness put us in powerful positions to choose what to do about it."

Our risk-taking experiments and conversations (in the next pages and chapters) were consciousness-transforming.[7] Brushing off sticky shadows of shame, we took more risks, with the group at our backs—growing to love the Jews around us, and ourselves a bit more in the process. "The learning together is so alive," Jessie marveled. "It comes from the heart."

"Only connect"[8] —E. M. Forster

Groups can be cutting-edge updates of quilting bees, political affinity groups, even the Jewish settlement houses where early-1900s immigrants found services, and sometimes also stimulation, politics, community. The glue for connection, to build closeness, trust? Check-ins, confidentiality, expansive meeting time. Time for noshing, cavorting, music-making—also for dancing, journaling, poetry/spoken word, art projects, skits, meditation, visualizations—tools to access inner voices and open us up, laying the groundwork for authentic bonding.

The closeness can feel risky. It *is* risky; we get hurt, because we're human. "The kind of survivor I learned to be," Emily admitted, "was 'You tough it out.' You're so scared you're gonna be hurt, you don't let anybody in. A lot of that has to do with internalized anti-Semitism. You feel like you don't have the luxury of being soft; you're fighting on the front lines. But when you're being tough, people can't get in close."

"Meeting over time, though, builds trust," she noticed, so she could develop "vulnerability and softness, letting people in." Judith found herself "become braver, exposing myself." Peeling back defenses constructed over a lifetime, going for real connection, showing each other we're wanted, even loved.

A testimonial from my friend Lynne, whose Washington, D.C., group still meets monthly after thirty-plus years: "Sticking it out over the long haul" gave time to work through issues from childhood, like trying to speak at family gatherings but being "ignored, treated with sarcasm, or asked to prove what we [the women/girls in the family] were saying." So "the feeling that my opinions were not worth much" hounded her. "But, our group, dynamic women with strong opinions, gave me the chance to express myself, even disagree with the prevailing view. To work through hard feelings in a safe place, watching other Jewish lesbians do the same."

Also, as a baby-boomer, growing up "feeling that being Jewish was not a good thing," working in the group helped her "heal from confusion about who I was as a Jew, giving me back the joy and strength that comes from being a very Jewish-identified woman."[9]

In Gale Berkowitz's study on women's friendships, she found that when women are stressed out, our close bonds with each other (along with tending children) sustain us, even reducing risk of disease.[10] While men often isolate, we calm each other down, offer that shoulder to lean on. A related study finds that the more friends women have, the more likely we are to lead joyful lives.[11] No surprise really: in our kitchens women have been baring our souls to each other forever. "We need to have the unpressured space...[to] do the special kind of talk that women do when they're with other women," Berkowitz says. "It's...very healing."[12]

Jessie definitely found our closeness rejuvenating. Although "doubtful that would ever happen for me, feeling I wasn't good enough as a Jew," she learned, "making these deep connections with other Jewish women is incredible. It's amazing, I'm in this group and I'm not getting rejected!" Beaming at us sprawled around her cozy living room, her brown eyes moistened. Softly she asked:

> What is the process we have to go through, to get to be able to say, "I am a fat, disabled, Jewish lesbian and I love myself exactly the way I am? And I'm going to live my life fully as who I am, and it's fine and wonderful!" Because unless we can do that, we can't be agents of social change. If we're steeped in self-hate, it doesn't work. We have to love ourselves and heal from the damage. For me, being in this group is part of the healing, and being an agent of social change can also be part of the recovery process — it's how you get to the other side.

Trying a little tenderness

"The things that trigger me in other Jewish women," Kim realized, "are the behaviors I hate in myself. Like so-and-so rushing to be included, or to get attention. Her insecurities make my skin crawl! I feel all this judgment—and then I see I have the same stuff. I'm cringing because that's *me*." She paused, head bowed, curls cascading down her back. "I'm getting a chance to notice this, to see the behaviors, and Jews, more compassionately." Looking up, she half smiled. "I guess that's a step towards healing."

"Mmm, you're talking about separating out the person from the behaviors that don't look so pretty," said Emily. "Sure, the behaviors may still need to be examined. But it's taking into account, what have people felt they had to do, to survive?"

"When we really grasp that," Deena mused, "maybe we won't need to push each other away."

Extending empathy, kindness, creates safety to face shame. "If you bring out into the light that which is inside you," the *Nag Hammadi* (early

Christian Gnostic texts) say, "that which you bring out will save you. If you do not do this, it will be your destroyer."[13]

And another part of lens-shifting? Revising language. "You might say this woman is 'struggling' or 'troubled' or 'scared,'" Emily pointed out, "rather than calling her 'crazy' or 'neurotic,' or even 'difficult,' words laced with [stereotypical] stigma and judgment."

Also important: loving contact and touch—nurturing responses to anxiety, hurt, and "internal ravages of the Holocaust experience."[14] Groups can be places to grieve about the Shoah, to face the terror, but not alone. "There's a lot of crying and screaming to do," says third-generation survivor Liat Weingart.[15] Bottom line: a little tenderness and patience can go a long way in soothing Jewish panic and urgency.[16]

Activist/author Jyl Lyn Felman pleads for human connection; shaping a just social policy isn't enough. "The measure of our commitment to one another will be revealed in our ability to offer food and shelter in the...intimate personal way—not just to a political cause, but to a loved one who is temporarily unable to nourish herself...Can I trade my fifteen minutes of fame for fifteen minutes of your arms around me while I cry?"[17]

Appreciation

In our group, when Judith told us she was afraid she'd been too vulnerable at our last meeting, Amy reached out to squeeze her hand. "Don't you see? When one person is open, it leads the way. I know how that internalized fear kicks in, after we show our full selves. That's exactly the time we get to validate each other, to say 'You're amazing!'"

Visibly appreciating one another counters the dismissive/critical voices, so we sometimes ended our meetings with Appreciations: Elly's ability to speak out without blaming, Amy's playfulness, Judith's depth, Emily's l'chayim (joy of life), Jessie's creativity, Deena's commitment to justice. But even though (deep inside) we longed for the accolades, it could be hard to take them in, showing "just how raw our stuff is."

When Geri said that she felt weak because she craved being told she was valued, Elly jumped in. "How many negative messages do you suppose you got as a little girl?"

"Probably a lot."

"A few million?"

"Yeah, maybe a few million."

"So," Elly continued, "how many positive messages do you think you'd need to counter those?"

"But do most people need that?" Geri asked.

"*Which* people?"

Geri giggled nervously, "Regular, non-pathological people."

"Ouch!" someone whispered.

"I think *you* need it," Elly replied, smiling. "That's what's important. Because of the intensity of the bad stuff, you need five to ten positive messages for each negative. We need to catch up here, we're behind!"

Geri grinned sheepishly, "Thanks"…with a dash more self-acceptance.

Appreciation takes many forms. Judith and Deena created our group's closing ritual, validating ten months of work. "We've grown together, like a grove of giant redwoods," they began, later leading us in singing "*Ay-li, Ay-li*" — "May these blessings never end" — written by young Jewish freedom fighter Hannah Szenes. We closed with the prayer, *Baruch atah adonai, elohaynu melech ha'olam, sh'asani isha: Praised are You Holy One who made me a woman.*

〜〜

One Mother's Day, in my monthly meeting of activist Jews (women and men), I suggested we each say something we liked about Jewish women. The reactions: surprise, nervous laughter, embarrassment. But most rallied, responding: "strong and opinionated," "beautiful," "chutzpah," "bold and tender," "makes me feel like home," "the way we lead everyone." And "I appreciate everything my mother did for me."

Reclaiming our power: more strategies
Reframing

"And if you must see me as that bloodsucking Jew, see me as that pesty mosquito that bites and sucks the prejudice right out of you."[18] –Vanessa Hidary

How would it be if we looked at Jewish difference as something positive? Even desirable? If we recontextualized hurtful experiences so we're not acting from a sense of victimhood?

Scrolling back to her awakening about internalized sexism, Kay Leigh Hagan tells of ambling through the lush oaks and maples at the Michigan Womyn's Music Festival and coming upon a banner hung from the branches: "Celebrate Womyn." "I was stunned," she remembers, "and suddenly tearful, imagining what the world might be like if the messages surrounding us… exhorted us to 'Celebrate Womyn,' instead of "Drink Coke.'"[19]

We can choose a new perspective, uprooting and reframing the hostile inner voices, "decision by decision."[20] Pop singer Pink cuts to the chase: "Change the voices in your head/make them like you instead." Realizing how we were shaped by the dominant (Christian male) culture, we can rewrite the story, reclaiming our lovable Jewish-woman-ness. Reframing messages may not vanquish the demons, but we can discredit/ even laugh at them, then direct our attention elsewhere. "This is a *process*, a skill," says Hagan, "not a sudden religious conversion after which we are instantly transformed."[21] (Italics added) Aren't support groups a terrific place to practice?

Take the ever-popular topic of our bodies. Rani mischievously shared her mantra for reclaiming Iraqi body hair, chanting, "I am a Jewish American warrior princess, defying malls, swiftly growing body hair where no one in my [Ashkenazi] family has grown it before!"

"And we need a movement saying 'Jewish noses are beautiful!'" Deena laughed. "Big hairy stomachs and arms are awesome!" Ophira Edut's black friends helped her embrace her own body, modeling "their own girth with a confidence that shattered everything I'd been taught to believe."[22] So, too, can the "Jewish face in the mirror," suggests therapist Rachel Siegel, become a face reflecting "Jewish pride and self-respect…an empowering link between generations of Jewish women."[23]

Reframing, reclaiming, affirming—and resisting. U.K. antiracism educator Leah Thorne's strategy is to risk being attacked as "pushy… [rather than] tone down what I do and say."[24] While activist Mady Shumofsky turns on its head the shame narrative about purported Jewish passivity, charging, "My people were said to have 'gone like sheep to the slaughter'…Even if you do…that does not mean you deserve to be slaughtered…The shame should be to the slaughterer."[25]

Check it out: in every classroom, office cubicle, picket line, bedroom or bar, our sisters, friends, and compañeras model resistance and affirmation.

> "Choosing life
> I walk upright
> and hope my brown curls
> do not hide the Mogen David
> around my neck."[26]
> —Nina Rachel

Acting in opposition

"There's only so far you can go with reflection and reading," Amy said in our group one day. "The best way I know to heal is by acting in opposition to the internalized voices—to just decide, then *do it!*" Acting "as if," even pretending. Making the effort to think and behave differently: reclaiming power.

"Figuring out how to act so that I feel different *internally*, even if nothing changes outside of me," Emily added. "The idea that as we do personal work, it ripples out into the world." Squinting her eyes, Judith interjected, "So what is the most healing word for each of us? And how do we *live* that? *Creating* something, not avoiding something."

Like behaving "as if" we are safe, letting down our guard. Moving towards each other, beginning to trust. "For me," Deena realized, "it's 'what would I do if I felt powerful right now?' It might mean calling someone, rather than waiting for them to call. Or deciding to run for the school board."

"Yes!" Elly cried. "When you ask, 'If I knew I were enough, what would I do and how would I be?' your mind comes up with the answer. It shifts your thinking."

I remember being on a panel of women speaking about racism, I was the only white Jew. All the questions were going to the women of color, and I started to sink. "The attention should go to them," I thought. "I'll just be invisible." But then I stopped myself, asking "What would I do if I felt powerful right now?" Without diverting the focus, I figured out how to say something I was thinking about fighting racial injustice. Later, a few folks

thanked me, appreciating what I said. It was a reminder: when I begin col-
lapsing into 'victim' mode, I can decide, "I don't need to go there."

"It's like choosing an interpretation that empowers me," Amy pointed
out.[27] "Either I can 'gather evidence' for interpreting a situation as 'They
don't want me'—*or* I can interpret that same situation as 'Something is
going on for them right now, it has nothing to do with *me*.' Thinking
about it that way," she continued, "I feel better about myself, more powerful, so it doesn't matter what 'the truth' is…just that I don't have to carry
those painful feelings around."

"An opportunity to climb out of victimhood!" Emily nodded. "To
chart some new pathways. Most days, I'm willing to give it a whirl."

And she did. Next meeting, Emily told us about teaching at a women's
music camp, which she worried would bring up feelings of "not belonging.
But when I began to withdraw," she grinned, "I'd bring myself back. Different from *pushing* myself to do it. I'd just ask 'How would I feel if I knew I
belonged here?' And then I really shared myself, showed who I was. It was
scary. But by mid-weekend, I didn't even have to say it anymore—and by
the end, I felt I had met extended family, that there's *totally* a place for me
here! It was one of the best teaching experiences I've ever had."

Jewish liberation/ envisioning a world without anti-Semitism

"Another world is not only possible, she is on her way. On a quiet day,
I can hear her breathing."[28]—*Arundhati Roy*

Years ago, at a women's spirituality camp in the Sierra foothills, writer/
teacher Deena Metzger challenged us to envision the world we wanted,
as a vital step towards making that happen. Gloria Steinem has the same
idea: "Imagining anything is the first step toward creating it. Believing in
a true self is what allows a true self to be born."[29]

"I find that if I just have a concept in my consciousness," Elly said,
"it shifts me." So how would our lives be different, we wondered, without anti-Semitism or internalized oppression? Emily mused, "I'd hold my
Jewishness differently. Not expecting someone to clobber or belittle me.
Just being who I am, no matter what. Seeing arms open wide, welcoming

me." Deena pictured "telling people what I need—and what I'm not going to tolerate." "We could let our Jewishness be what it *is*," Amy said, "as opposed to a reaction to prejudice or ignorance."

Rachel Wahba imagines "the chip gone from my shoulder, the bitter taste of invisibility gone from my mouth."[30]

Holding out a big picture, April Rosenblum writes: "A truly radical remaking of the world will include Jewish liberation: the condition in which Jews...live free from fear, free from threat of being targeted as Jews, and where our safety never depends on pleasing or remaining useful to any 'side,' be it powerful elites or peoples' movements. In which we will live free of pressure...to blend in or assimilate; unashamed of our Jewish looks, languages, rituals and distinctive behaviors; and Jewish culture will be nurtured in all its diversity...In which Jews will be...shown solidarity by groups around the world."[31]

"True Jewish liberation," she concludes, "...is incompatible with the oppression of any other group: because no human group is expendable in revolutionary change."[32]

How to move towards this feast of possibility? The late, highly acclaimed, prolific writer/poet/activist June Jordan believed, "We need, each of us, to begin the awesome, difficult work of love: loving ourselves so that we become able to love other people without fear so that we can become powerful enough to enlarge the circle of our trust and our common striving for a safe, sunny afternoon near to flowering trees and under a very blue sky."[33]

Writing a new story

Elly said our work together shook her up, giving her "a new filter for seeing our patterns," a filter that helped her move through the world "standing stronger as a Jew. Because if it's not my personal pathology, I don't have to be so ashamed." She paused. "Now I can minimize the impact of internalized Jewish oppression, and not give it any more power. So I can move on."

"So along with changing what I'm doing as a strategy, like using compassion rather than criticism," Judith's eyes lit up, "it's transforming who I am. Becoming the fullest person I can be. *That's* what healing is about."

Understanding that the core healing is cherishing our Jewish women-selves. We are more than what we have inherited, or what has happened to us;[34] we can write ourselves a new story.

> "Give birth to me sisters, in struggle we transform
> ourselves, but how often, how often
> we need help to cut loose, to cry out, to breathe!...
> Change is qualitative: we are
> each other's miracle."[35]
>
> —*Marge Piercy (excerpt)*

13

Jewish-Positive

"I will use my gift to only uplift and maybe change just one heart tonight I'm...the nonconspiracizing always-questioning hip-hop-listening
torah-scroll-reading all-people-loving pride-filled jewish girl."[1]

—*Vanessa Hidary*

"SAY IT LOUD," Deena shouted, "Jewish and proud!" Laughing, "I have
James Brown in my head!" Tagging onto Deena and Vanessa Hidary:
what do twenty-first century "Jewish-positive" lives look like?

Cultivating new eyes, or polishing up lenses tarnished by self-disdain.
Celebrating hyphenated identities, our bodies, our relationships. Digging
into multiculturalism and music, maybe secularism and spirituality. Passing
these to our children in ways that delight and intrigue. Building bridges,
not walls.

Going for joy over suffering, relinquishing victimhood. Taking pride
in our flourishing, reclaiming what assimilation stole from us, and then
focusing forward. Shining a light on inclusivity, opening up our tent;
blasting minority voices from rooftops. Celebrating resistance based on an
ethical tradition of justice, focusing on who has fought *for* us. Relishing
our resilient complex past, our privileged present, our future brimming
with possibility.

Noticing that our struggles count, *that Jews are worth fighting for, while
not at the expense of other precious peoples*—seeing how our interests are
bound together in one dazzling fabric. And although our up-front presence
can invite anti-Semitism, welcoming the chance to hone skills at taking it on.

Above all: reveling in the diverse richness of Jewishness, of *tikkun olam*, of healthy self-love as a people (casting off superiority, exceptionalism). "There are so many good things about being a Jew," says Jamaican-born director of the Center for Afro-Jewish Studies, Lewis Ricardo Gordon.[2] "Beautiful things...that you cherish and want your children to remember."[3]

Joy! in Jewishness!

"We...are hardwired for joy."[4] — *Rabbi David J. Cooper*

In our group, Rani stood out: "I'm so proud of being Jewish and Iraqi," she grinned. "I'm ecstatic! I've never felt too Jewish. I've felt *outstandingly* Jewish." Chuckling, she added, "The idea of being gentile would be disappointing. I'm considering having a Jewish star tattooed on my arm; I want to flaunt it!"

But Elly admitted, "When you asked, 'What brings me joy as a Jewish woman,' I wondered 'What language is that? Does not compute!'" Exactly why we need to excavate fear, self-hatred: to make room for repressed exuberance: Radical amazement.[5] The more we focus there, the more we feel it.

For Emily, the high is playing North African/Middle Eastern Jewish music, "where I feel my roots," while Amy is inspired by Jewish resistance fighters who transformed Yiddish songs into political anthems. Walking into the overflow theater of the San Francisco Jewish Film Festival is a yearly highlight, Amy adds. "Seeing the older folks, the queers, the straight-looking, they're all there."

Or delighting in Jewish humor. When Judith went to a "hysterically funny" evening called *Faegele/Shmagele* (Yiddish for "silly fag"), she loved it, "cuz I got the jokes, you know?" The crowd reminded her of the belonging she felt in Jewish youth group days, "where I felt popular, was looked up to, felt some esteem." Deena also adored her Jewish youth group. "It was so nurturing; it saved me after the horrible anti-Semitism in seventh grade. People there thought I was beautiful *before* I had my nose job, I couldn't believe it! I still have close friends from that time."

At Rabbi Julie Saxe-Taller's synagogue on Friday nights, congregants share *"simchas*—sources of happiness big or small."[6] Often, she says, eyes twinkling, "a certain couple of seven-year-olds" jump up and down, "hands raised, awaiting their turns to share simchas...barely able to contain themselves."[7]

"Collective effervescence"[8]—Émile Durkheim

Then there's that special quality of Jewish holidays, like Passover liberation *seders*, that weave issues of climate change, gender equality, and Middle East peace into traditional liturgy. Or Chanukah parties "with lots of kids, wild *dreidel* [a Jewish top] games. It's a blast!" laughs Emily. And despite sexist gender roles, Rani relishes holiday cooking with women relatives, having "catch up" time in the kitchen: "a power can be taken from it."

Elly loves the sense of community at High Holiday services, "being part of rituals practiced around the world," especially the "collective effervescence" that draws everyone together, embracing wonder, caring for each other. Joyous spirituality—like in ancient times, we are told, when giant lamps lit the sky for *Sukkot*, and Rabbi Shim'on ben Gamliel juggled eight torches, kissing the ground in between without missing a beat.[9] In Rabbi David J. Cooper's childhood in Brooklyn, exuberant conga-lines danced from shul to shul for blocks, for *Simchas Torah* at the end of Sukkot. Now, his Oakland synagogue has started a "joyfully Jewish" program for kindergartners.

Although not observant herself, Jessie loves the Orthodox practice of "saying a blessing over everything, like being able to get up in the morning, to have your body parts move. Or eating a meal. It makes ordinary things become extraordinary." Also amazing, she muses, pouring tea, "is a kind of Jewish spirit, like in *Fiddler on the Roof*. Even after the tragedy of the pogroms, the joy is still there, the aliveness. Jews can be beaten down, and still we come up and say there's beauty in the world."

"What's a Jewish woman?"

While we're at it, think Jewish-*women*-positive. It's a no-brainer: Jewish flourishing entails equality and liberation for women. Edgy provocateurs "Jewish Women Watching" published a front-page ad in the *New York Times* one year, just before *Rosh Hoshana*, "Jewish Women/Girls: Hold your community accountable. Sexism is a sin."[10] Their button? "We are the Jewish vote."

Opening up synagogue life to women's leadership, the late writer/ritualist Esther Broner created a seder table of women's voices with her groundbreaking *Women's Haggadah*, sparking feminist seders world-wide. And it's terrific that women rabbis are being ordained in record numbers, affecting our spiritual practices[11]—but as of 2011, most major, mainstream Jewish communal organizations were still male-run (though we know who does the grunt-work), and women leaders earned sixty-one cents for every dollar earned by male counterparts.[12]

Bent on multiple ways to value ourselves, also to validate our diverse challenges, Jewish/Women's studies professor Bonnie Morris generated variations on "What's a Jewish Woman?"[13] A woman:

- who plays in a Klezmer band
- who is the only Jew in her small town...
- who is a Jew of color preserving the cultural traditions of her Ethiopian, Yemenite, Iraqi, Moroccan, Syrian, or Sephardi community...
- who will not use her electric wheelchair on Shabbat
- who grew up speaking Yiddish...
- who challenges her Jewish friends and family to examine their...racism
- whose employer will not give her time off for Rosh Hoshana or Yom Kippur
- who was raised in an Orthodox home and who has chosen to abandon all religious traditions
- who moans "Oy!" in bed
- who feels guilty for enjoying Christmas
- who grew up in the 1940s and '50s being asked to leave "whites only" beaches
- who...supports the struggle for Palestinian self-determination
- who speaks Ladino...
- who incorporates Wicca, goddess worship, and recovery steps into her personal Judaism
- who was raised in a nonobservant, socialist Jewish home and who has chosen to embrace ultra Orthodoxy...

- who is fired from her job as a Hebrew teacher after coming out as a lesbian
- who finds much of Judaism patriarchal and uncomfortable, but who still keeps kosher
- who is under constant pressure to marry a nice Jewish boy and have children
- who loves her Jewish self even when she is frustrated with Judaism.

And Joy with our Jewish Bodies? *Really?* Absolutely. Emily's mom, a phys. ed. teacher, taught her it was good for girls to be physical, strong. Today, Emily carries forty pounds of tools on her job, reveling in "hard labor where I really sweat."

To shift her body image, Amy improvised a dance, clapping hand-bells as she swayed, chanting, "These are my hairy Jewish legs, they're ugly, shave them, be ashamed." *Then* singing, laughing, "I *like* my legs; I *like* their hair, my sturdy powerful Jewish legs!" Next came "The heavy Jewish thighs, so flabby, don't jiggle, tone them down!" Followed by, "They're large and round, they jiggle and shake, they're sooo fine, my Jewish thighs!"

Although Judith dropped over a third of her weight, accepting her body was still challenging. On a life-sized body outline she wrote: "I am stocky and fat, I have big bones. I am dark and smelly. I have voice, I have pain. I don't know what everything in my body means. I am earthy, I have history. I embody my ancestors, I am what is left of them; I am their hopes and dreams."

Valuing Jewishness

Remembering the group I co-led of less assimilated Jewish women, for a film on racism: how they valued their Jewishness, how outspoken they were about it. I guess it was contagious, I began to value my own in a new way. I hoped that growing my hair long, giving the curls somewhat free rein, that I would look "more Jewish."

On Rabbi Margie Jacobs' computer screen saver are the words *ahava* (love), *rachamim* (compassion), *chesed* (loving-kindness), and *v'shalom* (peace)—also a reminder of when these were chanted as she walked down her wedding aisle.[14] The late singer-songwriter Debbie Friedman raised her voice "to the unknown Jewish women throughout time, whose wisdom and patience she felt formed the bedrock of Jewish community";[15] Friedman's work also helped open Jewish community gates to lesbian/gay inclusion. And when Shoah survivors of Albuquerque congregation *Nahalat Shalom* were "tired of being seen as icons of death...and then left alone for the rest of the year ('No one remembers what happened before,'" they said), they devised the Anne Frank Café, to explore the rich cultural life *before* genocide.[16]

Looking forward, Judith contemplated structuring her life around the Jewish calendar. "I'm seeing Judaism not just as something I do, but as a shift from being an American who is Jewish, to seeing Judaism as central and legitimate." The first woman in her congregation to blow the *shofar* (ram's horn) on High Holidays, she initiated a *Rosh Hodesh*/Jewish women's spirituality group. "I've been a spiritual searcher for a long time," she realized, stroking her kitty. "Now I'm getting it in a Jewish way."

In another J-positive slant, Melanie Kaye/Kantrowitz calls for claiming *this* country as our (Jewish) home, *Diasporism*. Meaning: to decenter Jewish ultra-nationalism (Zionism) as well as assimilation, instead emphasizing the multi-braided vibrancy of our peoplehood—an inclusive, antiracist Jewishness, "love across the borders."[17] In their 2007 study of young adult Jews' alienation from Israel, sociologist Steven M. Cohen and Cultural Studies scholar Ari Y. Kelman also found, "Many American Jews are claiming... their identities as proud, equal, Diaspora Jews who do not necessarily believe that Israel is the center and America the periphery of a global Judaism."[18] Kaye/Kantrowitz shares liturgy from her friends' baby-naming ceremony:

> We hope that you will...embrace this gift [Jewish identity] without thinking that you are better than others...Your name contains our deep hope that you will explore and celebrate your Jewish identity without confusing it with nationalism...[that] you will develop an appreciation of the cultures being handed down to you, along with a willingness to challenge traditions that seem oppressive, even things that we hold dear.[19]

Jewishness/Judaism 2.0

An emergent spin: post-baby-boomer millennial Jews who are crafting innovative identities and activism, fresh cultural/religious expression.

"Unlike their parents and grandparents," wrote one reporter, "who may have gathered to fight anti-Semitism, remember the Holocaust, rally around Israel and liberate Soviet Jews, many Gen-X and -Y Jews see their worlds as wide open," often choosing "to re-engage in the world as Jews, but not solely for Jewish causes."[20] Like *The Great Schlep* 2008 YouTube video, where comedian Sarah Silverman roused thousands of young (and older) Jews to troop to Florida and convince their *bubbes* (grandmothers) to support Obama for President.

Naomi Less founded (queer-friendly) "Jewish Chicks Rock," "where girls can rock, express your Jewish identity, and be exactly who you want to be"; while JDub Records produces Israeli folk blended with hip-hop, Yiddish punk, and Sephardic rock, urging cross-cultural musical dialogue. Wilderness Torah mixes sustainable living with Jewish traditions, holding *Pesach* seders in the desert; and in Baltimore, 5000 flocked to a free "*Rosh Hoshana* Under the Stars." *Heeb* magazine, rather than making Jewish "cool," tries to make it "fun," because "in a world in which Jewish periodicals outdo themselves" to portray "how endangered Jews are, there should be one...that actually makes its readers smile."[21] On a Listserve, a note about a Jewish softball team, The Stars of David: "What's our battle cry? One player shouts 'Oy!' The rest yell back 'Gevault!'"

Meanwhile, the Congress of Secular Jewish Organizations celebrates *bat* and *bar mitzvahs* without God, Torah, or even Hebrew. The celebrant's teaching might focus on a grandparent's escape from Nazis...or on Jewish humor. The focal point is Jewish identity vis-à-vis ethics, history, music, attracting twenty-somethings in droves.

Many post-boomers, turned off by the Herzl/Hitler focus,[22] support a Palestinian state and prefer to raise funds for solar-powered ovens in Darfur than for trees in Israel.[23] And with no disrespect to Shoah victims, a trend is afloat: tattooing overtly Jewish symbols (just like Rani) asserting, "I'm Jewish, I'm proud."[24]

Educating 101: anti-Jewish prejudice

"I often react to prejudice, or ignorance, by being offended and shocked," Amy admitted. "But if that's all I do, nothing's going to change. I need to assume most folks want to do the right thing — then do some education, just be willing to explain things."

Great plan. And the educating, sometimes confronting, works best based on thoughtful strategy rather than emotional reaction, often as part of relationship-building. Speaking up, even with a laugh or smile, combats the voice inside, which mutters "we don't matter"—plus, advocating for ourselves is practice for being an ally. Working through feelings that come up, not letting these stop us. Jewish-positive, big-time.

Emily ripped through the remnants of shame to educate her daughter's Oakland public school about Jews. "There are only about twenty Jewish children out of 450. The rest are Christian, some Muslim and Buddhist. It's challenging to show up with my Judaism," she shrugged. "I find myself wanting to shrink. But," her eyes blazed, "this is important to me, and to my daughter. So I remind myself, 'These folks might have stereotypes about Jews, well I'm here to break them!'"

At Deena's job, a young coworker just read *The Protocols of the Elders of Zion*. "Wow," he told her, "you must feel good, Jews really have it together!"

"This book was a real document in his mind," Deena shuddered, "showing how brilliant Jews were, that we could mastermind control, like a model for other groups." Sighing, she shook her head. "I don't know if he has met many Jews, yet he's gotten the messages about us. I understand the context, but I don't want to excuse it." With wit and care, she challenged his ideas, without blaming him. "He grasped it right away," she smiled. "And that felt good."

A friend, T., told of asking her boss (back in the 1980s) for time off for Jewish holidays. She was refused, and then fired. To prove the anti-Semitism, she asked two Jews—one "Jewish-looking" with a "Jewish name," another "non-Jewish-looking" with a "non-Jewish name"—to go to the Wisconsin restaurant separately and apply for work. Guess who got the job offer? Weeks later, two more were fired, one black, one gay. When research revealed the franchise owner had Nazi ties, T. wrote an exposé in her university paper, "No Jews, Blacks or Gays Allowed," creating a stir. Later, the restaurant closed.

Probably toughest of all is (gently) bringing up the A-word (anti-Semitism) when the offender is a friend.[25] "Explaining to them what they've said is giving a gift," insisted Elly. "If I hurt someone I love, I'd want the opportunity to make amends, the chance to learn. As embarrassed as I might be, it would help me from doing it again."

∽

My anxiety mounting, I rushed uphill to the planning meeting about our anti-Semitism workshop, for staff at the Michigan Womyn's Music Festival. Would any facilitator-allies show up? Within minutes, I was amazed to see the twenty-plus faces surrounding me: (gentile) movers and shakers, multi-generational, spanning class/race backgrounds. The courtyard buzzed with energy, ideas, questions. Unbelievable! Inside me, a boulder of internalized anti-Semitism began to crack, dislodge.

That night, as dinner was ending, I heard Liz's voice above the din, "As a non-Jew, this is a place I get to work on my anti-Semitism." My head snapped up to see Liz announcing our workshop to the worker community. Karen jumped in, "And I personally want to invite my African American sisters, so we can work on our stuff." This time the tears came. My friends were standing up there, telling everyone that anti-Semitism was worth paying attention to at the festival. A tiny flame ignited deep inside, as if this public acknowledgment validated not only my people, but me as well. Liz came back to our table, quivering with nervousness. "That was scary!" But she'd done it anyway.

The moment arrived, and nearly 200 women gathered in a lopsided circle as more straggled in. Marcey started, giving a brief herstory of anti-Semitism. Then I spoke about cycles of scapegoating, stereotyping. New words began spilling out of my mouth, reflecting sudden insight: that Jews have been targeted for being Jews, but it's also deeply embedded in class, about diverting attention from the ruling Christian elite. Heads nodded; many in this group understood all too well the experience of class oppression. I finished by explaining how so many Jews carry inside the terror of the centuries, wondering when will it happen again? I felt them all taking in my words. I loved talking here about my people, loved feeling my Jewishness flood through me.

Then Darby stood, a gentile ally. Slowly, deliberately, she asked the Jews, "Stand up if you have ever been called names because you are Jewish...If you've ever heard jokes about Jews...If you've ever been treated unfairly at school or work...Not asked for what you want for fear of being called pushy or loud...Been afraid to wear something that identified you as a Jew...Been the target of violence because you were Jewish...Dreamed of being in a concentration camp...Imagined dying a violent death?" As Jews, we stood up, sat down, stood again, for what seemed like forever. Fear thundered in my ears: were the others bored? Impatient? Only later did I learn how many non-Jews wept as they watched us stand, again and again.

When Darby finished, the night air hung with a shocked stillness. Then Mel invited Jews to share our experiences of anti-Semitism, at the festival and elsewhere, and the stories began. Afterwards, we broke into separate groups of Jews and gentiles, asking non-Jews to remember the earliest messages they'd heard about Jews, and to consider how to be allies. When we reconvened, the gentile women spoke: "I thought I knew you," D. said slowly. "That we were close friends. But I didn't know about this. How could I not have known?" I heard the same refrain for days after: "We had no idea, we just didn't know." Amazing, that so many of them cared this much.

We had become visible at the festival—as Jews. For at least a moment, the isolation was broken, a fragile layer of trust forged. The rest of the festival was different for me than in years past. The flame inside burned brighter, stronger, shooting up, melting heavy chunks of self-hatred. I was learning to value and love my Jewishness, my Jewish self, in a way I never had before.

Embracing visibility

Jewish-positive means allowing our full Jewish (ethical) selves to be seen. Visibility is empowering. And sure, it can trigger bias, even bigotry, but coming out of hiding counters toxic shame, and (understandable) fear leads to self-acceptance; the emotional cost of concealment takes a whopping toll.

When Jessie decided to "go public" as a Jew, she was sometimes sneered at, even shoved, "scaring the hell out of me." But it also strengthened her resolve, "not to let them win, not to be invisible." And silence has never quelled anti-Semitism. (Though in times of real danger, hiding can make sense.) We just need to assess the circumstances, while becoming first-rate practitioners at confronting ignorance or scapegoating.

In our group, struck by the power of how "those Holocaust residuals" were holding us back, Amy experimented. She remembered years earlier at a women's peace encampment, seeing someone wearing a *kippah*. "Why would anyone advertise that? I held her at arm's length. But now," Amy wondered, "how would it be if somebody could tell that I was Jewish from forty feet away?!" Springing into action, she bought a *yarmulke* to wear out and about on *Shabbat*—uncommon for nonobservant Jews to wear publicly, especially women—to see what would happen.

And boy did stuff happen! I don't often feel so scared, but I did when I had the yarmulke on. Just walking to the bus stop, this woman looked at me over her shoulder, and I thought, "She thinks I'm menacing her because I'm a Jew!" When I got to the bus stop, the bus was late. We were waiting and waiting, and people were getting in a progressively worse humor. The thought flashed into my mind, "They're gonna blame me for the late bus, 'cause I'm a visible Jew."

It was the wildest thing! I felt like I was making myself into a target, even though I knew no one was gonna come after me with robes and torches. But it was the first time I ever came out that way and publicly identified as Jewish.

Pausing, Amy scanned our circle. "I was hit with a tidal wave of fear," she admitted. "There were people who found out I was Jewish that day, who hadn't known before. But it was hugely positive. I learned that there's nothing shameful about being a Jew." And now, she beamed, "I feel this Jewish pride and confidence that I never had before!"

Ever since, Amy wears her yarmulke in public throughout Shabbat. "I make great connections because of it," she grinned. Like at a rural potluck, where "It provoked this solidarity. One woman told me, 'No one talks about anything Jewish in this town!' She felt like the only Jew within forty miles."

"Solidarity, because of you talking about it?" we asked.

"That I'm willing to be that visible," Amy replied. "It feels important now to just insist on being Jewish. Like 'Yeah, you noticed I'm Jewish. Isn't that great?'"

Another day, Amy traipsed through her neighborhood on stilts, wearing her Hebrew *Ch'ai* necklace. "Popping in" to the nearby preschool, she said "the kids were thrilled." She grinned. "And I bent down so that they could give me a high five. This one girl was so beautiful. She asked 'Are you Jewish?'"

"Yes I am," I said. "How did you know?"

"I saw your necklace," she smiled.

"Oh, well, are you Jewish?" I asked.

"Yeah!" she shouted.

"Awright!" I said. "Put 'er there!"

"I loved it," Amy said, with a dreamy look. "It was total unqualified approval of being Jewish—from both of us."

And she shared more evidence of her changes: upon meeting a (gentile) Iranian woman who admired her Ch'ai necklace, Amy had "a big reaction," worrying "Is she gonna hate me, is the world gonna blow up right here?'" In the past, Amy admitted, "I would've turned tail to run. But this time I stayed. And it turned out to be a great interaction!" Another day, she was standing in line at the store, when a man snickered at her yarmulke, asking was she proud of being Jewish?

"Sure I'm proud of being what I am," I answered, "which is Jewish."

When he snickered again, I asked, "Don't you feel it's important to be proud of whatever you are?" And this time a guy behind me chimed in with, "Yeah, that's right. You should be proud of who you are."

As much *chutzpah* (nerve) as Jewish visibility sometimes calls for, the payoff remains self-respect. Queer human-rights leader Julie Dorf tells of donning her *Mogen David* necklace to combat bigotry, when her professional job challenging homophobia required travel to countries known to have blatant anti-Semitism. "I was often the first Jew that some of my colleagues had ever met," Dorf explains. In Japan, someone was surprised that horns weren't literally growing out of her head.[26] She continues wearing her star to keep her "mindful of the interconnection of oppressions and my role in countering injustice."[27] And given how "Jewish LGBTs are often made invisible, due to our community's share of ignorance and at times, genuine anti-Semitism...I will keep wearing my star in my gay day job."[28]

We never know when our Jewish visibility inspires others. Writer and poet Louise Bernikow remembers her first feminist seder in New York. What moved her most? "The fact that Gloria Steinem was there talking about her Jewish grandmother and identifying as a Jew, when she is half-Jewish and had the choice not to."[29] On the labor front, when New

England strikers are picketing, Marya Axner grabs her neon Jewish Labor Committee sign and joins them. Folks come up to thank her, telling her their stories; "We make a connection."[30]

I had a different kind of first-night seder one year. Instead of reclining around a table, I celebrated with 600 people in Atlanta, Georgia, at a multi-faceted, multiracial women's spirituality event, "Praises for the World," which included performers like Olympia Dukakis. I was a stage manager, and when I asked that we acknowledge Passover, my producer/ musician friend Jennifer suggested I say something brief from the stage. Introduced as a board member of Jewish Voice for Peace, I began:

"Tonight we remember how in ancient Egypt, Pharaoh was afraid of the growing number of Jewish slaves and so commanded that Jews kill their male babies. The two heroic midwives Pu'ah and Shifrah refused, and so began the rebellion. When Pharaoh asked why there were still so many Jewish babies, the midwives shrugged, 'The Hebrew women are lively and they deliver before we can get to them.' This allowed Moses and other Jewish infants to survive.

And in escaping Pharaoh, it was Miriam who led the people in song as they crossed the Red Sea, giving people strength to keep going. So on this first night of Passover, we remember and follow their leadership, to never lose our voices, but instead to keep singing, both songs of praise and resistance, as the dynamic element which can part oceans of injustice."[31]

When I ended by explaining how important it is on this holiday of liberation to speak out against anti-Semitism, AND against the occupation of Palestinians — the audience burst into applause. I stopped counting how many people came up later to thank me.

When we are visible as activist *Jews*, we remind each other and those around us of our long tradition of fighting for a better world, whether our T-shirt says "Jews for Fair Trade," "Jewish Unity for A Just Peace," or "*Mensches* in the Trenches."

Jewish multiculturalism: the politics of inclusion

"When we recognize that each of us is a link in a vibrant Jewish chain that wraps around the world and reaches back in time, we find that Judaism takes on an extraordinary life force with infinite possibilities...We rediscover our role as the *ivrim* — 'Hebrews,' which means 'border crossers' — transcending barriers between color, language, land, and custom."[32]—*Loolwa Khazzoom*

Put another way, by Rachel Wahba, "Jews are really multi-cultural, and the healing is in getting that we are."[33] Inclusivity is valuing "our incredibly textured cultural tapestry, with all its diversity, depth, and brilliance," and committing to inform about and reflect this diversity.[34] Supremely Jewish-positive. Case in point: Deena was thrilled to meet a Dominican person of color "who knew Iraqi Jews existed. It was so wonderful that he knew." And how unacceptable that, for her, this experience was so rare.

Inclusivity means the obvious: educating about multiple strains of Mizrahi and Sephardic cultures, historical tragedies and triumphs—as well as those in Uganda, India, China, elsewhere—along with the European Yiddish ones, a multicultural curriculum. Embracing the minor key of Judeo-Arabic melodies, and also white Western Jewishness. It strengthens us all to know the breadth and depth of who we are. And when organizing "Jewish" events, ensuring that these gatherings address the diversity of our peoplehood, that the planning team reflects this richness as well—or else specify *which* Jews the event is speaking about or to.

Also part of inclusivity, in Phoenix a rabbi conducts a Ceremony of Return, welcoming back to Judaism "crypto [hidden] Jews," or *anusim* ("the forced ones"), those pressured to convert by rulers in various countries but who secretly kept practicing Judaism. Succeeding generations passed on Judaic customs, though often unaware of their Jewish ancestry. Although his Puerto Rican family practiced Christianity, Carlos Padilla explained, "The first thing my father taught me was the *Shema*" (Judaism's most sacred prayer, affirming the Oneness of God).[35] Carlos grew up eating pita bread and nailing *mezuzot* to doorposts; researching his background, he connected the dots, uncovering his Jewish roots.

Strengthening multicultural Jewish flourishing, the San Francisco-based *Be'chol Lashon* (In Every Tongue) has nationwide programs, bringing together racially and ethnically diverse Jewish families who create community. In *The Colors of Jews*, Kaye/Kantrowitz showcases other ongoing key groups and programs: Temple University's Center for Afro-Jewish Studies; *Beta Israel* of North America's (BINA) support of Ethiopian Jewish heritage;

and Los Angeles' Levantine Cultural Center, promoting North African/Middle Eastern cultures, including Jewish ones.

Rabbi Capers Funnye is a Hebrew Israelite rabbi (a movement of African Americans who believe they are descendants of the original Hebrews) and is chief rabbi of Chicago's (very diverse) *Beth Shalom B'nai Zaken* Ethiopian Hebrew Congregation, one of the largest black U.S. synagogues. Leading in the Jewish mainstream, and promoting dialogue between white and black Jews, Rabbi Funnye battles for a seat at the table for his black, Jewish constituency, enlightening others about "what they perceive to be the Jewish community."[36] Also assisting as a spiritual leader in Africa, he said, "My dream is to help bring interested communities back into normative Judaism...We've always been a global people...When I say the *Shema*, I close my eyes and hear the voice in many tongues. Faces might look different, but the words are all the same."[37]

For white-ish Ashkenazi Jews, our homework includes changing the dynamics of domination that center our experience as *the* Jewish experience. A step in the right direction is the East Coast-based grassroots Jewish Multiracial Network, "because Jews come in all colors"; the network cofounders—white Ashkenazi parents of African American children—relinquished their leadership, so that the organization is now run by, and for, Jews of color.

"What kept me going" remembers Loolwa Khazzoom, "was singing the beautiful Iraqi-Jewish songs and prayers" she had learned as a child.[38] Because "with knowledge came pride."[39] "When our heritage is not represented at the local JCC [Jewish Community Center]" or in Jewish newspapers or schools, she urges, "let us use our anger to...offer... alternatives to Jewish leaders and educators"[40]—like her own trailblazing anthology *The Flying Camel*, centering on North African and Middle Eastern Jewish women's voices. The bottom line for Ashkenazi women? Figuring out how to love ourselves, Khazzoom suggests, "side by side" with "social action and respect for non-Ashkenazi women."[41]

Claiming All Jews: "These are my people"

No matter how different we are from one another, Jewish-positive includes recognizing our connection, simply because we are Jews.

(Ever notice how our turning on each other can mirror the prejudices of a Christian society?) This in no way means we need to get along with every Jew. Disagreeing openly, with respect and integrity, is healthy; we're astute enough to deliver constructive feedback without demonizing.

For all of us who are dismayed at Israeli government policies towards Palestine, we can show care for Israeli Jews as people (whether or not they are peace activists), not denying our Jewish link. Claiming this relationship can only deepen our work for real peace and justice. Referring to a headline "Israeli claims self-defense in slaying of a Palestinian teenager," Emily moaned, "Do they *have* to be Jews?" Yet "These are my people too," she realized, clasping her hands and continuing: "In my twenties, I shunned Jews because I couldn't deal with them, which was like shunning part of myself. My goal now is to claim all Jews. The separation, between Jews I like and Jews I don't, is part of the internalized anti-Semitism: 'Those behaviors are Jews I don't want to be with, and these behaviors are Jews I want to be with.'"

Aikido founder Morihei Ueishiba speaks to this dynamic, common in so many targeted groups: "As soon as you concern yourself with the 'good' and 'bad' of your fellows, you create an opening in your heart for maliciousness to enter. Testing, competing with, and criticizing others weaken and defeat you."[42]

In our group, to experiment with claiming all Jews, admittedly a novel idea, we applied the phrase "These are my people" to Jews in our lives. Jessie focused on sitting with congregants at her mother's mainstream Reform synagogue in San Francisco, whispering to herself, "You are my people."

"I gagged on the words. I could hardly stay in my body. I kept thinking 'This is just a social gathering for them; they're talking through the service. All they care about is the kind of clothes they're wearing.' These are my people. I felt, 'Let me out of here!' It upset me that my feelings are so strong."

But then, thinking about two close friends, she realized, "There's a bond because we're Jewish. When I say to myself, 'You are my people,' I feel 'Oh, *this* is what it's supposed to feel like. It doesn't have to feel awful.'" And towards a work colleague, Jessie noticed, "I love this woman! We talk about everything. So I said to myself, 'You are my people.' And when I got home, I started to sob. Why couldn't my family have been like her? She's a wonderful person. And part of the reason why she's so wonderful is because she's Jewish."

Reflecting back, Jessie realized that she never ran from Jewishness on a sociopolitical level, and injustice towards Jews angered her. But, "on the personal level I ran, feeling 'I'm not like them.' What I was really saying was 'I'm not like my family.' But all Jews are not my family, and I'm finally getting that. Making myself sit with 'You are my people,' and looking at how the negative stuff gets sparked, has been so healing. Though it's not like all that stuff is gone, it's an ongoing process!"

When Elly experimented with "These are my people," she didn't find what she expected. "I felt relaxation, acceptance; almost affection. *Truly* unexpected. So I think the first step," she concluded, brushing back a strand of hair, "has something to do with acceptance. Like 'what I resist, persists.' Maybe even *embrace* Jews a little."

Resistance: the shoulders we're standing on

"We are the children of those who survived, and our existence is their redemption."[43]

That we still exist as a people "is proof that we have always resisted anti-Semitism."[44] When we believe that Jews are *worth* fighting for, resisting mistreatment comes naturally. Remembering that we stand on a long line of Jewish revolutionary shoulders…like those of U.K. folksinger Leon Rosselson's grandmother:

"And when the drunken peasants got together,
and yelled 'Let's kill the Jews for killing Christ,'
His mother grabbed the rolling pin
she used to make the Sabbath bread,
and ran to crack their skulls,
my father said."[45]

Or the shoulders of intrepid visionary (and Portuguese converso) Dona Gracia Nasi. After failing to persuade the pope to stop the Portuguese Inquisition, she openly declared her Jewishness and mobilized an "underground railroad" to help hundreds escape.[46] In Ancona, Italy, when the pope burned twenty-four conversos at the stake, she organized Jewish merchants to boycott the city. "She knew how to dream without boundaries."[47]

And former priest James Carroll tells us that when the pope forced Jews to attend mass, the Jews put wax in their ears. In the 1920s, after Henry Ford published his anti-Semitic diatribes, many Jews (plus sympathizers) boycotted his cars; the following decade, U.S. Jews, and others, joined a worldwide anti-Nazi boycott. And in 1956, Groucho Marx danced the Charleston atop the bunker where Hitler committed suicide.[48]

Reclaiming Jewish identity alone can be an act of resistance. Fighting back "Jewish 2.0 style" means calling on audacious creativity as loud proud Jews, whether through Vanessa Hidary's spoken word, or the Muzzlewatch blog's defense of Jews who call for human rights for Palestinians.

Jewish liberation is inextricably linked with resisting injustice. Let's finally unpack the myth of Jewish passivity in the midst of genocide. When Holocaust scholar Raul Hillberg wrote his pioneering history about the destruction of European Jews, he relied on German sources.[49] *Finding "no sign of Jewish resistance in official German documents," he "concluded that none existed"*—and formulated his theory of Jewish passiveness.[50] (Italics added) The real question, says Elie Wiesel, "is not why all the Jews did not fight but how so many of them did," given their circumstances.[51] Anti-Semitism feeds the meekness myth, and Jews have internalized it; but as Shumofsky reminds us, the shame should be to the slaughterer—not to the slaughtered.

The truth lies in the countless stories of revolts, uprisings, and sabotage, of unimaginable earthshaking courage: narratives to hold close, a source of inspiration and pride. We will never even know all those who fought back. And at least early on, many Jews only boarded trains to the camps to escape slow certain death in the ghetto; they couldn't fathom that rumors about gas chambers could be true.

Within most European ghettos, underground networks of schools and soup kitchens, clinics and libraries, orchestras and theaters, were created through spirit, skill, nerve. Clandestine groups sustained morale and committed sabotage, often building fighting organizations that collected weapons, mobilized escapes, carried out revolts. Many of the young leaders trained in Communist, Socialist, or Zionist youth groups.

Every act was one of resistance. Like the Jewish tailors: forced to sew uniforms for their persecutors, they sent off trousers with the legs sewn together.[52] Or *Oneg Shabbat* (Shabbat Joy, so named because they met on Saturdays), code for young Warsaw Ghetto documentarians, led by Dr. Emanuel Ringelblum. Determined to record the annihilation of Polish Jews and to preserve remnants of their vibrant culture, they buried artifacts and reports, the sacred and the mundane. The recovered materials tell us what the dead no longer can.

When I was at Birkenau, our guide told us about Jewish prisoners who saved morsels of food, who smuggled clothing and medicine, directing these to the poets, musicians, painters, actors, and writers among them—believing "the artists will ensure the survival of Jewish identity; they are more important than we are." Also because the culture and creativity the artists shared gave strength to them all.

Resistance was communal, also individual—like the survivor who leapt off the last train to Belzec camp, slipped back into the ghetto, and rescued her little sister, leading her out through the sewers. Viktor Frankl helped save hundreds from suicide and despondency in Theresienstadt, surviving to write the classic *Man's Search for Meaning.*[53] At Birkenau, a guard known for choking prisoners to death ordered a woman to completely undress during the strip-down; slamming her shoe in his face instead, she grabbed his gun and shot him in the stomach—signaling other women to attack SS men at the gas chamber entrance, ripping off one's nose, scalping another.[54] (The women were later all gunned down—but they were already at the ovens.)

Janusz Korczak was a Warsaw pediatrician and founder of two orphanages: when the children were captured, he was offered escape, but refused. Instead he accompanied 200 children to the gas chambers so they wouldn't be alone, cradling them in his arms as more huddled around him, singing to give them courage. My friend B.'s mother was on the final death march from Auschwitz when her friends—exhausted, frozen, starving—were ready to give up. B.'s mother pushed them on, insisting, "If we survive this, there will be something good at the end. So we're going to make it." They did.

In 2008 Munich, Bavarian Jewry chose the 68th anniversary of Kristall-nacht to dedicate their magnificent new Jewish community center and synagogue. "Kristallnacht was the beginning of what many believed to be the end," said Rabbi Noam Marans, "but now there is a new beginning."[55]

"It was possible to do something": revolts against the Nazis

Fighting back ranged from creative defiance to armed defense and attacks. Though terrorized by Nazi brutality and decimated by hunger, thousands revolted in ghettos and camps, "snatching from the very gates of death the slender possibility of survival."[56] Still, writes Michael Berenbaum, "Resistance was, at bottom, a choice between forms of dying. Whatever Jews did, they would be killed," but one could choose "to defend oneself to the last breath."[57] Thousands escaped to the forests, joining Jewish (and Soviet) partisans, blowing up munitions trains, capturing supplies, even saving Jewish lives.[58]

We know of at least twenty-five ghetto or death camp uprisings.[59] And not just in the Warsaw and Bialystok ghettos, but in Tuchin, Lvov, Chenstochov, Minsk, more. In Lachwa Ghetto, without one revolver, 800 Jews fought with knives, hatchets, bare hands, killing or wounding 100 Nazis.[60] In Auschwitz, the *Sonderkommando* (who cleaned the crematoria) blew up one of four crematoria, killed four SS men, and cut holes through the wire fence, freeing 600, though these were then hunted down and murdered.[61] Two hundred escaped in Treblinka, half were not recaptured;[62] and while nearly all those in the Sobibor revolt fled, many were soon killed, but the Nazis then liquidated the camp.[63]

On the first night of Passover, April 1943, twenty-four-year-old Mordecai Anielewicz led roughly 750 fighters in holding off the Nazis for three weeks in the Warsaw Ghetto Uprising, the first open urban European revolt. "The dream of my life was realized," he wrote to a comrade on the Aryan side: "The Jewish Self-Defense in the Warsaw ghetto became a fact...I am a witness to this grand, heroic battle of the Jewish fighters."[64] When the Germans finally discovered his Mila 18 bunker, control center of the uprising, they piped in lethal gas; Mordecai and others committed suicide.

The largest of several hundred bunkers, Mila 18 (below Mila Street) was literally under the Nazis' noses. At the memorial, I read the hundred-some names of those who died below, likely in their teens and twenties, many women. Among them: Rachelka, Chaim, Jardena. Szmuel and Arie, Heniek and Mira. How many are unlisted? Placing a stone above the rough slab, tears slip out as I see inscribed above the names, "An everlasting symbol of Warsaw Jews' will to live!"

Marek Edelman, also twenty-four and a socialist, helped direct the uprising. At the end, leading fifty fighters to escape. "All night we walked through the sewers," he later wrote, often "crawling...where the water reached our lips, we waited forty-eight hours...to get out."[65] In "The Ghetto Fights," Edelman describes the preceding years of terror, humiliation, hunger—as Bundist activists, struggling "to overcome our own terrifying apathy...our own acceptance of the...prevailing feeling of panic. Even... small tasks... required truly gigantic efforts."[66] But in the fall of 1942, the Socialist Bund, the Communists, and the Socialist Zionists coordinated efforts, forming the Jewish Fighting Organization (ZOB), which led to the ghetto's first armed resistance—what Edelman calls the "psychological turning point," when "the Jew in the street realized that it was possible to do something."[67]

Rejecting the theory that ghetto fighters were defeated partly because of Polish anti-Semitism, Edelman remained in Poland, becoming a heart surgeon, continuing to save lives. He later joined the independent Solidarity trade union movement that overthrew the Stalinist regime in the 1980s, and in his last decades wrote solidarity letters to the Palestinian liberation struggle.

Women: "a daily heroism"

Among the resisters were women "from all backgrounds: poor, working class, middle-class and wealthy...Hassids, Orthodox, Reform and assimilated [also secular]... Zionists and leftists; certainly some were lesbians."[68]

There was Gisa Fleishmann, who smuggled out initial eye-witness testimony about the camps. Vitka Kempner, from the Vilna Ghetto, blew up a Nazi military train and later led hundreds through the sewers to the forests, forming a partisan brigade (which helped free Vilna). Twenty-three-year-old Hannah Szenes parachuted behind enemy lines to help Hungarian

Jews; when she was captured, the Nazis threatened to kill her mother if Hannah didn't reveal the names of others. She refused, telling her mother she couldn't betray the resistance—and her mother replied that not giving in to the fascists proved her love. Hannah was then executed.

One of Niuta Teitelboim's students said that no one could smuggle weapons into the ghetto, or lead Jews out, better than Niuta, whose code name was "Wanda." From a Hassidic family, she joined the student Left; in the ghetto, she organized a women's detachment. At age twenty-four, with long blond braids, she one day "lowered her large blue eyes demurely" to a Gestapo guard, whispering the name of an elite officer she needed to see "about a personal matter."[69] Upon entering his office, she pulled out a gun and killed him, then smiled bashfully as she exited. Later captured and killed, she smuggled out a note reassuring comrades she would not betray them.

One of the "most courageous unsung heroes of the Jewish resistance," nineteen-year-old Rosa Robota organized the smuggling that supplied dynamite to blow up the Auschwitz crematorium, after seeing her own family marched to the ovens.[70] Working in the camp munitions factory, for months Rosa and her friends "carried out little wheels of dynamite, which looked like buttons, in small matchboxes which they hid in their bosoms or in...the hems of their dresses."[71] (Our Auschwitz guide said they smuggled the dynamite in their fingernails.) After her capture, Rosa was tortured: her hair matted, "her face...bruised beyond recognition, her clothes torn. She could not walk, and had to be dragged."[72] As she and her friends were hanged, she shouted *"Khazak v' hamatz,"* "Be strong and of good courage."[73]

Rozka Korczak, one of the chief partisans of Vilna, described her companions:

> When I review the course of our work...I think constantly of the wom-en...with some of whom I grew up, and with some of whom I shared the days of danger. It was they who maintained the contact between the ghetto and the city...with false papers, though the penalty was instant death; it was they who spread the idea of resistance from city to city. It was they who carried on the technical work in the ghetto, and...who later took their place among the partisans. I can think of no part of the work with which the name of some girl comrade is not associated.

I want to tell you something about them: they were not extraordinary women. They were not women with special training or qualifications...We saw how human beings rose to the needed height in the daily execution of their tasks. And that was the hardest, the fact that the work had to be done every day...That requires the greater courage than a heroic exploit which lasts a few minutes. Those girls had to have a daily heroism—and they had it.[74]

Noticing allies

"If it's an unsafe world," Elly speculated, "what makes it safer are our connections with other people." Allies. Offering solidarity, protection, affirming that we are valued. As non-Jews, they help us see the world at a different tilt, a check against our own (sometimes skewed) perspectives.

In our group, Emily told about her gang of women artists, black and white, Jewish and gentile, who committed to fight prejudice against the other. Christian President Obama (whose father was Muslim) hosted a White House Passover seder, offered Rosh Hoshana blessings, and held the first-ever White House celebration of Jewish America Heritage Month (which included the first U.S. black woman rabbi, Alyssa Stanton). In World War II, thousands—including Muslims—risked their lives to speak out, to shelter Jews: sometimes entire communities, twice whole countries.

World War II

Recognizing that during the Shoah some Christians protected Jews, "there should have been more," Kim pointed out. Because when it happened, Jews survived. For example: in Poland, Lithuania, and Latvia, nine out of ten Jews were killed. But in Denmark, nine out of ten were saved. In Bulgaria, no Jews were sent to death camps.

The Denmark rescue, "mostly quiet but stunningly effective," still brings chills.[75] For two weeks, fishermen, police, and the coast guard risked their lives to ferry over 7200 Jews to sanctuary in Sweden. The 464 who remained—mostly old, disabled, and/or too poor to pay for the trip—were sent to Theresienstadt camp, where all but fifty-one survived. Why the rescue? "Danish Jews...were regarded as Danes, like any others."[76]

Less well known is Nazi ally Bulgaria's refusal to deport its 48,000 Jews to death camps, saving their lives—thanks to public outcry and defiance by the population, politicians, the Bulgarian Orthodox Church, an archbishop, and King Boris III himself—all of whom, again, considered the Jews to be Bulgarians like themselves.[77]

In England, the Quakers/Society of Friends persuaded Prime Minister Neville Chamberlain to accept 10,000 Jewish refugee children from Germany, Czechoslovakia, Austria, and Poland in the *Kindertransport*. Within Germany, the White Rose—student intellectuals and their philosophy professor—wrote anonymous leaflets condemning Hitler; they were caught and beheaded. Sixty thousand Dutch citizens hid up to 300,000 Jews, while Mexican diplomat Gilberto Bosques Salvidar, as consul general in Marseille, issued nearly 40,000 visas to Jewish (and other) refugees, chartering ships to help them escape to Africa. Maria Skobtsova, a Parisian nun, organized garbage collectors to smuggle Jewish children to safety in trash cans (she herself later died in Ravensbruck camp).

Cofounding the Emergency Rescue Committee in Marseille was young U.S. journalist Varian Fry, helping Marc Chagall and Hannah Arendt escape, plus thousands of other Jewish artists, writers and intellectuals: "I stayed because the refugees needed me. But it took courage...a quality that I hadn't previously been sure I possessed."[78] Also in France, the Mosque of Paris gave sanctuary to over 1700 Jews and others.[79] And across the Mediterranean in Morocco, King Muhammed V insisted "There are no Jews or Arabs in Morocco, there are only Moroccans,"[80] saying the Nazis would have to kill him before he made Jews wear the yellow star.

Polish health worker Irena Sendler, a member of the Underground, smuggled 2500 children from the ghetto in potato sacks, coffins, and ambulances. Although captured and tortured herself, she escaped. When asked why she did it, she said that was how her parents had raised her. In *The Zookeeper's Wife*, Diane Ackerman weaves a fascinating tale of how Warsaw zookeepers Antonina and Jan Zabinski successfully hid Jews in their home, also in empty animal cages, though Nazis hovered close by. *Zegota*, the Polish code name for the Council to Aid Jews, procured false papers, also money and hiding places. And Daniel Mendelsohn reports that despite atrocities, every Jewish survivor he met from Ukraine "had been saved by a Ukrainian."[81]

What motivated them all? Repeatedly, many, like the French *Hugue-nots* (Protestants who hid 5000 Jews), emphasized that they did "what had to be done...It was the most natural thing in the world to help these people."[82] Jorgen Keller, from the Danish resistance, agreed: "Jews don't owe us gratitude; rather, we owe each other mutual friendship."[83]

Not in our town

Recent allies continue reminding Jews they have our backs. A stirring documentary, *Not in Our Town*, tells the story of Billings, Montana. In 1993, townsfolk rallied to support the few local Jews in response to anti-Semitic hate crimes (that followed attacks against people of color), including a brick thrown through six-year-old Isaac Schnitzer's bedroom, where his Chanukah menorah glowed. After Isaac's parents pushed for front-page coverage, churches, civic groups, and shopkeepers mobilized. Ten thousand gentiles taped drawings of menorahs to their own windows in solidarity, stopping the hate violence. If this had happened to her Native American or gay/lesbian neighbors, Isaac's mother Tammie said, she hoped townsfolk would have done the same. "Today, not in our town" the film ends. "Tomorrow, not in our country."

After three Sacramento synagogues were firebombed in 1999, also destroying Holocaust documents and 5000 books and films, Judith told us about the Shabbat service held the following Friday. One of the congregants had e-mailed her an article, explaining that "even though he doesn't usually go to Shabbat services, after the arson he thought, 'They rented a 2000-seat hall, that's gonna swallow us up, I'll go and be one of 200 people there.'"

"Well 1800 people showed up!" Judith continued. "Jews, Protestants, Catholics, Hare Krishnas, including folks from Black and Asian churches, as well as Methodists at a national conference. After the sermon, a woman representing the Methodists announced, 'You know, we really support you—and here's $6000 we raised to help you rebuild.'"

"Oh my god!" we gasped. Judith recounted, "The man writing the article said he felt, 'Everybody's against bad things happening to other people.' But when the Methodist woman produced this check, he was dumbfounded. 'What's this?' he thought. 'No Christian has ever given

Jews money like this before.' At that moment, everything changed. People started crying. This was different than just talking; it became very real."[84]

And when the students' sukkah at Stanford University was vandalized, a Muslim group offered to raise funds for a new one, just one show of support among many. Overwhelmed, the Jewish Student Association president invited the whole campus for Shabbat dinner in the sukkah, explaining, "This is a reminder that no matter how rooted...we may seem, each individual, each community is depending on something larger than itself. What grounds the sukkah is not the canvas and metal that make up the frame. It is the people and community that fill it."[85]

Being allies

As tough as it can be to navigate bigotry or bias, the lessons are invaluable: we have a hunch what others may need. In being allies, we self-educate, notice our privilege, speak out as Jews—sometimes making mistakes, then taking responsibility for them. When we're given a platform because of our privilege, we use that opportunity to speak out, even to share that platform with voices being muzzled or ignored. Above all, when the going gets tough, we stick around: committing to relationship.

A conversation with her Japanese-American friend S., whose people were forced into U.S. internment camps during World War II by President Roosevelt, resonated with Deena. "Japanese-Americans were integrated into society here, they had friends from other backgrounds—and then they were imprisoned in concentration camps. Their citizenship was taken away, and their neighbors and friends didn't try hard enough to stop it. I realized I could be an ally to S. from knowing what I would want as a Jew: allies committed to the end, who won't turn their backs."

Schmoozing at a Jewish event, I mention to an acquaintance, D., about my book on internalized anti-Semitism. He begins telling me about his volunteer work as a public speaker, raising funds for queer homeless youth. D. is white, straight, middle-aged, and I raise my eyebrows inquisitively. No, he says, his son is not gay, nor anyone else in his family. But he grew up small for his age, a "terrified" Jewish boy, in a Christian neighborhood in Chicago. His eyes fill up. "I know what it's like to feel vulnerable, alone. I have some idea how these kids might feel. That's why I do this work."

Among the most targeted these days? Along with young black men, south-of-the-border immigrants, and abortion clinics—are Arab and Muslim Americans, blamed by those who feel unsafe in any way. We can offer a hand, ask what they need, remind them they're not alone…and organize against Islamophobia and anti-Arabism. After 9/11, when a Los Altos, California, Arab-American church went up in flames, hundreds gathered in support—including rabbis who committed to help rebuild the site, and children from a Jewish school who brought a check to the church's director. When eleven young Muslim students at the University of California at Irvine heckled (nonviolently) Israeli Ambassador Michael Oren's 2010 speech, decrying Israeli army 2008-09 attacks on Gaza, they were found guilty of misdemeanors in criminal court; Jewish Voice for Peace delivered 5000 signatures to the district attorney's office protesting the mistreatment, and JVP leader Estee Chandler, plus thirteen rabbis, spoke out in solidarity.[86]

To create an alliance with her Arab Muslim friend M., Terry Fletcher tells of her first visit to a mosque. Other Muslim friends lent her a *hijab* (headscarf) and long robe.

> During a break in the prayers, I agreed to take J. [her former student] to a store down the street to buy some sweets. The errand seemed innocuous enough at first, but as we stepped out onto the dark street, I realized with fright that I was walking around in public in full Muslim attire just two months after 9/11, when hate crimes against Muslims were rampant. Thankfully, nothing untoward happened, but walking that block to the store and back turned out to be far more terrifying than anything I experienced as a Jew. [Fletcher is the daughter of a Shoah survivor.][87]

After Fletcher's mosque visit, M. accompanied her to synagogue. What made the friendship with M. work, Fletcher concluded, was that they were willing to reach across a divide, question their assumptions, and learn about each other's politics and cultures—to relinquish comfort zones. When Fletcher asked M. how it felt to be at her synagogue, he replied: "The way you Jews pray is really different…from how Muslims pray. But…what we pray for…is exactly the same."[88]

⁇

Noticing allies, being allies. Aligning with joy, inclusion, visibility, resistance. Jewish-Positive.

> "This Jewish spirit is still unbroken.
> It's like the candle that mocks the darkness
> It's like the song that shatters the silence.
> It's like the fool who laughs at the dragon.
> It's like the spark that signals rebellion
> It's like the dance that circles unending."[89]

> —*Leon Rosselson*

14

Liberatory Healing

"When we move and put our voices together, it connects us physically, cutting through defenses, reaching what can be hard to get to otherwise. And it's heart-connected! For me, the real shift doesn't happen unless my whole body is involved."

—*Emily*

A CRUCIAL PART OF OUR RECOVERY? Unplugging those emotions, activating our bodies, checking out holistic tools. "For a lot of Jews," Emily mused, "it's comfortable to be in our heads, figuring things out, even worrying— disconnected from our bodies. Unless we're pushed, we often don't go to those scary edges. But it's working those edges that helps us heal."

Art, movement, psychodrama, music, all can reach in where internalized oppression hides...touching feelings we're scared to face, maybe places that make our skin crawl, realms sometimes hard to access cognitively. Breathwork and somatics (body-centered therapies) can help us let go of trauma passed through our families. Cutting through hurt and armor, these modalities overlap, lancing wounds...like the Jewish "Grief and Growing" weekend (near San Francisco) for mourning loss, whose healing program involves not just support groups and workshops, but massage, hiking, meditation; also singing and art projects, community ritual and prayer—and laughter.

Just because there's a dominant-culture rule about stuffing our feelings— consider how Hillary Clinton shook things up when her voice quivered after losing the 2008 Iowa presidential primary—doesn't mean that makes sense.

Feminist psychotherapist Miriam Greenspan bluntly charges, "This patriarchal style of dissociating from emotion is killing us."[1] Even *New York Times* columnist David Brooks wrote, "We emphasize things that are rational... and are inarticulate about the processes down below."[2] Trauma theory also reports the danger of keeping toxins bottled up. Healing calls for releasing grief, anger, and fear—also taking risks, trying holistic strategies.

"I used to only exist above the neck," Elly confided ruefully to our group. "My mind was my best tool, so I focused on developing it. Only in the last few years have I started feeling my body. And although it's sometimes scary and uncomfortable, it's also healing. For example, breathwork is fabulous because the head never gets involved!"

Full-bodied engagement and experiential practices integrate our whole selves, ground us—freeing us up, letting us play. Especially: helping us reclaim aliveness, self-value. This is what transformation looks like.

Whole person healing: holistic modalities

"We have five senses," folk artist Judy Collins once told Gloria Steinem, "because we're supposed to use them. I think we each come out of the womb with some unique way of looking at the world, and if we don't express it, we lose faith in ourselves."[3] Free-association writing, dance, drumming, more—all can be antidotes to our Jewish wounds, giving us information, helping us treasure different parts of ourselves. We restore balance, reigniting the vitality and wonder we were born with.

Psychotherapist Alice Miller painted her way through healing her "spirit-breaking" childhood.[4] "It was only the free, tactile act of painting," she remembers, "that finally broke through a protective shield of denial."[5]

"So give yourself an opportunity," says Gloria Steinem, "to discover your own imagery. Walk through an art store and see what attracts you: using a sketchbook and soft pencils, getting your hands in wet clay, smelling oil paints on real canvas, sloshing brushes over watercolors, feeling finger paints, or scrawling with big crayons. The images you create *can bypass the intellect and go straight to emotion*, and so can the tactile feel of the medium you make them in."[6] (Italics added)

She recalls a young friend, "an anorexic former dancer who gained weight and health during six months of flinging paint on big canvases... troweling it into the shapes of larger-than-life women's bodies. Having created females who had breasts and hips, and were still strong, beautiful, and safe, she stopped starving herself out of being a woman."[7]

"The more regularly you create," Steinem adds, "the more you will notice an image often repeated in varying ways. That is your true self made visible."[8]

A Tunisian painter living in France in 2005, Linda Ellia, responded to the devastating memory of Hitler's (attempted) Final Solution by inviting hundreds worldwide to express themselves artistically, by altering the book pages of *Mein Kampf*. She compiled their submitted pages "covered in ink and paint, torn, burned, sewn, glued, collaged" into a book she named *Notre Combat* (Our Struggle).[9] Collaborative art of contemporary resistance, the project transformed "the worst kind of ugliness" into "collective healing, something of beauty."[10]

Another pathway for peeling back the onion's layers, to make the unconscious conscious and find the way forward, is writer Julia Cameron's "Morning Pages" exercise: to spontaneously write three pages (longhand) first thing each day to express yourself, for your eyes only.[11] Writing as meditation, while still sleepy-eyed and vulnerable, can channel your soul's voice, before the mind's defenses report for duty.

This can also be a time, says Cameron, to *kvetch* (complain) to "the Universe instead of just suffering unconsciously. I call it meeting the Shadow and asking for a cup of coffee. When we ventilate the negative, we make room for the positive."[12] Uncensored writing can reveal where we're off-kilter, inviting us to brainstorm action steps rather than wallowing in victimhood. Shifting lenses, we see our lives with fresh eyes, tap into new dreams, shape up for adventurous risk-taking.

And maybe a communal escapade? In our group, Amy seized upon the idea of writing a skit: what would a world look like without internalized anti-Semitism? After acting out her script, we improvised, bringing our family patterns into the fray—while Amy's character valiantly tried intervening, suggesting self-loving approaches. "It got tense," Emily admitted, "but it was so creative! It opened us in this different way." Psychodrama.

When Deena beat herself up for getting triggered during the improv, Judith jumped in. "What I saw you doing," she tossed her head, "was ask for what you needed. When you did, your whole body changed. Your voice got louder, stronger. You didn't seem *angry*, you seemed *centered*. You were setting limits in a clear unshakable way."

"Well, what I learned," said Amy, rubbing her chin, "is that it takes something drastic to break our patterns. And theater can be just the thing! A therapeutic way to try new behaviors, ones we don't do every day. It was a bold splash in the pond—and hey, it shows we can change."

Body-based healing

Early on, many of us learned to split our minds from our bodies, so we don't pay attention when the body sends out a flare. But body-based modalities can rejoin that mind/body rupture—from movement and meditation to yoga and chi gung[13]—showing that suffering *can* be diminished, repaired. By way of example, Rabbi Lynn Gottlieb's Albuquerque synagogue offered klezmer music and dance to their community's Shoah survivors, who delightedly "rediscovered a source of healing and joy."[14] While some strategies zero in on healing trauma and rebuilding aliveness, others broaden the context, connecting personal transformation to social justice.

Dance

"I get up. I walk. I fall down. Meanwhile, I keep dancing." —*Rabbi Hillel*

In her Yom Kippur sermon, high school senior Natalie Boskin described how dancing keeps grief from "sucking the joy out of...my life."[15] When she lost a number of family members and friends, she understood that sitting *shiva* (a seven-day communal mourning ritual) was only the first step in coping with her pain. "Shiva was the time to let grief take control, but I needed to figure out how to regain it."[16] And she did. "My body craves dance," she said.[17] "I need my body, lungs, brain, and heart to feel that electricity reminding me I'm still here."[18] Then "By getting the emotions...into my web of muscles, I can get the space to understand them."[19]

After one funeral, she drove straight to her dance studio: "Simply entering the studio was...entering into sacred space...Then I start to move; the grief is...replaced by the rhythm of the drums. The movement starts to fill me up like water fills up a balloon, pushing the grief out...By no means am I trying to deny myself feeling loss...In the face of death, this process simply allows me to feel...the radical joy of passion and life...*The goal is to feel what you need to feel as deeply as you can allow and then feel alive when the joy comes back.*"[20] (Italics added)

Movement

Bored with headiness, our group prevailed upon Emily's expertise as a sound-and-movement teacher to help us explore antidotes to feelings we'd been wrestling with. She started us clapping and tapping rhythms on our bodies to "open up this place, reeducate your body." The next exercise confronted "how we get pulled in to other people."

"So take a deep breath," she instructed, "notice where you are in your body, and stay with your*self*."

Emily then devised a follow-the-leader/tag game, to give us experience "taking up space." "Throw out your thinking mind," she dared. "Be your best five-year-old self, let yourself *play*!" Whoops of laughter, wild noises, racing around ensued. After a chaotic while, our bodies now fully engaged, Emily directed us to take turns shouting out (whatever), and then echoing each other:

"Speak loudly!" ("Speak loudly!")

"Loud!" ("Loud!")

"Don't leave me alone." ("Don't leave me alone.")

Our voices softened. "I need you." ("I need you.")

"Show me that you like me." ("Show me that you like me.") Nervous laughter.

"Let me get close to you." ("Let me get close to you.")

"We just want to be together."

Now we stood in a circle, arms around each other. No more echoing.

"Very very close." Sighs.

"I feel how scared I get!"

"But we love you!"

"I don't know what the fear is."

"We're all terrified."

"Let's just take some deep breaths," Emily interjected. "And notice how close we are."

"If I felt people really wanted to be close to me, I wouldn't be fighting for my life. I could relax."

"What are we afraid of?"

"I'm scared of being rejected."

"Why does it feel so devastating if someone says 'No'?"

"Because then I'm alone. It feels safer not to take the risk..."

We dropped to the floor to sit, still in the circle.

"I'm sitting here thinking how deeply I care for each of you," Judith said quietly. Pause. "And how vulnerable I feel to have you know that. It's so right-here-now for me, it's scary. I'm not used to feeling so much permission to be caring."

"Judith, your whole face has opened up! It's beautiful to see."

"So maybe one of our healing strategies is saying how much we care for each other."

"Yeah, taking that risk, even if it *feels* like life or death."

"Mmm, maybe that's where the Jewish stuff comes in: feeling like if someone doesn't want us, that maybe we could be killed."

"Oy!"

This experiment was a high point. Emily chuckled afterwards: "We're not a group I would define as touchy-feely. We're political, we disagree. But when we were standing so close, this openness and love was *right* there. I can tangibly feel us when we had our arms around each other. There was a softness and a sweetness that felt like an amazing reward for all the hard work."

"And it took us nine months to get there," Amy nodded. "The more I think about it, at least to do the healing, it's in community. It's building closeness and trust, which just takes time. It's using our bodies, letting out feelings."

"And what's interesting," Deena half smiled, "is that we often feel 'I don't wanna do a skit,' or that we're 'too grown-up' to make silly noises. But in doing those things, you get new info about who you are."

Somatics: experiencing ourselves from the inside

Philosopher Thomas Hanna created the word "somatic" to describe the dynamic of experiencing yourself from the inside: *paying attention to the body's messages.*[21] Somatics teaches body awareness, using the senses to access our body's memory, also to release blocked energy, often to heal trauma.[22]

And anything we *perceive* to be life-threatening can be traumatizing. The restorative process? Not a quick fix. It means revisiting the trauma, not reliving it; noticing symptoms that are wake-up calls; learning relaxation and well-being. And with children (as with all of us), helping them move through their emotions, not trying to talk them out of their feelings, no matter how uncomfortable for us.

SOMATIC EXPERIENCING (SE)

Trauma pioneer Peter Levine developed Somatic Experiencing, a process that replaces a "trauma vortex" with a "healing vortex," relevant for personal or collective trauma.[23] The key, he says, is learning the language of body sensation, tuning in to how we physically feel in the moment—whether inhaling ocean spray, arguing with a lover, or spilling chocolate sauce on a pink suede jacket—and tracking the sensation.[24] Noticing, for example, is the felt sense like butterflies? Or a knot, a tingling, or a racing heart? Does it burn or feel icy? By paying attention, we can learn not to automatically freeze when afraid, liberating the spot where instincts were first thwarted. Thoughts that once created intense emotion lose their grip; we can exit trauma and move towards life. A wise healer counseled me to use the thought: "My body may be afraid, but I'm not."

Exercises are used to ground and center us, thawing emotions, releasing painful memories through the body...to move us from rage or numbness to a new middle ground, helping us channel aggression in healthy ways, reintegrating fragmented parts, learning resiliency. We rebuild connection to our bodies, ourselves, and our communities—regaining self-worth, "because trauma is about loss of connection."[25]

Practitioner Gina Ross, an Israeli-American Syrian-born Jew, uses Somatic Experiencing with Israeli Jews and Palestinians. "Peace can only come from balanced collective nervous systems," she points out. "This is where creative solutions to daunting problems come from."[26]

GENERATIVE SOMATICS:
SOMATIC TRANSFORMATION AND SOCIAL JUSTICE

"The aim of healing is to create more choice, more well being and the ability to take more powerful and effective action in our lives and in the world."[27] —*Staci Haines*

Staci Haines, trauma-healing leader and activist, developed Generative Somatics to strategically build on Peter Levine's work. Exploring the dynamic interdependence between social and personal transformation, Haines points out that the *social context* of trauma, from the Nazi Holocaust and wartime combat to incest, can't be separated out from the frozen feelings.[28] Such trauma helps shape our identities, our reactions, our worldview; but we can develop resilience, and reshape ourselves.

A trauma survivor herself, Haines then discovered body-oriented therapy, which worked the trauma out of her body, reopening her emotional life. At Oberlin College, she found a socially and politically savvy community, and discovered it was empowering to learn she wasn't alone in surviving abuse.[29]

Incorporating principles from aikido, meditation, neuroscience, and systems change, Generative Somatics works with shame, hypervigilance, and numbing, helping politicized healers/practitioners stay present while feeling deep emotion and learning new ways of being. The goal? Creating systemic change by bringing embodied transformation to movement-building. "Somatic practices," says Haines, "support flexibility and boundaries,...increase trust and connection, and inspire meaningful action toward justice...We don't see healing as separate from our participation in our communities, the world, and social change, but rather as an essential part of it."[30]

BREATHWORK

In her Ph.D. dissertation, transformative leadership teacher Taj Johns describes how her group, SASHA—Self-Affirming Soul-Healing Africans—developed "a process for healing internalized racism that pairs body-based techniques with cultural knowledge" using breathwork.[31] Their aim: for African Americans to be "in action with the world, not reacting to it."[32]

Breathwork can help excavate and express repressed feelings. When a "warning" tells us to hold our breath, sensation is blocked and the parts of ourselves that express caring and love become cut off.[33] Breathwork teaches breathing into the tension, unlocking emotions, releasing energy, creating healthy breathing patterns.

SASHA members used breath work to grasp how their bodies held memories of racism. "With each breath," writes Johns, "one relaxed into a memory."[34] In one (potent) example, participants lay on the floor spooning-style, "lying stomach to back."[35] Holding one another, while listening to Aretha Franklin sing "Amazing Grace" (written by slave ship captain John Newton who ultimately turned his ship around), Johns writes: "We held onto one another with more force, as if we were holding on for dear life...I remember my eyes filling with tears because I was having a body memory of being in this position once before. I felt the body of the person I was holding, heaving with a release of tears. I felt the person holding me responding in a similar manner. In a few moments we all were in tears, the sounds of sighing were rippling throughout the room..."[36]

"We were able to...release deep feeling about slavery," SASHA member Wazir recalls, "as if our souls were remembering our ancestors. What was remarkable for me was that there was...a oneness of our spirits."[37]

With an awareness of new choices, Johns points out, group members would likely no longer store in their bodies the memory of ongoing racism, and instead could become self-affirming "active participants in shaping our destiny."[38]

"I felt whole," remembers Tony, another SASHA member, "and...the more experiences you have where you feel whole...the longer you can feel whole in between those experiences."[39]

Accessing emotion

"I love analysis," Elly announced, arms wrapped behind her head. "It's exciting, especially in conversation back and forth. But over time, it's not enough. For me, personal growth work has to be on an emotional level, because I'm so comfortable in my head. Sharing our stories is the nugget; the challenge is knowing the questions to ask to get underneath the story. Going deeper."

For Amy, our emotional work had the most impact of all our group processes. "Like releasing the fear of being killed," Deena agreed.

Amy nodded. "Before, I was more ruled by fear. Like I wanted to be visibly Jewish, but it felt too scary."

"And now?" we asked. "Now I feel freedom. I'm more aware of my feelings and the ability to decide how much power I want to give to them. So my emotions aren't running the show."

If we really want to build a progressive U.S. Jewish agenda, Cherie Brown urges, we have to take time to heal by releasing feelings—"so that we can come up with fresh thinking, unencumbered by internalized fear."[40]

Some studies show that repressing feelings can be lethal. Referring to a ten-year study of women in unhappy marriages, Dr. Gabor Maté explains that those who did not express much emotion "were four times as likely to die as those women who...did express their feelings" (presumably within that ten-year span).[41] And women who rarely show healthy anger or say "No," who are nonstop caregivers, adds Maté, are also more prone to disease.[42]

Re-evaluation Counseling (RC)

"RC differs from therapy in that instead of attempting to make human beings adjust to society, it aims at liberating human beings and changing society to better support them."[43]—*Stephanie Abraham*

In our group explorations, we talked about a myriad of therapies, workshops, modalities for moving through emotions. Most of us found Re-evaluation Counseling exceedingly well matched for healing internalized Jewish oppression.

Multiple choice: What is Re-evaluation Counseling, better known as "co-counseling" since it's usually done with a peer?

1. A potentially cathartic practice used to help people transform their lives.
2. An experiential tool for exchanging help with others to release emotion, freeing us up from past pain, enabling us to think more clearly and flexibly. Not about advice-giving.
3. A social liberation theory to dismantle oppression, a theory that assumes we've all been tossed around by adversity, which has

muddled our thinking and led to some poor decisions, but that we're all doing the best we can.

You guessed it: all of the above. The premise is simple. By using the healing gifts of release we were born with—crying, laughing, shaking, screaming, sweating—while someone listens with awareness and kindness, people recuperate and flourish. "Going through this process," notes one practitioner, "I have seen people begin to reclaim the loving, intelligent, joyful, powerful people we truly are." As emotional release occurs, we can see reality in a new light, increasing our potential effectiveness at fighting injustice.

The theory goes like this: From the time we burst from the womb, full of zest and potential, damaging messages hit us, even though we may have caring parents or caregivers: "Bad girl!" "What's wrong with you?!" We resist taking these in, but at some point we start believing them. (Almost all of us are maltreated in some way as children: Adultism.)

In response to angry words, mishap, or social oppression, children use a natural healing process—such as crying—to release terror, frustration, loss. Emily confirmed, "Kids spit, scream, get mad. And then, if it's not interrupted, it's *gone*. They have no more processing to do. They're role models for us."

But when this process is constantly disrupted ("Stop crying right now!"), as children our feelings become blocked, dulling our brightness. A painful memory gets locked inside. And then similar (new) events trigger memories, bringing back the time when we first felt afraid, alone, powerless. The *old* feelings take over; we again feel victimized, confused about what is actually happening in the present. We may take out our upset on each other, on ourselves, or ultimately on our own children. Key to recovery is being listened to thoughtfully, even tenderly—countering the harshness of internalized voices, and for Jews, the urgent thrust of Jewish anxiety—then *re-evaluating* what's really going on right now, and what we can do about it.

I remember reading about pogroms, the Nazi Holocaust, then beginning to write about it. But I felt stuck, the words wouldn't come. So I called R., a co-counselor, and as I started analyzing what might be wrong,

R. stopped me. "Just tell me what you're feeling," she suggested. "I'm afraid!" I blurted out—and immediately started crying. Understandable, given all I'd been reading. After about ten minutes, with R. listening quietly, warmly, encouraging me to keep crying, I felt much lighter, my perspective shifted. I still faced a huge writing task. But now it felt possible.

Peer counselors bring empathy, patience, and belief in each other's ability to gain insights and reclaim power. *The strategy is to evoke emotional release*—not by comforting feelings away, but by listening. Also by helping each other notice that sometimes the places where we are upset right now link back to being mistreated as Jewish children by a prejudiced society, one that influenced our parents as well. Another tactic: offering a contradiction to the feelings. Like being playful, to counter the heaviness Jews often feel, because of a challenging past. Repeat: *past.*

A core tenet is the inherent decency of us all (a concept sometimes tough to hang onto, but ultimately hopeful). We're talking non-demonizing—just as Martin Luther King, Jr. spoke of opposing evil systems, rather than the individuals caught up in those systems.[44] In terms of the Middle East, for instance, remembering that Jews are good human beings, as are Arabs and Palestinians, as are U.S. policy makers…which doesn't discount that some have been responsible for, and/or colluded in, horrific behaviors and decisions; and that one group is occupying another; and that some have succumbed to manipulation, confusion, fear. But there is no *inherent* conflict between any peoples.

One day in our group, Jessie told us she was on the verge of tears, remembering all the Jewish children killed. "The sadness is unbearable. When I read about the Shoah, I feel like I'm missing an arm or a leg. Why do so many people hate Jews?" She was *talking about* her feelings, but they were still bottled up inside of her.

"Would you be willing to try something?" Emily asked, bringing in the co-counseling process. "Try saying, 'Hey, guess what? We survived!'"

Jessie tried it: "Hey Emily, guess what? We survived! The Jews survived!" Taking a deep breath, she murmured, "It's true, isn't it? We're *still* here."

Emily repeated, "The Jews are still here. We survived."

And Jessie echoed, "We survived," this time adding, "Despite everything."

Jessie's tears began to flow. After a minute, Emily asked gently, "What are you feeling?"

"Feeling for the ones who didn't survive," Jessie wept.

"So just feel that," said Emily. "Let your heart break." Lots more sobs. When Jessie again brought up the "needless suffering and death, just because we're Jews," Emily responded softly, "Guess what? The Jews survived!" Which Jessie repeated, tears streaming.

"It's not about denying the tragedy," Emily explained later. "It's just *also* noticing, 'we've survived.' It's part of our healing, to remember that, along with the unbearable things." By lovingly contradicting the message of Jewish suffering, Emily opened up space to unlock Jessie's grief, so she could move through her feelings.

"And for me," Jessie realized, "I'm saying at the same time '*I* survived. I'm here.'" At the next meeting, she brought a song she had written, of empowerment and resistance.

> "Hitler's death camps functioned day and night,
> Killings and torture in plain sight...
> And though we suffered and millions of us died,
> We fought for freedom and our people survived!
> Hitler tried to kill us all, but this he could not do,
> We would never be destroyed, we would live as free proud Jews!"

The song ended in solidarity with the Tibetan struggle for liberation: "Many tried to silence you, but this they cannot do. All your voices will be heard, and you'll survive just like the Jews!"

Another co-counseling story: As part of her recovery journey, Deena shared her "acting as if" watercolor. She had painted the affirmations *"You need to know me"* and *"I belong"* to counter the ways she felt invisible as Mizrahi/Ashkenazi. And the phrase *"I'll tell you how to treat me right"* was a call to herself "to speak, not to stay quiet and resentful."

Remembering how Deena had been ridiculed for what the teacher called her "annoying" voice, and how she had shrunk into silence, we urged her to say her mantras *loudly*. Laughing, she repeated them, raising her voice. But we *still* couldn't hear her, we said. Laughing harder (laughing is also emotional release), she spoke louder, and again we egged her on. Finally she shouted, "I talk quietly because I'm afraid of being loud, of being attacked again. But you *need* to know *me*, you *need* to want *me*! I belong here!"

With that she burst into long-suppressed tears. "Just some internalized anti-Semitism" (and racism), Amy suggested softly. "We're right here with you. You're great! Push those feelings out of your body, they're just old junk!"

Now Deena pushed against Amy, laughing, shoving the feelings out. "You need to know me!" she shouted. Cheering her on, Amy cried, "I *do* need to know you!"

Afterwards, Deena realized, "I never got to express rage or grief about that before. I was silenced, or I silenced myself. It was numbing." But in our group she felt supported to take up space, to ask for what she needed. Soon after, at a mostly Ashkenazi gathering, Deena organized a large group discussion about Mizrahi issues—which Emily applauded as "a big leap into visibility, in a really courageous way."

I am at a co-counseling workshop in Warsaw, Poland, "Healing from World War II," with people from Europe, Israel, the U.S., Australia. Today, in small groups we are releasing feelings about anti-Semitism. I choose Peter's group, a (self-described) descendant of Nazis.[45] I've been watching him the past few days; I trust him. (Note: Names used here are pseudonyms.)

My turn. I talk about the terror I felt when we were in Birkenau: seeing the "selection platform," where Jews designated as "not useful" were marched directly to the gas. Now I'm crying, sobbing. Peter hugs a thick pillow to his chest, tells me to hit it—him—and to keep my eyes on his, to help me get the feelings out, also to keep me present. I pound as hard as I can. "Yell!" he encourages me. Now I'm screaming, slamming the pillow, grief and terror pour out of me. Then exhausted, I collapse in sobs, clinging onto Sima, a Mizrahi Jew from Israel, as she holds me. Now back again to pummeling Peter, now crying with Sima.

In ten minutes, my time is up. Unbelievable. Enormous waves of relief wash through me, I feel lighter than I can remember. Catharsis. Afterwards the six of us, Jews and gentiles, hug and then laugh together, with connection, closeness. I think to myself, "It doesn't get any better than this."

Liberatory healing

Recovery from internalized oppression, using whatever modalities fit best, is a Can Do, a Must Do—to free up our spirits, and so that we get on with building a better world. Releasing feelings, experimenting with holistic modalities, learning sensory awareness: these all purge toxins and help us gain fluency in our body's unique language. Reclaiming our intact/amazing selves buried under debris, we can reappraise, realign, even bring these tools to other Jews and allies.

Pushing those edges, generating insights, we usher in new consciousness: liberatory healing. "Since I've committed my life to social change, the more that I work through and release," Deena realized, "the more powerful I become. That feels like a huge shift—the potential to increase my power."

]

Hope into Practice: Choosing Justice Despite Our Fears

"How wonderful it is that nobody need wait a single moment before starting to improve the world."

—Anne Frank

"THERE'S A NEW JEWISH IDENTITY," says activist leader Cecilie Surasky, one that is "multigenerational, multiethnic, multisexual, a united front against bigotry and xenophobic nationalism, and for all forms of equality."[1] Our recovery is in no way isolated from global movements for justice, peace, and environmental sustainability.

Drawing on the (Ashkenazi) Yiddish concept *doikayt,* "the right to be, and to fight for justice, wherever we are,"[2] we use our Jewishness as a social justice platform.[3] Speaking out against crimes targeting our people, we speak out just as strongly against crimes committed in our name. For us, activism is putting hope into practice.

Tikkun olam (mending the world) spills out of Jewish prophetic and mystical traditions: the prophet Micah asks us to do justice, love mercy; Leviticus says to love our neighbors as ourselves. In the sixteenth century, Rabbi Isaac Luria created the cosmology myth of regathering holy sparks—to restore the world.[4] Today, Rabbi Alissa Wise speaks of *Mussar,* the ethical thread in Judaism she links with "radical responsibility."[5] One of our most compelling thinkers, medieval philosopher Moses Maimonides, taught: people should not oppress each other, individually or collectively, nor should one people occupy another.[6]

Doikayt was a guiding principle of the Jewish Socialist Bund, Melanie Kaye/Kantrowitz reminds us. It means coalition-building, big-time, for universal equality: addressing anti-Semitism *and* racism, including anti-Arab/Muslim bigotry, including marginalizing of Jewish minorities. Also organizing to stop scapegoating of immigrants, hate crimes against queers, violence against women—plus ending economic injustice, corporate greed, abuse of Palestinians.

Paraphrasing Rabbi Tarfon: We do not need to complete The Work in this lifetime, but neither can we refuse to do our unique part.[7] My friend Henri Picciotto told me that his father taught him as a boy in Lebanon, "In Judaism, the synagogue is just a building. The rabbi is just a person, a teacher but still just a person. The essence of being a Jew is to strive to do the right thing."

Our ongoing strategy: visibility, compassionate resistance, creative visioning. "We are activists, and we do not keep silent," insists Kaye/Kantrowitz.[8] "We recognize the...range in what gets categorized as anti-Semitism: from ignorance to extermination and everything in between, including conspiracy theories, stereotypes, hate crimes, Christian Zionism, rampant Christianity, and ridicule of Jewish identity or culture...It is...essential to resist anti-Semitism and simultaneously to oppose...injustice inflicted on others."[9]

Jewish liberation means choosing justice, *tzedek*, in spite of inherited fear—also truly valuing our Jewish-woman-selves.

So what's Jewish self-love got to do with it?

"It is simply impossible to struggle successfully against hatred outside ourselves, while ignoring its messages within."[10]—*Alice Miller*

If we're hanging on to feeling that something's wrong with us, it can blind us to seeing how beautiful we are, make us doubt ourselves, limit the impact of our change-making. Brush those messages aside (*Feh!*); leap into who we can be. When our outrageous Jewish woman's/genderqueer life-force is unleashed, what can possibly stop us?

Absolutely, let's intertwine self-love with social justice, braiding through both a "strategy of generosity."[11] When we resist self-loathing or fear, and act anyway, it boosts our self-esteem, our gutsy-ness—whether we are working-class, Mizrahi, however-hyphenated. It's a natural step to use that confidence to intervene against police brutality or attacks on undocumented workers...to fight Israeli seizure of Palestinian land, nuclear energy, or the roll-back of abortion rights.

Learning to feel good about who we are, to disregard the inner critic, is an *ongoing* practice; and then we're more likely to feel loving towards others.[12] To treat each other respectfully—even when we're exhausted, broke, discouraged. Even when we feel betrayed. When our calls aren't returned or our e-mails aren't answered, when the printer breaks, when there's no food in the fridge and the laundry piles up...when a lover leaves us, or the baby is sick, or we're having hot flashes, or our boss doesn't get it that organizing this event comes first and our job responsibilities will have to wait. Let's remember, we have similar fears and needs. Leadership trainer Akaya Windwood asks, "What if we...stopped nit-picking at each other, and...lifted each other up instead?"[13]

Ultimately, deciding to act—both for ourselves *and* for other groups—counters both our internalized victimization and the mistreatment of others, benefitting our neighborhoods, our workplaces, our world...and us. Realizing that even though we aren't perfect (who is?), we are enough; loving ourselves is an everyday project, after all. Valuing ourselves, we're more effective allies, can take bigger risks for world-changing. It's a deep-down inside-outside process.

And we get it, feeling hopeful feels better. Celebrating victories, no matter how small, we dust off our joy. Supporting one another to be our fullest Jewishly visible selves, we cherish each other, also ourselves—yes, *cherish*. We can do this. Challenging internalized Jewish oppression strengthens our communities: with empathy for Jewish insecurities, understanding how fear is manipulated by some Jewish and Christian leadership, we build better bridges, helping our people heal, fueling societal transformation. Young Israeli protest leader Daphne Leef articulated the "new discourse" they were creating, after bringing half a million into Tel

Aviv's streets for weeks in 2011, replacing: "the word 'charity' with the word 'justice'...the verb 'to wait' with the verb 'to change'...the word 'alone' with the word 'together.'"[14]

Jewishness: a platform of social action

"If we remember those times and places—and there are so many—where people have behaved magnificently, this gives us the energy to act, and at least the possibility of sending this spinning top of a world in a different direction. And if we do act, in however small a way, we don't have to wait for some grand Utopian future. The future is an infinite succession of presents, and to live now as we think human beings should live, in defiance of all that is bad around us, is itself a marvelous victory."[15]—*Howard Zinn*

We're talking Jewish-positive, loud and proud. "Many of us complain about the lack of leadership," says cultural historian Dr. Bernice Johnson Reagon.[16] "If you are missing something, it is the sound of your own voice."[17] Speaking out wherever we are; as Chip Berlet urges, raising "hell in the streets and in the suites."[18]

Taking action—fighting back, working across differences, or launching new visions—taps into our power, helps alleviate despair, and creates conditions for others to empower themselves. Radical historian Howard Zinn reminded us it is everyday people like ourselves, ordinary but persistent and determined, who achieved some of the most profound change, despite overwhelming odds. On the 40th anniversary of Dr. Martin Luther King's assassination, Senator Barack Obama had the same idea: "Dr. King once said that the arc of the moral universe is long but it bends towards justice. But what he also knew was that it doesn't bend on its own. It bends because each of us puts our hands on that arc and bends it in the direction of justice."[19]

Realizing how massive the problems are, "sometimes we think that we have to be massive people."[20] Not true—though "activism is hard," cautions Letty Cottin Pogrebin, taking "hours, days, nights of dogged effort."[21] Like what we've seen in Cairo, Tunisia, Madison (WI). More than just signing one petition, activists "organize hundreds of thousands" of others to sign it, then mobilize folks "to show up...at the office of the person with the power to effect change."[22] Small actions piled together lead to big ones, build a movement.

Also key, as veteran change-maker Barbara Smith points out, "Successful organizing depends a lot upon the quality of the relationships we build."[23] Echoing Smith, new-ish activist Rachel Brown reflects about a successful Philly protest: "The most important thing I learned was that my anxiety about stepping forward had been misplaced, because it had never been about me. I could never have willed the demonstration into being; I was only laying the groundwork to make it possible. In the end our success was built entirely on people's relationships, and the support of activist networks doing...parallel work for justice."[24]

At Occupy Wall Street, Naomi Klein noted her favorite sign: "I care about you."[25] "Let's treat each other," she suggests, "as if we plan to work side by side in struggle for many...years to come."[26] Also remembering, it is in relationship with each other that minds and hearts change.

Jews have helped change hearts and minds—and laws—as abolitionists and suffragettes, labor agitators, freedom riders in the Civil Rights Movement, antiwar mobilizers, playwrights and music-makers, whistle-blowers, leaders in women's and gay liberation and the ending of South African apartheid. Historian Aurora Levins Morales says we've been "disproportionately present in movements for social justice wherever we have landed."[27] Today, in Jewish groups and as Jews in other organizations/coalitions, we're tackling breast cancer and transphobia and sexual abuse, strategizing for better schools and bike lanes, marching to end wars and poverty and the death penalty. We're rapping for indigenous rights, exposing unexamined Christian dominance. Our clergy block streets on behalf of same-sex marriage, our synagogues are going green.

Sometimes this translates to defying policies of power brokers who happen to be Jews, who own the sweatshops or nursing homes or drug companies, or who run Jewish institutions. Sometimes it means challenging Jewish conspiracy theories from Right or Left. Jews have also launched a vibrant new wave of activism to end the Israeli occupation of East Jerusalem, the West Bank, and Gaza, what Cecilie Surasky calls "the Jewish civil rights cause of this era"[28]—combatting violations of rights that were institutionalized as international law after World War II, in response to Nazi crimes.

And hardly a surprise, another "disproportionate number" of Jewish social justice leaders are women.[29] In the early 1900s, it was especially Jewish *women* who championed rights of prisoners and prostitutes, migrant workers, women and children. A personal hero of mine from the 1960s-'70s, feminist firebrand Bella Abzug, funny/loud/boat-rocking—and the first Jewish woman elected to Congress—helped launch Women Strike for Peace. This group mobilized 50,000 women who poured into the streets, a significant factor in adopting the Limited Test Ban Treaty.[30] Abzug also supported the Equal Rights Amendment, and in 1974 introduced the first federal gay rights bill.

Writing in 2007, Melanie Kaye/Kantrowitz pointed out: "Since the Civil Rights movement, Jews are commonly assumed to have moved to the right, but this shift—to the extent that it exists—is sharply gendered. I do not hear the same sarcasm, pessimism, rejection, and dejection in the voices of leftist Jewish women of my generation—or of the generation of women now in their twenties and thirties."[31]

❦

Weaving politics with ritual

Grounding their activism, a plethora of Jews across genders and generations, are tying in their politics with "Judaism 2.0" rituals, updating, reinventing. For *Tisha B'Av*, when Jews mourn exile from Jerusalem/Spain/Iran, activist leader Susan Lubeck wrote that we can also grieve horrific inequities in our criminal justice system that especially target young black men. Tisha B'Av can be a time "to understand...our well-being is linked to the well-being of all."[32] At a San Francisco rally protesting the murder of nine Gaza Freedom Flotilla members, Rae Abileah organized a *kaddish* service; Jews and gentiles gathered around an altar on the Code Pink table, publicly praying together.

Queer activist/artist Wendy Elisheva Somerson emphasized "how important it is for radical Jews to create alternative spiritual and political spaces, instead of begging to be let into Jewish institutional spaces that offer us inclusion only when we leave our anti-Occupation politics behind."[33] Celebrating Passover with the political Jewish community she helped build in Seattle, she "felt an internal shift...like I was taking a deep nourishing breath after years of shallow breathing."[34]

During the 2006 High Holy Days, after shootings at the Seattle Jewish Federation, Somerson's Jewish Voice for Peace chapter held a *Tashlich L'Tzedek* ceremony, combining social justice and spiritual healing, to address "the complicated intersection of anti-Semitism and anti-Occupation work."[35] Tossing stones into Lake Washington on a sparkling sunny day, participants cast off sins of the Israeli occupation. Then allies cast away sins of anti-Semitism—"ignorance about Jewish history and historical trauma, not speaking up against anti-Semitism, and equating all Jews with the policies of the Israeli government."[36] The tashlich idea? Not just to rid ourselves of shortcomings, the husk of prejudice around our best selves—but to set a transformational intention, recommitting to something bigger.

Occupy Judaism:

"Bring the Jews to Occupy Wall Street, bring Occupy Wall Street to the Jews."

The 2011 phenomenon birthed "Occupy Judaism" right on time for *Kol Nidre* (the beginning of Yom Kippur) at Occupy Wall Street—beginning with a "Tweet," and ending with 1000 people, secular to Orthodox.[37] Picture this: sandwiched between the skyscrapers of Manhattan's financial district, Jews chanting Kol Nidre, in public, on the holiest night of the year, wearing kippas/prayershawls/jeans/hoodies. Heartfelt "civil disobedient *davening* [praying]" for economic justice, people's-mic style: loudly echoing back the prayer-leader's words, so that everyone could hear.[38] What change-maker Rebecca Vilkomerson called the "most meaningful religious experience of my life...the first time that I felt my Judaism and my politics were completely in tune. It was breathtaking."[39]

For *Succot*, L.A. staged "Not Just A Succa: A JUST Succa at Occupy LA," decrying home foreclosures, lack of health care, unequal distribution of wealth. The next spring in NYC, an Occupy-Interfaith-Freedom-Seder-&-Palm-Sunday-Processional to symbolic "pyramids of power"—a bank, an immigrant detention center, the New York University financial aid office (signifying crushing student debt)—insisting to "pharaohs of government and industry 'Let our people go!'" and ending with a Freedom Seder.[40]

This juicy new weaving of protest with ceremony continues a trajectory from the Revolutionary War, abolition, civil rights and anti-Vietnam War movements.[41] Now mobilized "bottom up" via social media, this "audacious display of empowered Judaism" thrives "without the authorization of Jewish officialdom."[42] Points out organizer Daniel Sieradski, "Most Jewish institutions are dominated by their wealthiest donors, whose views might not be in line with that of the wider Jewish community; it's… our tradition as much as it is anybody's, and they need to make space for us."[43] So while we're at it, let's rethink Jewish institutions. This is what Jewish liberation looks like.

Activism from secular to synagogue

"How do we manage spiritually during hard times? The most subversive thing that a synagogue or community organization can do is to affirm that the problems lie not with ourselves…but with a system that is more concerned with short-term gain than with people and with the health of the planet."[44] — Rabbi David J. Cooper

To whet your appetite, a coast-to-coast (micro) sampling of change-making groups, secular to synagogue.[45]

- *Jews for Racial and Economic Justice* (NYC) helped win a landmark NY Domestic Workers Bill of Rights;[46] organizes with Jews Against Islamophobia; also fights for housing justice and quality long-term care—focusing where Jewish support can help win victories. Their founding act was a public Shabbat service in Nelson Mandela's honor when he visited the U.S. after being freed from prison, raising $30,000 for the African National Congress. Cultural work is also key, weaving theater, history, hilarity, politics (also glitter) into Jewish celebrations.

- *Shalom Bayit* (peace in the home) (San Francisco Bay Area) breaks the silence about domestic violence in the Jewish community. Empowering battered women and children, they build Jewish families that are respectful, loving, and violence-free. They also wrote a teen dating violence-prevention curriculum, *Love Shouldn't Hurt*, recalling

Lilith's message "I demand to be treated as an equal. I have the right to say no."

- *Bend the Arc* (a national partnership of Progressive Jewish Alliance [PJA] and Jewish Funds For Justice) met at the White House in 2012 about a Jewish justice agenda,[47] to increase the religious left's impact in policy debates. Investing in Boston foreclosure prevention, fighting for fair immigration reform, and training change-makers, they're also organizing for a California Domestic Workers Bill of Rights and creating a national interfaith multiracial organizing network. As PJA, they won an anti-sweatshop ordinance in Los Angeles, wrote a *No Shvitz* (no sweat) guide to sweatshop activism, and helped pass an L.A. resolution condemning anti-Muslim bigotry, the first city to do so.

- *TransTorah* members are educators, rabbis, and cultural workers who raise trans Jewish voices to build diverse, loving, expansive Jewish communities—transforming traditions, creating all-gender resources.

- *Fair Trade Judaica* encourages Jews to use our purchasing power to create a more just trade system, supporting artisans from Guatemala to Thailand to Uganda in becoming self-sufficient—offering fair trade products like Jewish blessing flags from Nepal, a hand-crocheted kippah, a recycled paper dreidel.

- When *Jews United for Justice/St. Louis* fought union-busting in a Jewish nursing home, they linked the elders' welfare with that of the mostly African American staff. In the process, they were able to notice, and so to address, "how...our internalized anti-Semitism, and our history of oppression...get in the way of our ability to think clearly and to feel positive about ourselves in a way that allows us to understand racism and to form partnerships with people of color."[48]

- Youth-led *Jewish Youth for Community Action* (JYCA) (San Francisco Bay Area) initiates teens in self-selected activist projects, like teaching youth empowerment workshops at Occupy Oakland, or urging people to "break up" with big banks on Valentine's Day and join credit unions instead. At JYCA, Sasha Petterson learned "what activism can do... build not just safety, but connection...Not just friendship, but love."[49]

- Combatting racism, poverty, and anti-Semitism since the 1960s, the *Jewish Council on Urban Affairs* (Chicago) partners with communities of color, Christians, and Jews to help groups feed their communities, to fight for housing and schools.

- President Obama lauded *American Jewish World Service* for the $6 million they immediately raised for Haitian earthquake relief. Their projects challenge poverty and champion human rights in the Americas/Asia/Africa, including raising a Jewish voice for Lesbian, Gay, Bisexual, Transgender, Intersex (LGBTI) rights,[50] also for life-saving food aid/food justice policies in the U.S.—always recognizing women's critical role in community change.

- *Urban Adamah* (earth) operates an organic community farm in Berkeley (CA), distributing produce to those in need, integrating social justice into Jewish environmental education.

- *T'ruah: The Rabbinic Call for Human Rights* (formerly *Rabbis for Human Rights-North America*) fights human trafficking and torture, also works to end forced labor in the Florida tomato industry.

- Celebrating progressive secular Yiddish culture for 100-plus years, *Workmen's Circle* backs labor struggles nationwide, plus immigrant and health care rights.

- The *Shalom Center* (Philadelphia), which got its start leading Jewish opposition to nuclear weapons/power, also builds interfaith peace work.[51] Condemning Big Oil, Big Coal, Big Gas, they train activists in policy change, like fighting "fracking" (smashing shale rocks into releasing natural gas, which pollutes drinking water). They celebrated *Tu B'Shevat*, the Jewish festival of trees, by defending ancient redwoods against corporate devastation.

- *Hazon* (vision) mobilizes Jewish environmental bike rides to spur fresh thinking about transportation, connect with nature, build empowerment. Coleading the Jewish Food Justice Movement, they push for sustainable farming/ethical food systems.

- *Jews United for Justice/Washington, D.C.*, wrote a "Green & Just Celebrations Guide" for planning socially conscious events. They fight for D.C. voting rights, living wage legislation, and immigrant rights.

- Highlighting connections between (sometimes Jewish-organizational) anti-Muslim hate speech, racial-profiling "stop and frisk" police practices and surveillance, and government policies, *Jews Against Islamophobia* (NYC) fights hate-mongering ads in New York subways and organizes educational panels.[52]

In the last decade, a burst of congregation-based organizing of synagogues and churches has hit the national scene, mobilized by four community organization networks,[53] catalyzed by the Jewish Funds for Justice Foundation. Shunning charity, thousands of members approach healthcare, housing, and education struggles in "a shift from a patronizing 'Look what I can do for you,'" explained Rabbi John Linder, "to a 'What can we do together?'"[54] Organizer Renee Wizig-Barrios affirms, "In the moments when I doubt my capacity and act anyway, I live out my Judaism."[55]

Jewish Community Action (Minneapolis-St. Paul) highlights congregational activism because synagogues have power that "can…make a difference."[56] Their focus on loving the stranger (an admonition appearing in the Bible far more than rules about the Sabbath) led to helping pass immigrants rights protection, and they won accolades for their campaign fighting foreclosures, allying with communities of color.

In the room-for-improvement category? Most organizations have yet to develop "a full-blown political practice that…reflects, incorporates… Jewish diversity."[57]

When asked his message for young people, Rabbi Abraham Joshua Heschel replied, "Let them be sure that every deed counts…and that we…do our share to redeem the world, in spite of all frustrations…"[58] Responding to Heschel's call, *The Jewish Week* annually spotlights "36 Under 36,"[59] just a few of millennial social justice movers and shakers: like rabbinical student Shmuly Yanklowitz, who launched *Uri L'Tzedek* (Awaken to Justice) to mobilize Orthodox communities. Or Ronit Avni, founder of Just Vision, which documents Israeli and Palestinian nonviolent projects to end the conflict, initiated by her award-winning documentary *Encounter Point*.

After fleeing Ethiopia, Beejhy Barhany founded Beta Israel of North America (BINA), to help Ethiopian Jews transition to the States—"If we empower each other we can…be stronger"—and to educate the Jewish world that "There is more than one shape and color for Jews."[60] Sheva Tauby started iVolunteer, matching up volunteers with isolated Nazi Holocaust survivors; and when Brazil native Rabbi Mendy Weitman saw the need to give South American Jews a "home away from home," he created the Latin Jewish Center in Manhattan.[61] Eli Winkelman launched Challah for Hunger to support Sudan relief—while Nati Passow cofounded the Jewish Farm School, focused on food justice. And as Gal Beckerman won a National Jewish Book Award for his history of Soviet Union suppression of Jews, Rabbi Rachel Kahn-Troster led Rabbis for Human Rights-North America (now T'ruah) in challenging Islamophobia.

"And may our actions be faithful to our words," writes poet Marcia Falk (excerpt)

"That our children's children may live to know:
Truth and kindness have embraced,
Peace and justice have kissed and are one."[62]

℘

Like the Seattle activists in their tashlich ritual, inherent in our change-making is confronting anti-Jewish prejudice. Holding that intent, in her excellent pamphlet "The Past Didn't Go Anywhere: Making Resistance to Anti-Semitism Part of All of Our Movements," April Rosenblum adds a cautionary note: "When white gentiles or white Jews have trouble confronting white privilege, it can look more attractive and less uncomfortable to make an issue of anti-Semitism. Sorry—it won't be possible to choose between the two. Anti-Jewish oppression cannot be dealt with in a movement that isn't also utterly dedicated to fighting the oppression of people of color, both in the larger world and in our movements."[63]

For those of us who are white Ashkenazi, this means nonstop awareness of our privilege: catching that urge to run the show, to control (because we "know best"). Instead: sliding over, stepping back, making room—always—for the voices of the less-enfranchised, be they African American, Mexican, Palestinian, Sephardi.

And in sync with our frontline tikkun olam organizations, as we take back the *progressive* fight against anti-Semitism, we need to keep battling U.S. imperial policies that harm millions worldwide and that drain our economy of funds so desperately needed at home—an economy *New York Times* columnist Bob Herbert calls "rigged to benefit the rich and powerful."[64] Let's shift astronomical disparities in resources, in opportunity, in human rights: transforming systems. As long as inequality is accepted as status quo, we won't end injustice, internalized oppression, or all the *tsuris* (troubles) blocking a brighter future. Let's build a society, a world, grounded in fairness and generosity, in empathy and caring community, in participatory democracy and human dignity...one that values our interdependence with all things living.

"Hope still lives here in America," shouted 2011 Mario Savio Young-Activist Award-winner Josh Healey, to 10,000 folks at UC Berkeley's Sproul Plaza, in the midst of Occupy Cal:[65] "She [hope] has always lived here with us/and now she is back before our eyes/marching head high, fist higher/and whispering.../Thank you./You're bringing me back./Take my hand,/feel my pulse joined with yours./Trust my taste on your tongue,/my strength in your lungs,/and let's see how far we can go/together."[66]

Focus: Israel-Palestine

"All land is holy. All people are chosen."—*Alan Senauke*

Longtime feminist nonviolence leader Rabbi Lynn Gottlieb asks us to "find the...courage to soften our hearts and seek an authentic peace based on justice and love for both Palestinians and Israelis."[67] Where there is no longer occupier and occupied, where everyone has an equal seat at the table. Winning fairness and freedom for the Palestinian people will bring peace and security to Israelis as well. And as long as legitimate critiques of Israeli policies are blocked by charges of anti-Semitism, says Gottlieb, it's "the responsibility of Jews committed to universal justice to speak up."[68]

We need to face the Israeli government's refusal to dismantle settlements, to end the occupation, to grant Palestinians democratic rights—and build a movement to push our government, hard, to pressure Israel to implement these goals.[69] Not allowing fear to derail us, we remember that silence = consent. When the Jewish establishment presses for misguided U.S. policies that support subjugating and disenfranchising Palestinians, our speaking out for Palestinian rights—as visible Jews—has an impact far beyond our numbers.

And as we make our voices heard, April Rosenblum points out: "You keep things clear when you describe accurately and specifically...*actions and policies* as unjust—not people or nations."[70] (Italics added) For example: distinguishing between the accuracy of the statement "The Israeli government systematically confiscates Palestinian land" from the anti-Jewish idea that Israel is the "root of the world's problems."[71]

Conversely, says Rosenblum, "when people suggest that they see targeting of Jews in something you're saying or doing [in critiquing Israeli policies], don't shoot them down: seek out useful information in what they're saying that might help you give your message even more clarity and impact."[72]

As Jews, when we publicly act against Israeli state abuses—whether bombing civilians, using white phosphorous, or depriving Gazans of clean drinking water[73]—we decrease anti-*Jewish* bigotry. Anytime our outcry can lessen brutality towards Palestinians, this also diminishes hatred of Israel/ hatred of Jews, so such speaking out is a way to fight anti-Semitism. Yet even though explicitly Jewish voices are crucial in our anti-occupation movement, as activist Rachael Kamel points out, "*a peaceful and democratic future for everyone in the Middle East is not an ethnic but a human issue.*"[74]

Vital Jewish voices like:

- Hedy Epstein: whose parents sent her to England on the *Kindertransport* before they were murdered in Auschwitz. Now in her eighties, she said that one way she alleviates her suffering is by responding to the suffering of others (Palestinians), crediting "my experiences as a Holocaust survivor as the leading influence behind my efforts to promote human rights...I know what it is to be oppressed."[75]

- Alice Rothchild: physician and author, who wrote: "While I am totally appalled by violence of any kind, how can I not understand resistance? I frequently ask myself, if Jews were living under occupation, would we not also resist?"[76]

- Judith Butler: Adorno-prize-winning philosopher/professor, who testified to the UC Berkeley student senate, to support asking the university to divest from General Electric and United Technologies, because their weapons are used by the IDF against Palestinian civilians. "The point is to leave the discourse of war and to affirm what is right. You will not be alone...you will, actually, be making a step towards... peace."[77]

    In a subsequent speech, she added, "Perhaps the word 'justice' will assume new meanings as we speak it, such that...what will be just for the Jews will also be just for the Palestinians...since justice, when just, fails to discriminate, and we savor that failure."[78]

- Rabbi Margaret Holub: (from an unpublished Passover letter to her congregation): "It really doesn't help to say 'It's too complicated.' Sometimes we have to...do our best with what we do understand... And wise people...may hold positions quite unlike my own. I welcome conversation and challenge...I've dedicated my life work to helping the Jewish people grow and blossom. I believe that...occupying another people has wounded our people at the root of our collective soul. I see in BDS [Boycott, Divestment, Sanctions] the hope for healing—most importantly for the Palestinian people whose homes, livelihoods and lives are harmed, but also for our own people...I take great hope in the Jewish people and our capacity to do good."[79]

- Anna Baltzer: Gen-Y activist/author interviewed on Jon Stewart's *The Daily Show*, with Palestinian leader Dr. Mustapha Barghouti. "We're part of a large movement of Palestinians and Jews working together," explained Baltzer.[80] Added Barghouti, "Jewish Americans have been in the avant-garde struggling for justice."[81]

- Or all the voices echoed in the YoungJewishProud Declaration, collectively written as a "call to action for both our peers and our elders," towards justice in Israel and Palestine.[82] Launched at their protest at the 2010 Jewish Federation General Assembly in New Orleans, the activists wrote (excerpt):

We speak and love and dream in every language. We pray three times a day or only during the high holidays or when we feel like we really need to or not at all. We are punks and students and parents and janitors and Rabbis and freedom fighters. We are your children, your nieces and nephews, your grandchildren...We remember brave, desperate resistance...We remember the labor movement. We remember the camps...We remember solidarity as a means of survival and an act of affirmation, and we are proud...We refuse to knowingly oppress others, and we refuse to oppress each other... We will not carry the legacy of terror...We won't buy the logic that slaughter means safety...We commit to equality, solidarity, and integrity...We seek breathing room and dignity for all people.[83]

∞

"[The Occupation] is not just, is not moral, and is not Judaism."
—*Rabbi Michael Melchior, "Peace: a Jewish Value"*

Over a score of Jewish-identified U.S. groups across a moderate-to-radical spectrum are also raising voices and dollars to support a just/secure peace. National organizations range from J Street (see Chapter Three) to T'ruah: The Rabbinic Call for Human Rights, Americans for Peace Now, and Partners for Progressive Israel (formerly Meretz USA). Rabbis Brian Walt and Brant Rosen coordinate the Jewish Fast for Gaza, *Taanit Tzedek*, endorsed by over eighty rabbis; Jewish tradition calls for communal fasting during crises, and this initiative seeks to end Jewish community silence over Israel's collective punishment of Gazans.[84]

Jewish Voice for Peace is the only national grassroots U.S. Jewish peace organization, 130,000-plus online activists strong (as of 2013), inspired by Jewish tradition, that explicitly (loudly) calls for full equality, security, human rights, and dignity for Israelis *and* Palestinians, backing nonviolent efforts—such as economic activism[85]—to secure Palestinian rights. Also working in the Jewish mainstream, as well as side by side with non-Jews, JVP published the primer *Reframing Anti-Semitism*. Supporting a Middle East policy based on international law, JVP condemns attacks on *all* civilians, also mobilizes against the censoring (and jailing) of Palestinian rights advocates, be they Israeli, Palestinian, or worldwide.

"We're dissenters, yes," says JVP Deputy Director Cecilie Surasky, "but we're dissenting patriots. Disagree with us, fine. But we actually care what being Jewish stands for; we take time every day to manifest our universalist Jewish values. We are not the threat to a Jewish future. We are a pillar of that future."[86]

YoungJewishProud (YJP)

JVP organized the training institute that birthed the YoungJewish-Proud protest—which Surasky called "an earthquake in the center of the Jewish world"[87]—when five activists consecutively interrupted Netanyahu's speech at the largest gathering of U.S. Jewish leaders (the 3000-strong Federation General Assembly in 2010), lifting banners and chanting that the occupation, the settlements, and silencing dissent all delegitimize Israel.

Protestor Rae Abileah, of Israeli descent, wrote afterwards: "When the traditional routes of civic engagement fail us, we turn to nonviolent action, and the time-honored tactics that secured women the right to vote, an eight-hour day for workers, and civil rights protections for people of color... We made visible the unsettling disconnect between Jewish values of social justice and current Israeli policies...We opened up the possibility for people to have genuine dialogue about these issues, and we are part of a seismic generational shift in the Jewish community."[88]

For seventeen-year-old Swarthmore student Hanna King, a YJP activist, Israeli actions go against the values she learned in Jewish day school. "Oppressing people in refugee camps is not Tikkun Olam."[89] As she honors "the memory of the Holocaust and the terrible experiences of our ancestors," King points out: this horror can "blind people to the conflict they're perpetuating."[90]

Not missing a beat, with the advent of Occupy, YJP urged young Jews to occupy "Jewish institutions that actively obstruct human rights of Palestinians," including AIPAC, the federations, Birthright, and the Jewish National Fund, also Hillel and right-wing foundations.[91] King implores: "We are the next generation of American Jews, proud of our heritage... committed to Jewish life...We want...the American Jewish community to stand up and say that Israel's ongoing violations of Palestinian human rights are wrong and that we will not continue to support it."[92]

∽

Some synagogues are indeed including diverse perspectives. Like *Kehilla* in Oakland, CA, which cosponsored a program at the synagogue marking Israel's sixtieth birthday as well as the Palestinian *Nakba* (catastrophe). Incorporating *both* narratives, in his 2011 *Kol Nidre* sermon, Rabbi David J. Cooper named Israel-Palestine "the single greatest ethical issue facing the Jewish people in the 21st century."[93] New York City's Congregation *B'nai Jeshuru* organized a panel on "what's legitimate to talk about in the Jewish community," including perspectives on boycott/divestment/sanctions against the occupation and Israel.

And Rabbi Brant Rosen (one of *Newsweek*'s 2008 top twenty-five pulpit rabbis) led nineteen members of his Chicago *Jewish Reconstructionist Congregation* to the West Bank and East Jerusalem, where they spent nights in Palestinian homes. Israeli reporter Orly Halpern wrote Rabbi Brant, "It was great meeting your open-minded and courageous congregation... Courageous because they were willing to hear the Other."[94]

To our allies: in theologian Marc Ellis' words, we need both your assurance and your critique.[95] Whenever Jews are attacked, blamed, or silenced, we need you to speak out—to bear in mind our history and not abandon us. Otherwise, understandably, says Levins Morales, some Jews will hold back from joining the anti-occupation movement, "just as people of color don't rush to join white-led organizations where racism isn't actively challenged."[96]

One inspiring (complex) example: when a Jewish-born writer who championed the Palestinian cause also strongly espoused offensive (internalized) anti-Semitism and racism in the process, Palestinian leaders publicly disavowed the writer's statements. "Our struggle was never... with Jews...," the Palestinians wrote.[97] "Our struggle is with Zionism, a modern European settler colonial movement, similar to movements in... other parts of the world that aim to displace indigenous people and build new European societies...We reaffirm that there is no room in this analysis of our struggle for any attacks on our Jewish allies, Jews, or Judaism;

nor denying the Holocaust; nor allying…with any conspiracy theories… Challenging Zionism…must never become an attack on Jewish identities."[98] (Italics added)

At the same time, Israeli-American activist Liat Weingart asked Presbyterian Church allies, "We…need you to persist in seeing the best in us and…expecting…it of us…Don't let us get away with anything less than what we're capable of. We know you feel bad about what has happened to Jews…[but] We need you at our side as partners in our liberation. And we will not be truly liberated as long as we are occupying…the Palestinians."[99]

Where do we go from here? Scrape up the *chutzpah* to initiate the thorny conversations at family dinner tables, with friends and acquaintances—to risk discomfort, reach minds and hearts, examine what's at stake.[100] Find whatever routes we can to pressure the Israeli government *as well as our own* to end the occupation, dismantle settlements, and grant Palestinians (in Palestine and in Israel) full democratic and human rights, based on international law, also creating security for Israelis. Integrate this activism into the rest of our lives, nestled right in the center of our Jewishness.

In "Latkes and Laments," organizer Lynn Pollack described her dilemma: after Israel launched the devastating December 2008 attack on Gaza, what to do about the Hanukkah party she had planned? "My phone started ringing… 'Was the party still on?' I told people that we might as well get together and eat. That's what Jews do when tragedy hits. We'd turn it into a shiva/ wake, I said, craft press releases between courses and make signs for a demo after dessert."[101]

So, a bit dazed, Pollack grabbed "my great-grandmother's latke smasher, and began peeling potatoes," meanwhile following the news on her laptop.[102] After guests arrived, one by one they "lit a candle and spoke of their hopes for peace, for an end to the suffering…in Gaza, hopes for a true miracle"—and by evening's end, "we were ready, fed, and united for a demo the next day."[103]

Keep wrestling, mounting campaigns, writing Op Eds…also lobbying and marching. Keep backing the Israeli peace movement and Palestinian nonviolent strategies, coalition-ing with churches and mosques, messaging on Facebook…keep supporting organizations here doing the work, circulating petitions, sitting-in at federal/corporate offices and Israeli consulates—movement-building/unleashing our power, big-time, to make our government change its policies.

"I always wonder," says Rabbi Lynn Gottlieb, "which terrible rendition of loss and grief will tip the balance…so that a flood of compassion will wash away our fear and create the resolve to not turn away. In times of profound sadness, I gather…hope from…those Israeli Jews and Palestinians, who in spite of the worst kind of loss…reach out to each other for the sake of peace…Aware of all the complexities, they refuse to be enemies, they speak out against occupational brutalities, construct bridges across the abyss. For the sake of our children, how can we not do the same?"[104]

Solidarity

"If you have come here to help me, you are wasting your time. But if you have come because your liberation is bound up with mine, then let us work together."[105] —*Aboriginal activists group, Queensland, Australia, 1970s*

In the summer of 1999 "season of hate," a neo-Nazi, ex-security guard critically wounded three children at an L.A. Jewish day care center, later that day killing a Filipino letter-carrier. The same summer, after two white supremacist brothers burned down three Sacramento synagogues, they murdered a gay male couple in bed—and torched an abortion clinic. And that July, a white-power fanatic shot and wounded six Orthodox Jews walking home from shul in Chicago; the same weekend, he killed an African American basketball coach in front of his children, wounded an African American minister, and murdered a young Korean doctoral student. Can we doubt the links? Although our advantages (or lack of these) vary, people of color, queers, feminists, Jews, all understand being demonized, and many feel the common ground we share: Jews yesterday, Muslims today. Who tomorrow? We are natural allies.

"*Tonight for Passover,*" I read, "*we drink a cup of wine for those who reached across chasms for a shared humanity. For the Egyptian, knowing the Hebrews were leaving, who gave her neighbor gold earrings and a kiss, veiling her face to hide her tears. For the woman in Georgia who opened her door to escaping slaves, tucked them under hay in the wagon, and rode them to the next station on the Underground Railroad, knowing she risked prison if caught. And today, for the Jewish Israelis who escort Palestinian children to school, under a hail of stones from extremist Jewish settlers."*

Let's remember the connections between our own immigrant pasts and those trying to slip across U.S. borders to escape grinding poverty, often persecution. The connections between today's racial profiling and our own histories…between pogroms or forced exile and current Immigration and Customs Enforcement (ICE) raids/deportations, wrenching apart families. Between coerced service in the tsar's army and the recruitment of young people of color to fight U.S. wars, when no other jobs can be found, much less affordable education. Between our own exodus from tyranny in Egypt, and liberation struggles the world over.[106]

Our security as U.S. Jews lies in our relationships with our allies and with each other, our hope in what we can create together: solidarity rather than separation. Because confronting *all* unfairness and bigotry builds a social justice movement—including holding ourselves (and our government) accountable, making sure that we "rely on the vision and efforts of those who [most directly] suffer the pangs of systemic injustice to articulate the way forward."[107] As this book goes to press – despite extremist rhetoric, xenophobia, right-wing Republicanism (including a war on women's reproductive rights), and jarring racial injustice—and as unpleasant as anti-Jewish prejudice remains, U.S. Jews, as Jews, are in much less peril than many others. Our overall privilege and security (for most of us) is almost unparalleled in Jewish history.[108]

Whenever we say NO—to the backlash of racism and Islamophobia, the surge of hate crimes and bullying, the scapegoating of immigrants and gays—we break a consensus built of fear/greed/ignorance; we encourage others to openly resist, to lead. As (white) Jews we can use our privilege to raise issues, fight hard…and make a point to link with those who share a herstory of dispersion: South Asians, Africans, Chinese, and Palestinians, among others.[109] Aurora Levins Morales pens a Passover liberation liturgy (excerpt):

"They say that other country over there
dim blue in the twilight
farther than the orange stars exploding over our roofs
is called peace...
We would cross the water if we knew how.
Everyone blames everyone else for barring the way...

This time...We cannot cross until we carry each other
all of us refugees, all of us prophets...
No more taking turns on history's wheel,
trying to collect old debts no one can pay.
The sea will not open that way.

This time that country
is what we promise each other,
our rage pressed cheek to cheek
until tears flood the space between,
until there are no enemies left,
because this time no one will be left to drown
and all of us must be chosen.
This time it's all of us, or none."[110]

⸜⸝

Solidarity's cousin is Inclusion. Diversity consultant Linda Holtzman speculates, "If I were to fantasize about how inclusion would feel, it would be that [for] *everybody*...when they participated in the Jewish community, that it felt like home."[111] (Italics added)

Meanwhile, let's encourage Christian allies to cook up fresh initiatives, outspokenness. Like Judy Andreas, who organized two bicoastal conferences on Anti-Semitism and the Left, and who is naming her dissertation on this topic "The Forbidden Compassion." Or James Carroll, who said in the video about his book *Constantine's Sword*, if you want to understand anti-Semitism, don't study Jews: study non-Jews.

And absolutely, let's stretch both ways across the generational divide. Reach out, listen, team up. Though times always change, older Jews have precious experience to share, perspective. While "Some of the bravest political work," writes Kaye/Kantrowitz, "has happened because people often too young to grasp their own mortality stick their necks out. The job of the rest of us is to rise to the occasion of their bravery...This doesn't mean that youth are always right...It does mean the rest of us need to check our impulse to control, to say we know best..."[112]

As Dr. Bernice Johnson Reagon wrote in her inspirational anthem "We Who Believe In Freedom Cannot Rest" (officially titled "Ella's Song"): "The older I get, the better I know that the secret to my goin' on, is when the reins are in the hands of the young who dare to ride against the storm."[113]

When we dare to be powerful...

"Beneath self-hate...something more solid and luminous reveals itself as deepest longing, for a just, generous, beautifully diverse world. My task...is to...welcome my strength, to believe that I, I in all my...identities...can help create this world—not in spite of who I am, but because of it."[114]—*Melanie Kaye/Kantrowitz*

To build a better planet—with imagination, determination, scrappiness and sparkle, knowledge of our herstory, belief in possibility. Unstoppable, while caring for life at every turn.[115]

Although the visionary Audre Lorde is gone, her spirit still guides activists across generations: "When I dare to be powerful, to use my strength in the service of my vision, it becomes less and less important whether I am afraid."[116] And even when we are afraid, Warsaw Ghetto survivor Irena Klepficz writes: "My Jewish fears remind me that I have not left the tribe...I need to convince ...[others] of what I have to convince myself again and again...*That we must choose justice, despite our fears.* That our fears are real, rooted in history, but that they cannot control us or stop us from making just choices."[117] (Italics added)

Using our privilege to shift power, challenging bigotry and violence and repression, let's tackle dehumanization and midwife social justice. Embracing diasporism, let's shove nationalism and assimilation to the margins. Along the way, sing and strategize. Collaborate. Envision. Simultaneously we can build Jewish-positive self-love, (diverse) community, and compassionate resistance—and create solidarity that is accountable, resilient, and shot through with great swaths of love.

The third cup of wine on Tu B'Shvat is mostly red, but still has a tinge of white, reminding us that the world is always unfinished...there is always work to be done.

Action-Oriented Reader's Guide

WELCOME TO THE READER'S GUIDE for *Hope into Practice: Jewish Women Choosing Justice Despite Our Fears*, a tool for exploring these chapters more deeply, especially for making meaning of your own experience. The suggested exercises and questions are points of departure to use in a Jewish circle or study group, a book club or classroom, with a friend, or by yourself. Whichever route you choose, I suggest keeping a journal to chart insights: to map your thoughts and stories, jotting down poetry, adding sketches or other art. Try journaling at least several pages per chapter.

The richest learning, I have a hunch, will come from engaging in this material with others, getting to kvetch and kvell, to think and reflect, together. If used in the classroom, I suggest focusing on small group work, working with the same peers over time. You'll also find it useful to share in pairs or triads, processing feelings and ideas. Check in often with a buddy about how the material is affecting you.

My hope is for groups of Jewish women, and Jews across the gender spectrum, to use this book together—creating communities of closeness, trust, and learning, building cultures of resistance and healing (see Chapter Twelve). May you find joy in Jewishness, counter mantras of suffering, help each other reframe, reclaim, and create justice.

Since this Guide will be used in different venues, I'm providing a skeletal structure and sequence—divided into separate modules, or meetings—but please adapt this to whatever form suits your needs. That said, I encourage allowing time to really work through the material, (for groups) spending several meetings on each of the longer chapters. (Remember that slowing down, patience, is a wonderful antidote to Jewish feelings of urgency!) Consider sharing food, which translates into relationship-building time. And whether working with others or by yourself, explore at least some of the experiential activities, to delve more deeply, or check out a new modality or angle. *If you are using this by yourself, consider the journal as your partner: try writing/drawing/responding to the various questions and projects. See what emerges.*

Forming a group: first meeting

First: forming a meaningful group is totally doable. If you've picked up this book, you can pull a group together. I suggest recruiting a somewhat diverse gang—in terms of class, ethnicity, background—and definitely those who are open-minded, soulful, willing to take risks, interested enough to commit time. Decide what level of political diversity works for you; if group members cover a spectrum, make sure everyone is willing to listen, to maintain respect during disagreement. An ideal group size is six to nine members, meeting at least three hours (even more) at a time.

I suggest an initial getting-to-know-each-other meeting, before engaging with the book's material. Devote time to sharing about yourselves, why you were drawn to this book and this group. Also decide what kind of process you will use, and make sure everyone is on board: will you share or rotate leadership, or have one leader/facilitator? How will you make decisions? Agreeing to clear guidelines establishes firm grounding for your process. For example, confidentiality is key (meaning that outside the group, not repeating the names of who said what, or anything that might identify them); and verbal attacks (harshness/ meanness) are unacceptable. Another excellent guideline is assuming that everyone is an expert on their own experience—yet not on the experience of others. Then decide on logistics: How often will you meet, when and where, for how long?

Also important: how will you respond to emotions that inevitably surface with this material? I suggest a guideline of allowing feelings to be there, not trying to "comfort" them away. When a conversation becomes tense or painful, it helps to break into pairs and take turns sharing feelings for a few minutes: one person talks while one listens, *without interrupting*. Ideally a few of you have facilitation and processing skills—though the ability to listen goes a long way.

Opening with time for each group member to briefly check in creates connection, brings everyone into the room. Encourage full participation, to benefit from each member's thinking; draw out quieter voices. Toning down interruptions allows shyer voices to enter the fray and makes it possible for the group to hear everyone's complete thoughts and stories. This is not to dampen disagreement; devil's advocates are part of meaning-making.

Art, music, poetry, movement, and skits enrich learning, build community, guarantee fun—and are welcome outlets during edgy moments. So don't forget to bring butcher paper, markers, basic art supplies, and percussive musical instruments to enliven your gatherings.

I also suggest drawing on an action research strategy called Cooperative Inquiry, which incorporates the ideas above, simply because it provided an excellent structure for my own project.[1] You can access the resource "A Short Guide to Cooperative Inquiry" by Peter Reason and John Heron (also called "A Layperson's Guide to Cooperative Inquiry") at http://www.human-inquiry.com/cishortg.htm.

At your first meeting, try taking turns sharing what would make the group work for you: What would help you feel visible and supported, so that you can bring your whole Jewish self? Also share, in turn, where you feel vulnerable in your Jewish identity: as a woman? Genderqueer or trans? As Mizrahi, Sephardic, or other Jewish minority? As working class, poor, young or old, disabled? Other? And at the same time, share where you are aware of privilege: as white? Ashkenazi? Middle or upper class? Heterosexual? Able-bodied? Educated? Male?

In the modules below, I intentionally suggest activities in specific modes: from whole group discussions, to each person sharing in the whole group (for a few minutes each, given time constraints) or with one or two others, to individual journaling. Hardly set in stone, these ideas are based on my experience of fruitful learning, as well as which setting can provide safety. Also, since we each learn differently, mixing up modalities serves various learning styles. Of course anyone can sit out any exercise, and you will decide what makes sense for your group. But dare to risk...

Now, ready, set? *Adelante!*

∽

Chapter One: ANTI-SEMITISM 101

MODULE 1 (Ch. 1) *You are now beginning the section*
"How Did Things Get So Hard?"

After check-in, break into pairs and each share for three minutes:

- What has been good about growing up as a Jewish girl, or as a Jew?
- What has been difficult?
- What are the earliest messages you remember receiving from your family about being Jewish?

These opening exercises are key to getting to know each other, for laying the ground-work for the rest of the learning and community building. Allow significant time, including for questions after each person shares. And remember to listen well.

~

In the whole group, take turns sharing (for several minutes each):

- Where your people come from, who they were/are, what you know about their struggles.
- Include your responses to the questions you discussed in pairs too, about growing up Jewish.

~

After everyone has shared and answered a few questions, discuss as a group: do you notice any common themes? Any differences?

Action: Pick one or two key themes from your discussion. Pay attention to these in your life until the next meeting. Notice how these themes come alive: journal about them, discuss with others, consider creating a collage or art or a song to bring to the group.

Action: Watch a movie, documentary, or TV show with Jewish content (examples: *Gentlemen's Agreement, The Longest Hatred, Fiddler on the Roof, Azi Aiyma (Come Mother), Yentl, Liberty Heights, Sophie's Choice, Routes of Exile: A Moroccan Jewish Odyssey, Schindler's List, The Pianist, Life Is Beautiful, The Partisans of Vilna, The Last Marranos, Yoo Hoo Mrs. Goldberg, Hollywoodism, Trees Cry for Rain, The Wedding Song, Borat, Seinfeld*). You could do this with others in the group. See what themes you notice, journal about your responses.

MODULE 2 (Ch. 1)

After check-in, take turns (for a few minutes each) telling any stories or fresh insights about the themes that arose at the last meeting. Discuss as a group.

~

Form triads and take ten minutes each to share:

- What role has anti-Semitism played in your life/how does it affect you today? (At home, school, work, with partners/friends, in political/social groups, on the Internet?)

- Have you ever been violently threatened or attacked (verbally/physically) as a Jew, or has this happened to any Jew you know? If so, how have you responded?

- Have you heard offensive statements (possibly masquerading as humor) about Jewish mothers, Jewish American Princesses, Jewish women?

- What would you like to never hear or read again, as a Jew?

~

Discuss in the group what you learned in your triads. Make sure everyone shares with the group what you never want to hear or read again, as a Jew.

~

Discuss as a group: how is the Nazi Holocaust similar to other genocides? How is it different?

~

Action: Before the next meeting, visit http://www.christianhegemony.org/ hosted by Paul Kivel. Journal about whatever you learn, whatever it brings up for you.

Action: Before the next meeting, spend an hour researching on the Internet, or reading a book chapter, about a Jewish ethnic minority group (Mizrahi, Sephardic, Ethiopian) other than your own (not Ashkenazi). How has this group been oppressed as Jews from outside the Jewish community? (Note: this is distinguished from racism within the Jewish community, which comes later.) Consider bringing this info back to the group as a poem, song, art, or in another creative form.

MODULE 3 (Ch. 1)

After check-in, take turns sharing your research (from last time) about anti-Semitism against Jewish ethnic minorities/Jews of color. Discuss.

~

Discuss as a group:

- In your life today, where do you see Jews functioning in a middle-role position?
- Are they representing decisions they are not actually making?
- Are they targeted as Jews in this role?

- Do you see ways they are colluding with decision-makers at the top, participating in dominating and/or exploiting other people?

~

In pairs or triads, for three minutes each:

- Compare anti-Semitism with discrimination against two other U.S. groups regarding: physical safety, economic security, communal solidarity.

~

Discuss as a group your insights from reading Kivel's Christian Hegemony website.

MODULE 4 (Ch. 1)

After check-in, share in triads for an hour or more, dividing up the time, each person choosing the questions which most resonate:

- Do you think that anti-Semitism has been discussed plenty, so you feel embarrassed to bring it up? Are you concerned that by asking others to deal with anti-Semitism you are "draining the movement" of precious energy that would be better used elsewhere?

- What examples can you remember of anti-Semitism that you did not confront, and why you didn't?

- What would you have needed to confront these? Did not confronting it cost you anything?

- If you have raised issues of anti-Semitism, did anyone say that you were being too sensitive, even paranoid? How did that affect you?

- If you strongly disagree with Israeli policies, are possibly also ashamed of those policies, do you feel that, as a result, you can't defend Jews wholeheartedly against anti-Semitism?

- Do you associate the struggle against anti-Semitism with conservatism? Why?

~

Discuss as a group. *Remember to listen well and avoid interrupting, to allow for different perspectives without attacking:*

- Have you been part of progressive groups where you felt attacked as a Jew, and/or where you felt Jews were invisibilized, disparaged, or snickered at if anyone raised a "Jewish issue" or brought up anti-Jewish attitudes or behavior?

- Have you seen signs at peace demonstrations that you consider anti-Jewish? Anti-Israel?

- What is the difference between these and signs that are pro-peace-and-justice? Explain and discuss why you think so.

- What examples do you notice of the misuse of the term anti-Semitism, where sincere critiques of unjust Israeli policies are dismissed as anti-Jewish?

Take turns sharing in the group what had the most impact for you in this chapter, and why?

~

Action: For the next meeting, journal about, and/or bring to the meeting, music, poetry, art, or movement to share the story of your racial identity. Respond to the questions:

- How would you place yourself on a continuum with white privilege on one end and racism on the other?

- How do you think others perceive you on this continuum?

- Have you been targeted by racism: if so, how and by whom?

- Have you benefitted from white privilege?

- Have you participated in racism yourself?

- How do the above interact with any vulnerability/how safe you feel as a Jew?

Chapter Two: INSIDER/OUTSIDER—Jews, Race, and Privilege

MODULE 1 (Ch. 2)

After check-in, take turns presenting the stories of your racial identities as described in the action from the last meeting (roughly ten minutes or less each). If by yourself, meet with a Jewish friend and talk about this, based on ideas in the chapter.

~

After everyone has shared, discuss as a group. Include any ways your experience differed in the region/ town/city where you grew up as opposed to where you live now?

~

Everyone journal about new insights you may have about the interplay in your life of race and racism, privilege, and Jewish vulnerability.

~

Share in ethnically/racially similar pairs. Depending on the composition of your group, decide what makes sense. (As pairs of Ashkenazim? As pairs of Mizrahi/ Sephardic/Jews of color/ethnic minority Jews?)

- How did you respond to this chapter? If you are white and Ashkenazi, did it give you any insights about your own attitudes and behavior towards Mizrahim, Sephardim, Jews of color, Jews of other racial/ethnic backgrounds? About anti-Semitism from gentiles of color?

- Whatever the ethnic/racial mix of the group, how does it feel for you being in this group?

- How is it feeling in your body to share about this?

~

If you are willing—Jews who are Mizrahi, Sephardic, multiracial, of color, of other Jewish ethnic/racial minorities—take turns sharing with the rest of the group:

- One thing you never want to hear again from a white Ashkenazi?
- What do you need from your allies?

~

Action: For the next meeting, read one chapter/section from *The Colors of Jews* (Chap 1, Note 52) and one chapter from *The Flying Camel* (Chap 1, Note 34). Come prepared to share something you learned that may have moved or surprised or triggered you: via poem, song, music, movement, skit, art, dance, or story.

MODULE 2 (Ch. 2)

After check-in, take turns sharing from your reading about Jewish multiculturalism and/or Jewish antiracism activism. Discuss as a group.

~

As a group, give yourselves an hour or more to discuss the following questions:

- Did the G.I. Bill have any effect on your family of origin?
- How is anti-Semitism similar to, and different from, U.S. racism?
- What examples have you noticed of Jewish racism against people of color, either organizationally or individually?
- What examples have you noticed of anti-Semitism by non-Jewish people of color towards Jews?
- Describe a situation in which you saw white Jews and people of color pitted against each other. How could this have been turned around, or still be turned around?

~

Discuss in pairs:

- When issues of Jewish racism come up, do you ever feel defensive?
- Do you feel guilty and/or ashamed of Jewish racism in this country and, as a result, feel that you can't defend Jews wholeheartedly against anti-Semitism?
- Can you acknowledge Jewish racism, work to combat it, and still feel Jewish pride? And still confront anti-Semitism?
- How is it feeling in your body to share about this right now?

~

Action: Consider going as a group to an event about Jewish multiculturalism or one that focuses on Jews who are Mizrahi, Sephardic, Jews of color, and/or from Africa or Asia. At the next meeting, present what that was like for you. If by yourself, do this with a friend.

Action for Ashkenazim: Consider supporting/getting involved with an organization led by Mizrahi or Sephardic Jews, Jews of color, Jews whose heritage is from Africa or Asia. And/or ask any Jews in your life from these backgrounds what they want or need from Ashkenazi allies.

MODULE 3 (Ch. 2)

After check-in, if you were able to go to an event about Jewish multiculturalism, or that focused on Jews who are Sephardic, Mizrahi, of color, and/or from Africa or Asia, share what that was like for you.

~

Devise and act out role-plays about how to interrupt racism against Jews of color (see examples in the chapter). You can do this as one group, or you can break into separate groups of white Ashkenazi and Jews of color/Jews who are Sephardic, Mizrahi, of African/Asian heritage, and do this as two groups. Then discuss together.

~

At the end of the meeting, shine a light on each group member in turn, while the group spends two or three minutes saying what they appreciate about that person. Not everyone needs to say something about each person, and these need not be long—but everyone gets a turn being appreciated.

Chapter Three: LET'S TALK ABOUT "JEWISH POWER": Rethinking Stereotypes

MODULE 1 (Ch. 3)

After check-in, brainstorm together and write all the Jewish stereotypes you can think of on a piece of newsprint:

- What common themes do you see?
- Are these characteristics true of any other groups? *The point is that these are rigidly attributed to all Jews, and most of them are in contrast to Christians and in response to Christian hegemony. Remember a key point in Chapter One: that stereotypes help justify the scapegoating, by making the group (Jews, in this case) seem deserving of mistreatment.*
- Now go through each stereotype and ask why it exists, how it functions/who it serves.
- Finally, take each stereotype and rename it in a positive way. For example, "cheap" could be reframed as "frugal." Write these reframed characteristics next to the original stereotype.

~

In triads, reflect on this exercise.

- Also share about any way this chapter speaks to your life.
- Do you disagree with any of the thinking in this chapter?

~

Discuss as a group: did reading this chapter give you anything new to consider?

~

Action: Before the next meeting, journal about your class background. As a Jew, what was good and what was difficult about it? What early messages did you get about class? What is both good and difficult about your current social class?

MODULE 2 (Ch. 3)

After check-in, take turns sharing in the group, five to ten minutes each:

- What was your parents' social class? Your grandparents'? Your great-grandparents'?
- What work did they do in their home country; what work did they do when they immigrated here? Make sure to include women's work, both inside and outside the home.
- What was your class background growing up: what was good, and what was difficult about that as a Jew?
- What early messages did you learn about class?
- Describe: your social class now, what work you do, and what is both good and challenging about being a member of this class?

~

Share in dyads:

- If you know someone is a Jew, do you tend to make assumptions about their class background?
- Has anyone made assumptions about your class background if they know you are Jewish?
- Were these assumptions correct? How did that feel?
- Have you ever tried to hide your class background?
- If you have assets and/or wealth, do you try to hide this? If so, why?
- How do you feel in your body right now?

~

Discuss all of the above as a group, including the question: why is class so important in discussions of anti-Semitism, especially regarding the stereotype of Jewish power?

MODULE 3 (Ch. 3)

After check-in, discuss in the group:

- What examples have you seen of Jewish power or influence being exaggerated, while the majority of white predominantly Christian power is less discussed?

- Are there any ways that you think allegations of "Jewish power" or influence may be justified, or where you feel confused about this?

- What examples of scapegoating Jews can you think of?

- Are there ways that you feel Jews have prospered in this country and so shouldn't complain?

~

Devise and act out role-plays using examples of accusations of Jews controlling Hollywood, the media, the financial system, and/or U.S. foreign policy. Respond in the role-play to those accusations. (Note: three people can all be in the responder role together, which is more engaging and less scary.)

~

Break into pairs to share how it felt both doing that and watching that. Then discuss as a group.

~

You have now finished the first section of the book, "How Did Things Get So Hard?" Journal for five minutes:

- How is reading this book and being in this group affecting you?

- What are you learning about yourself, about Jews? Be specific.

Discuss in the group.

Chapter Four: THE TRICKSTER IN OUR HEADS: *Internalized Jewish Oppression*

MODULE 1 (Ch. 4) –*You are now beginning the section "Wrestling with the Voices."*

After check-in, share in triads: three key messages in your head that try to convince you there is something wrong with you, as a Jew; possibly to try to make you believe you are "weird" in some way.

~

Create a brief impromptu skit about these (go for humor!) and present to the group.

~

Get back into your triad and share for five minutes each:

- Any ways the behavior of another Jew has triggered you

- Do you try to avoid acting like this person acts, feeling that you don't want to be like this person?

- Who does this person remind you of? (This may provide a clue about your internalized anti-Jewish prejudice: could your feelings be less about this person, and more about how you learned to feel bad about your people and yourself?)

~

Journal for five minutes about your insights.

~

Discuss as a group:

- Your learnings about the above.
- Does this chapter offer you new perspectives?
- What overlap do you see between internalized anti-Jewishness and voices of internalized racism, sexism, homophobia/transphobia, ableism, ageism, classism?

~

Action: Before the next meeting, if possible, interview at least one adult in your family about how anti-Semitism has affected them. Also ask what Jewishness means in your family, from their perspective. This can provide insights into messages you likely received as a child. Notice key themes (possibly including fear, shame, denial, ambivalence, upward mobility, anger, silence, powerlessness, guilt).

MODULE 2 (Ch. 4)

After check-in, take turns sharing what you learned from your family interview(s) and how you felt about that.

~

Stand up Exercise.[2]—This is a powerful exercise, an opportunity to directly see what kind of anti-Semitism Jews face, and how different Jews internalize it. How, as Jews, we are not alone in what we have experienced. It's important to remember that this is the result of living in a Christian-dominated society, and none of these experiences or feelings are our fault. It can be eye-opening to non-Jews to see the effects of anti-Semitism, to understand why we feel vulnerable.

~

Whoever leads this exercise reads the following:

For the Jews, if you are able, stand anytime a statement applies to you; otherwise, if you are able, raise your hand. Stay standing (or keep hand raised) until I ask you to sit back down, or lower your arm. If the statement applies to you, but you do not want to stand or raise your hand, that's fine.

For everyone, please remain silent. Look around and notice who is standing or has an arm raised. Pay attention to any thoughts, feelings, reactions that you have.

(**Note to leader:** Allow plenty of time, do not rush. After reading each statement, while people are standing or have an arm raised, wait a few seconds: then say gently: "Thank you, please sit down, or lower your arms.")

ACTION-ORIENTED READER'S GUIDE

Please stand up (or raise your hand) if:

1. You have ever been called names because you are a Jew, including J.A.P., or Jewish mother.

2. You have heard demeaning jokes told about Jews.

3. You have been treated unfairly at school or work because you are a Jew.

4. You have ever felt out of place because you are a Jew.

5. You have ever felt responsible for, or felt the need to apologize for, the actions of other Jews or of Israel.

Everyone take a few deep breaths...

6. You ever felt the need to hide or downplay being Jewish for fear of being judged or treated differently.

7. You have ever been told that the Nazi Holocaust did not happen, or that Jews should stop making such a big deal about it.

8. You have ever been told that Jews in Arab countries had an easy time of it.

9. You did not ask for what you want or need for fear of being called too pushy, loud, or demanding.

10. You had to choose between a religious observance and a work or school requirement.

11. You have been told that anti-Semitism is not that important.

Everyone take a few deep breaths...

12. You have been afraid to wear something that visibly identified you as Jewish.

13. You have been told that you "look Jewish."

14. You have been told that you "don't look Jewish."

15. You learned that Jewish men are nerdy, intellectual, not athletic, not sexual.

16. You learned that Jewish women are domineering, smothering, unattractive.

17. You have wished you weren't Jewish.

18. You have pretended you weren't Jewish.

19. You have been told that all Jews like lox and bagels and matzoh ball soup, so what's wrong with you?

Everyone take a few deep breaths...

20. Non-Jews or other Jews have ever seemed to perceive you as "too Jewish."

21. You ever felt grateful that you weren't as visible as "those other Jews."

22. You ever felt that anti-Semitism gets too much attention.

23. You ever felt you weren't really "Jewish enough" because you:

- Don't know Hebrew or Yiddish, Ladino or Judeo-Arabic

- *Don't know Jewish songs, prayers, dances*
- *Didn't have a Bar/Bat Mitzvah*
- *Didn't celebrate some/many/enough holidays*
- *Don't like or aren't familiar with "Jewish" (whatever that means to you) foods*
- *You have been told you can't be Jewish, because you are black or Arab or Latino or Native American or Asian/Pacific Islander or mixed*

24. *You ever felt that other Jews complain too much.*

Everyone take a few deep breaths...

25. *You ever felt uncomfortable when you saw someone wearing a yarmulke in public.*
26. *You've ever had dreams or waking nightmares about being in prison or in a concentration camp.*
27. *At times you imagine dying a violent death.*
28. *You worry that people resent you for being too smart or too talkative.*
29. *You find yourself working very hard on every liberation issue other than anti-Semitism or Jewish liberation.*

Everyone take a few deep breaths...

30. *You ever worked in a social justice movement/organization/project where proportionately there were more Jews in the organization than in the U.S. population (around 1.8 percent) and the Jews did not visibly identify as Jews.*
31. *You ever felt or heard that Jews should be held to a higher standard.*
32. *You ever heard or have been told that:*

- *Jews have lots of money*
- *Jews are sneaky, stingy, greedy, dishonest, conniving*
- *The "Jewish lobby" controls U.S. foreign policy*
- *Jews control the banks, media, Hollywood*

33. *You often feel like you aren't doing enough.*

Everyone take a few deep breaths...

~

Break into pairs and take turns sharing how it felt for you to do this. Notice what you are feeling in your body. If this is a mixed group, make sure that Jews are with other Jews.

~

Discuss as a group.

~

Action: Take some time soon after this exercise to journal about any other feelings or insights that come up. Make sure to check in with someone else in the group to share these before the next meeting.

Chapter Five: SUCKLED ON WORRY

MODULE 1 *(Ch. 5)*

After check-in, take ten minutes to journal about any ways that fear has played a significant role in your life:

- Does this connect to your being a Jew?

- In your family did you notice dynamics of worry, urgency, anxiety, hypervigilance, panic? Of fear masquerading as control? How did this affect you as a child?

- Do you see this pattern in yourself now? How does it affect your life?

- If you are descended from a Nazi Holocaust survivor, do you feel a connection between your life now and whatever happened to your parent/grandparent/family member?

- If you are not descended from a Nazi Holocaust survivor, do you feel a connection between your life now and the Holocaust?

- Can you envision confronting your fear, especially the part related to your Jewish identity? What kind of support would you need? Can you ask your group, or your community, for support?

~

Everyone take turns sharing about this in the group, as much as you feel willing to, up to ten minutes each. *Feel free to use movement, sound, art, dance, to express yourself. When it is your turn to share, go slowly, take your time. Allow any feelings to be there: shake if you feel like it, or if tears come, then let them. When you are not the one sharing, listen with care, avoid interrupting, do not try to "comfort" anyone out of their feelings, so they get a chance to fully express and release their pain.*

~

Break into pairs for any other sharing people want to do, including releasing feelings. Notice how you feel in your body. Can you distinguish between *feeling* fear, but not *acting* on it?

~

Discuss as a group:

- What resonated for you in this chapter, triggered you, or gave you a new perspective?

- Do you relate at all to Emily's experience about not having the luxury of feeling "soft," like you are always fighting on the front lines?

Chapter Six: "HELLO ASSIMILATION, GOODBYE PERSECUTION"

MODULE 1 (Ch. 6)

After check-in, introduce the "shame scarf" (someone needs to bring a transparent scarf for the group to use).[3] *If everyone is willing, from now on if you want to share about something, but you feel some shame and can't look others in the eye, or do not want to be seen, you can put the "shame scarf" over your head while you talk. Then whenever you can, remove the scarf and look others in the eye: a key step to self-acceptance.*

Someone reads this part aloud slowly, pausing for a minute between each question:

Please close your eyes, and take some deep breaths. Think about your childhood growing up as a Jew. Notice the first thoughts and associations that come up.

- Are there any ways you would describe your family of origin as assimilated? As unassimilated? Think of specifics.

- What do you know of your family's history that might have led to this?

- Did your family encourage assimilation? If so, did you benefit from that? Did you lose anything?

- If you and your family are white, are there any ways your family might have colluded with racism to play it safe?

- Did your family resist assimilation? If so, what was that like for you as a child?

- Does your class background play a role in this picture?

- Was your family upwardly mobile?

- What was it like for you as a Jew growing up in your neighborhood? Who was there?

- How did others respond to your family?

- Is your current family and/or lifestyle more or less assimilated than when you were a child?

- How does this relate to how you feel as a Jew today?

Take ten minutes to write or draw any insights in your journals.

~

Take turns sharing in the group, up to ten minutes each. Feel free to use art, sound, movement, dance. Remember that the "shame scarf" is available if anyone wants/needs to use it.

~

Break into dyads to share any feelings that arose. Notice how you feel in your body. Or if the group prefers, discuss as a group.

MODULE 2 (Ch. 6)

After check-in, discuss as a whole group—or break into two smaller groups, with each team choosing two or three of these questions to focus on:

- Do you relate at all now, or did you growing up, to the concept: "keep your Jewish self hidden"?

- Are there ways you feel that anti-Semitism exists, but is "not really important"? Explain.

- What do you see as the differences between self-hate and assimilation?

- What do you think of the idea that "No Jew is ever completely assimilated"?

- Did you get messages in your family or community about the importance of having Jewish children, to not let the Jewish people die? If so, has this affected your life?

~

Take a few minutes to reflect and write in your journal about any decisions you make in your day-to-day life to stay safe: physically, emotionally, or in other ways. How do you feel about that?

Share in pairs.

Chapter Seven: "THERE IS A 'REAL' JEWISH WOMAN AND I AM NOT HER": Too Much/Not Enough

MODULE 1 (Ch. 7)

After check-in, journal for five minutes about the following questions:

- In what ways (if any) do you feel "too Jewish"? Does this relate to feeling "not Christian enough"?

- Do you repress yourself in hopes that no one will identify you with Jewish stereotypes?

~

Break into triads and share from the above.

- Strategize together: how could you rename/reframe these, from something negative to positive?

- Now take turns responding:

  Do you feel that Jews draw too much attention to themselves? Which Jewish stereotypes most make you cringe? Give examples, being sensitive to who is in your group.

- Discuss together: notice any similarities in what you have shared about yourselves.

As a large group, share insights from examining the questions above.

- Do you have any new learning about the influence of Christian hegemony on our lives?

- Then together devise an exercise about embracing different stereotypes that make your skin crawl. Spend time trying it out, with everyone participating — and pay attention to how your body feels.

~

Action: Before the next group, spend fifteen minutes doing free-association writing in your journal about your Jewish body, whatever comes up spontaneously.

Make sure to bring a large roll of newsprint and lots of crayons and markers to the next meeting, and find a space for the next session that feels particularly safe and private, not where someone else could walk through or see from outside.

MODULE 2 (Ch. 7)

After check-in, everyone is going to do an exercise that tells the story of your Jewish body. *Approach this exercise with special care. Some of us have eating disorders related to our bodies. Some of us have had surgeries to change our bodies; some of our bodies have changed due to disease. Some of us are disabled. Some of us have lost or gained large amounts of weight. Some of us have been physically or sexually abused. We hold a lot in our bodies, and we want to be sensitive to each other and to ourselves. Of course anyone is free to sit this out — but remember, we are in this for the healing!*

~

In pairs, take turns lying down and outlining each other's bodies on the butcher paper.

- Then spend half an hour coloring in your drawing, telling the story of your Jewish body, whatever that is. Note the parts of your Jewish body you feel good about, and the parts you struggle to feel good about. *If any feelings come up while doing this, let them be there; be present for one another, while not trying to comfort anyone out of their feelings.*

- If by yourself, do this with a friend and share as suggested below.

- Get back into your pair to share, including how your body feels.

~

In the whole group, take turns using your drawing to tell a story of your body, whatever you are willing to share. If possible, include what you feel good about and what feels hard.

~

Discuss as a group:

- Did you notice any patterns in what people liked or didn't like about our bodies?
- Did you notice any standard of beauty that as Jews we unconsciously learn to refer to?

~

As a group, end by going around the circle and asking everyone to give an Appreciation of the person to their left—and then to give an Appreciation of themselves.

~

Action: Soon after this meeting, journal about what this experience was like. Did you gain insights? Before the next meeting, check in with someone in the group about how you felt, anything you learned.

MODULE 3 (Ch. 7)

After check-in, take five minutes and journal about all the ways (if any) you feel "not Jewish enough." Then make a list of everything Jewish you want to learn more about.

~

In the group, take turns sharing any ways you feel "not Jewish enough." Then also share your list of anything Jewish you want to learn more about. Find out if anyone in the group has resources/information that other group members would like to learn. Spend the bulk of this meeting time sharing with each other in whatever ways make sense (either all-group or divided into interest groups): Teaching songs or dances, including from different ethnic traditions? Mizrahi chants? Explaining rituals or prayers? History lessons? Stories of Yiddish theater? Sharing recipes? Hebrew/Judeo-Arabic/Yiddish/ Ladino lessons? If there is interest, make plans to meet outside the group to share more. *Remember: there are as many different ways to be Jewish as there are Jews.*

~

Discuss anything else in this chapter that resonates or gave you something new to think about.

~

Action: Consider subscribing to Jewish magazines or journals, reading blogs, attending organizational meetings or events. Consider going with someone in the group.

Make sure to bring art supplies, percussive musical instruments, dance music, even sports equipment, to the next meeting.

Chapter Eight: PUSH/PUSH/PUSH FOR PERFECTION

MODULE 1 (Ch. 8)

Take turns doing in-depth check-ins about how your life is going. Since you are now about halfway through the book, how is reading it and meeting in the group affecting your life?

~

Discuss as a group:

- In your family, did you ever feel others were disappointed in you because you made mistakes, were not perfect? What effect has that had?
- Did you ever feel that you needed to know everything before you could speak about a topic?
- Shout out any topics related to anti-Semitism and/or Jewishness that you haven't brought up because you were afraid of being criticized for not having a good enough analysis.

~

Share in pairs:

- Are there other ways that this chapter relates to your own life? Explain.
- Did it give you anything new to think about?

~

Bring out the art supplies, percussive musical instruments, dance music, sports equipment. Spend some time together (inside or outside) just playing! Without an agenda or game plan or anything you need to accomplish.

~

Action: For the next week or more, go easy on yourself. Give yourself room to mess up—and still be feel good about who you are. Journal (or not!) about how this feels.

Chapter Nine: "WHERE DO I BELONG?"

MODULE 1 (Ch. 9)

After check-in, take turns sharing all together:

- How do you feel similar to other Jews in the group?
- How do you feel different, maybe even "the only one"?
- Who are the "real" Jews? Are you one?

~

Someone reads this aloud, slowly:

Please close your eyes, take a deep breath. Now think of a time when you felt you belonged, as a Jew. Was it because someone reached out to you? Or what made you feel that way? And how did it feel? (Pause for ten seconds or so.)

Take another deep breath. Now think of a time when you felt you didn't belong as a Jew. What made you feel this way? Have you ever felt you didn't belong, period? Or that you didn't belong with other Jews? (Possibly as a Jew of color, or because you were Mizrahi, or Sephardic or with African or Asian heritage. Or because you were working class, poor, genderqueer or trans, disabled, old or young?) (Pause for ten seconds or so.)

Everyone journal, or draw, or move around for five minutes.

~

Now break into pairs and take turns sharing what came up for you. Notice how you feel in your body.

~

Discuss in the group the concept suggested by Kyla Wazan Tompkins, that "Home, I have learned, is where we sit down and decide to build it." How could this relate to your own Jewish life?

Chapter Ten: TAKING EGYPT OUT OF THE JEWS

If you are in a group, please approach these next three meetings with special care. Remember to listen well, avoid interrupting, tolerate differences. Practice "trying on" new perspectives. Again, disagreements are fine, verbal attacks are not.

One suggestion: try all-group discussions by going around the circle for several rounds, everyone taking turns speaking (okay to set time limits), without people "cross-talking" or specifically referring to what someone else said. The focus is on sharing, not on all agreeing to one conclusion. Then break into pairs to release feelings that come up.

MODULE 1 (Ch. 10)

After check-in, everyone journal for five minutes about all the ways you feel like a victim, as a Jew (including as a Jewish woman, genderqueer, old/young, disabled, struggling economically or with chronic illness, an abuse survivor, other). Be honest, give examples.

Share in pairs.

~

Next, altogether, everyone create a movement, a body stance, or a sound that shows how "victim" feels to you as a Jew. Hold it/express it for thirty seconds. Notice anything you feel in your body.

Then take turns sharing:

• How is it to feel like a victim in any way? How does this manifest for you specifically?

- Does it get in your way?
- Does fear of extermination live anywhere inside of you? Even if this does not feel conscious, how could such underlying fear actually be showing itself?

~

Discuss as a group the words of Warsaw Ghetto survivor Irena Klepfisz, that keeping the Nazi Holocaust "at the center of our Jewishness" leaves us "stuck in the past," committed to "a lifetime of mourning," so that we are unable to "engage with the present." Instead, Klepfisz urges us to recontextualize the Shoah— to move "toward a Jewish future that is *informed, but not defined*" by it. How do you respond to this idea?

~

Share in pairs any ways you have noticed how 'hurt people hurt."

Discuss in the group.

~

Action: Before the next meeting, spend half an hour visiting/reading at least one Israeli feminist peace activist website (Women's Coalition for a Just Peace, Who Profits, New Profile, Israeli Women in Black, Machsom Watch), or one other Israeli human-rights website (Israeli Committee Against House Demolitions, Gush Shalom, Breaking the Silence, Combatants for Peace, Rabbis for Human Rights, B'Tselem, Ta'ayush). ALSO, spend half an hour visiting/reading one Palestinian human-rights website (the Jerusalem Center for Women, the Palestinian Counseling Center, the Gaza Center for Mental Health, The Palestine Center for Rapprochement Between People, MIFTAH, Palestinian Centre for Human Rights, Palestinian BDS National Committee). Journal your reflections about what you read, what you learn.

Action: If you have time: read one or two chapters of Sandy Tolan's book *The Lemon Tree.*

MODULE 2 (Ch. 10)

After check-in, share in pairs:

- How do you feel when you hear the word "Israel"?
- When you hear the word "Palestine"?
- Do you feel connected to Israelis? To Palestinians? If so, how?

~

Everyone take five to ten minutes to journal your own perspective, in response to key ideas in this chapter about Jews projecting (and being manipulated to project) our fears onto Palestinians. Also include what "never again" means for you.

As a group, take turns sharing some of what you wrote.

~

Take turns reading aloud in the group the Chapter Ten subsection "Let Gaza Live," up until the "Gaza Freedom Flotilla" subsection.

~

In pairs, share:

- How did you respond to the Israeli invasion of Gaza in 2008–2009?

- How do you see Jews functioning as oppressors today?[4] How do you feel about that?

- What can be done about it?

~

In the group, discuss:

- Anything you want to share from the questions above.

- Responses from reading the Israeli and Palestinian websites, and/or *The Lemon Tree*, as well as anything you know about the Israeli peace movement and the Palestinian liberation movement, including the movement for Boycott, Divestment, and Sanctions.

- Any ways you notice that U.S. Middle East policy uses Israel?

~

Action: Before the next meeting, scan Chapters Four–Ten. Journal about how these chapters are impacting you.

MODULE 3 (Ch. 10)

After check-in, share in pairs:

- What is your experience in the U.S. institutional Jewish community, if any?

- Do you agree or disagree with one of this chapter's points, that these institutions perpetuate ideas that Jews are still victims, and that the U.S. Jewish establishment believes this is true?

~

Discuss in the group any reflections from sharing in pairs.

- How can we work with any Jewish communities in our lives to become more aware of how internalized victimization operates in us, and how we allow our fear to be manipulated? Think of actual Jewish communities you know.

- How can we, as Elly said, "get out from under that way of thinking?"

~

Share in pairs:

- Did any of this chapter challenge, or upset, or confuse you?

- Has this reading led you to any new perspectives?

- In the group, take a chunk of time for everyone to share two key reflections from this section "Wrestling with the Voices": what impact the reading or group is having on you, what you are learning.

~

Go around the circle and offer an Appreciation of the person to your right.

~

Action: If applicable, for the next meeting bring any photos, songs, or memorabilia of your social justice activism as a visible Jew.

Chapter Eleven: ON THE FRONT LINES: An Activist's Vignettes

MODULE 1 (Ch. 11) *You are now beginning the section "Creating a Future."*

After check-in, take turns sharing in the group:

- Have you ever felt "on the front lines" as a Jew? If so, share a highlight from that experience.
- What was difficult?
- What have you learned?
- Share any photos, songs, memorabilia that you brought to illustrate.
- If you are a social justice activist, though not on the "front lines," respond to the same questions above.

~

Discuss as a group:

- Are there any ways that being a Jew brings up complexities for you in your activism? Explain.
- Do you relate to the concept of activism as therapy, of taking action partly to help you deal with/work through feelings about injustice in the world?

~

Share in pairs:

- How did you respond to this chapter?
- Did it give you any new perspectives?

~

Action: Before the next meeting, journal about the internalized anti-Jewish messages in your head right now that have the most sting. What purpose have they served?

Make sure someone brings rolls of newsprint and bright markers to the next meeting.

Chapter Twelve: CRACKING THE CODE OF OUR CONDITIONING

MODULE 1 (Ch. 12)

After check-in, break into triads. Choose two internalized anti-Jewish messages that really affect you now (even if you have used them before in these exercises):

- Strategize together: how could you positively express these messages? (Examples: "I'm loud!" "I trust my thinking.")

- Write out the reframed messages in LARGE print on newsprint, using BRIGHT markers. Tape these onto the wall, so everyone can see.

~

With the whole group:

- Take turns saying out loud what you wrote on the butcher paper. Ask the group to shout it back to you!

- Discuss other ways to resist your various internalized messages (such as humor: "Thank you for sharing—now goodbye!" to the voice in your head).

~

Back in your triad:

- Think of a key struggle that is connected to your being a Jewish woman or Jewish trans/genderqueer.

- Strategize together to imagine looking at your situation differently, compiling the "evidence" to lead to a different conclusion, choosing an *interpretation* that *empowers* you (see examples in the chapter).

- Choose a way to "act in opposition" to your most debilitating internalized messages (perhaps the one above): to act "as if." For example, "How would I be if I felt powerful, or knew I belonged, or knew I mattered? Right now?"

~

Take five minutes to write both of these in your journal. **Action:** Try to live these until the next meeting; see what comes up.

~

Action: Journal for ten minutes about "What would my life be like without anti-Semitism and internalized oppression?" Take half an hour and use music, poetry, dance, movement, art, or a skit to play with this idea. Bring whatever you come up with to share with the group; it doesn't need to be polished, just something that expresses your sense of possibility.

MODULE 2 (Ch. 12)

After check-in, take turns sharing:

- Your experience since the last meeting, based on reinterpreting/reframing a significant struggle for you.
- Your experience "acting in opposition."
- How did this go, what did you learn?

~

Reflect together in the group about everyone's experiences. Can you make any meaning from this?

~

Now take turns in the group sharing your project about what your life could be like without anti-Semitism and internalized anti-Jewishness. Have fun, enjoy!

~

Action: Try bringing the concept and practice of appreciating each other to another Jewish group you are part of.

Make sure someone brings rolls of newsprint and markers to the next meeting.

Chapter Thirteen: JEWISH-POSITIVE

MODULE 1 (Ch. 13)

After check-in, take turns sharing in the group:

- What you love about being a Jewish woman, or about being Jewish trans/ genderqueer?
- What you appreciate about Jews in general?
- What brings you joy as a Jew? What do you notice in your body as you say this?

Discuss as a group. What do you notice?

~

Brainstorm together and write on newsprint: what can you add to Bonnie Morris' list about "What's a Jewish Woman?" Have fun with this!

~

In triads, share:

- Three ways you appreciate yourself as a Jew.
- Something that you do in your life that you consider Jewish-positive. (One example: do you use the structure of the Jewish calendar and rituals to help you navigate the process of conscious Jewish living?)
- How does this add to your life?

~

Discuss as a group:

- In your day-to-day life, are you 1) usually around other Jews, 2) sometimes around other Jews, 3) often the only Jew? How does that feel?
- What is the quality of your relationships with Christians in your life? With Muslims, or other gentiles? Are these relationships different than with Jews, and if so, how—or can you even generalize about this?
- Strategize ways to raise Jewish issues that you care about in Christian or gentile environments, and about how to make sure you have support. Be specific.

~

Action: Before the meeting ends, make plans with someone in your group, perhaps with the whole group, to attend a Jewish event that you wouldn't ordinarily go to (whether a film, concert, lecture, ethnic event, benefit, political event), even if it is in the future.

If by yourself, do this with a friend.

Action if you have time: Spend an hour on the Jewish Women's Archive website (jwa.org), investigate whatever sparks your interest.

Action if you have time: Before the next meeting, read poetry, a story, an article, a play—by a Jew, something that appeals to you but that you haven't read before. Journal about it: are there ways that it strikes you as "Jewish"? If so, what do you like/not like about that?

MODULE 2 (Ch. 13)

As part of your check-in, if applicable, share your experience attending the Jewish event suggested as an Action at the previous meeting.

~

Take turns sharing in the group:

- How are you Jewishly visible? When does that feel good? Difficult?
- Can you remember times when you consciously stayed invisible as a Jew? Why? How did that feel?
- What do you think you would never do, that would make you visible/more visible as a Jew? Why not? How does it feel in your body to say this?

~

Discuss together any ways you are willing to risk being more visible as a Jew. (Some possibilities: wearing a kippah, jewelry, speaking out as a Jew at a meeting/public event, writing an Op-Ed/letter to the editor as a Jew, organizing a Jewish event and inviting gentiles.)

~

As a group, think about ways that anti-Semitism can appear in your life, both personally and organizationally, from the Right and the Left. Develop a few role-plays and try these out together, about thoughtful strategies for intervening and educating about anti-Semitism—with several of you playing the "responder" role at one time, to try out different responses. Discuss how it feels to do this.

~

In pairs, notice any groups you are part of and their awareness of Jewish issues and anti-Semitism. If it is not high, what can you do to raise awareness? Who can support you?

~

Action: Choose one of the two below to do before the next meeting, or soon:

1. Make a date with a Jewish elder. (A relative is fine, if you don't already know much of their story.) Ask about their Jewish life: what have they enjoyed, what has been particularly difficult? (Obviously you cannot expect a whole life story, unless you are planning to spend more time together.) Journal about the impact this has on you.

2. Talk to some Jewish children or young people you know (including your own children or relatives). Find out what Jewish culture means to them, if they relate to it at all.

MODULE 3 (Ch. 13)
After check-in, reflect for a few minutes about a Jew who has had a positive influence on you. Then take turns sharing in the group. Feel free to use movement, music, or other creativity.

~

Journal for five minutes:

- Who are some of the hardest Jews for you to feel connected to, either individuals with certain traits, or specific groups? Why?

- What would it take to claim your connection to them as Jews, to find any common ground? Thinking about this, how does it feel in your body right now?

- How could you experiment with claiming your connection to all Jews?

~

Take turns sharing in triads your responses to the above.

~

As a group, practice critiquing the positions/policies of other Jews without demonizing them as individuals, without playing into a Good Jew/Bad Jew dynamic. This can be challenging. Discuss.

~

Share in pairs:

- Can you imagine deciding to never again turn your back on any Jewish woman?

- To accept her for whoever she is, as a person, even if you disagree with her behavior?

- To consider the idea that these characteristics, this behavior, may be what she has developed to survive anti-Semitism? Sexism? Some other oppression?

~

As a group, discuss Melanie Kaye/Kantrowitz's idea of Diasporism, touched on in this chapter and throughout this book.

- What would it mean to your Jewish life to de-emphasize a nationalist focus on Israel and Zionism as core to U.S. Jewish identity?

- To actively try to counter assimilation in your life?

- How do you respond, instead, to focusing on creating Jewish-positive lives right here, to emphasize a vibrant diverse antiracist Jewishness as core to your identity?

~

Journal about the impact this discussion has on you.

~

Action: Until the next meeting, practice living with the idea "These are my people," applying it to Jews you encounter. Journal about what this brings up for you.

MODULE 4 (Ch. 13)

As part of your check-in, share what happened for you in living with the phrase "These are my people." Discuss together.

~

Break into pairs and brainstorm a step you could take toward making Jewish multiculturalism more visible.

~

Take turns sharing this step in the group. Commit to doing it by a given time and reporting back to the group.

~

Divide into two groups: white Ashkenazim; and Mizrahim/Sephardim/Jews of color, Jews of African/Asian heritage, mixed (or however you identify). In each group, brainstorm ways to build inclusivity of Jews who are not white Ashkenazi into predominantly Ashkenazi organizations, at events, on planning teams and boards.

~

In the whole group, report on the plans each team came up with.

Then discuss together:

- Consider organizing a cultural event that includes representation by several different Jewish ethnicities.
- Brainstorm: How would you design such an event?
- How would you pull together the planning group?

~

Break into pairs and share any feelings that came up in talking about these issues together. Notice any feelings in your body right now?

~

Action: Before the next meeting, spend an hour researching one Jewish resistance story from any period in history, by any Jews, and plan to bring it to the group, using poetry, song, movement, art, theater, story-telling.

Action: If time: make a plan to attend a class at your synagogue, Jewish community center, or elsewhere about a Jewish topic that interests you. Find someone to go with you!

Have someone check out from your university or other library a copy of the video Not in Our Town, *(based on the true story of allies taking action in Billings, MT) and bring it to the next meeting.*

MODULE 5 (Ch. 13)

After check-in, take turns sharing your Jewish resistance story.

~

In the whole group, one person leads this exercise, taking your time: *Please close your eyes and take a deep breath. Feel your body. Now think of a time when someone was an ally to you—either as a Jew or in one of your other identities. Maybe when you were a small child, maybe in school? Maybe at work, or in your neighborhood? Or at an event? Or in your relationship? What did they do? How did that impact you? How does it feel in your body remembering this?* Take turns sharing in the group.

~

Discuss as a group any ways that you have been an ally to someone else.

- Have there ever been hate crimes in your community?
- Next time, how could you respond, individually and/or as a group?

~

Watch *Not in Our Town* together, and then discuss what you could do if something like this happened to Jews or to other groups.

~

Action: For the next meeting, delegate one or more members to bring some group movement or voice exercises to do together—or possibly a group (not individual) art or psychodrama project—that relates to a Jewish theme your group has been working on.

Action if you have time: Find a Jewish cultural event you want to attend, and ask a gentile friend to join you (not someone who often comes to such events with you). Afterwards, talk about what that was like for both of you, and report back to the group.

Action for the future: Consider organizing a group potluck, and ask everyone to bring an ally who is not Jewish. At the potluck, make time for everyone to share what you appreciate about your ally and why you invited this person. Also, create a simple way to share some of what the group has learned, and how that has affected you.

Action for the future: Consider having a special session of the group, and bringing in a practitioner to teach breathwork or somatic practices, aikido or co-counseling, art or music therapy, yoga or meditation.

Chapter Fourteen: LIBERATORY HEALING

MODULE 1 (Ch. 14)

As part of your check-in, if applicable, share your experience going to a Jewish event with a gentile friend.

~

In pairs, take turns sharing:

- What was your response to the various modalities suggested in this chapter: art, dance, movement, psychodrama, co-counseling, somatic, and breathwork?

~

Discuss as a group:

- Do you use/have you ever used any of the holistic tools suggested in this chapter? If so, what has that experience been like for you?

- What is one healing process you might consider using, and why?

- What do you think of the idea that it is important to involve your whole body in the recovery process?

~

As a group, experiment during the meeting with the voice/movement/art/psychodrama exercise(s) or project(s) that any group members are leading for this session, related to a Jewish theme you have been working on (as suggested at the end of the previous module).

Afterwards reflect on this experience together:

- How did it affect you? Did you notice any feelings in your body?

- What was it like to do this as a group?

~

Action: Before the next meeting, try Julia Cameron's Morning Pages exercise, for one week. Afterwards, journal about what this was like for you.

Action: Spend an hour before the next meeting reading about/researching one example of Jewish social justice activism in the U.S. that happened before you were born, AND one that is occurring now. For both of these, choose something that you didn't know much about already.

- Who led/is leading it?
- What do you find powerful, possibly surprising, about what they are doing?
- How does it relate to Jewish values?

For the next meeting, everyone bring art supplies, scissors and glue, and old magazines that can be cut up.

Chapter Fifteen: HOPE INTO PRACTICE: Choosing Justice Despite Our Fears

MODULE 1 (Ch. 15)

After check-in, take turns sharing from last meeting's action your research of Jewish social justice activism, Then and Now:

- Who is/was leading it?
- What is/was particularly powerful, possibly surprising?
- How does/did it relate to Jewish values?

~

Journal in response to the paraphrased version of Rabbi Tarfon's quote: "We do not need to complete The Work in this lifetime, but neither can we refuse to do our unique part."

- What does it mean to you to do your "unique part"? How does this feel in your body?
- If you are not doing so already, what is one step you would be willing to take, to work on a social justice issue as a visible Jew?
- If you are already doing this work, what would be a bold new step you could take to move the work forward?
- Also: how can you help broaden community support for a Jewish justice issue?

In the group, take turns sharing the above.

~

At the meeting, use any of the art supplies you've brought and spend time together creating a collage or other art project about how you use, or can use, your Jewishness as a platform for social action. Some folks may want to work together to write a song or spoken word about this. Share with the group.

~

Action: Before the next meeting, learn about a Jew under 36 who is helping lead social justice work, either in a Jewish group or visibly as a Jew in a non-Jewish group—ideally in your community. Consider reaching out to this leader to learn more about what this leader is doing; ask how you can support the work.

MODULE 2 (Ch. 15)

After check-in, take turns sharing anything you learned about a leader under 36, any impact this had on you.

~

Share in pairs:

- Imagine an example for yourself, of choosing justice despite fears you may have.
- What is one step you could take to speak out as a visible Jew to help bring justice to an oppressed (non-Jewish) group in your community?
- Can you imagine encouraging the Jewish community to support this issue?

In the group, take turns sharing about the above.

~

Then, as a group, discuss any responses you have to this chapter overall, except for the part about Israel-Palestine, which you will work on in the next meeting.

~

Action: Before the next meeting, spend half an hour reading the website of a U.S. Jewish group working for justice in Israel-Palestine (see examples in the chapter, including YoungJewishProud.org, or you may have others in your community).

Action if you have time: Try to learn about someone in your community who is working for justice in Israel-Palestine as a visible Jew. Plan to meet and listen to their perspective. Consider inviting this activist to speak to any Jewish or other group you are part of. Consider also asking how you can support the work.

Action for the future: Perhaps volunteer for a Jewish social justice group in your area, even briefly. Ask to interview one of the Jewish staff about the work and how it connects to their Jewishness.

MODULE 3 (Ch. 15)

After check-in, share in pairs:

- Whatever you learned from reading the website of the U.S. Israel-Palestine group, how you felt about it.
- What is one step you would be willing to take to help bring justice and security to Israel and Palestine?
- Notice any feelings in your body right now.

~

In the group, take turns sharing the step you will take for justice in Israel/Palestine.

Discuss at length as a group:

- What response did you have to the website of the U.S. group?
- Any concerns, questions, or ideas you have as a Jew about Israel-Palestine, and what the role is for U.S. Jews in working for peace.

~

In pairs, think of another step you will take, based on issues covered in this book or in your groups—whether recovering from your internalized Jewish oppression, getting involved in a social justice project, confronting anti-Semitism—and commit to that.

Write this in your journal.

~

Action: Before the next meeting, journal about:

- your ideas for bringing the various practices in this book to any Jewish communities. What would your next steps be? Notice any feelings in your body this brings up.
- a few key learnings from reading the book and being in the group. Include what has been most challenging for you? Most rewarding?

Action: Before the next meeting, ask someone you know who identifies as Christian to read this book as your ally. Explain why this is important to you. Then once they read it, plan to talk together about it. Journal about what this process is like for you.

MODULE 4 (Ch. 15)

After check-in, discuss as a group:

- How it was for you to ask someone you know who identifies as Christian to read this book as your ally?
- Ideas you have for bringing the concepts and practices in this book to Jews and Jewish communities. (Such as: internalized anti-Semitism, Jewish multiculturalism, Israel-Palestine, Jewish-positive, support groups, Jewish racism, healing modalities, Jewish activism, resistance stories) Perhaps introducing some of these as a synagogue workshop, at High Holidays, or another time? Or to your Jewish group, or Jewish community center? *Consider processes that allow people to say what is in their minds and hearts, and to listen to each other,*

without articulating conclusions—based on the idea that it can be healing just to be listened to, that once we feel heard, we can often hear someone else's pain. And being listened to can help clear up our own thinking.

~

Journal your reflections about the recovery processes described in this "Creating A Future" section:

- What impact has this whole section had on you?
- What new learning, new perspectives?

~

In the whole group, take turns sharing two key learnings from reading the book and participating in this group.

Also share what has been most challenging for you? Most rewarding? How does your body feel talking about this?

~

If this is your last group meeting, take turns sharing:

- A gift that you got from engaging in this process.
- Something you contributed to the group, a gift that you brought.

~

Take a couple of minutes appreciating each person (although not everyone needs to speak about each member). Everyone should also appreciate something about themselves.

✎

Suggested reading and videos (not already suggested in the text of this Reader's Guide)—see Bibliography on www.PennyRosenwasser.com for details as well as other resources:

Books, articles, pamphlets

Anti-Semitism in America by Leonard Dinnerstein

Dreams of an Insomniac: Jewish Feminist Essays, Speeches, and Diatribes by Irena Klepfisz

How the Jews Became White Folks and What That Says About Race in America by Karen Brodkin

"How to strengthen the Palestine solidarity movement by making friends with Jews" by Guy Yizhak Austrian and Emma Goldman (2003) (especially useful for allies)

"Jews in the U.S.: the rising cost of whiteness" by Melanie Kaye/Kantrowitz

Living in the Shadow of the Cross: Understanding and Resisting the Power and Privilege of Christian Hegemony by Paul Kivel

Nice Jewish Girls: A Lesbian Anthology by Evelyn Torton Beck (ed.)

"Reflections by an Arab Jew" by Ella Shohat

"Split at the root: An essay on Jewish identity" by Adrienne Rich

The Ethnic Myth: Race, Ethnicity and Class in America by Stephen Steinberg

The Lost by Daniel Mendelsohn

The Tribe of Dina: A Jewish Women's Anthology by Melanie Kaye/Kantrowitz and Irena Klepfisz (eds.)

They Fought Back by Yuri Suhl

Toward the Final Solution: A History of European Racism by George Mosse (out of print, but very worth tracking down a copy)

Trail Guide to the Torah of Nonviolence by Rabbi Lynn Gottlieb

Understanding the Palestinian-Israeli Conflict by Phyllis Bennis

Wrestling in the Daylight by Rabbi Brant Rosen

Yentl's Revenge: The Next Wave of Jewish Feminism by Danya Ruttenberg (ed.)

Yours in Struggle: Three Feminist Perspectives on Anti-Semitism and Racism by Elly Bulkin, Minnie Bruce Pratt, and Barbara Smith (eds.)

Videos

Constantine's Sword by (former priest) James Carroll (2007). Documentary exploring Christianity's oppression of Jews, http://www.imdb.com.

Encounter Point (DVD). Award-winning documentary about the everyday Palestinian and Israeli Jewish leaders who work together against violence and for peace, http://www.justvision.org/en/home.

Israel & Palestine: A Very Short Introduction, 6 minutes, http://www.youtube.com/watch?v=Y58njT2oXfE&feature=youtu.be, or www.jewishvoiceforpeace.org.

The Courage to Care. An examination of individuals whose courageous acts against the persecution of Jews in Nazi Germany made a difference. http://en.wikipedia.org/wiki/The_Courage_to_Care.

The Longest Hatred [VHS] (1993). Two segments, 150 minutes, directed by Rex Bloomstein, an excellent history of anti-Semitism, www.Amazon.com.

The Tribe: An Unorthodox, Unauthorized History of the Jewish People and the Barbie Doll by Tiffany Shlain and Ken Goldberg, narrated by Peter Coyote, 15 minutes. Explores what it means to be Jewish today, confronting stereotypes, assimilation, and historic persecution, yet also using humor to explore complexity. (Note: I have not personally seen this, but it sounds intriguing.)

The Way Home by Shakti Butler, 90 minutes (1998). Multiracial councils of women, including Jews, explore racism and internalized oppression. (New Day

New Films, 190 Route 17M, P.O. Box 1084, Harriman, NY 10926). Also see world-trust.org/the-way-home.

Young, Jewish and Left by Irit Reinheimer and Konnie Chameides, 70 minutes (2006). "Weaves queer culture, Jewish Arab history, secular Yiddishkeit, anti-racist analysis, and religious/spiritual traditions into a...tapestry of Leftist politics...Grab your Bubbe (grandmother) and your habibi (loved one) and check it out," http://youngjewishandleft.org/.

Notes

NOTE TO THE READER

The BIBLIOGRAPHY for this book is on my website (in the interest of being space-efficient here): www.PennyRosenwasser.com, or www.Hope-into-Practice.com.

For the same reason, where not included, many of the online link addresses and dates accessed for the NOTES that follow can be found on my website, see above. Readers should be able to access any of these sources below by googling the article titles, authors, dates written, and websites.

INTRODUCTION

1. Hidary, V. "The Hebrew Mamita." Excerpt from her signature poem, performed as part of Def Poetry Jam HBO, 9/7/2010. http://www.youtube.com/watch?v=yAeWyGGTdEE.

2. Bizarre: when my parents ordered the writing on the bracelet, they wrote "Jewish," but it came back as "Hebrew."

3. As I will explain, throughout this book my analysis is most precise about Ashkenazi Jews. Regrettably, due to Ashkenazi centrism, I have less information about internalized anti-Semitism for Mizrahi, Sephardic, and Jews of other ethnicities and that is a limitation of this book; but from what I do know, some of the effects are similar.

4. Gilligan, C. (1993). Letter to Readers. *In a different voice: Psychological theory and women's identity* (Rev. ed.) (p. xxiv). Cambridge, MA: Harvard University Press.

5. Lawrence Bush notes that the National Council of Jewish Women has been "by far among the most liberal and activist organizations within the Jewish mainstream," and today has about 90,000 members; see "Hannah G. Solomon," (1/14/13), www.jewish currents.org.

6. A *shtetl* was a small town or village in Eastern Europe, usually Jewish.

7. He moved south to work in a relative's store in Manning, SC. Then with savings and his sister's help, he opened his own store in Denmark, SC. My father's father, from Stropkov (then Austria-Hungary, now Czechoslovakia), became the first Jewish judge in Westchester County, NY. Both my grandmothers were born in the U.S., their parents fled from Russia.

8. Again, these are (mostly) Ashkenazi messages. I suspect many hold true for at least some other Jewish ethnic groups as well, but I don't know for sure.

9. For excellent resources to learn more about Cooperative, or Collaborative, Inquiry, see Chapter 12, Note 6.

10. *Kvetch* is complain, *kvell* is rejoice.

11. Heschel, A. J. (1983). *I asked for wonder*, (p. 8). Samuel Dresner (Ed.). New York: Crossroad Publishing Company.

12. This is the translation of the *"V'ahvata"* section, part of the *Shema* prayer, in the 2009 Shabbat Siddur of Kehilla Community Synagogue (Oakland, CA), p. 19.

13. *Tikkun olam* is Hebrew for the repair and healing of the world. See Chapter Fifteen. Also see Schwartz, H. (3/28/2011), "How the Ari Created a Myth and Transformed Judaism," www.Tikkun.org.

CHAPTER ONE: ANTI-SEMITISM 101

1. Kempton, S., in Hagan, K. (1993). *Fugitive information: Essays from a feminist hothead*, 127. New York: HarperCollins. I do not know if Kempton is Jewish.

2. Adams, M. & D'errico, K. (2007). Antisemitism and anti-Jewish oppression curriculum

design. In M. Adams, L. A. Bell, & P. Griffin (Eds.). *Teaching for diversity and social justice*, 2nd ed. (p. 291). New York: Routledge. I do not know if Adams and D'errico are Jewish.

3. Reason TV (10/12/2011), http:www.youtube.com/watch?v=IMjm4Lx.

4. Thomas, P., Date, J. and Cook, T. (2009, June 11). Alleged museum shooter: 'The Holocaust is a lie.' ABC News.

5. Referring to Glenn Beck. Elliott, J. (9/9/10). Beck attacks Soros as "Puppet Master," www.Salon.com. The media watchdog group Media Matters also documents Beck hosting various authors whose books espouse anti-Semitic ideas: "Fox News anti-Semitism Problem," (October 14, 2010), www.mediamatters.org.

6. Jewish Telegraph Agency. (12/18/09). Philly students dunked after Holocaust taunts, www.JTA.org.

7. Stelter, B. (10/1/10). CNN fires Rick Sanchez for remarks in interview, www. nytimes.com.

8. Jews on First! (6/25/07). Southern Baptists rely on deception in effort to convert Jews, www.jewsonfirst.org.

9. Shamir, Y. (2009). *Defamation* (film documentary), www.defamation-thefilm.com. This occurred in 2007.

10. *Democracy Now* Headlines (5/9/12) 10 white supremacists arrested in Florida for "race war" plot, www.democracynow.org. Ten alleged members of the group American Front were arrested.

11. Rothchild, A. (2007). *Broken promises, broken dreams*, (p. 3). Ann Arbor, MI: Pluto Press.

12. New World Encyclopedia. Viewed 1/16/11 from http://www .newworldencyclopedia.org/entry/Ashkenazi. Jewish diversity organization Be'chol Lashon reports wide discrepancies in the number of Jews reported by reputable sources, coming up with the overall figure of 13-15 million worldwide: viewed 1/16/11 from http://bechollashon.org/population/today.php.

13. Some excellent sources of information on multiracial Jewry include: Ammiel Alcalay's *After Jews and Arabs: Remaking Levantine Culture*; back issues of *Bridges: Sephardi and Mizrahi Women Write About Their Lives* (1997-98) and *Bridges: Writing and Art by Jewish Women of Color* (2001); Ruth Behar's 2002 film *Adio Kerida*; Ophira Edut's essay "Bubbe Got Back" in *Yentl's revenge* (Danya Ruttenberg); Loolwa Khazzoom's *The flying camel: Essays on identity by women of North African and Middle Eastern Jewish Heritage* (and anything in this book's bibliography by Khazzoom); Ella Shohat's essay "Reflections by an Arab Jew"; Melanie Kaye/Kantrowitz's *The colors of jews*; and Diane and Gary Tobin and Scott Rubin's *In every tongue: Ethnic & racial diversity in the Jewish community*.

14. Levins Morales, A. (2005). Latino Jews in the United States. *The Oxford Encyclopedia of Latinos and Latinas in the United States*. New York: Oxford University Press. Morales writes, "Genetic testing has shown that some Jews do...descend from people who lived thousands of years ago in what is now Israel, but many Jews are also related to their non-Jewish neighbors, and look like them. Jewish identity, religious and cultural, is something that people of any background can acquire, while Jewish ancestors are not."

15. Kraemer, J. (1997, July). Comparing crescent and cross. [Review of the book *Under crescent and cross* by Mark Cohen]. *The Journal of Religion*, 77, 3, 449. (The crescent of Islam, the cross of Christianity.)

16. In his article "The Becking of Rep. Gabrielle Giffords," (1/9/11), Chip Berlet offers an excellent description of scapegoating (from the book he co-authored with Matthew Nemiroff Lyon, *Right-wing populism in America*): "the social process whereby the hostility and grievances of an angry, frustrated group are directed away from the real causes of a

social problem onto a target group demonized as...wrongdoers. The scapegoat bears the blame, while the scapegoaters feel a sense of righteousness and...unity. The social problem may be real or imaginary, the grievances legitimate or illegitimate, and members of the targeted group may be...innocent or partly culpable. What matters is that the scapegoats are wrongfully stereotyped as all sharing the same negative trait, or are singled out for blame while other major culprits are let off the hook."

17. Although a few Jews colluded in the attack on Jesus, it was the Roman governor of Palestine who spearheaded the execution. See Glen Hauer's "How the system of Anti-semitism can derail progress towards peace & justice in Israel and Palestine, and what to do about it," www.glenhauer.com.

18. Kivel, P. Challenging Christian hegemony. www.christianhegemony.org. In his Winter 2010 newsletter, "Getting Together for Social Justice," Kivel adds that Christian hegemony "is not a critique of individual Christians, many of whom do not see the world this way or promote this perspective," and some Christians "have contributed greatly to human well-being." But Christian hegemony, Christian power and privilege "is a...system of oppression that has greatly impacted our lives in the West...[and] has been terribly destructive," http://www.paulkivel.com/newsletters/2010-1-email.html. See Kivel's 2013 book, *Living in the shadow of the cross: Understanding and resisting the power and privilege of christian hegemony.*

19. Rosenberg, E. (2000). *But were they good for the Jews?* 183. Secaucus, NJ: Citadel Press.

20. Carroll, J. (3/9/10) Preach peace in holy week, www.boston.com/bostonglobe. In "Launching the Crusades." (11/18/12), Lawrence Bush notes in JewishCurrents.org that in 1095, Pope Urban II called on French knights to make war on Turks who had occupied Palestine, and "God wills it" became their battle cry; in the First Crusade, "Jews almost single-handedly defended Haifa against the Christians," fighting alongside Muslim soldiers to defend Jerusalem. The Crusades lasted for 600 years.

21. According to historian Walter Laqueur, there have been over 150 recorded "blood libel" accusations against Jews, beginning in 1144 in Norwich, England. See Lawrence Bush, (9/4/11), The Blood Libel, *www.Jewishcurrents.org.*

22. Luther, M. In Bloomstein, R. (Producer), (1991), *The Longest Hatred* [film documentary]. WGBH Boston Video.

23. Levins Morales, A. (3/11/12). Latinos, Israel and Palestine: Understanding anti-Semitism, www.auroralevinsmorales.com. Levins Morales notes that middle-agent-to-ruler roles were one of few options offered to Jews, "often under duress."

24. After 9/11, Internet rumors circulated that thousands of Jews had been warned to stay home that day, and/or that the Israeli secret service orchestrated the attacks. And although this pattern manifested in the U.S. in 20th-century economic depressions, Jews have not been scapegoated in a major way in the 2008-plus recession (see Chapter Three).

25. Levins Morales, A. (personal communication, 9/19/04).

26. Dinnerstein, L. (1994). *Anti-semitism in America.* New York: Oxford University Press.

27. Ibid.

28. Trotsky, L., (1971), 1905, pp. 131-134, New York: Vintage Books (as cited in Zirin, 2002).

29. Spiro, Rabbi K. The Spanish Inquisition, http://www.aish.com/jl/h/cc/48951681. html. The exact number of Spanish Jews exiled is disputed, but this is a likely estimate. This edict also exiled the thriving Muslim culture of the Moors.

30. Mendelsohn, D. (2006). *The Lost,* p. 87, New York: HarperCollins.

31. Bush, L. (2012, July 30). Farewell to Spain. www.jewishcurrents.org. Bush cites Rabbi Joseph Telushkin in Jewish Literacy, 1991. Also see (9/20/10, September 20), Auto-da-fé, www.jewishcurrents.org, in which Bush explains that the Portuguese Inquisition introduced the auto-da-fé, or "act of faith," consisting of a public Catholic mass followed by torture and burning at the stake of "secret Jews." Nearly 500 of these took place over three centuries, until 1850, in France, Spain, Portugal, Mexico, Brazil, Peru, and Ukraine, killing thousands.

Bush also reports that Ferdinand and Isabella actually invited the Inquisition into Spain in 1480 (under Tomás de Torquemada's leadership, a descendant of Jews), to "purify the blood" of Spanish nobility–because Jews had converted en masse after anti-Semitic massacres on the Iberian Peninsula in 1391, so many aristocratic/wealthy families had "Jewish blood" in their ancestry. See (10/19/12), Ferdinand and Isabella, www.Jewishcurrents.org.

32. Adams, & D'errico. Antisemitism and anti-Jewish oppression. (p. 288) (Chap 1, Note 2)

33. Shlaim, A. (8/30/10). Professor Avi Shlaim reviews "In Ishmael's House." [Review of the book In Ishmael's house by Martin Gilbert]. Financial Times, http://www.politics.ox.ac.uk/index.php/news/avi-shlaim-reviewing-qin-ishmaels-houseq.html.

34. Wahba, R. (2003). Benign ignorance or persistent resistance? In Khazzoom, L. (Ed.). The flying camel (p. 50). New York: Seal Press. Estimates of Jews killed in the Farhud vary; some scholars say up to 600 were murdered. Lawrence Bush writes (2012, June 1), The Farhud, www.Jewishcurrents.org, that this "marked the beginning of the end for a Jewish community that had existed in Iraq (Babylon) for 2600 years."

35. Ibid.

36. Adams, & D'errico. Antisemitism and anti-Jewish oppression. (p. 286) (Chap 1, Note 2)

37. Gilman, S. (1991). The Jew's body (p. 69). New York: Routledge.

38. Ibid., p. 173.

39. Estimates vary regarding the total number of Jews worldwide when the Nazis came to power. Be'chol Lason (In Every Tongue) says 16.6 million, and I will go with that figure (http://bechollashon.org/population/today/php), given that the common estimate is that the Shoah killed approximately one-third of the world's Jews. But in "Anti-semitism curriculum design" (1997) (In Adams, Bell, & Griffin. Teaching for diversity. [p. 188], [Chap 1, Note 2], Weinstein and Mellen say the Nazi genocide killed nearly one-half of the world's Jews, citing Boonstra et al (Eds.) (1989, Antisemitism, a history portrayed. Amsterdam: Anne Frank Foundation.)

Just one illustration of such 20th-century racism against Jews, written by Austrian Jewish writer and Auschwitz survivor Jean Amery in At the mind's limits: Contemplations by a survivor on Auschwitz and its realities: "Daily, for years on end, we could read and hear that we were lazy, evil, ugly...our bodies–hairy, fat, and bow-legged–befouling swimming pools, yes, even park benches. Our hideous faces, depraved and spoilt by protruding ears... disgusting to our fellow men." Thanks to Annette Herskovits for sharing this with me.

40. Berenbaum, M. (1993). The world must know: The history of the holocaust as told in the United States Holocaust Memorial Museum (p. 16). New York: Little, Brown.

41. Mendelsohn. The Lost. (p. 353). (Chap 1, Note 30)

42. Ibid., p. 125.

43. Ibid., p. 227.

44. Ibid., p. 221.

45. Berenbaum, M. (1990). A mosaic of victims: Non-Jews persecuted and murdered by the Nazis. New York: New York University Press. Also Small, M. and Singer, J. D. (1982). Resort to arms: International and civil wars 1816–1980. Beverly Hills, CA: Sage. Including

Roma, gays, lefties, Catholics, those with physical/mental disabilities. Including Soviet civilians and prisoners of war, and more.

46. Steinberg, S. (1989). *The ethnic myth: Race, ethnicity, and class in America* (p. 13) (Rev. ed.). Boston: Beacon Press. In "Split at the root: An essay on Jewish identity" (1982), Adrienne Rich wrote about growing up in 1930's nd '40's Baltimore: "it was white social christianity…that the world was founded on. The very word *Christian* was used as a synonym for virtuous, just, peace-loving, generous, etc.…Anti-Semitism was so intrinsic as not to have a name."

47. Dinnerstein. *Anti-semitism in America.* (Chap 1, Note 26)

48. Anti-Defamation League (2011). ADL poll on anti-Semitic attitudes in America. Viewed 1/9/12 from http://www.fighthatred.com/fighting-hate/reports/915-adl-poll-on-anti-semitic-attitudes-in-america. In terms of popular culture, see the "Shit Christians say to Jews" http://www.youtube.com/watch?v=51dFlpwKkBM&feature=related, actual comments made to Allison Pearlman–such as "I'm gonna miss you when I'm in heaven," or "Is there a Jewish church? Do you want to come to a real church with me?"

49. The ad on San Francisco MUNI buses in 2012, sponsored by the American Freedom Defense Initiative (defined as a hate group by the Southern Poverty Law Center): "In any war between the civilized man and the savage, support the civilized man. Support Israel… Defeat jihad." See "Hate group places Islamophobic advertisements on San Francisco buses" by Nora Barrows-Friedman, 8/16/12, electronicintifada.net; and "'Jews against Islamophobia' condemns latest round of Geller ads in NYC" by Adam Horowitz, 12/17/12, mondoweiss.net.

And in April 2013, after the terrorist attack on the Boston Marathon, "speculation about the backgrounds of those behind the bombings prompted at least two violent attacks": one against a Palestinian woman who was punched in the shoulder and harassed while walking with her infant daughter in Malden, MA; and a Bangladeshi man brutally beaten in NYC and called a "F-ing Arab." See *Democracy Now* headlines (4/19/13).

50. Kivel. Challenging Christian hegemony. (Chap 1, Note 18)

51. Kaye/Kantrowitz. (1996). Jews in the U.S.: The rising costs of whiteness. In B. Thompson & S. Tayagi (Eds.), *Names we call home: Autobiography on racial identity* (p. 125). New York: Routledge. She says that although "anti-Semitism in this country is distinct from racism," it has "everything to do with racism."

52. Kaye/Kantrowitz, (2007). *The colors of Jews* (p. 28). Bloomington, IN: Indiana University Press.

53. Lyons, M. N. (2003). Parasites and Pioneers: Antisemitism in White Supremacist America. In J. Alexander, L. Albrecht, S. Day, and M. Segrest (Eds.), *Sing, whisper, shout, pray!* edgework.com: EdgeWork Books.

54. Ordover, N. (2003). *American eugenics: Race, queer anatomy, and the science of nationalism* (p. 42). Minneapolis: University of Minnesota. In Kaye/Kantrowitz. *Colors of Jews.* (p. 16). (Chap 1, Note 52)

55. Ibid., p. 9.

56. Dinnerstein. *Anti-semitism in America.* (p. 126). (Chap 1, Note 26)

57. Prell, R.-E. (1999). *Fighting to become Americans: Assimilation and the trouble between Jewish women and Jewish men,* (pp. 164) Boston: Beacon Press.

58. Ibid., p. 32.

59. Beck, E. T. (1992). "From 'Kike to Jap': How misogyny, anti-semitism and racism construct the Jewish American Princess," 6. In Anderson, M. and Collins, P. H. (Eds.) *Race, class and gender.* Belmont, CA: Wadsworth.

60. Prell. *Fighting to become Americans* (p. 143) (Chap 1, Note 57)

61. Ibid., p. 145.

62. Beck, E. T. (1995). Judaism, feminism and psychology: Making the links visible. In K. Weiner & A. Moon (Eds.), *Jewish women speak out* (pp. 11-26). Seattle, WA: Canopy Press.

63. Beck, E. T. "From 'Kike to Jap'" 6 (Chap 1, Note 59). Here Beck refers to research by Syracuse University sociologist Gary Spencer.

64. Rizzo, R. (2000, June 12). What your CI leaders don't want you to know. *The GW Hatchet*, 4.

65. Belzer, T. (2001). On being a Jewish feminist valley girl. In D. Ruttenberg (Ed.), *Yentl's revenge: The next wave of Jewish feminism* (p. 184). Seattle, WA: Seal Press.

66. Gaynor, A. (1996). *Jewish American Princess jokes: A disparaging humor cycle as a vehicle for hate speech.* (p. 87). Unpublished bachelor of arts honors thesis, Bates College, Lewiston, ME.

67. Kaye/Kantrowitz, M. (1992b). To be a radical Jew in the late 20th century, 113. In *The issue is power: Essays on women, Jews, violence and resistance*. San Francisco: Aunt Lute Books.

68. One Jewish woman who fought back was Texan Sherry Merfish who convinced the Houston Rabbinical Association to pass a resolution, "no more JAP crap in synagogues." Crusading to synagogues nationwide, she would ask audiences to shout out "characteristics" of a JAP, scribbling these on the blackboard. "Then I'd erase 'JAP' and substitute 'Jew', making the anti-Semitism clear. "Were Jap jokes a justification for intermarriage?" by Lenore Skenazy, (2/23/11), www.Forward.com.

69. Rubin, J. (2004, Fall/Winter). Once you go JAP. *Heeb*, 44

70. Siegel, R. (1995), Jewish women's bodies: Sexuality, body image and self-esteem, 48. In K. Weiner, *Jewish women speak out*. (Chap 1, Note 62)

71. Lerner, M. (1992). *Socialism of fools* (p. 65). Oakland, CA: Tikkun Books. Also, in the U.S. today, Koreans and Palestinians are often in middle person economic roles as well.

72. Weinstein, G., & Mellen, D. (1997). Anti-semitism curriculum design. In Adams, Bell, & Mellen, D. (1997). Anti-semitism curriculum design. In Adams, Bell, & Griffin. *Teaching for diversity*. (p. 190).(Chap 1, Note 2)

73. Dinnerstein. *Anti-semitism in America*. (p. 33). (Chap 1, Note 26) Dinnerstein footnotes Korn, *American Jewry and the Civil War*, p. 177; Berman, *Richmond's Jewry*, pp. 181-184; and Lonn, *Foreigners in the Confederacy*, p. 336, among others.

74. Ibid., p. 32.

75. Ibid., p. 105.

76. Ibid., p. 128. For example: Noam Chomsky reports that in his German/Irish Philadelphia neighborhood, sympathies were mostly pro-Nazi (Robert Barsky, *Noam Chomsky, a life of dissent*, 1997). While in *Old men at midnight*, 2002, Chaim Potok refers to Father Coughlin's outrageous broadcasts: "The anti-Semitic neighbors would turn up their radios so you would hear him when you walked down the street."

77. Rosenblum, A. (2009 May/June). Offers we couldn't refuse: What happened to Jewish secular identity? *Jewish Currents*, 16.

78. Sanders, R. (ed.) (2004) March. "Father Charles Edward Coughlin" in "Facing the corporate roots of American fascism," *Press for Conversion* magazine, #53, http://coat.ncf.ca/our_magazine/links/53/coughlin.html.

79. U.S. Holocaust Museum exhibit, Washington, D.C., December 1999.

80. Dinnerstein. *Anti-semitism in America*. (p. 119). (Chap 1, Note 26). Dinnerstein footnotes David S. Wyman, *The abandonment of the Jews* (New York: Pantheon Books, 1984), p. 8; Charles H. Stember, *Jews in the mind of America* (New York: Basic Books, 1966), p. 138.

81. Piercy, M. (2002) . *Sleeping with cats* (p. 56). New York: HarperCollins.

82. In 2011, Israel passed a law cutting off state funding to any group that discusses the Nakba.

83. Kivel, P. Christian Zionism (p. 5), http://www.christianhegemony.org/articles.

84. Rosenblum, A. Offers we couldn't refuse. *Jewish Currents*, 16. (Chap 1, Note 77) And some Jews named other Jews as well.

85. Kaye/Kantrowitz. Jews in the U.S (p. 125). (Chap 1, Note 51)

86. Ibid. Korean-Americans are also blamed for financial crises.

87. Kaye/Kantrowitz. To be a radical Jew (p. 149). (Chap 1, Note 67)

88. Steinberg, S., *The ethnic myth* (p. 236). (Rev. ed.). (Chap 1, Note 46)

89. Goldberg, J. J. (1996). *Jewish power: Inside the American Jewish establishment* (p. 236). Reading, MA: Perseus Books.

90. Rosenblum, A., Offers we couldn't refuse. *Jewish Currents*, 15. (Chap 1, Note 77)

91. Ibid.

92. John Hope Franklin interviewed on the *Charlie Rose TV Show*, December 1, 2005.

93.Wyman, D. (2000). The setting: Europe and America. In M. Adams, W. Blumenfeld, R. Castaneda, H. Hackman, M. Peters, & X. Zuniga (Eds.), *Readings for diversity and social justice: An anthology on racism, anti-Semitism, sexism, heterosexism, ableism, and classism*, (p. 166). New York: Routledge.

94. Another key example: in 1939, the U.S. refused to let the S.S. *St. Louis*, carrying 930 Jewish refugees from Germany, land in the U.S. after Cuba refused entry. "As the ship sailed along the Florida coast, the passengers could see the lights of Miami," but "the U.S. Coast guard ships patrolled the waters to make sure that no one jumped to freedom." The ship returned to Europe where few of its passengers survived the Holocaust. Berenbaum, M., *The world must know* (p. 58) (Chap 1, Note 40)

95. Dinnerstein. *Anti-semitism in America*. (Chap 1, Note 26). Also, J. J. Goldberg *(Jewish Power*, p. 111) cites a 1939 *Fortune* magazine poll which found that 83% of Americans opposed lowering immigration quotas. Yet First Lady Eleanor Roosevelt tried to persuade her husband to help the Jews. See also David Oshinsky's (4/5/13) *New York Times* article, "Congress Disposes," a fascinating book review of *FDR and the Jews* by Richard Breitman and Allan Lichtman. Oshinsky writes that the authors conclude, "While saving the Jews of Europe was never a high priority for Roosevelt, he did more for them than any other world leader at the time, despite the enormous obstacles he faced at home." He didn't intervene to lift immigration bans because jobs were so scarce "and Jews were among the least popular of those seeking admission." But he did recall the U.S. Ambassador to Germany to protest Kristallnacht and encouraged efforts to settle European Jews in Latin America. The authors also recount U.S. presidents' ignoring other genocides: Woodrow Wilson and the slaughter of Armenians, Jimmy Carter and Pol Pot's extermination of Cambodians, Bill Clinton's lack of confronting mass murder in Rwanda, George Bush and Barack Obama not combatting atrocities in Darfur.

96. Associated Press. (8/27/2000). USA: Behavior in Nazi Era Examined, http://www.corpwatch.org/article.php?id=594.

97. Dobbs, M. (11/30/98). Ford and GM scrutinized for alleged Nazi collaboration. *Washington Post*, p. A01. Opel was a "100% GM-owned subsidiary."

98. Ibid.

99. Associated Press. (8/27/2000). USA: Behavior in Nazi Era Examined.

100. Black, E. (2/28/12). IBM at Auschwitz, new documents. *Reader Supported News*, http://readersupportednews.org/news-section2/328-121/10198-focus-ibm-at-auschwitz-new-documents. This article updates Black's 2001 book *IBM and the Holocaust, The strategic*

alliance between Nazi Germany and America's most powerful corporation. For example, the IBM number 8 designated Jew, 3=homosexual, 12=Gypsy, 4=death by execution, etc.

101. Ibid.

102. Berenbaum. *The world must know.* (Chap 1, Note 40)

103. Ibid., p. 162.

104. Medoff, R. (5/25/12). Jan Karski, from hell on earth to recipient of U.S. presidential honor, www.JTA.org. Before that, British Foreign Minister Anthony Eden showed "little interest" when meeting with Karski, and Winston Churchill was "too busy" to meet him at all, though the BBC and British press did print his accounts. The book he published was called *Story of a secret state.* See also, *Democracy Now* (2012, June 5), Polish resistance figure Jan Karski, honored with posthumous Medal of Freedom, in his own words, www.Democracynow.org.

105. Berenbaum. *The world must know.* (p. 164). (Chap 1, Note 40). See also Oshinsky, Note 95 above: Oshinsky says that Roosevelt consistently maintained "the best way to save the Jews of Europe was to defeat the Nazis as quickly as possible, and that was exactly what he intended to do."

106. Piercy. *Sleeping with cats.* (p. 28). (Chap 1, Note 81)

107. Berenbaum. *The world must know.* (p. 164). (Chap 1, Note 40)

108. Kaufman, M. (7/15/2000). Jan Karski Dies at 86; Warned West about Holocaust, www.nytimes.com. Also Goldberg, J. J., *Jewish Power*, and Berenbaum. *The world must know.* Also, Wallenberg was Christian.

109. Wyman. The setting: Europe and America. (p. 166). (Chap 1, Note 93)

110. Goldberg. *Jewish power.* (p. 116). (Chap 1, Note 89)

111. Ibid., p. 113. Goldberg cites, for example, Arthur D. Morse who wrote *While Six Million Died* (1968). Melanie Kaye/Kantrowitz also speaks of this in *The colors of Jews.* . See also Oshinsky, Note 95 above.

112. Lichtblau, E. (11/13/10) Nazis were given "safe haven" in U.S., report says. www.nytimes.com.

Operation Paperclip was a U.S. program that recruited former Nazi scientists, including war criminals; see "CIA Mind Control–and Stanley Gottlieb," (4/13/13), www.Jewishcurrents.org.

113. Berenbaum, M., *The world must know.* (Chap 1, Note 40). Also see Oshinsky, Note 95 above; Oshinsky refers to Roosevelt's "notoriously anti-Semitic State Department."

114. Ibid. (Berenbaum and Oshinsky)

115.Dinnerstein. *Anti-semitism in America.* (p. xiii). (Chap 1, Note 26). Meanwhile, over 1000 blacks were lynched in this region between 1900 and 1917: Belth, N. (1981) *A promise to keep: A narrative of the American encounter with anti-Semitism,* NY: Schocken Books.

116. Sawyer, K. (6/20/2000). A lynching, a list and reopened wounds. *The Washington Post,* pp. A1-A2.

117. Ibid.

118. Close to half of the U.S. Communist Party in the 1930s were Jews, though some were expelled for attending religious services. Liebman, A. (1979), *Jews and the left,* New York: Wiley & Sons. Also, in personal communication with Robert Meeropol (younger son of the Rosenbergs) on September 21, 2009, he said that the book *Exoneration: The trial of Julius and Ethel Rosenberg and Morton Sobell, prosecutorial deceptions, suborned perjuries, anti-Semitism, and precedent for today's unconstitutional trials,* (2010) by David and Emily Alman, Green Elms Press, argues that anti-Semitism played a much bigger role than has been previously discussed

119. Rosenberg Fund for Children. (5/31/07), http://writing.upenn.

edu/~afilreis/50s/meeropol-on-rosenbergs.html. Robert Meeropol also makes the point, (9/23/10) in "Julian Assange, My Parents and the Espionage Act of 1917," "the only evidence...against my mother was David and Ruth Greenglasses' testimony that she was present at a critical espionage meeting and typed up David's...description of a sketch. Although this testimony has since been shown to be false, even if it were true, it would mean that the government of the United States executed someone for typing." Rosenberg granddaughter Ivy Meeropol's 2004 documentary "Heir to an Execution" says the Rosenbergs were innocent of what they were charged with, and they trusted history would absolve them. See also Robert Meeropol's (2/23/12) article, "60 years too late," on the Rosenberg Fund for Children's Directors' blog, http://www.rfc.org.

120. Kaye/Kantrowitz, M. (2007, March.) Some notes on anti-Semitism from a progressive Jewish perspective, www.jewishcurrents.org. The sign she was referring to read "Sharon=Hitler."

121. Picciotto, H. (2004). Bogus charges. In *Reframing anti-Semitism: Alternative Jewish perspectives* (p. 48). Oakland, CA: Jewish Voice for Peace. For an excellent six-minute animated summary of the Israeli-Palestinian conflict, see *Israel & Palestine: A Very Short Introduction*, http://www.youtube.com/watch?v=Y58njT2oXfE&feature=youtube, or http://www.JewishVoiceForPeace.org.

122. Thanks to my friend and scholar Sarah Anne Minkin, who points out, for example, the similarities between the Nuremberg "race laws" of the 1930s that enforced the isolation, segregation, and exploitation of German Jews – and Israeli laws, policies, and practices that deprive Palestinians of legal rights and protections for property, livelihood, mobility, and other civil rights.

123. Levins Morales. Latinos, Israel and Palestine. (Chap 1, Note 23)

124. Klein, N. (2003). Sharon, Le Pen, and anti-Semitism. In Kushner, T., & Solomon, A. (Eds.). (2003), *Wrestling with Zion*. New York: Grove Press. Such examples, which continue to crop up, are unsettling indeed! For one example of clearly standing up to anti-Semitism on the left, see JVP statement on Greta Berlin and allegations of anti-Semitism, October 7, 2012, http://jewishvoiceforpeace.org/blog/jewish-voice-for-peace-statement-on-greta-berlin-and-allegations-of-an.

125. Plitnick, M., Reclaiming the struggle, 5. In *Reframing anti-Semitism: Alternative Jewish perspectives* (Chap 1, Note 121).

126. Pogrebin, Letty Cottin. (1982). Anti-Semitism in the women's movement, www.jwa.org.

127. Ibid.

128. Fletcher, T. (2004). What is "anti-Semitism" and does it still exist? 40. In *Reframing anti-Semitism: Alternative Jewish perspectives*. (Chap 1, Note 121)

129. Rosenblum, A. (2007). The past didn't go anywhere, www.scribd.com/doc/81712788/The-Past-Didn-t-Go-Anywhere-April-Rosenblum. A 2012 example: when California gentile activists tried to cancel a workshop on anti-Semitism (by progressives) at a Palestine-Israel peace conference. One organizer justified, "Don't get me wrong, we know the Holocaust happened."

Of course there is room on progressive agendas to oppose all oppressions; in addition to Rosenblum's excellent booklet, Guy Izhak Austrian and Ella Goldman make this same point in their equally well-done article "How to strengthen the Palestine solidarity movement by making friends with Jews," http://www.soaw.org/resources/anti-opp-resources/111-anti-jewish-oppression/606-how-to-strengthen-the-palestine-solidarity-movement-by-making-friends-with-jews. Both of these are a must-read for allies and Jews alike.

130. Ibid.

131. Loeb, D. (2010). Sundown to sundown. In *Birkat Ha-Gomel, A survivor's blessing*, contact dyanna.loeb@gmail.com. Used with permission. Loeb notes that this poem is recorded and featured on *Change the Nation* (2006), Youth Movement Records' compilation album.

132. ADL (2011 November 3). ADL poll finds anti-Semitic attitudes on rise in America, http://www.adl.org/NR/exeres/A546CBC4-266F-4B64-B325-56FD4E34E309,0B1623CA-D5A4-465D-A369-DF6E8679CD9E,frameless.htm. Conversely, a November 2012 ADL poll found that anti-Semitic incidents in the U.S. declined by 13 percent in 2011, the lowest number of such incidents reported by the ADL in two decades (and the 15 percent figure cited in this chapter still held); see "Anti-Semitic incidents in U.S. declined by 13 percent in 2011, ADL audit finds," (11/1/12), jta.org, and Markoe, L., (3/21/12) Anti-Semitism on the rise in Europe, www.huffingtonpost.com.

133. Carroll, J. (3/29/10). Preach peace in holy week, www.boston.com/bostonglobe.

134. A *sukkah* is a temporary shelter Jews construct and spend time in during the week-long Sukkot festival, usually made of branches and leaves. It commemorates the time God provided for the Israelites wandering in the wilderness after escaping slavery in Egypt.

135. Finkelstein, N. (2009). In Shamir, Y. (2009). *Defamation* (film documentary. Finkelstein is a historian, the child of Auschwitz survivors, and an outspoken critic of Israeli policies against Palestinians. His full quote in the film: "I'm sure lots of people I meet... deep down inside them have this queasy feeling about Jews. I'm sure that's true."

136. Kivel, P. (2004). *You call this a democracy? Who benefits, who pays and who really decides?* (p. 132.) New York: Apex Press.

137. Shefler, G. (12/23/10). Vote for the biggest Jewish world news event of 2010, http://www.jpost.com/JewishWorld/ JewishNews/Article.aspx?ID=200543&R=R1.

138. Biale, D. (1986). *Power and powerlessness in Jewish history*. New York: Schocken Books.

139. Ibid.

140. Plitnick. Reclaiming the struggle. (p. 4). "In Reframing Anti-Semitism," (Chap 1, Note 121)

141. Pew Research Center. (9/17/08). Unfavorable views of Jews and Muslims on the increase in Europe, http://pewglobal .org/2008/09/17/unfavorable-views-of-jews-and-muslims-on-the-increase-in-europe/. See also "Uncovering latent anti-Semitism in Germany" by Samuel Salzborn (Summer 2008), Moreshet 5. Also, in 2005, 500 prominent Russians wanted to ban Judaism, half a century after Stalin's vicious persecution of Soviet Jews. See (1/28/05), "Deputies Urge Ban on Jewish Organizations, Then Retract-Bigotry Monitor." Volume 5, Number 4. Published by UCSJ. Editor: Charles Fenyvesi. In *Wikipedia*, History of the Jews in Russia.

142. Ibid. And in 2012, a Berlin rabbi was brutally beaten by four young men as he walked down the street with his six-year-old daughter; see "Attack on Rabbi in Berlin draws outrage," (8/30/12), www.spiegel.de. A 2013 Tel Aviv study on world anti-Semitism noted that 40 percent of 2012 attacks involved violence against people; see "Report: Anti-Semitic incidents surged in 2012," by Ariel David, 4/7/13, AP.

143. ADL Survey in Ten European Countries Finds Anti-Semitism at Disturbingly High Levels, (3/20/12), www.adl.org. Note that the ADL indicates Polish anti-Semitism has remained at 48 percent since 2009 while the 2008 Pew poll reported Polish anti-Semitism at about one-third of the population. See also "Report: Anti-Semitic incidents surged in 2012," by Ariel David, 4/7/13, AP.

144. Furedi, F. (1/19/09). After Gaza: what's behind 21st century anti-Semitism? http://www.spiked-online.com/ index.php/site/article/6117/.

145. Ibid.

146. Human Rights First 2008 Hate Crimes Survey: Anti-Semitism, Chapter IV: The Causes and Sources of Antisemitic Violence, p. 51, FD-081103-hate-crime#332325.pdf. Roger Cukleman was former leader of France's Representative Council of Jewish Institutions. Case in point: the horrific 2006 torture/murder of Ilan Halimi, a young Moroccan working-class Jew by a group of mostly Muslims, who admitted to kidnapping Halimi for ransom, believing all Jews are rich; 19 were imprisoned for the crime, and 100,000 Parisians demonstrated against the murder. 2011 showed a number of violent assaults in France against Jews, also increased anti-Semitic attacks in Sweden and Australia, and consistent incidents in Argentina. In 2012 Chilean websites blamed Jews and Israel for deliberately igniting a fire in an environmental preserve.

147. Loeb, D. (2010). Never stop. In *Birkat Ha-Gomel, A survivor's blessing*, contact dyanna.loeb@gmail.com. Also, in Greece, in December 2010, in an interview on the country's largest television station, a leading priest blamed world Jewry for the country's financial crisis and claimed Hitler was used to establish the state of Israel.

148. Plitnick, M. (6/30/10). Those we can talk to and those we cannot, *The Third Way*, www.mitchellplitnick.com. The leader referred to is Hassan Nasrallah.

149. *B'tselem*. Fatalities during operation "cast lead." http://www.btselem.org/english/statistics/casualties.asp?sD=27&sM=12&sY=2008&eD=18&eM=01&eY=2009&filterby=event&oferet_stat=during.

150. ADL. (6/1/09) Anti-Semitic incidents decline for fourth straight year in U.S., according to annual ADL audit, http://www.adl.org/ PresRele/ASUS_12/5537_12.htm.

151. Furedi, F., After Gaza, (Chap 1, Note 144)

152. Ibid.

153. Regarding anti-Semitism in 20th-century South America, the bombing of a Jewish community building in Argentina in 1994 killed eighty-five and injured hundreds; and between 1976- and 1983, 10 percent of those murdered/kidnapped by the Argentine military were thought to be Jews, although Jews were only 1 percent of the general population.

154. The children's names were Aryeh and Gavriel Sandler (4 and 5) and Miriam Monsonego (7). The shooter was killed after a firefight with police; he was connected to a jihadist group and also claimed links with al-Qaida. Local Jewish leaders expressed surprise at the outpouring of support from Jews and gentiles worldwide, and French President Sarkozy asked citizens not to confuse the violence with France's Muslim community. In the same time period of these crimes, a U.S. marine in Afghanistan was charged with murdering sixteen Afghani children and women; and in central Florida, (white/Latino) George Zimmerman killed 17-year-old, unarmed, African American Trayvon Martin, who was 80 pounds lighter—to my mind, all hate crimes.

155. Furedi, F., After Gaza. (Chap 1, Note 144) My colleague Sina Arnold, a white German gentile activist and Ph.D. candidate who is researching anti-Semitism, concurs with Furedi's analysis. As we go to press in 2013, the *Tablet* documents a spike in incidents that target Jews for the actions of the Israeli government, in Denmark— a country known during World War II for its dramatic rescue of most of its Jews; see "Hiding Judaism in Copenhagen" by Michael Moynihan, (3/28/13), www.tabletmag.com.

156. Surasky, C. (5/12/09) Durban Review Debate, http://www.muzzlewatch.com/?s=Durban+Review+Debate. The Jewish Council on Urban Affairs explains that human rights are international standards, composed of several treaties, which articulate the universal treatment of all human beings—including civil, political, economic, social, and cultural rights.

157. Snyders, M. (10/3/07) Banning Desmond Tutu, http://www.citypages.com/2007-

10-03/news/banning-desmond-tutu/. A counter-campaign by Jewish Voice for Peace cleared his name and the invitation was reissued. Similarly, in 2011 the Zionist Organization of America brought a class action lawsuit against former President Jimmy Carter for his book *Palestine: Peace not apartheid*, claiming it to be anti-Israel. Various academics have been terminated from their university jobs for their critiques of Israel and Zionism (Norman Finkelstein, Joel Kovel, Terri Ginsberg, more), and journalists are attacked as well (like M. J. Rosenberg). But in 2012, the California State University system refused to cave to pressure to dis-invite anti-Zionist Israeli historian Ilan Pappe from speaking at their schools. Even the right-wing David Project issued a "white paper" in 2012, "A Burning Campus? Rethinking Israel Advocacy at America's Universities and Colleges," admitting that most college environments are not hostile to Jews; it advised accusing peace-and-justice faculty members of "academic malpractice" as a more effective strategy to get them fired, than of accusing them of Israel-bashing.

158. Surasky, C. (4/14/09). It's official: Abe Foxman has lost his mind on Tutu, http://www.muzzlewatch.com/ ?s=it%27s+official%3A+abe+foxman+has+lost+his+mind+on+tutu.

159. Tutu, Desmond. (4/13/10). Divesting from injustice, http://www.huffingtonpost.com/desmond-tutu/divesting-from-injustice_b_534994.html. Under international law, the Israeli occupation of Palestinian lands–the West Bank, Gaza, and East Jerusalem–is illegal, because it was acquired during the June 1967 War. According to the Fourth Geneva Conventions established after World War II, it is inadmissible to acquire territory by war.

160. "University of California student union votes to condemn California Assembly Resolution H.R. 35, encourages free speech in higher education," (9/15/12), http://calsjp.org/?p=1272. H.R. 35 followed a report on Campus Climate by the University of California that conflated criticism of Israeli policy with hate speech. See Stephen Zunes (8/30/12) article, "California State Assembly seeks to stifle debate on Israel," HuffingtonPost.com, in which he also notes that the bill attacks "the rights of students and faculty to raise awareness about human rights abuses by U.S.-backed governments." See also Jewish folklorist Steve Koppman's 9/27/12 Op-Ed, www.Jweekly.com, "Protesting against Israel–valid or anti-Semitic?: Organized community conflates policy, values," which notes "the incompatibility between Israel's policies towards the Palestinians and the historic values of our people."

The UC Berkeley Graduate Assembly later passed a resolution similar to the UC Student Association. Jewish Voice for Peace supported the student resolution, writing "Many Jewish UC students and professors have been very clear—efforts like HR35 aren't about protecting Jewish students. They are about trying to protect the right-wing government of Israel from the criticism of others, many of whom are Jewish." See "Hate speech on campus—against whom? Misrepresenting campuses as anti-Semitic is a disservice," by Carol Sanders, (9/20/12), www.Jweekly.com.

A letter submitted by the Center for Constitutional Rights and other civil rights groups to the UC president additionally speaks to the problematic comparison of student activism for Palestinian rights to "truly anti-Semitic and racist incidents on campus, such as noose-hangings and graffiti disparaging Jews, Muslims and the LGBTQ community"; see "Letter to University of California President advising him of need to protect pro-Palestinian speech on campus," www.ccrjustice.org.

Finally, see the excellent *Daily Californian* Op-Ed, (10/16/12 by UC Berkeley senior, Isaiah Kirshner-Breen: "UCSA resolution was merely one reaction to bill: why we should be focusing on HR35, not the UCSA reaction to it," www.dailycal.org. The author disapproves of boycott and divestment campaigns, for example, but "will absolutely defend the right of students to use them," adding that equating "valid political protest…with hate speech, effectively… [silences] a community of students on campus…We are bright people, and we should strive for a thoughtful dialectic…it is only through open, intellectual discourse that we can possibly grasp the truth."

161. Levy, G. (9/17/09). Disgrace in The Hague, www.haaretz.com. This news source, *Haaretz*, is considered the *New York Times* of Israel.

162. Falk, R. (9/24/09). Why the Goldstone report matters, www.zcommunications.org.

163. B'tselem and some other groups backed the main recommendations of the report but criticized some parts as flawed: for example, blaming Israel for the possible commission · of crimes against humanity, a claim made without factual basis or hearing Israel's version (because Israel refused to cooperate with the study), http://www.btselem.org/node/120754. Others disagreed with some key conclusions while supporting parts of the study, taking a nuanced careful approach—in stark contrast to those who dismissed the report carte blanche.

164. Rosen, B. (5/11/10). Alan Dershowitz and the politics of desperation, www.huffingtonpost.com.

165. Blumenthal. M. (7/25/10). IDF report confirming Goldstone's key findings is suppressed inside Israel, http://maxblumenthal.com/2010/07/ idf-report-confirming-goldstones-key-findings-is-suppressed-inside-israel/. The report itself, *Gaza Operation Investigations: Second Update, July 2010*, can be found at GazaUpdateJuly2010.pdf.

166. Shamir, S. (2/5/10). Nobel Prize laureates back Elie Wiesel anti-Ahmadinejad ad, www.haaretz.com. Wiesel consistently conflates critiques of Israeli policies with anti-Semitism. Significantly (as recounted by physician/author Gabor Maté), as a boy, Wiesel was imprisoned in Auschwitz, along with his father. When the Nazis beat his father to death on a top bunk, Wiesel cowered below on the bottom bunk, afraid that if he moved or cried out, he would be next. Throughout this book I argue that unhealed traumatic experiences can then be projected onto innocent "others." Chapter Ten explores this theme in depth.

167. Rosen, B. (5/11/10). Alan Dershowitz and the politics of desperation. www. huffingtonpost.com. Dershowitz called the report's main conclusions "entirely false," and Goldstone "evil," http://www.haaretz.com/news/dershowitz-goldstone-is-a-traitor-to-the-jewish-people-1.265833.

168. Blumenthal, M. (3/13/10) Inside the Lawfare Project: Netanyahu's attack on human rights NGO's hits the States, http://maxblumenthal.com/2010/03/inside-the-lawfare-project-netanyahus-attack-on-human-rights-ngos-hits-the-states/. The specific charge came from David Mataas, senior legal counsel to B'nai B'rith Canada.

169. Otterman, S. (10/22/09). Gaza report author asks U.S. to clarify concerns, www. nytimes.com.

170. Cook, J. (10/6/09). How Israel buried the U.N.'s war crime probe, www.counterpunch.org.

171. Kucinich, D. (11/3/09). Standing against the "wrong is right" Goldstone Resolution, www.huffingtonpost.com.

172. Falk, R. (9/24/09). Why the Goldstone report matters, www.mondoweiss.net.

173. Pogrebin, L. C. (2010, January/February) Jewish McCarthyism strikes gold(stone). www.momentmag.com.

174. Kaiser, J. E. G. (5/4/10). Rabbi and editor Michael Lerner's home found vandalized, www.forward.com.

175. Levy, G. (9/17/09). Disgrace in The Hague, www.haaretz.com.

176. Goldstone, R. (4/1/11). Reconsidering the Goldstone Report on Israel and war crimes, www.washingtonpost.com. Significantly, Goldstone was only one of the Report's four authors, and the only one to partially backtrack from this official U.N. document.

177. Horowitz, A. (4/4/11). Judge Goldstone retracts part of his report on Israeli assault

on Gaza, leaves rest intact, www.democracynow.org. Horowitz is coeditor of the 2011 book *The Goldstone report: The legacy of the landmark investigation of the Gaza conflict.*

178. The bulldozer driver said he did not see Rachel, even though she was wearing an orange fluorescent vest, and witnesses said she had been speaking to the driver shortly before.

179. Pazornik, A. (7/9/09). Film festival under fire for scheduling "Rachel," inviting mom, www.jweekly.com. The quote is from festival director Peter Stein.

180. "Film festival, sponsors respond to 'Rachel' controversy," (7/21/09), www.jweekly.com. The foundations referred to were the Taube and Koret Foundations. "Rachel" later played in Tel Aviv and at Haifa's prestigious International Film Festival without incident.

181. Surasky, C. (3/31/12). Jewish Community Relations Council of SF to young Jews: You can't speak here, www.muzzlewatch.com. The quote is from the panelists' letter to the Jewish Community Library, who cancelled the panel in consultation with its parent organization, the Bureau of Jewish Education, and with the Jewish Community Relations Council, consultant-advisor to the local Jewish Community Federation Endowment. Abileah was also ostracized for personally challenging Netanyahu about his policies, in a congressional hearing a year earlier. Congregation Sha'ar Zahav later hosted the event.

Full disclosure: I was also targeted by these guidelines in April 2012 when the Jewish Community Center of the East Bay withdrew as cosponsor of a KPFA-radio-sponsored event with Peter Beinart—because I was to moderate the event and was a founding board member of Jewish Voice for Peace, which supports withdrawing economic support from Israel's occupation. After the JCC withdrawal, Beinart cancelled the event. See http://jewishvoiceforpeace.org/blog/beinart-berkeley-talk-cancelled-mccarthyism-in-jewish-world and http://www.jweekly.com/article/full/64734/zionism-author-cancels-kpfa-talk-in-berkeley/.

182. Brostoff, M. (5/6/10). Academic question, www.tabletmag.com.

183. Pine, D. (3/4/10). Pluralism panel morphs into debate over new JCF rules, www.jweekly.com. Yet another example: Deborah Kaufman reports that in trying to screen the documentary she coproduced with Alan Snitow, *Between Two Worlds: The American Jewish Culture Wars*, many Jewish Film Festivals from Boston to Calgary couldn't screen the film "because of a funder, board member, or community member who warned of dire consequences for crossing some kind of political line." See her July 2012 *Tikkun* article, "The Jewish community's drift toward the right."

184. Levy, S. (10/27/09). Bridging the gap with honesty and transparency, www.muzzlewatch.com. Elissa Barrett acknowledged that Progressive Jewish Alliance lost funders because of its positions on Israel.

185. Wikipedia. Louis Brandeis, http://en.wikiquote.org. And nationally, the tide is turning. In early 2013, when award-winning philosopher Judith Butler (on the Advisory Board of Jewish Voice for Peace) and Palestinian leader Omar Barghouti were scheduled to speak at Brooklyn College about BDS (Boycott, Divestment, Sanctions against Israeli human rights abuses), alum and Harvard law professor Alan Dershowitz complained that the event was unbalanced–and ten City Council members threatened to cut financing for the college. But college president Karen Gould held firm, citing the principle of academic freedom, despite her personal opposition to BDS; and signaling a sea change in mainstream opinion, in the *New York Times*, and in an Op Ed in the *LA Times*, Mayor Michael Bloomberg, and Governor Andrew Cuomo (among others) backed Gould, and the event took place as planned. See "Litmus Tests," (2/4/13), www.nytimes.com.

186. Wind, M. and Mishly, N. (9/24/09). From a letter posted on the Code Pink listserve written by the refusers, or *shministim* (twelfth-graders), Maya Wind and Netta Mishly.

187. Fleischman, D. and Klein, D. (10/13/11). "Occupy Wall Street" movement brings Jewish ethos to demonstrations, www.jweekly.com.

188. Anti-Defamation League (11/1/11). "Occupy Wall Street" demonstrations: anti-Semitic incidents surface, www.adl.org.

189. Burke, K., Rotondo, C., and Siemaszko, C. (11/11/11). Vandals torch three vehicles in Midwood, Brooklyn, scrawl anti-Semitic graffiti, www.nydailynews.com.

190. OWS official statement against anti-Semitism (11/12/11), http://blog.occupy-judaism.org/.

191. Personal correspondence from Sina Arnold, December 2011.

192. Prominent Jews defend OWS from anti-Semitism claims, (11/1/11), www.thejewish-week.com.

193. Jewish Voice for Peace. (11/13/11). Jewish groups stand up for free speech at Occupy Wall Street, http://jewishvoiceforpeace.org.

194. Rosenberg, M.J. (10/14/11). Opinion: Exploiting anti-Semitism to destroy Occupy Wall Street, www.jewishjournal.com.

195. West, C. (10/24/10). Dr. Cornel West: "We are in a magnificent moment of democratic awakening," www.democracynow.org.

196. Berlet, C. (6/10/09). Holocaust museum shooting, anti-Semitic conspiracy theories, and the tools of fear, www.huffingtonpost.com.

197. Wise, A. and Rosen, B. (2/2/12). A statement in support of the Penn BDS conference. http:// palestiniantalmud.com.

198. Ibid.

199. Herbert, B. (6/12/09) The way we are, www.nytimes.com. I do not know if he is Jewish.

200. Berlet, C. (9/17/09). Vast conspiracy of leftist parasites and traitors, www.huffingtonpost.com. Berlet is Christian.

201. In 2012 the Supreme Court struck down three of the law's four provisions, that made it a crime for undocumented folks to be in the state, to work or look for work, and that allowed warrantless searches by police. Significantly, although it upheld the "show me your papers" provision, requiring police to check the immigration status of people they stop before releasing them, the court left open the possibility of later challenges to this section of the law after it goes into effect.

202. Krugman, P. (6/11/09). The big hate, www.nytimes.com. Krugman is also a Pulitzer Prize winner.

203. Berlet, C. (6/10/09). Holocaust museum shooting, anti-Semitic conspiracy theories, and the tools of fear, www.huffingtonpost.com.

204. Ibid.

CHAPTER TWO: INSIDER/OUTSIDER: Jews, Race, and Privilege

1. Greenberg, C. (1998). Pluralism and its discontents (p. 60). In D. Biale, M. Galchinsky, & S. Heschel (Eds.), Insider/outsider: American Jews and multiculturalism. Berkeley: University of California Press.

2. Rosenwasser, P., & Gatmon, A. (2000). Crosscurrents of Jewish women in a journey towards healing. Bridges, 8, 119.

3. Personal communication, 7/20/10. Windwood is an African American gentile.

4. Kaye/Kantrowitz, M., To be a radical Jew in the late 20th century (p. 145). (Chap 1, Note 67)

5. Kaye/Kantrowitz, M., Jews in the U.S. (p. 125). (Chap 1, Note 51)

6. Marder, D. (5/5/07). Black Jew illuminates diversity of Judaism. The Inquirer, http://articles.philly.com.

7. Levins Morales. Latino Jews in the United States. (Chap 1, Note 14)

NOTES TO CHAPTER 2

8. Rosenwasser & Gatmon, Crosscurrents of Jewish women, 118, (Chap 2, Note 2)

9. Ibid.

10. Edut, O. (2001). Bubbe got back: Tales of a Jewess with caboose (p. 30). In D. Ruttenberg (Ed.), *Yentl's revenge: The next wave of Jewish feminism*. Seattle, WA: Seal Press.

11. Rosenwasser & Gatmon. Crosscurrents of Jewish women, 118. (Chap 2, Note 2)

12. Personal communication, 7/19/10, used with permission.

13. Ibid. Sephardim also settled in Greece, North Africa, the Caribbean; and some returned to the Middle East from Spain, so the terms Sephardim and Mizrahim mean different things to different people.

14. Piercy. *Sleeping with cats*. (p. 43). (Chap 1, Note 81)

15. Brodkin, K. (1998). *How the Jews became white folks and what that says about race in America*, (p. 17). New Brunswick, NJ: Rutgers University Press. Her book is excellent in regard to white Ashkenazi Jews.

16. Rosen, B. (11/8/11), From the American South to the West Bank: A Freedom Rider bears witness to human rights in Israel/Palestine, http://mondoweiss.net. Ironically, Brom's Freedom Rider, African American colleague Marjorie, fair-skinned and green-eyed, who also refused to state her race, was booked as white and put in the white women's "tank." Broms notes "If we did nothing else during that ride, we did succeed in briefly integrating the jail."

17. Elly illustrates a key aspect of white privilege: when you have it, you don't have to think about it.

18. Ululating is flicking the tongue against the roof of the mouth, while cheering. Intifada is the name of specific Palestinian uprisings (1987-1993 and 2000-2005), resistance struggles against the Israeli occupation.

19. Personal communication, 1/20/11, used with permission. Thanks to Loolwa Khazzoom for initially sending me Linda's quote.

20. Elly Bulkin explains that these Sephardic Jews managed to remain in New Amsterdam (which became New York) even though Governor Peter Stuyvesant objected. In (1984), "Hard ground: Jewish identity, racism, and anti-Semitism," in E. Bulkin, M. Pratt, & B. Smith (Eds.), *Yours in struggle: Three feminist perspectives on anti-Semitism and racism*, p. 107. Brooklyn, NY: Long Haul Press.

21. Stoval, T. (1/25/06), Funny, you don't look Jewish: Local synagogue explores the changing face of Judaism, *The Montclair Times*, http://www.jewishresearch.org/. The statistic is from Paul Golin of Boston's Jewish Outreach Institute.

22. Khazzoom, L. (2009 March). Esther is *our* queen: expanding our vision of the Jewish family. In *Wise, Beneath the Masks We Wear, Who Are We?* (p. 6), www.wisela.org/WorkArea/downloadasset .aspx?id=38120, March 09@wise for web.pdf.

23. Khazzoom, L (1995). When Jewish means Ashkenazi: an exploration of power and privilege in the Jewish community. *Response Magazine*, www.loolwa.com.

24. Khazzoom. Esther is *our* queen. (p. 6). (Chap 2, Note 22)

25. Be'chol Lashon: In Every Tongue. Counting Jews of color in the United States. www.bechollashon.org/.

26. Kaye/Kantrowitz. *The colors of Jews*. (p. 100). (Chap 1, Note 52)

27. Ibid., p. 36. Kaye/Kantrowitz cites Michael Gelbwasser, "Organization for black Jews claims 200,000 in U.S.," *Boston Jewish Advocate* (4/10/98): 38. She says estimates range from 100,000 to 250,000.

28. The Southern Poverty Law Center reports that a black supremacist wing of Hebrew Israelites preach that Christ is returning to enslave or kill whites, Jews, queers, others. However, this extremist wing does not represent the Hebrew Israelite community, and lacks ties

to both the power structure and the Black community.

29. Setton, R. (2003b). The life and times of Ruth of the Jungle (p. 5). In Khazzoom. *The flying camel.* (Chap 1, Note 34)

30. Ibid

31. Levins Morales. Latino Jews in the United States (p. 9) (Chap 1, Note 14)

32. Kaye/Kantrowitz. *The colors of Jews.* (p. 38). (Chap 1, Note 52)

33. Ibid. p. 36.

34. Barshad, A. (2010 June). *Heeb.* Drake: The Heeb interview, www.heebmagazine. com. Schvartze is a derogatory Yiddish word for black person.

35. Wahba. Benign ignorance or persistent resistance?. (p. 52) In Khazzoom. *The flying camel.* (Chap 1, Note 34). See also Ella Shohat's excellent essay, "Reflections by an Arab Jew," http://www.bintjbeil.com/E/occupation/arab_jew.html.

36. Ibid., p. 53.

37. Ibid., p. 56.

38. Ibid.

39. Khazzoom, L., Esther is *our* queen, (p. 7) (Chap 2, Note 22)

40. Personal communication, October 1997, used with permission.

41. Khazzoom, L. (2001). United Jewish feminist front (p. 168). In Ruttenberg. *Yentl's revenge.* (pp. 168-180). (Chap 1, Note 65)

42. Ibid.

43. Rosenwasser & Gatmon. Crosscurrents of Jewish women, 122. (Chap 2, Note 2). This group was the council Anna Gatmon and I recruited and cofacilitated for Shakti Butler's film *The Way Home,* about what holds oppression in place. Loolwa reminded me that she had to pressure me and Anna (also Ashkenazi) into adding group members, so that it would not be so Ashkenazi-dominant. I had conveniently forgotten about that.

44. Ibid.

45. Khazzoom, L., Esther is *our* queen, (p. 6) (Chap 2, Note 22)

46. Ibid., p. 7.

47. Ibid. Racism by Ashkenazi Jews against Mizrahim is also prevalent in Israel.

48. Fishkoff, S. (10/13/09) Jews of color come together to.explore identity. *Jewish Telegraph Agency,* http://jta.org/.

49. Kivel, P. *Uprooting racism: How white people can work for racial justice* (Rev. ed.). Gabriola Island, British Columbia, Canada: New Society.

50. Brodkin, K., *How the Jews became white folks,* (p. 60) (Chap 2, Note 15)

51. Ibid., p. 58.

52. Steinberg, S., (1989). *The ethnic myth: Race, ethnicity, and class in America* (Rev. ed.). (Chap 1, Note 46) Boston: Beacon Press.

53. Ibid. Steinberg refers to *The Reports of the Immigration Commission,* vol. 3, op. cit. pp. 98-178.

54. Ibid. Steinberg points out, though, that the literacy rate for Jewish immigrants was similar to that of other immigrants from industrial backgrounds, such as northern Italians.

55. Ibid., p. 99.

56. Ibid., p. 71. Additionally, regarding the significance here of the Great Compromise, Brodkin cites Lieberson, S. (1980) *A piece of the pie: Blacks and white immigrants since 1880* (p. 5). Berkeley: University of California Press, which cites the Report of the National Advisory Commission on Civil Disorders, pp. 143-145 (1968). In an interview on KPFA radio in Berkeley, CA, 9/25/10, journalist Isabelle Wilkerson (who documents the story of African Americans' "great migration") reports that a $25,000 fine was charged in 1918 to anyone recruiting a black worker from the South. Steinberg adds that part of the rationale

was that most immigrants were unwilling to work in the cotton fields.

57. Ibid., p. 200.

58. Brodkin, K., *How the Jews became white folks*, (p. 61) (Chap 2, Note 15)

59. Ibid., pp. 61-62. Brodkin refers to Howe, I. (1980), *World of our fathers* (pp. 156-57), abridged edition, New York: Bantam.

60. Ibid., p. 53. I do not know whether or not Taylor is Jewish.

61. Steinberg, S., *The ethnic myth*. (Rev. ed.) (Chap 1, Note 46)

62. Ibid., p. 132.

63. Ibid., p. 103.

64. Ibid., p. 176.

65. Brodkin, K., *How the Jews became white folks*, (p. 76) (Chap 2, Note 15). For example, in 2013, researchers at Brandeis University found that "Tracing the same households over 25 years, the total wealth gap between white and African-American families nearly triples," and also that this dramatic racial U.S. racial gap "cannot be attributed to personal ambition and behavioral choices, but rather reflects policies and institutional practices that create different opportunities for whites and African-Americans." See "Heller study finds public policy widens wealth gap," www.brandeis.edu.

66. Ibid., p. 63.

67. Ibid., p. 38.

68. Wikipedia. History of the Jews in the United States, http://en.wikipedia.org.

69. Kaye/Kantrowitz. *The colors of Jews*. (p. 11). (Chap 1, Note 52)

70. Brodkin, K., *How the Jews became white folks*, (Chap 2, Note 15)

71. Ibid.

72. Ibid.

73. Ibid.

74. Ibid.

75. Ibid., p. 51.

76. Rosenwasser & Gatmon. Crosscurrents of Jewish women. (Chap 2, Note 2)

77. Loeb. Sundown to sundown (excerpt). (Chap 1, Note 131)

78. COINTELPRO was an FBI-created Counter Intelligence Program in the 1960s-'70s, which illegally spied on, infiltrated, disrupted, and weakened leftist political groups, including imprisoning (for decades) and murdering Black Panthers and American Indian Movement activists. Agents wrote Rev. Martin Luther King, Jr. a letter encouraging him to commit suicide. See the 2011 video documentary *Cointelpro 101* by Claude Marks of the Freedom Archives, http://freedomarchives.org/Cointelpro.html.

79. Brodkin, K., *How the Jews became white folks*, (p. 152) (Chap 2, Note 15)

80. Thandeka. (1999). *Learning to be white: Money, race, and God in America* (p. 29). New York: Continuum.

81. White, K. (2006, November 17). Know your rightwing speakers: Norman Podhoretz, http://campusprogress.org/.

82. Although Miller won a Pulitzer Prize for drama, he was targeted by the House Un-American Activities Committee.

83. Thandeka, *Learning to be white* (p. 32). (Chap 2, Note 80).

84. Levins Morales. Latinos, Israel and Palestine. (Chap 1, Note 23)

85. Personal communication, 6/24/10, used with permission.

86. Rowley, R. & Soohen, J. (2010). *White power USA* (film documentary), www.democracynow.org/ 2010/1/11/ white_power_usa_the_rise_of. Although extremist, they are trying hard to enter the U.S. mainstream.

87. Levins Morales. Latino Jews in the United States (pp. 6-7). (Chap 1, Note 14)

NOTES TO CHAPTER 2

88. In *The colors of Jews* (p. 28), Kaye/Kantrowitz quotes Karen Brodkin Sacks, "How did Jews become white folks?" in Gregory and Sanjek, Race, 87.

89. Kaye/Kantrowitz. *The colors of Jews*. (p. 207). (Chap 1, Note 52)

90. Kivel. *Uprooting racism*, (p. 162). (Rev. ed.) (Chap 2, Note 49)

91. Lerner. *Socialism of fools* (p. 121). (Chap 1, Note 71). For an excellent analysis of the complex intersections between racism and anti-Semitism. See Bulkin. "Hard ground," in Bulkin, Pratt & Smith. *Yours in struggle*. (pp. 91-230). (Chap 2, Note 20).

92. Bearing in mind that racism is an involuntary by-product of living in U.S. society. And not to excuse the behavior, but believing that no one would oppress someone else unless they themselves had somehow first been hurt. In *Privilege, power and difference*, Allan Johnson points out, "Oppression and dominance name social realities that we can participate in without being oppressive or dominating people." Also, check out The Catalyst Project in Oakland, CA, which works in majority white communities to deepen antiracist commitment and build multiracial movements for liberation, "where all people are free from all forms of oppression and are able to live in sustainable relationship with the earth."

93. Greenberg. Pluralism and its discontents, (p. 75). In Biale, Galchinsky, & Heschel. Insider/outsider. (Chap 2, Note 1). In *Going south: Jewish women in the civil rights movement*, Debra Schultz writes, "Jewish racism has its own dynamics. It often derives from a sense of victimization and consequent commitment to protecting oneself and one's family from harm." p. 26.

94. Ibid., p. 61.

95. This exercise "Stand Up/Sit Down: Anti-Semitism" (p. 164) was developed by Michael Taller and printed in the invaluable resource by Hugh Vasquez and Isoke Femi, Vasquez, (1993). *A manual for unlearning oppression and building multicultural alliances*. Oakland, CA: TODOS Sherover-Simms Alliance Building Institute. See Action-Oriented Reader's Guide in this book for a full version of this exercise.

96. Cited by Evelyn Beck, (Ed.). (1989). *Nice Jewish girls: A lesbian anthology* (p. xxiii) (Rev. ed.). Boston: Beacon Press. Moraga and Barbara Smith are not Jewish, I don't know about Perez or Beverly Smith.

97. Fred Phelps heads the über-homophobic, anti-Semitic Westboro Baptist Church, an extended-family, Kansas-based hate group, which pickets various events nationwide. David Duke was a former Ku Klux Klan Grand Wizard, and in the 1990s served as a Republican in the Louisiana House of Representatives.

98. Lyons. Parasites and Pioneers. In Alexander, Albrecht, Day, et al. and M. Segrest (Eds.), *Sing, whisper.* (Chap 1, Note 53)

99. This was Rabbi Hillel's succinct response when a skeptic asked him to describe Judaism while standing on one foot. Hillel followed these words by adding "All the rest is commentary."

Referring to Jewish racism, for an exposé of the links between extremist Jewish hate-group funders, Islamophobia, and the far right in Israel, see "Follow the money: From Islamophobia to Israel right or wrong," (10/3/12,) by Elly Bulkin and Donna Nevel. Another powerful article by Nevel and Bulkin documents anti-Muslim campaigns by the (Jewish) Anti-Discrimination League towards U.S. groups: "ADL's pro-Israel mindset leads it to perpetuate anti-Muslim worldview," (2/4/13). Also see Note 91 in Chapter 15.

100. Kershner, I. (2/10/10). Museum creates new Jerusalem divide, www.nytimes.com.

101. Central Conference of American Rabbis. (2/24/09). CCAR Resolution on the Jerusalem Location of the Museum of Tolerance, http://data.ccarnet.org/cgi-bin/resodisp.pl?file=museum&year=2009.

102. Lawler, A. (10/21/11). Jerusalem's Museum of Tolerance under Fire—for intolerance. *ScienceInsider*, http://news.sciencemag.org/. The Center for Constitutional Rights notes that the burial ground was active until the new Israeli state appropriated this part of Jerusalem in 1948.

103. Surasky, C. (4/25/09). Communication to Jewish Voice for Peace listserve. Used with permission.

104. Ibid.

105. Klein, N. (2009, September). Minority death match: Jews, blacks and the "post-racial" presidency," (p. 62). *Harpers Magazine*, 319.

106. Ibid., p. 60.

107. Ibid., p. 54. Thanks also to trusted friends who participated in the NGO Forum for clarifying some of this info, Elizabeth Seja Min and Susan Freundlich.

108. World Conference Against Racism. (9/3/01). NGO Forum Declaration, #419, http://i-p-o.org/racism-ngo-decl.htm.

109. Klein. Minority death match. (p. 54). (Chap 2, Note 105). Specifically, then-U.N. High Commissioner on Human Rights Mary Robinson condemned the NGO document.

110. Ibid., p. 55.

111. Ibid.

112. Zunes. S. (4/22/09). Missing an anti-racism moment. *Foreign Policy* in Focus, www.fpif.org.

113. Israeli Ministry of Foreign Affairs. (9/9/01). The conclusion of the Durban conference—comments by Israeli leaders and officials, http://www.mfa.gov.il/MFA/MFAArchive/2000_2009/2001/9/ The Conclusion of the Durban Conference—Comments.

114. Surasky, C. (5/13/09). My word: Rebranding of U.N. conference undid years of human-rights work. *Oakland Tribune*, http://www.highbeam.com/doc/1P2-20252974.html. The Badil Resource Center (www.badil.org) reports that the Jewish National Fund (JNF) was created in 1901 to acquire land and property rights in Palestine and beyond for exclusive Jewish settlement. In 2011, the JNF continues to destroy Bedouin villages (over 200,000 Palestinian shepherds living in Israel, usually in the Negev), to plant forests overtop the remains.

115. Surasky, C. (4/23/09), Personal communication, used with permission.

116. Klein. Minority death match. (p. 63). (Chap 2, Note 105)

117. Ibid.

118. Ibid., p. 64.

119. Ibid.

120. West, C. (2000). On Black-Jewish relations (p. 179). In Adams, Blumenfeld, Castaneda, et al. *Readings for diversity.* (Chap 1, Note 93)

121. Ibid.

122. Ibid., p. 180.

123. Pomerance, Rachel. (1/14/05) "Jewish-Black Ties Loosen over Years." *The Jewish Journal*, Jewish Telegraphic Agency. Cited in Kaye/Kantrowtiz. *The Colors of Jews.* (p. 53).

124. Smith, B. (1984). Between a rock and a hard place: Relationships between Black and Jewish women (p. 85). In Bulkin. "Hard ground" in Bulkin, Pratt & Smith. *Yours in struggle.* (pp. 65-88). (Chap 2, Note 20).

125. Kaye/Kantrowitz. *The colors of Jews.* (p. 57). (Chap 1, Note 52)

126. Davis and Baldwin resigned from the advisory board of the black journal, *The Liberator*, because of its argument of Jewish conspiracy theories (Bulkin, "Hard Ground.")

127. Kaye/Kantrowitz. *The colors of Jews.* (p. 51). (Chap 1, Note 52).

128. Ibid., p. 35. In an endnote, Kaye/Kantrowitz adds (p. 233) "Though the plaintiff named was a different person with the same surname, a black man named Oliver Brown."

She cites Nussbaum Cohen, Jewish Telegraph Agency, 1/14/2000, discussing Rabbi Marc Schneier's book, *Shared Dreams: Martin Luther King, Jr. and the Jewish Community*. Esther Brown was a 30-year-old housewife when she initiated this suit; see also "May 17th: Esther Brown v. Board of Education," www.jewishcurrents.org.

129. Ibid.

130. Ibid., p. 63.

131. *Democracy Now* (3/30/12), Adrienne Rich (1929-2012): Alice Walker & Frances Goldin on the Life of the Legendary Poet & Activist, www.democracynow.org. Rich and Allen Ginsburg were both white, Jewish, and gay.

132. Ibid.

133. Ibid.

134. De Veaux, A. (2004). *Warrior poet, a biography of Audre Lorde*. New York: Norton, p. 133.

135. Aurora Levins Morales, personal communication, 2/11/12, used with permission.

136. One survivor still remembered the teddy bear that arrived in a care package for her fourth birthday.

137. Segev, T. (7/16/10). The makings of history/A personal and collective war, www. haaretz.com.

138. Ibid. Another example, June 2012: when the LA Jewish Federation allowed anti-Muslim hate blogger Pamela Geller to give a speech, an interfaith coalition (including Jews) denounced her appearance and succeeded in pressuring the Federation to cancel Geller's talk.

139. Wikipedia explains "Stand your ground" as a "self-defense" law that gives people the right to use "reasonable force" to defend themselves, without any requirement to evade or retreat from a dangerous situation.

140. When I told my African American upstairs neighbor about this, she replied "In a few years one of those boys will be gone [murdered] too."

CHAPTER THREE: LET'S TALK ABOUT "JEWISH POWER": Rethinking Stereotypes

1. Zunes, S. (1995, March). Anti-semitism in U.S. Middle East policy. Z *Magazine*, www.zcommunications.org. Zunes is Episcopalian.

2. Structural advantage and power here refers to how more than a few individual Jews have significant decision-making roles in key institutions, from corporations to government, and so are part of the U.S. power structure. Examples are given in this chapter. I also mean that as predominantly white and middle/upper-middle class, sometimes owning class, more Jews than not have systemic advantage, meaning *power that we can tap into by virtue of our positions within the structure*. In general we are on the "upside" of power dynamics in this country, as opposed to the "downside." Sociologist G. William Domhoff defines "structural economic power" as "the basis for dominating the federal government through lobbying, campaign finance, appointments to key government positions, and a policy-planning network made up of foundations, think tanks, and policy discussion groups." See WhoRulesAmerica. net, http://www.ucsc.edu/whorulesamerica/power.

3. Newport, F. (12/24/12). In U.S., 77% identify as Christian, www.gallup.com. A year earlier, a 1/17/12 Forward article by N. Zeveloff put the figure at 1.8 percent ("U.S. Jewish population pegged at 6 million," http://forward.com). Two new independent studies found that there are between 6.4 and 6.6 million Jews living in the U.S. as of January 2012. However, the United Jewish Communities say "there is no definitive estimate that everyone agrees on."

4. Pogrebin. Anti-semitism in the women's movement. (Chap 1, Note 126)

5. Kivel. *You call this a democracy?* (p. 17). (Chap 1, Note 136)

6. Ibid., p. 32.

7. Ibid., p. 20.

8. Ibid.

9. Domhoff, G. (2011). Wealth, income, and power. WhoRulesAmerica.net, http://www2.ucsc.edu/whorulesamerica/ power/wealth.html. Domhoff adds that in 2007 "the average white household had 15 times as much total wealth as the average African-American or Latino household." In 2010, CEO's in all industries made about 100 times as much as their workers (and much more in the Dow-Jones companies); "CEOs now are able to rig things so that the board of directors, which they help select — and which includes some fellow CEOs on whose boards they sit — gives them the pay they want."

10. Kivel. *You call this a democracy?* (p. 21). (Chap 1, Note 136.) Kivel refers here to the thinking of sociologists C. Wright Mills, in *The power elite*, and G. William Domhoff, in *Who rules America: Power and politics in the year 2000*. In 2013 Kivel said that the power elite numbers 7,000-10,000 (in his 4/20/13 workshop on Christian Hegemony at the Jewish Voice for Peace National Membership Meeting, Berkeley, CA). See also Domhoff's excellent 2006 article, "Mills's the Power Elite, 50 years later," http://www2.ucsc.edu/whorulesamerica/ theory/mills_review_2006.html. In WhoRulesAmerica.net (2012), Domhoff specifies the power elite as the biggest corporate CEOs working together with top execs at foundations, think tanks and policy discussion groups, adding that sometimes "they do fight among themselves," http://www.ucsc.edu/whorulesamerica/power.

11. Described by Peter Phillips and Mickey Huff in their excellent Op-Ed, (12/27/09), Inside the military-industrial-media complex: Impacts on movement for social justice, www.truth-out.org.

12. Kivel. *You call this a democracy?* (p. 21). (Chap 1, Note 136). Kivel cites Parenti, *Democracy for the Few*, 36.

13. Richard Alba (The University of Albany, SUNY) refers to these "narrow class interests" in his promotional quote on the cover of Zweigenhaft & Domhoff's 1998 book, *Diversity in the power elite*. Also relevant, from the Declaration of Occupy D.C.: "The rotation of decision makers between the public and private sectors cultivates a network of public officials, lobbyists, and executives whose aligned interests do not serve the American people."

14. Paul Kivel, personal communication, 9/1/04, used with permission. Also see: Letty Cottin Pogrebin's 1982 article "Anti-semitism in the women's movement," (Chap 1, Note 126; also Aurora Levins Morales' 2012 article, "Latinos, Israel and Palestine: Understanding Anti-Semitism": (Chap 1, Note 23), "...the real power structure of this country which is solidly white and Protestant."

15. Prell. *Fighting to become Americans.* (p. 125). (Chap 1, Note 57); also Dinnerstein. *Anti-semitism in America.* (p. 131). (Chap 1, Note 26)

16. Dinnerstein. *Anti-semitism in America.* (p. 126). (Chap 1, Note 26)

17. Zweigenhaft, R., & Domhoff, W. (1998). Jews in the power elite. In *Diversity in the power elite: Have women and minorities reached the top?* (pp. 12-40). New Haven, CT: Yale University Press.

18. Dinnerstein. *Anti-semitism in America.* (p. 238). (Chap 1, Note 26)

19. Ibid. Dinnerstein cites Robert A. Bennett, "No Longer a WASP Preserve," 6/29/86, III, 1, 8.

20. Dinnerstein. *Anti-semitism in America.* (p. 129). (Chap 1, Note 26)

21. Goldberg, J., *Jewish power*. (p. 117) (Chap 1, Note 89)

22. Zweigenhaft & Domhoff. Jews in the power elite. (p. 22). (Chap 3, Note 17). I do not know if Zweigenhaft and/or Domhoff are Jewish. Then (Presbyterian) venture capitalist Steven Pease published *The Golden Age of Jewish Achievement*, which listed 31% of the 2007 Forbes 400 "High Tech Entrepreneurs and CEO's" as Jews. This means 69% of the CEOs were gentiles.

23. Pew Forum's U.S. Religious Landscape Survey, 2007, religions.pewforum.org/portraits. Data for Muslims is from the Pew Research Center, 2007, "Muslim Americans: Middle Class and Mostly Mainstream" (cited in Pew survey.)

24. Popper, N. (10/8/2004b). Nearly a million living in poor Jewish households: Study challenges longstanding views of need. *The Forward*, CVIII, 1 & 3.

25. In the 2007 Pew survey, earning less than $14,000 (the lowest end of the scale): 9% were Hindus, 14% Jews, 25% from "mainline churches," 31% Catholics, 35% Muslims, and 47% from "historically black churches." Pew Forum's U.S. Religious Landscape Survey, 2007, religions.pewforum.org/portraits. Data for Muslims is from the Pew Research Center, 2007, "Muslim Americans: Middle Class and Mostly Mainstream" (cited in Pew survey).

26. Muller, J. (3/24/10). *Forward*. Antisemitism and this recession: The dog that didn't bark, http://forward.com. Muller notes that of the four surviving Wall Street firms in 2010, three were led by Christians, one by a Jew. I do not know whether or not Muller is Jewish.

27. *Democracy Now Headlines* (4/26/10). Goldman Sachs execs bragged of profiting from housing crash, www.democracynow.org.

28. Meaning just as some Jews can act as oppressors, they can also be oppressed. Even still, it would be classic bigotry to hold all Jews responsible for the misdeeds of a few.

29. Do you need a $100 Bernie Madoff doll? (2009, February 17). *Daily Finance*, http://www.bloggingstocks.com/2009/02/17/do-you-need-a-100-dollar-bernie-madoff-doll/.

30. *Forward* editor J. J. Goldberg calls Madoff "a villain," while also explaining "he was doing things that are illegal, but not that different from everybody else…Everybody…lost money. Which is a lot better than the people at Bear Stearns and Bank of America, who took the whole world down with them. The big difference between him and them is that the things that they were doing weren't illegal anymore." See Nathan-Kazis, J. (5/18/09). Why it matters that Madoff is Jewish, www.newvoices.com.

31. Leopold, L. (7/17/09), Wall Street and anti-Semitism, www.huffingtonpost.com.

32. Scherer, M. (5/24/10). The new sheriffs of Wall Street. *Time*, 24.

33. Ibid. Of course some women also bear responsibility for the breakdown and/or profited from it.

34. ADL. (11/4/11). ADL poll on anti-Semitic attitudes in America, www.fightthatred.com. The exact statistic here was 19%, while 20% said "Jews have too much power in business." A 2011 example (reported by *JTA* on 2/15/11): flyers distributed at a Chicago subway station against mayoral front-runner Rahm Emanuel read, "I will run Chicago as I ran Freddie Mac, PROFITABLE (for me, me, me) thirty millions$$$$$$. I was entitled to it, being a Holocaust survivor (I mean my family)."

35. Wise, T. (8/19/03). When paranoia meets prejudice: debunking the notion of a Jewish conspiracy, www.timwise.org.

36. Kivel. *Uprooting racism*. (p. 163). (Chap 2, Note 49)

37. Ibid.

38. Goldberg, J., *Jewish power*. (p. 280). (Chap 1, Note 89)

39. Fox network and more. Interesting: when Rupert Murdoch's son James stepped down from overseeing News Corp's newspapers, after the 2011 phone-hacking scandal, British Labour Party leader Ed Miliband said the scandal highlighted why new rules were

needed to limit media consolidation. In May 2012, a British parliamentary report found Rupert Murdoch himself unfit to run a major international media company, as a result of the same scandal.

40. Graham, R. & Alford, M. (1/29/09). The power behind the screen. *The New Statesman*, www.newstatesman.com/ film/2009/01/disney-hollywood-interests.

41. Phillips, P. & Huff, M. (12/26/09), Inside the military-industrial-media complex: Impacts on movement for social justice, www.truth-out.org.

42. Ibid., also Graham & Alford. The power behind the screen. (Chap 3, Note 40)

43. Phillips & and Huff. Inside the military-industrial-media complex. (Chap 3, Note 41). I do not know if Phillips and/or Huff are Jewish.

44. Paul Kivel, personal communication, (9/1/04), used with permission.

45. Kivel, P. (1998, February). I'm not white, I'm Jewish. But I'm white: Standing as Jews in the fight for racial justice. Paper presented at the Whiteness Conference, University of California at Riverside. Also check out the 2012 documentary *The Koch Brothers Exposed* by Robert Greenwald.

46. Immigrants Hall of Fame. Hollywood moguls, http://slalli.tripod.com/archives. htm#Hollywood%20Moguls. Thanks to Paul Kivel for telling me about this.

47. Thanks to Sandy Butler for this insight.

48. Stein, J. (2008, December 19). How Jewish is Hollywood? *LA Times* Op-Ed, www. latimes.com.

49. Graham & Alford. The power behind the screen. (Chap 3, Note 40)

50. Ibid. Also Phillips & Huff. Inside the military-industrial-media complex. (Chap 3, Note 41)

51. Zunes, S. (2/2/09). Personal communication, used with permission. Examples: nearly every U.S. president for quite a period of time was Episcopalian; Zweigenhaft and Domhoff cite a 1992 study by Ralph Pyle showing the overrepresentation of Episcopalians as corporate directors; and my colleague Jesse Bacon references Nicholas Lemann's book, *The big test*, about the SAT test history and the drive to create an education-based meritocracy with a subtext of Episcopalian dominance.

52. Berkman, J. (10/4/09). At least 139 of the Forbes 400 are Jewish. *JTA*, http://blogs.jta. org/philanthropy/article/2009/10/05/. Again, this means two-thirds are not Jews. *The Jewish Telegraph Agency* reports in the 2013 Forbes annual world billionaires list, five Jews were among the top twenty-five, led by Oracle's Larry Ellison in the fifth spot. For an analysis of American Jewish economic success, historian Debra Schultz recommends *Jews and the New American Scene*, (1997), by Seymour Martin Lipset and Earl Raab.

53. Paul Kivel, (10/19/09), personal communication, used with permission.

54. Ibid.

55. Kivel. Challenging Christian hegemony. (Chap 1, Note 18)

56. Fox News. (11/10/10). Glenn Beck: The puppet master, www.foxnews.com.

57. Elliott, J. (11/9/10). Beck attacks Soros as "Puppet Master," www.salon.com. Salon. com notes that Beck's show was watched regularly by over 2 million people.

58. Schell, J. (12/20/10). And now: Anti-Semitism. *The Nation*, 20-22. Beck ended up leaving Fox in spring 2011. Ironically, Beck's far-right views on Israel also got him invited as a speaker at the 2011 (Christian Zionist) Citizens United for Israel Conference, sharing the podium with Jews from the Israel Lobby.

59. Kaye/Kantrowitz, M. (3/25/06). Talk at "Facing the Challenge Within," www. diasporism.net/files/Antisemitism_on.doc.

60. Ibid.

61. Feldman, K. (11/10/11). Consider Birthright Israel occupied, http://wagingnonvio-

lence.org/. "Mic check" refers to an Occupy movement tool for ensuring everyone can hear if there is no microphone: a speaker shouts out a short phrase, and those who can hear, echo it back.

62. Krugman, P. (11/3/11), Oligarchy, American style, www.nytimes.com. I also like the way political economist Robert Reich said it, during "Occupy Cal" at UC Berkeley, on 11/15/11: "It is not wealth that is the problem. It is the irresponsible use of wealth being used to undermine our democracy."

63. Biale. *Power and powerlessness.* (p. 181). (Chap 1, Note 138)

64. Mearsheimer, J. & Walt, S. (3/23/06). The Israel lobby. *London Review of Books.* Analyst Mitchell Plitnick also argues that a "small number of wealthy Jews...put up a great deal of money in campaign contributions" towards ongoing, unconditional support of Israel "no matter what actions Israel takes and whether or not those actions serve American interests." In "Lobbies, pro and con," (6/24/2000), "The Third Way: Finding Balance in the Middle East" blog. These are often the funders that candidates do not want to antagonize.

65. Walzer, M. (1998). Multiculturalism and the politics of interest (p. 96). In Biale, Galchinsky, & Heschel. *Insider/outsider.* (Chap 2, Note 1)

66. Goldberg. *Jewish power.* (p. 117). (Chap 1, Note 89). Ron Kampeas of the Jewish Telegraph Agency wrote in June 2011, "Estimates over the years have reckoned that Jewish donors provide between one-third and two-thirds of the party's money." See "Democrats launch major pro-Obama pushback among Jews," www.jta.org. The 60 percent figure comes from M. J. Rosenberg's (4/2/13) article, "Democrats Not So Into Israel Anymore," www.tikkun.org–an excellent/hopeful article about how the Democratic party is changing and the potential of grass roots activism. Rosenberg says this amount dwarfs "the contributions of a few highly publicized Republican donors like Sheldon Adelson."

67. Mearsheimer & Walt. The Israel lobby. (Chap 3, Note 64)

68. Stone, P. (12/03/12) Sheldon Adelson spent far more on campaign than previously known, www.huffingtonpost.com. Also *Democracy Now* (7/18/12), As Senate GOP blocks DISCLOSE Act, top donor Sheldon Adelson probed for bribery and mob ties, www.democracynow.org; quote is from journalist Peter Stone describing Adelson's characterization of Obama's economic policies. Also Plitnick, M. (2/15/12), Updating anti-Semitism, http://mitchellplitnick.com. Adelson has close ties to Netanyahu and spends millions monthly distributing a free Israeli right-wing daily paper, *Israel Hayom*, with one of the largest readerships in Israel.

69. *Democracy Now,* (8/31/12). Amy Goodman questions top GOP donor David Koch: does concentration of wealth subvert democracy?, www.democracynow.org. Other gentile megadonors include Texas billionaire Harold Simmons who, as of early 2012, gave $16.2 million to super PACs and campaigns backing Republicans: see McGregor, R. (3/19/12), Billionaire floods super-PACS with funds, *Financial Times,* www.ft.com. Also from *Huffington Post,* 12/03/12, check out "Donors giving $500,000 plus to Super PACS."

70. *The Forward,* (1/27/12), Editorial: The Adelson factor, www.forward.com. Specifically, individuals and corporations can give unlimited funds to political action committees supporting candidates, superPACs, as long as these are independent and do not coordinate with the candidate.

71. CBS News. (10/7/09). Jews responsible for all "wars in the world," but Mel Gibson not responsible for DUI anymore, www.cbsnews.com

72. Goldberg, J. J. (5/9/10). The vaudeville routine that has taken over American Jewry, www.haaretz.com. Stanford University Middle East Studies professor Joel Beinin explains that the Lobby's role became greater after the Cold War, and the Christian Zionists' role became greater under President George W. Bush: personal communication, 2/14/12.

73. Although Mearsheimer and Walt argue that oil interests were not a factor in the U.S going to war in Iraq, other analysts disagree: Peter Beinart, Dr. Joel Beinin, Mitchell Plitnick, Cecilie Surasky.

74. Greenwald, G. (12/12/07). New poll reveals how unrepresentative neocon Jewish groups are, www.salon.com.

75. Zunes, S. (12/20/07). The Israel lobby revisited. *Foreign Policy in Focus*, www. organicconsumers.org.

76. Analyst Michael Parenti defines imperialism as a process in which a country imposes its economic and military power on another country/region "in order to expropriate its land, labor, natural resources, capital, and markets—in such a manner as to enrich the investor interests"; see "What Do Empires Do?" by Michael Parenti. Both Stephen Zunes ("The Israel Lobby, *Tikkun*, November/December 2007) and Noam Chomsky ("The Israel Lobby," *Znet*, 3/28/06) agree that U.S Middle East policy has been similar to U.S foreign policy elsewhere.

77. Plitnick, M. & Toensing, C. (2007 Summer). "The Israel lobby" in perspective. *Middle East Report*.

78. Zunes. The Israel lobby revisited. (Chap 3, Note 75). Also, Zunes, S. (5/16/06). The Israel lobby: How powerful is it really? *Foreign Policy in Focus*, http://motherjones.com.

79. Buruma, I. (8/21/03). How to talk about Israel. *New York Times Magazine*, 4, www. nytimes.com.

80. Analysts dispute exactly which Jewish groups comprise the Israel Lobby, but generally included are: the Orthodox Union, the ADL, the American Jewish Congress, the American Jewish Committee, B'nai Brith, Hadassah, the Wiesenthal Center, the Jewish Federations, the United Jewish Appeal, the various Jewish Community Relations Councils, most of the campus Hillels, the Zionist Organization of America, the Conference of Presidents, J Street, Americans for Peace Now, the American Israel Public Affairs Committee, the National Jewish Defense Council, the United Jewish Communities, and various media.

81. Plitnick, M. (3/8/11). The UNSC veto and "The Israel Lobby," http://mitchellplitnick.com. The Lobby also promotes itself this way, see Plitnick & Toensing. "The Israel lobby" in perspective. (Chap 3, Note 77). Noam Chomsky argues that the Israel Lobby, however, is "dwarfed by the business and military lobbies." See his 1/3/11 Op-Ed in *Truthout*, "Breaking the Israel-Palestine Deadlock."

82. Mearsheimer & Walt. The Israel lobby. (Chap 3, Note 64). In a speech he gave in Oakland (5/8/13), "Palestinian Hopes, Regional Turmoil," Professor Noam Chomsky challenged whose interests were "U.S. interests" anyway; he argued that these are primarily the interests of large corporations.

83. Plitnick & Toensing. "The Israel lobby" in perspective. (Chap 3, Note 77). In "The system of anti-Semitism," peace activist Glen Hauer writes, "To argue that absent pressure from U.S. Jewish establishment, the U.S. government would naturally side with the angels in the Middle East is laughable," http://glenhauer.com/.

84. Mead, W. (2008, July/August). The new Israel and the old: Why gentile Americans back the Jewish state. *Foreign Affairs*, www.foreignaffairs.com. Mead's father is Episcopalian; I do not know Mead's religion. Professor Noam Chomsky also spoke about "substantial" Christian fundamentalist/Christian Zionist influence on U.S. policy regarding Israel (calling them "extreme anti-Semites") in a 4/28/13 interview on KPFA radio in Berkeley with Phillip Maldari (the interview was taped 4/25/13).

85. Zunes, S. (7/20/04). The influence of the Christian Right on U.S. Middle East policy. *Foreign Policy in Focus*, http://www .politicalaffairs.net.

86. Rubin, N. (7/17/12). In Christian version of AIPAC conference, CUFI draws 5600

NOTES TO CHAPTER 3

to Washington for pro-Israel lobbying. *Jewish Telegraph Agency*, www.jta.org. Also, according to the Pew Forum on Religion and Public Life, one in five in the U.S. (60 million) consider themselves evangelicals.

87. Plitnick. Reclaiming the struggle, (p. 8) (Chap 1, Note 125). Christian Zionism is part of the Christian Right, which refers to a wide spectrum of groups with ultra-conservative beliefs on everything from abortion to homosexuality to Israel-Palestine.

88. For example, the Conference of Presidents leadership (Malcolm Hoenlein) has attended CUFI rallies, and in 2007 AIPAC chose Hagee as their conference keynote.

89. Kivel, P. Christian Zionism, www.christianhegemony.org.

90. During 2011 summer recess, eighty-one reps plus spouses traveled to Israel for free trips sponsored by the American Israel Education Foundation, an ostensibly-charitable affiliate of AIPAC, but which CODEPINK charges may be an illegal AIPAC front group. AIPAC also recruits and trains students to speak out in support of their policies.

91. Cooper, David J. (2011, October). Hillel, Israel, Palestine and me, www.kehilla-synagogue.

92. Plitnick & Toensing. "The Israel lobby" in perspective. (Chap 3, Note 77). I do not know if Toensing is Jewish. Plitnick adds in his 2011 article, "The UNSC veto and 'The Israel Lobby,' "There are instances where what we might consider bad decisions are caused by the Lobby and somewhere they're caused by such other considerations."

93. Friedman, T. (12/13/11). Op-Ed: Newt, Mitt, Bibi, and Vladimir, www.nytimes.com. For an illustration of the power of some segments of the Israel Lobby, see "Follow the money: From Islamophobia to Israel right or wrong," 10/3/12, by Elly Bulkin and Donna Nevel.

94. Chomsky, N. (2006, March 28). The Israel Lobby? *ZNet*. Retrieved February 6, 2011, from http://www.zcommunications.org/the-israel-lobby-by-noam-chomsky. The second quote is from a 4/28/13 interview aired on KPFA radio in Berkeley, CA, with Phillip Maldari (taped on 4/25/13). Chomsky reiterated this idea in a speech at Oakland, CA's Paramount Theatre on 5/8/13, "Palestinian Hopes, Regional Turmoil."

95. Bennis, P. (2003a). Of dogs and tails: The changing nature of the pro-Israeli lobby, the unchanging nature of the U.S.-Israeli alliance (p. 121). In T. Kushner & A. Solomon (Eds.), *Wrestling with Zion: Progressive Jewish-American responses to the Israeli-Palestinian conflict*. New York: Grove Press. Bennis reiterated this theme in a 9/25/11 interview on KPFA with Philip Maldari, that the U.S. role and Lobby goals are intertwined. And as explained, these goals are also shared by defense contractors, oil interests, and Christian Zionists. Noam Chomsky expressed this same perspective as Bennis in a speech at Oakland, CA's Paramount Theatre on 5/8/13, "Palestinian Hopes, Regional Turmoil."

96. Paul Kivel, 1/25/09, personal communication, used with permission.

97. Massad, J. (3/ 25-26/06). Blaming the Israel lobby, www.counterpunch.org. Massad is not Jewish.

98. Ibid.

99. Mearsheimer & Walt. The Israel lobby. (Chap 3, Note 64). Also, Zunes, S. (12/31/10). Could U.S. Foreign Policy in the Middle East be worse? *TruthOut*. According to Bravenewfoundation.org, in 2010 alone the Northrop Grumman CEO made $22.84 million, the Lockheed Martin CEO made $21.89 million, and the Boeing CEO made $19.4 million—putting them in the top 0.01 percent of U.S. income earners. And one example of close links between the government and the weapons industry: in 2011, William Daley left Boeing's board of directors to become President Obama's White House Chief of Staff.

100. Zunes. The Israel lobby: How powerful. (Chap 3, Note 78)

101. Ibid. Also, Mitchell Plitnick notes in "Actually, we CAN change things if we decide to try" (6/7/12), that "the amount of money the Israel Lobby can mobilize is big in terms of

361

special interests, but it is far, far less than what is raised by major industries like insurance and pharmaceuticals, and…by special interests groups like the NRA and the AARP."

102. In February 2011, leading Israeli peace activist/anthropologist Jeff Halper wrote, in "'Working Around America': a new strategy on Israel/Palestine": "The strategic funding and political support (or threat of withdrawing them) of candidates in both parties by AIPAC and the clout of the Christian Right in the Republican Party is matched by the influence of Pentagon defense contractors who keep members of Congress in line by arguing that any cut in the billions given to Israel, by extension, to the other countries in the region…will cost jobs in their states and districts."

103. Walt, S. (9/20/09). Settling for failure in the Middle East. *Washington Post*, www. hks.harvard.edu; 76 senators signed the letter as did 329 members of the House.

104. Zunes, S. (2007, November/December). The Israel Lobby: a progressive response to Mearsheimer and Walt, www.tikkun.org.

105. Ibid. Also various articles by Mitchell Plitnick, *The Third Way*.

106. Survey/Chosen for what? Jewish values in 2012. Public Religion Research Institute, http://publicreligion.org/research/2012/04/jewish-values-in-2012/. Significantly, when a 2012 Zogby poll asked what organization they most support, only 23% of U.S. Jews said that organization was AIPAC: see http://www.aaiusa.org/reports/is-peace-possible. Also see Mitchell Plitnick's 2013 article, "AIPAC on the Defensive", which posits that AIPAC's agenda is "increasingly out of touch with most Americans," www.lobelog.com.

107. Welchman, A. (6/10/08). Avnery on Obama: No I can, http://jewishpeacenews. blogspot.com.

108. Kampeas, R. (5/28/10). Welcome to Obama's Jewish America. *Jewish Telegraph Agency*, http://jta.org.

109. Rosenberg, M. (3/18/10). Public opinion backs Obama not Netanyahu, http://tpm-cafe.talkingpointsmemo.com/. The (right-leaning) Rasmussen poll reported that 49 percent of voters backed Obama.

110. Plitnick. The UNSC veto. (Chap 3, Note 81). See Rosenberg, M.J. (2/14/11), Obama pledges to veto U.N. resolution condemning Israeli settlements, www.huffington-post.com. Yet in July 2012, the State Department said, "We do not accept the legitimacy of continued Israeli settlement activity." See 7/10/12, "Wrong time for new settlements," www. newyorktimes.com. Regarding AIPAC's power, see also Mitchell Plitnick's 11/2/12 article "Unseating the Israel Lobby," *Souciant.com*.

111. Horowitz, A. & Weiss, P. (11/2/09). American Jews rethink Israel, www.thenation. com.

112. Traub, J. (9/13/09) The new Israel lobby. *New York Times Magazine*, www.ny-timescom. The quote is from J Street founder Jeremy Ben-Ami. Also, another take on "pro-Israel," from an interview with Cecilie Surasky in *Moment Magazine*, January/February 2012, "What does it mean to be pro-Israel today?": "Being pro-Israel means…acknowledging the painful histories of all of Israel's citizens, including the 75 percent who are Jewish and have histories of genocide…and the 20 percent who are Palestinian… and who experienced the Nakba."

113. Ben-Ami, J. (2/5/10). Jeremy Ben-Ami's remarks at J Street Local Launch, http:// www.jstreet.org/blog/?p=833.

114. Horowitz, A. (10/28/09). Squaring the circle and erasing the margins, http:// mondoweiss.net.

115. Ben-Ami, J. (9/9/11). J Street supports a Palestinian State. J Street listserve.

116. Fletcher. What is "anti-semitism." (Chap 1, Note 128).

CHAPTER FOUR: THE TRICKSTER IN OUR HEADS: Internalized Jewish Oppression

1. Lorde, A. (1984). *Sister outsider* (p. 123). Freedom, CA: Crossing Press. Lorde was not Jewish. Two excellent films with content about internalized racism and anti-Semitism by director/producer Shakti Butler: *The Way Home*, (1998) available from New Day Films, 190 Route 17M, P.O. Box 1084, Harriman, NY 10926; and *Cracking the Codes: the system of racial inequality* (2012), world-trust.org/the-way-home.

2. Freire, P. (1993), *Pedagogy of the oppressed* (Rev. ed.), New York: Continuum. Freire was not Jewish. Sander Gilman called this dynamic being "forced to internalize the projections of the dominant culture," (1991, *The Jew's body*, (p. 24), New York: Routledge.) Freedom fighter/martyr Stephen Biko explained this same dynamic in successfully rousing South African youth to fight apartheid.

Also check out the powerful work of pioneering neuropsychologist Dr. Mario Martinez in *The mind-body code*; although using different terminology ("the dynamic interplay between thoughts, body and cultural history") he speaks about various aspects of what I condsider to be internalized ageism.

3. Kaye/Kantrowitz. To be a radical Jew. (p. 84). (Chap 1, Note 67)

4. Weissglass, J. (2000). *Understanding and ending the oppression of Jews: What you can do* (p. 5). Santa Barbara, CA: National Coalition for Equity in Education. (Available from the Center for Educational Change in Mathematics and Science, University of California, Santa Barbara, CA 93106).

5. Brown, C. (1995b). Cherie's talks. *Ruah Hadashah*, 9, p. 8.

6. Schwartz, M. (1995). Truth beneath the symptoms: Issues of Jewish women in therapy, K. Weiner & A. Moon (Eds.), *Jewish women speak out*. Seattle, WA: Canopy Press.

7. Thanks to Dr. Wanella (Bola) Cofield for this idea, of self-love as an ongoing process. Check out her excellent 2012 dissertation, "Learning Circle–Sacred Space: A Case Study of African-American Women Cultivating a Self-Loving Attitude in the Midst of Systemic Oppression," California Institute of Integral Studies, San Francisco, CA.

8. Neumann, Y. (2004, August 21) Opening panel remarks, p. 77. In Judy Andreas' "In-depth report on the 2004 conference of - FACING A CHALLENGE WITHIN," http://www.google.com/search?ie=UTF-8&oe=UTF-8&sourceid=navclient&gfns=1&q=In-depth+report+on+the+2004+conference+of+-+FACING+A+CHALLENGE+WITHIN. Dr. Gabor Maté made a similar point, in an interview on KPFA with host Philip Maldari, 9/2/12: how important it is to become *self-aware* of emotions instilled in us from early childhood, that still affect our view of reality, to see how we all project our past onto the present, usually unconsciously. Maté says that becoming aware of these projections (usually distortions) can help us become more effective activists.

9. Levins Morales, A. L. Personal communication, 4/22/04, used with permission.

10. Abraham, S. (2005, Winter). I want my RC! A conscious community that keeps me going. *LOUDMOUTH*, 8, 10 (California State University, Los Angeles), http://www.google.com/search?ie=UTF-8&oe=UTF-8&sourceid=navclient&gfns=1&q=stephanie+abraham+-+I+want+my+RC!+A+conscious+community+that+keeps+me+sane, Loudmouth8.pdf). Also, as Guy Izhak Austrian and Ella Goldman point out in their excellent article, "How to Strengthen the Palestine Solidarity Movement by Making Friends with Jews": "Like all cultures, Jewish cultures are exciting and complex, as well as scarred by irrationalities that stem from oppression."

11. Hidary. Excerpt from "The Hebrew Mamita." (Intro., Note 1)

12. Ackerman, D. (2007). *The zookeeper's wife* (p. 155). New York: W. W. Norton.

13. Khazzoom. When Jewish means Ashkenazi. (Chap 2, Note 23)

14. Gilman, S. (1986). *Jewish self-hatred: Anti-semitism and the hidden language of the Jews*. Baltimore: Johns Hopkins University Press. He argues that self-hatred can be traced in Jews throughout history, and that it is a consistent aspect of identity formation in Diaspora groups worldwide. The actual term "Jewish self-hatred" was not popularized until 1939 in Germany by Theodore Lessing (Gilman, p. 393). This interesting/painful sourcebook focuses on European men.

15. Schwartz. Truth beneath the symptoms. (Chap 4, Note 6)

16. Brown, C. (1994a). Jewish parents and children. Ruah Hadashah, 8, 67.

17. Rothchild. *Broken promises., broken dreams,* (p. 4). (Chap 1, Note 11)

18. Kaye/Kantrowitz. Jews in the U.S. (p. 126). (Chap 1, Note 51)

19. I'm referring here to the critical lens of intersectionality, a term coined by African American legal scholar Kimberle Crenshaw, describing the idea that structural exclusion and disadvantage "can be based on the interaction of multiple factors rather than just one"–see the African American Policy Forum's "A primer on Intersectionality."

20. Hagan. *Fugitive information.* (p. 37). (Chap 1, Note 1). I do not know if Hagan is Jewish.

21. Tallen, B. (2000 June). "Who speaks for lesbians in NWSA?" Keynote at Dana Sugar Lesbian Institute, National Women's Studies Association Conference, Simmons College, Boston, MA.

22. Ibid.

23. Lewin, K. (1948). *Resolving social conflicts* (p. 189). (G. W. Lewin, Ed.). New York: Harper & Brothers. Lewin was a white European Jew who fled to the U.S. to escape Hitler.

24. Lipsky, S. (1995). Internalized racism. *Black Re-emergence*, 2, http://www.rc.org/publications/journals/blackreemergence/br2/br2_5_sl.html. I do not know if Lipsky is Jewish.

25. Anzaldua, G. (1987). *Borderlands/La frontera* (p. 200). San Francisco: Aunt Lute. Anzaldua was not Jewish.

26. Bell, L. (2007). Theoretical foundations for social justice education. In Adams, Bell, & Griffin. *Teaching for diversity.* (p. 10). (Chap 1, Note 2). Bell references Foucault, M. (1980). *The history of sexuality.* New York: Vintage Books. I do not know if Bell is Jewish.

27. Young, I. (2000). Five faces of oppression, (p. 36). In Adams, Blumenfeld, Castaneda, et al. *Readings for diversity.* (Chap 1, Note 93) I do not know if Young is Jewish.

28. Harro, R. (2000). The cycle of socialization (p. 18). In Adams, Blumenfeld, Castaneda, et al. *Readings for diversity.* (Chap 1, Note 93) I do not know if Harro is Jewish.

29. Vasquez, H. & Femi, I. (1993). *A manual for unlearning oppression and building multicultural alliances* (p. 23). Oakland, CA: TODOS Sherover-Simms Alliance Building Institute. Vasquez and Femi are not Jewish.

30. Kinnell, G. (1980). Saint Francis and the sow. Galway Kinnell – Online Poems, http://www.english.illinois.edu/maps/ poets/g_l/kinnell/online.htm. I do not know if Kinnell is Jewish.

31. Written by Bitch for the Opening Ceremony of the Michigan Womyn's Music Festival, August 2008. Unpublished, used with permission. Bitch is not Jewish.

CHAPTER FIVE: SUCKLED ON WORRY

1. Schnur, S. (2001, Spring). The anatomy of worry. *Lilith*, 26, 24.

2. Ibid.

3. Ibid.

4. Lerner. *Socialism of fools.* (p. 8). (Chap 1, Note 71)

5. Prell. *Fighting to become Americans.* (p. 125). (Chap 1, Note 57)

6. Dinnerstein. *Anti-semitism in America.* (p. 132). (Chap 1, Note 26).

7. Schwartz. Truth beneath the symptoms. (p. 140). (Chap 4, Note 6)

8. Brown, C. (2008, May/June.) Unnumbing from the Holocaust. *Tikkun*, 34.

9. Brown, C. (1995b). Cherie's talks. *Ruah Hadashah*, 9, 9.

10. Brown, C. (1991, March/April). The dynamics of anti-semitism. *Tikkun* 6, 26.

11. Fletcher. What is "anti-semitism." (p. 39). (Chap 1, Note 121)

12. Mennis, B. (2000). Jewish and working class (p. 189). In Adams, Blumenfeld, Castaneda, et al. *Reading for diversity*. (Chap 4, Note 27).

13. A *mezuzah* is a piece of parchment (often in a decorative case) inscribed with the Jewish prayer, the *Shema*. It is affixed to the doorframe in Jewish homes to fulfill the biblical commandment to inscribe the words of the Shema "on the doorposts of your house" (Deuteronomy 6:9).

14. Brown, C. (2000, July 20). Speech at National Jewish Fast for Peace and Justice, Washington, D.C.

15. I'd like to think that our class on Anti-Semitism/Anti-Arabism gave her the courage, as a Jew, to confront that anti-Semitic remark.

16. Schwartz. Truth beneath the symptoms. (p.140). (Chap 4, Note 6)

17. *Fox News*. (5/8/09). Wesleyan murder suspect wrote 'kill Johanna," "ok to kill Jews" in journal, police say, www.foxnews.com. In 2011, Stephen Morgan, 32, was found not guilty by reason of insanity (paranoid schizophrenia). He allegedly targeted other Jewish students, and a copy of the *Protocols* was found in his motel room. It's also important to acknowledge the obvious: women are killed by men every day just for being women.

18. Brown, C. (1995a, March/April). Beyond internalized anti-semitism: Healing the collective scars of the past. *Tikkun* 10, 44.

19. Eckberg, M. (2000). *Victims of cruelty: Somatic psychotherapy in the treatment of posttraumatic stress disorder.* Berkeley, CA: North Atlantic Books. Also Hammer, B. (1995). Anti-semitism as trauma: A theory of Jewish communal trauma response (p. 208), in K. Weiner & A. Moon, Jewish women speak out. (Chap 1, Note 62).

20. Hammer, B. (1995). Anti-semitism as trauma: A theory of Jewish communal trauma response (p. 208), in K. Weiner & A. Moon, *Jewish women speak out.* (Chap 1, Note 62). Hammer describes her thinking as a theory of Jewish communal trauma response.

21. Mendelsohn. *The lost.* (p. 391). (Chap. 1, Note 30)

22. Klepfisz, I. (1990b). Resisting and Surviving America (1982) (p. 61). In *Dreams of an insomniac: Jewish feminist essays, speeches and diatribes.* Portland, OR: Eighth Mountain Press.

23. *Democracy Now*, (2/3/10), Interview with Gabor Maté: In the realm of hungry ghosts, www.democracynow.org

24. *Democracy Now*, 2/15/10, Interview with Gabor Maté: When the body says no, www.democracynow.org.

25. *Democracy Now,* In the realm of hungry ghosts (Chap 5, Note 23)

26. Piercy, M. (1999). Growing up haunted (p. 108). In *The art of blessing the day.* Alfred A. Knopf: New York.

27. Butler, Sandra, & Rosenblum, B. (1989). Reverberations (p. 171). In M. Kaye/Kantrowitz & I. Klepfisz (Eds.), *The tribe of Dina: A Jewish women's anthology* (Rev. ed.). Boston: Beacon Press.

28. Weissglass. *Understanding and ending the oppression of Jews.* (Chap 4, Note 4).

29. Brown, C. (2011 Winter). Unhealed terror, www.tikkun.org.

30. Rachel, N. (1989). On passing: From one generation to another (p. 14). In Beck. *Nice Jewish girls.* (Chap 2, Note 96).

31. Weingart, L. (2005, March). Commentary: Speaking to the Presbyterians about

selective divestment. *Jewish Voice for Peace newsletter*, http://www.jewishvoiceforpeace.org/content/speaking-presbyterians-about-selective-divestment.

32. Kaye/Kantrowitz. *The colors of Jews*. (p. 215). (Chap 1, Note 52)

33. Ibid.

34. Thanks to white anti-racist organizer Chris Crass for this idea.

CHAPTER SIX: "HELLO ASSIMILATION, GOODBYE PERSECUTION"

1. Edut. Bubbe got back (p. 29). In Ruttenberg. *Yentl's revenge*. (Chap 1, Note 65). For a powerful/personal story about assimilation in 1930s-'40s Baltimore, see Adrienne Rich's 1982 essay "Split at the Root."

2. Wahba. Benign ignorance. (p. 52). In Khazzoom. *The flying camel*. (Chap 1, Note 34)

3. Klepfisz, I. (1990d) Secular Jewish identity: Yidishkayt in America (p. 159). In *Dreams of an insomniac: Jewish feminist essays, speeches and diatribes*. Portland, OR: Eighth Mountain Press.

4. Ibid., p. 151. April Rosenblum says this practice continued until the 1960s.

5. Lyons. Parasites and Pioneers (p. 317). In Alexander, Albrecht, Day, et al. *Sing, whisper*. (1, Note 53)

6. Ibid.

7. Rosenwasser & Gatmon. Crosscurrents of Jewish women, 120. (Chap 2, Note 2). The quote is from Sarah, working-class lesbian of Turkish heritage. Her last name is not identified in the article.

8. Jacobovici, S. (1997). *Hollywoodism: Jews, movies, and the American dream*. The National Center for Jewish Film, www.brandeis.edu. The quote is from this film, which appears to have morphed into the film by A & E Entertainment, *Hollywood: An Empire of Their Own*, http://www.newvideo.com/ae/hollywood-an-empire-of-their-own/.

9. Libo, K. & Skakun, M. All that glitters is not Goldwyn: Early Hollywood moguls. Center for Jewish History, http://www.cjh.org/p/52. The founding Hollywood "moguls" are considered to include Harry and Jack Warner of Warner Brothers, Louis B. Mayer and Samuel Goldwyn of MGM, Harry Cohn of Columbia, Carl Laemmle of Universal, Adolph Zucker and Jesse Lasky of Paramount, and William Fox of 20th Century Fox. In the 1930s, Laemmle paid expenses for hundreds of Jewish refugees, lobbying the U.S. government to let them in; he also unsuccessfully tried to save the Jewish refugees on the S.S. *St. Louis* who were forced to return to Europe. Warner Brothers (changed by a clerk at Ellis Island from Wonskolaser) also lobbied Congress and FDR to stop Hitler's rise to power; see the documentary, "The Brothers Warner," made by a Warner granddaughter, Cass Warner Sperling. Also see Jack Warner in Wikipedia.

10. Sorin, G. (1992). *The Jewish People in America*, 3. Baltimore: Johns Hopkins University Press. In Rosenblum. Offers we couldn't refuse. Jewish Currents, 63, 17. (Chap 1, Note 77)

11. Prell. *Fighting to become Americans*. (p. 24) "(Chap 1, Note 57)

12. Rosenblum, A. (2009 May/June). Offers we couldn't refuse. *Jewish Currents*, 63, 17. Yet Sarah Henry Lederman argues that settlement houses were also powerful political bases for some Jewish women, in "Settlement Houses in the United States," *Jewish Women's Archives*, http://jwa.org.

13. Horizontal hostility, meaning when targeted groups internalize dominant societal norms and prejudices, and also their anger at being oppressed, and project this onto their own group members.

14. Lyons. Parasites and Pioneers. In Alexander, Albrecht, Day, et al. *Sing, whisper*. (Chap 1, Note 53). Lyons cites Liebman, *Jews and the Left*, 150.

15. Hyman, P. (1995). *Gender and assimilation in modern Jewish history: The roles and representation of women* (p. 18). Seattle: University of Washington Press.

16. Rich, A. (1982). "Split at the root: An essay on Jewish-identity," www.public.asu. edu/. Even into the early 1960s, as Debra Schultz writes in *Going south: Jewish women in the civil rights movement,* "The primary injunction [for Jewish women] was not to make waves. Their job was to ensure that their family and the Jewish community would 'make it' in the United. States" (p. 14).

17. Ibid.

18. Rosenwasser & Gatmon. Crosscurrents of Jewish women 121. (Chap 2, Note 2).

19. Ibid.

20. Gaynor, A. (1996). *Jewish American Princess* jokes (p. 80). (Chap 1, Note 66)

21. Rosenblum. Offers we couldn't refuse. *Jewish Currents,* 63, 17. (Chap 1, Note 77)

22. Fremont, H. (1999). *After long silence: A memoir,* cited in Rosenblum. Offers we couldn't refuse. *Jewish Currents,* 63, 17. (Chap 1, Note 77)

23. Hyman. *Gender and assimilation.* (p. 14). (Chap 6, Note 15)

24. Bush, L. (10/5/11). Napoleon's Sanhedrin, http://jewishcurrents.org. Bush is explicitly speaking about France, but the process was similar elsewhere in Europe.

25. Kaye/Kantrowitz. *The colors of Jews.* (p. 13). (Chap 1, Note 52)

26. Ibid.

27. Dinnerstein. *Anti-semitism in America.* (Chap 1, Note 26) Specifies the ADL and the AJC (American Jewish Committee).

28. Hyman. *Gender and assimilation.* (pp. 16-17). (Chap 6, Note 15)

29. Dinnerstein. *Anti-semitism in America.* (Chap 1, Note 26). However, Marshall did urge President Coolidge to veto the 1924 immigration restriction act against Jews.

30. Kaye/Kantrowitz, M. (2007, March.) Some notes on anti-Semitism from a progressive Jewish perspective, www.jewishcurrents.org.

31. Dinnerstein. *Anti-semitism in America.* (p. 125). (Chap 1, Note 26)

32. Goldberg, J., *Jewish power.* (p. 118) (Chap 1, Note 89). Goldberg argues that McCarthy himself "bent over backwards to avoid anti-Semitism" (p. 118).

33. Bulkin. "Hard ground" in Bulkin, Pratt & Smith. *Yours in struggle.* (Chap 2, Note 20)

34. Jewish Virtual Library. Harvard's Jewish Problem, http://www.jewishvirtuallibrary. org/jsource/anti-semitism/harvard.html.

35. See Aviva Kempner's wonderful 2009 documentary *Yoo-hoo, Mrs. Goldberg!,* http:// www.mollygoldbergfilm.org/. Berg's original name was Tillie Edelstein. Philip Loeb, who played Molly's husband Jake on TV, committed suicide in 1955 after being blacklisted in 1951 and fired from the show. When Berg fought his firing, the show was cancelled for eighteen months.

36. Dinnerstein. *Anti-semitism in America.* (Chap 1, Note 26).

37. Richter, C. (2007). A note from the director of *Fiddler on the Roof.* Muhlenberg Summer Music Theatre Program, Muhlenberg College, Allentown, PA. *Fiddler* was written by Jerry Bock, Sheldon Harnick, and Joseph Stein.

38. Hyman. *Gender and assimilation.* (p. 123). (Chap 6, Note 15)

39. Ibid., p. 159.

40. Biale. *Power and powerlessness.* (p. 210). (Chap 1, Note 138)

41. Greenberg. Pluralism and its discontents, (p. 64). In Biale, Galchinsky, & Heschel. *Insider/outsider.* (Chap 2, Note 1)

42. In Prell. *Fighting to become Americans.* (Chap 1, Note 57), Prell cites Marshall Slare's study, (p. 160).

43. Brodkin. *How the Jews became white folks.* (p. 173.) (Chap 2, Note 15).

44. Prell. *Fighting to become Americans.* (p. 9). (Chap 1, Note 57). And in another example, from Adrienne Rich in her 1982 essay "Split at the Root: An essay on Jewish identity" about her college friends at Radcliffe in 1947: "For these young Jewish women…it was acceptable, perhaps even necessary, to strive to look as gentile as possible; but they stuck proudly to being Jewish, expected to marry a Jew, have children, keep the holidays, carry on the culture."

45. Biale, D. (1998) The melting pot and beyond: Jews and the politics of American identity. In Biale, Galchinsky, & Heschel. *Insider/outsider.* (pp. 17-33). (Chap 2, Note 1)

46. Sources such as: 2001 National Jewish Population Survey; Case, E. (11/9/10), Can the Jewish community encourage in-marriage AND welcome interfaith families?, http://www.interfaithfamily.com/news_and_opinion/synagogues_and_the_jewish_community/Can_the_Jewish_Community_Encourage_In-marriage_and_Welcome_Interfaith_Families.shtml; and Warikoo, N., (6/27/10), Do interfaith marriages threaten Jewish identity?, http://www.usatoday.com/news/religion/2010-06-29-jewish-interfaith-marriage_N.htm. Also sociologist Steven Cohen, cited in Ravitz, J. (10/28/09), "New Jews" stake claim to faith, culture. *CNN*, http://articles.cnn.com/ 2009-10-28/living/ new.and.emergent.jews_1_jewish-life-chosen-beer-rabbis?_s =PM:LIVING.

47. Lerner. *Socialism of fools.* (p. 76). (Chap 1, Note 71)

48. Marx, R. (1968). The people in-between (p. 16). *Reform Judaism.*

49. Moragh, G. (1997). Breaking silence: Israel's fantastic fiction of the holocaust (p. 150). In A. Mintz (Ed.), *The boom in contemporary Israeli fiction.* Hanover, NH: Brandeis University Press/University Press of New England.

50. Gilman, S., *Jewish self-hatred.* (Chap 4, Note 14)

51. Karen, R. (1992, February). Shame. *The Atlantic Monthly,* p. 41.

52. Thandeka. *Learning to be white,* (p. 33). (Chap 2, Note 80)

53. Kaufman, G., & Raphael, L. (1987, Spring). Shame: A perspective on Jewish identity (p. 33). In *Journal of Psychology and Judaism,* 11(1).

54. Jewish Liberation Draft Policy Statement No. 5 of Re-Evaluation Counseling. (2000). *Ruah Hadashah,* 10, 11.

55. Felman, J. (1996, July/August). Nurturing the soul. *Tikkun,* 11, 51.

56. Langman, P. (2000). Including Jews in multiculturalism. In Adams, Blumenfeld, Castaneda, et al. *Readings for diversity.* (Chap 1, Note 93). Langman cites Klein, J. (1976), "Ethnotherapy with Jews," *International Journal of Mental Health,* 5, 26-38.

57. Forshpayzn (Appetizers): Jews in SDS. (2008 January-February). *Jewish Currents,* 62, 4.

58. Ibid.

59. Rosenblum. Offers we couldn't refuse. *Jewish Currents,* 63, 23. (Chap 1, Note 77). Rosenblum says "the disproportionately high number" of young Jewish civil rights workers "did not generally identify as Jews," although they "recalled that their concern about racism stemmed from early awareness of the Holocaust as a racist persecution against their own people."

60. Lerner. *Socialism of fools,* (p. 86). (Chap 1, Note 71)

61. Abrahamson, A., & Pasternak, J. (1998, April 20). For U.S. Jews, era of plenty takes many far from roots. *The Los Angeles Times,* pp. A1, A10-11.

62. Loeb. Sundown to sundown. (Chap 1, Note 131)

63. For an exciting and original discussion of Diasporism, see Kaye/Kantrowitz's *The colors of Jews,* pp. 193-225, (Chap 1, Note 52). In 2006, the radical Jewish rock band The Shondes presented Melanie with a *Shonde to Love* Award for her work promoting diasporism and Jewish internationalism.

CHAPTER SEVEN: "THERE IS A 'REAL' JEWISH WOMAN AND I AM NOT HER": Too much/Not enough

1. Kaye/Kantrowitz. *The colors of Jews*. (Chap 1, Note 52)

2. Eve Ensler speaking in Berkeley, CA, 2/18/10, at King Middle School about her book *I am an emotional creature*.

3. Kleeblatt, N. (1996b). *Too Jewish?: Challenging traditional identities* (inside cover). New York: The Jewish Museum; New Brunswick, NJ: Rutgers University Press, p. 27.

4. Reichek, E. (1996). Untitled (p. 148). In Kleeblatt. *Too Jewish?* (inside cover). (Chap 7, Note 3)

5. Pogrebin. Anti-semitism in the women's movement. (Chap 1, Note 126)

6. Bulkin. "Hard ground" in Bulkin, Pratt & Smith. *Yours in struggle.* (pp. 91-230). (Chap 2, Note 20)

7. Kaye/Kantrowitz, M. (1992a). The issue is power: Some notes on Jewish women and therapy (p. 190). In *The issue is power: Essays on women, Jews, violence and resistance*. San Francisco: Aunt Lute Books.

8. Kaye/Kantrowitz. To be a radical Jew. (p. 149). (Chap 1, Note 67)

9. Edut. Bubbe got back (p. 27). In Ruttenberg. *Yentl's revenge*. (Chap 1, Note 65)

10. Austrian, G. and Goldman, E. (2003). How to strengthen the Palestine solidarity movement by making friends with Jews, http://www.soaw.org/ resources/anti-opp-resources/111-anti-jewish-oppression/606-how-to-strengthen-the-palestine-solidarity-movement-by-making-friends-with-jews.

11. Lieberman, R. (1996). Jewish Barbie (p. 108). In Kleeblatt. *Too Jewish?* (inside cover). (Chap 7, Note 3).

12. Ibid., p. 110.

13. Ibid., p. 109.

14. Ibid., p. 112.

15. Ackerman. *The zookeeper's wife*. (p. 220). (Chap 4, Note 12)

16. Piercy. *Sleeping with cats*. (p. 20) (Chap 1, Note 81)

17. Ibid.

18. Brodkin. *How the Jews became white folks*. (p. 166) (Chap 2, Note 15)

19. Steinem, G. (1992). *Revolution from within*, (p. 228). Boston: Little, Brown and Company.

20. Pogrebin, L. C. (3/26/10). The ten plagues – according to Jewish women. *The Forward*, http://blogs.forward.com/sisterhood-blog/126921/.

21. Wolf, N. (1991) The beauty myth. In Steinem. *Revolution from Within*. (p. 229), (Chap 7, Note 19)

22. Kushner, H. (1996). *How good do we have to be?* (p. 48). Boston: Little, Brown and Company.

23. Steinem. *Revolution from Within*. (p. 229). (Chap 7, Note 19)

24. Edut. Bubbe got back (p. 29). In Ruttenberg. *Yentl's revenge*. (Chap 1, Note 65)

25. Sh*t Christians say to Jews. (1/8/12). Allison Pearlman made this youtube, says all these comments were actually said to her, http://www.youtube.com/watch?v=51dFlpwKkBM.

26. Edut. Bubbe got back. In Ruttenberg. *Yentl's revenge*. (Chap 1, Note 65). Also Steinem, *Revolution from Within*. (p. 229), (Chap 7, Note 19).

27. Ibid. (Edut, p. 27).

28. Loeb, D. (2010). Never stop (excerpt), in *Birkat Ha-Gomel, A survivor's blessing*. Used with permission, contact dyanna.loeb@gmail.com.

29. Kleeblatt, N. (1996a). "Passing" into multiculturalism, (p. 16). In Kleeblatt. *Too*

Jewish? (Chap 7, Note 3)

30. Naidus, B. (1996). The Plates: What kinda name is that?, (p. 143). In Kleeblatt. *Too Jewish?*. (Chap 7, Note 3)

31. Kaye/Kantrowitz. Jews in the U.S. (p. 123). (Chap 1, Note 51). Also, in *The Jew's body*, (1991), Sander Gilman traces the history of nose surgery, which began in Austria and Germany in the late 1800s; Jews hoped that reducing their noses to "gentile contours" might heal the "disease" of Jewish visibility and so avoid attacks (p. 187).

32. Gilman. *The Jew's body.* (p. 179). (Chap 1, Note 37). Quote by Moses Hess, German-Jewish revolutionary, explaining how Germans hated Jews less for their religion, more for their race. Thanks also to Paul Kivel for telling me how Christians believed marks of sin could be seen on the body.

33. Berger, A. (1989). Nose is a country/I am the second generation, (p. 137). In Kaye/Kantrowitz & Klepfisz. *The tribe of Dina.* (p. 134). (Chap 5, Note 27)

34. Mendelsohn. *The lost,* (p. 228). (Chap 1, Note 30)

35. Significantly though, in the preceding story, it was an older man who intervened to ask my friend what *she* wanted to do for the yartzeit.

36. Stoval, T. (1/25/06). Funny, you don't look Jewish: *The Montclair Times*, http://www.jewishresearch.org/v2/2006/ articles/growth/1_25_06.htm.

37. Kaye/Kantrowitz. *The colors of Jews.* (p. 185). (Chap 1, Note 52). In 1999, Buchdahl became the first Asian-American worldwide to be ordained as a cantor; in 2001, she became the first Asian-American in North America to be ordained as a rabbi.

38. Ibid. Kaye/Kantrowitz refers to Nussbaum, D., (2002, December 6), Finding their voice, *Jewish Week.*

39. Taller, M. (1994). Judging ourselves as Jews. *Ruah Hadashah* 8, 31.

40. Johns, T. (2008) *We are self affirming soul healing Africans* (p. 323). Dissertation Abstracts International-A69/03. (ProQuest document ID. 1503397041). For another excellent contemporary study of internalized racism by an African-American woman, see Wanella (Bola) Cofield's doctoral dissertation, 2012, *Learning Circle-Sacred Space: A Case Study of African American Women Cultivating a Self-Loving Attitude in the Midst of Systemic Oppression.*

CHAPTER EIGHT: PUSH/PUSH/PUSH FOR PERFECTION

1. CBS News. (10/12/07). Jewish groups condemn, boycott Ann Coulter, http://www.cbsnews.com.

2. Gilman. *Jewish self-hatred.* (p. 270). (Chap 4, Note 14)

3. Kushner. *How good do we have to be?*(p. 10). (Chap 7, Note 22)

4. Weingarten, G. (8/8/2000). Ma, you're gonna kvell at this news. *The Washington Post*, p. C1. Son of Sam, or David Berkowitz, was a U.S. serial killer and arsonist whose crimes terrorized New York City from July 1976 until his arrest in August 1977. Monica Lewinsky was a young White House intern, then staffer, whose intimate relationship with President Bill Clinton between 1995 and 1997 involved sexual contact; Clinton's lying about it led to his Republican-railroaded impeachment by the House in 1998 and then acquittal by the Senate in 1999.

5. Cameron, J. (2006). *Finding water,* (p. 61). New York: Penguin Books. I don't know if Cameron is Jewish.

6. Ibid.

7. Ibid.

8. Kushner. *How good do we have to be?* (p. 37). (Chap 7, Note 22)

9. Ibid., p. 42.

10. Ibid., p. 54.
11. Ibid, p. 180.
12. Ibid., p. 7.

CHAPTER NINE: "WHERE DO I BELONG?"

1. Rothchild. *Broken promises, broken dreams.* (p. 5). (Chap 1, Note 11)
2. Smadja, C. (2003). The search to belong, (p. 155). In Khazzoom. *The flying camel.* (Chap 1, Note 34)
3. Ibid.
4. Ibid., p. 156.
5. Rosenwasser & Gatmon. Crosscurrents of Jewish women, 121. (Chap 2, Note 2)
6. Kleinbaum, S. (2011 Winter), "Do not hold back," *Tikkun*, 51. *Newsweek* also named Kleinbaum one of 150 Women Who Shake the World—and the *Huffington Post* named her one of the Top 10 Women Religious Leaders, also one of the 15 Inspiring LGBT Religious Leaders. In a 2013 example of Kleinbaum's commitment to inclusivity, when the rabbi of a Manhattan synagogue objected to a controversial event being scheduled there, Kleinbaum agreed to host the event at her shul, explaining, "I am disturbed by the trend in the Jewish community to censor discussions about Israel and Palestine. I feel it's my moral responsibility to make sure this burning issue that's facing us as a Jewish people gets a complete debate and discussion." See "Controversial Panel on Israel Moved from Ansche Chesed After Rabbi Balks," by Josn Nathan-Kazis, 3/14/13, wwww.forward.com. For an excellent article about Kleinbaum's outstanding social justice work overall, see "New York's New Firebrand Rabbi," (5/3/13) by Allison Hoffman, www.tabletmag.com: (for example, from Kleinbaum) "If we don't care about these issues, then I really think as a synagogue we might as well just close up our doors and become a laundromat...Because it's just bullshit to talk about God on the one hand and prayer and a beautiful sanctuary, and then not care whether working people get paid sick leave."
7. Ibid.
8. Obviously an African American track meet is not WASP-land, but the feeling of "not belonging" was there.
9. Tompkins, K. (2003). Home is where you make it, (p. 140). In Khazzoom. *The flying camel.* (Chap 1, Note 34)
10. Piercy, M. (1973). The Influence coming into play, THE SEVEN OF PENTA-CLES, (p. 90.) *To be of use.* Doubleday: NY.
11. Ibid.

CHAPTER TEN: TAKING EGYPT OUT OF THE JEWS

1. Biale, D., Galchinsky, M., & Heschel, S. (1998). Introduction, (p. 5) In Biale, Galchinsky, & Heschel. *Insider/outsider.* (Chap 2, Note 1)
2. Miller, A. (1997). *The drama of the gifted child: The search for the true self* (p. 129). (Rev. ed., R. Ward, Trans.). New York: Basic Books. (Original work published 1979). Admittedly, this doesn't excuse the abuse or explain why some who are abused don't themselves become abusers. I don't know if Miller is Jewish.
3. Tennenbaum, S. (8/5/06). Why doesn't Israel work for peace? *Newsday*, http://www.informationclearinghouse.info.
4. Melamed, A. (4/25/09). As victims, we're allowed. *Muzzlewatch*, http://jewishpeace-news.blogspot.com.
5. Baldwin, J. (1967, April 9). Negroes are anti-Semitic because they're anti-white (p.

3). *New York Times.*

6. In 2010, this statistic still held, whereas in many other communities "the dollar bill stays within that community and exchanges hands up to eight times, before it leaves that community." See Kadeem Lundy's article, "Patrick Freeman's Guide to Building Wealth," 5/5/10, in *Black Star News.* When Farrakhan spoke at UC Berkeley in 2012, espousing his "Jews control everything" rant (including the myth that Jews dominated the slave trade), a listener responded that what he got out of it "was how we as black students can take our education and utilize it to build the black community back up...We're looking at the minister's statements in terms of how to empower the black community, not all of the other controversial things..."; (See KTVU.com, 3/17/12), "Some students offended by Louis Farrakhan's UC Berkeley address."

7. Brown. Unnumbing from the Holocaust. (Chap 5, Note 8).

8. Ibid.

9. Klepfisz, I. (1990b). *Khaloymes*/Dreams in progress: Culture, politics and Jewish identity (pp. 204-5). In *Dreams of an insomniac: Jewish feminist essays, speeches and diatribes.* Portland, OR: Eighth Mountain Press.

10. Ibid.

11. Lerman, A. (3/7/09). Must Jews always see themselves as victims?, www.independent.co.uk.

12. Biale. *Power and powerlessness,* (Chap 1, Note 138). Biale argues that repressing memories of the war, and "collective trauma" (p. 209) prevented U.S. Jews from fully confronting the Holocaust until 1967.

13. Ibid., p. 200.

14 Ibid.

15. Goldberg, J., *Jewish power* (p. 147) (Chap 1, Note 89).

16. Ibid., p. 161.

17. Finkelstein, N. (2/13/08). A farewell to Israel: The coming breakup of American Zionism. Speech in Berkeley CA. Also see his book, *The Holocaust industry.*

18. Ibid. In a 4/28/13 interview on KPFA radio in Berkeley, CA, with Phillip Maldari, Professor Noam Chomsky agreed that 1967 was when the U.S. formed its alliance with Israel and that the U.S. continues to consider Israel a "valuable" ally.

19. Biale. *Power and powerlessness.* (pp. 160-16.). (Chap 1, Note 138)

20. Ibid., also Lyons. Parasites and Pioneers (p. 317). In Alexander, Albrecht, Day, et al. *Sing, Whisper.* (Chap 1, Note 53)

21. Karon, T. (12/16/09). Hannukah without the Taliban. *Rootless Cosmopolitan,* http://tonykaron.com.

22. Buber, M., 1921. (1983) A proposed resolution on the Arab question (p. 61). In *A land of two peoples: Martin Buber on Jews and Arabs,* (Ed.) Paul Mendes-Flohr, University of Chicago Press.

23. Biale. *Power and powerlessness,* (p. 161) (Chap 1, Note 138).

24. Ibid., p. 209.

25. Ibid., p. 137.

26.Legal scholar George Bisharat explained, for example, that "Palestinian citizens of Israel endure more than 35 laws that explicitly privilege Jews," in (9/3/10), "Israel and Palestine: A true one-state solution," *Washington Post.* Bisharat is not Jewish.

27. Rose, J. (2005). *The Question of Zion* (p. 82). Princeton, NJ: Princeton University Press. And elsewhere in the world are similar movements which try to displace indigenous populations and build European societies in their stead.

28. I borrowed this concept from Melanie Kaye/Kantrowitz, *The colors of Jews,* p. 193.

Also, the colonial enterprise of Israeli policy has been aided by the UK since the 1917 Balfour Declaration, as well as by France and the U.S. Peter Beinart imagines a more humane Zionism, one that does not wield power in Israel: see his article "The Failure of the American Jewish Establishment," 6/10/10, in the *New York Review of Books* as well as his more recent articles and books.

29. Hirt-Manheimer, A. (2003, Spring). The man who mistook his stereotype for himself: A conversation with Professor Sander Gilman on the origins and dynamics of Jewish self-hatred. *Reform Judaism*, 79.

30. Thanks to Kim Klein for telling me this specific phrase.

31.Brown, C. (1995a, March/April). Beyond internalized anti-semitism: Healing the collective scars of the past. *Tikkun* 10, 45.

32. Brown, C. (2003, February 12). *Anti-semitism*. Speech delivered at Hebrew College, http://www.btvshalom.org/resources/anti_semitism_brown.shtml.

33. Ibid.

34. Rabbis for Human Rights Hagadda Supplements 5770. (2009, April). Who sits with us at our Seder?, http://jfjfp.com/?p=11870.

35. Steinem. *Revolution from within.* (p. 81). (Chap 7, Note 19)

36. Katan, U. (2001). To open my mouth and speak what I know (pp. 156-7). In Ruttenberg. *Yentl's revenge.* (Chap 1, Note 65)

37. Ibid., p. 156.

38. Ibid., p. 155.

39. Ibid., p. 160. Additionally, although not ready to share their stories publicly, other Jewish incest survivors have made the link between their abuse, anti-Jewish oppression, and the Israeli government abuse of Palestinians–and the need to let go of their attachment to being victims.

40. Ibid., p. 155.

41. Okun, T. (12/31/08). I fear for the future of Judaism today. *Israeli Committee Against House Demolitions–USA*, http://icahdusa.org.

42. Levy, G. (2/8/09). Kahane won, www.haaretz.com.

43. They continue "And don't imply we should have gotten over it by now." Austrian and Goldman. How to strengthen the Palestine solidarity. (Chap 7, Note 10)

44. Goldberg, J., *Jewish power,* (p. 7) (Chap 1, Note 89). Goldberg is specifically referring to the gap between Jewish vulnerability and "the reality of Jewish power," but I think the meaning holds as I describe it here.

45. Norman, J. & Welchman, A. (3/8/09). Must Jews always see themselves as victims? http://jewishpeacenews. blogspot.com. They use these words to summarize and introduce the words of Antony Lerman, former director of the Institute for Jewish Policy Research.

46. Eckberg, M. (2000). *Victims of cruelty: Somatic psychotherapy in the treatment of posttraumatic stress disorder* (p. 88). Berkeley, CA: North Atlantic Books.

47. Shavit, A. (6/11/07). Avram Burg's case against Israel. Interview with Burg, www.zionism-israel.com. Shavit uses these words to describe the thesis of Burg's book *Defeating Hitler.*

48. Montell, J. (2001, January/February). The Al-Aqsa intifada. *Tikkun*, 16.

49. Berger, J. (2003, January/February). A war of ghosts: Trauma theories, traumatic histories, and the Middle East. [Review of the book *Writing history, writing trauma*.] *Tikkun*, 18, 75. A rabbi friend of mine put it another way, "Palestinians are bearing the brunt of anti-Semitism." Adding to the complexity, the trauma from Hitler is retriggered by Palestinian violence (which itself is a reaction to Israeli state violence). Jewish Israeli peace activist friends have confided in me, for example, of the daily/gripping fear they experienced riding

Israeli buses—when bus bombings by Palestinian suicide bombers were not infrequent...of having flashbacks about it years later.

50. Boyarin, D. (2008 May/June). Their Nakba and ours. *Tikkun*, 23, 33.

51. Gilman, S., *Jewish self-hatred*, (p. 391). (Chap 4, Note 14)

52. Brown, C. (1994b). Responses to Harvey's letter: Updating Jewish liberation. *Ruah Hadashah*, 8, 12.

53. Ephron, D. (9/5/01). "Our guns are only causing our misery": Palestinian human-rights activist Eyad Sarraj lobbies for new, nonviolent tactics. *Newsweek International*, http://www.gcmhp.net/File_files/interviewwitheyadinNewsweek.pdf.

54. Cohen, R. (2/12/10). Hard Mideast truths, www.newyorktimes.com.

55. Rothchild. *Broken promises* (p. 12). (Chap 1, Note 11)

56. Ibid., p. 8.

57. Ibid., p. 12. For an excellent/brief summary of what Rothchild is referring to, see the 2012 video, *Israel & Palestine: A Very Short Introduction*, http://www.youtube.com/watch?v=Y58njT2oXfE&feature=youtu.be, or http://www.israelpalestine101.org/ (or www.jewishvoiceforpeace.org.) As described in the video, "one group of refugees found a new home—creating a new group of refugees."

58. Barely a century old, because in 1917 the British issued the Balfour Declaration to encourage a national home in Palestine for Jews, followed by Jewish immigration from Europe, which began altering the demographic balance (with indigenous Arabs), creating tension in Jewish-Arab relations over the implications of Zionist immigration. A short excellent resource is Phyllis Bennis' 2003 primer, *Understanding the Palestinian-Israeli conflict*.

59. For example, the Fourth Geneva Convention bars occupying powers from settling their own populations in occupied lands. Also, Stephen Zunes points out that public opinion polls consistently show "that a majority of Americans believe U.S. military aid should be made conditional to human rights"; see his 12/14/11 article "Obama ad condemns Israel aid opponents," www.fpif.org.

60. Surasky, C. (9/1/09). Naomi Klein shows you can boycott Israel without cutting off dialogue over Palestine. Interview with Klein and Israeli publisher Yael Lerer, www.alternet.org. In his 5/8/13 speech at Oakland, CA's Paramount Theatre, "Palestinian Hopes, Regional Turmoil," Professor Noam Chomsky also urged an end to U.S. support for the Israeli occupation, as the best way to end it.

61. Hari, J. (2//6/09). The nightmare of Netanyahu returns, www.independent.co.uk. Hari is quoting from a 1982 essay Oz wrote in response to Menachem Begin comparing the Palestinian leadership to Hitler.

62. Ibid.

63. Horowitz, A. (10/30/09). Palestinian equal rights joins the progressive agenda on "The Daily Show," http://mondoweiss.net/2009/10/palestinian-equal-rights-joins-the-progressive-agenda-on-the-daily-show.html.

64. Reese, C. (2003). Four former heads of Israeli security speak out. King Features Syndicate, Inc., www.lewrockwell.com/reese/ reese10.html.

65. Herskovits, A. (2/11/09). Who remembers the Holocaust? http://www.berkeleydaily-planet.com

66. Ibid., For example, various historians suggest that if Israel apologized for the 1948 displacement of hundreds of thousands of Palestinians, it would go a long way towards peace.

67. Miller. *The drama of the gifted child*. (pp. 114-115). (Chap 10, Note 2)

68. Rose. *The Question of Zion*. (p. 144). (Chap 10, Note 27).

69. Lerner, M. (2004, March/April). Tikkun Passover Supplement 2004, www.tikkun.org/article.php/mar2004_lerner2. And the late Rabbi Alan Lew put it this way, in his 2003

book, *This is real and you are completely unprepared*: "We accept that to be human is to be…broken, and we realize that we don't have to project our brokenness onto someone else…We can fix it…The world is set up to heal itself. Our choice is to align ourselves with this healing or not."

70. Doctors report that increased cases of infant deformity, as well as miscarriages, are a result of the white phosphorous. See "Newborn in Gaza with severe defects," 1/28/10, *Palestine News Network*; also "New study finds strong correlation between birth defects and white phosphorous exposure of parents," 5/4/12, by Fablo De Ponte, http://www.uruknet. de/colonna-centrale-pagina.php?p=87802&colonna=m.

71. B'Tselem. Statistics: Fatalities during operation "Cast Lead," www.btselem.org. The majority of Gazans are under 18 years old.

72. Falk, R. (9/19/09)). Why the Goldstone Report matters, www.zcommunications.org.

73. Hass, A. (10/18/09). Family who lost 29 members in Gaza war: We envy the dead, www.haaretz.com. The number dead was later corrected to 21, but another 45 relatives were injured, most of them children. In May 2012, the Israeli military said its review of the massacre found no evidence of a war crime or deliberate targeting of civilians; see Democracy Now, 5/3/12, "Israeli military clears soldiers in killings of Gaza relatives."

74. Ibid.

75. Ibid.

76. Zunes, S. (11/4/09). Bipartisan attack on international humanitarian law. *Foreign Policy in Focus*, www.huffingtonpost.com. See also Max Blumenthal, (7/25/10), "IDF report confirming Goldstone's key findings is suppressed inside Israel," http://maxblumenthal.com.

77. Pine, D. (1/2/09). Local Jews defend, criticize Israel. *Jewish Weekly*, www.jweekly. com. Pine is quoting Mervyn Danker, director of the American Jewish Committee's Northern California chapter.

78. Cohen, R. (1/7/09). The dominion of the dead, www.nytimes.com.

79. Avnery, U. (1/10/09), Gaza: Uri Avnery, how many divisions? http://morris108. wordpress.com/2009/01/11/gaza-uri-avnery-how-many-divisions-100109/.

80. Barker, A. (12/28/10). Gazans mark two years since offensive, www.abc.net.au. Quoting award-winning Gazan psychiatrist Dr. Eyad El-Sarraj, Mehdi Hasan reports that four years later (11/15/12), one in five children in Gaza suffers from PTSD; see "Ten things you need to know about Gaza," www.huffingtonpost.co.uk. If you can bear it, watch the documentary *Tears of Gaza*, a Norwegian-made antiwar film that focuses on the effects of the assault on civilians, as seen through the eyes of Palestinian children, http://tearsofgazamovie. com.

81. Hauslohner, A. (8/13/10). Gaza's siege mentality: Not deprivation but desperation. *Time*, www.time.com.

82. Rosen, B. (9/27/09). A call to moral accounting. *Chicago Tribune*, http://articles. chicagotribune.com. Check out Rabbi Brant's 2012 book, *Wrestling in the Daylight*, Just World Books.

83. In 2012, this hateful rant was still chanted in a major race riot by hundreds of teen-aged Israeli soccer fans after winning a match in Beitar. Descending on a shopping mall, they spit on Palestinian women, yet it was barely reported by the media. A *Haaretz* commentator noted "If it was skinheads beating Jews the whole world would know about this." See "Hundreds of soccer fans crowd Jerusalem mall: 'Death to Arabs,'" *mondoweiss.net*.

84. Rose, J. (2005). *The Question of Zion* (pp. 130-131). (Chap 10, Note 27).

85. Lerman. Must Jews always see themselves as victims? (Chap 10, Note 11)

86. Derfner, L. (10/7/09). Rattling the cage: Our exclusive right to self-defense. *Columns. jpost.com*. http://fr.jpost.com.

87. Baltzer, A. (2/6/09). What may come of the tragedies. *OpEdNews*, www.opednews. com.

88. Ibid.

89. See the grassroots group in Sderot, The Other Voice, who collected signatures for a cease-fire during the Israeli onslaught, http://www.othervoice.org/welcome-eng.htm. Also see the moving plea by Sderot activist Nomika Zion, "War Diary from Sderot," 1/13/09.

90. Lerman. Must Jews always see themselves as victims? (Chap 10, Note 11)

91. B'Tselem. (5/8/13). B'Tselem's findings: Harm to civilians significantly higher in second half of Operation Pillar of Defense. www.btselem.org.

Veteran Israeli peace activist/negotiator Gershon Baskin reported that two hours before Hamas leader Ahmed Jabari was assassinated by Israel—which started the assault—he had received a proposal for a long-term truce developed by Israel and Hamas. See *Democracy now*, 11/16/12, "Israeli negotiator: Hamas commander was assassinated hours after receiving truce deal from Israel."

Also see: Noam Chomsky's 12/4/12 article, "Chomsky: what the American media won't tell you about Israel," www.alternet.org; Rabbi Brant Rosen's 11/16/12 blog article, "Outrage in Gaza redux," http://rabbibrant.com/2012/11/16/outrage-in-gaza-redux/; Phyllis Bennis' 11/20/12 article, "Israel's war on Gaza," www.thenation.com; Stephen Zunes' 11/26/12 article, "Abetting the carnage in Gaza," www.fpif.org; and various resources suggested by Jewish Voice for Peace, http://jewishvoiceforpeace.org/blog/gaza-news-and-social-media-sources-articles-etc.

92. Palestinian Center for Human Rights, (11/22/12), Israeli offensive on Gaza stopped following 8 days of attacks, http://www.pchrgaza.org/. My colleague Barbara Lubin delivered medical aid to children in Gaza in December 2012, immediately after this attack; upon returning, she reported that some children she visited there have been so traumatized by the 2008-09 and 2012 bombings, that they have stopped speaking.

93. Wright. Israel and Palestine: who is the victim. (Chap 10, Note 91). Palestinian journalists were specifically targeted in the attacks, as well as Gaza infrastructure; see *Democracy Now*, 11/19/12, "Live report from Gaza hospital: As civilian toll mounts, Israel again bombs Palestinian journalists."

94. Akram, F. et al, (11/19/12), Hamas leader dares Israel to invade Gaza amid airstrikes, www.newyorktimes.com. Those paying condolences to Dalou said his face was swollen from crying.

95. Bennis, P. (12/1/12). The Gaza ceasefire holds: a little bit to be thankful for, www. ips-dc.org. The IDF used U.S. weaponry made by Boeing, General Electric and Elbit U.S.A.; see "7 top things you should know about Gaza," 11/12, http://jewishvoiceforpeace. org/campaigns/take-action-for-gaza. Citing the *Common Dreams* website, *Democracy Now* (12/13/12) reported that the Pentagon confirmed plans to replenish $647 million of U.S.-made bombs and missiles used by Israel in the assault; see (headlines), "U.S. to replenish bombs used by Israel in Gaza attack."

96. Greenwald, G., (11/17/12), Stop pretending the U.S. is an uninvolved, helpless party in the Israeli assault on Gaza, www.guardian.co.uk.

97. Jewish Voice for Peace, (11/12), 7 top things you should know about Gaza, http://jewishvoiceforpeace.org/campaigns/take-action-for-gaza. Also, Israeli peace activist (and former army veteran/current army refuser) Amir Terkel wrote that the IDF bombs were "ten or twenty times more powerful" than the Gaza rockets—rockets which could destroy an apartment but not a whole building; and the Israeli Iron Dome defense system reportedly destroyed 85% of rockets headed towards populated areas. See Terkel's 12/2/12 article, "From Israel:...bomb shelters" http://groups.yahoo.com/group/TheEndTime2012/mes-

sage/3206.

98. Terkel, A., (12/2/12), From Israel:...bomb shelters, http://groups.yahoo.com/group/ TheEndTime2012/message/3206. Most Israelis were lucky to have bomb shelters to run to; still, it's terrifying to hear the siren and know you have 90 seconds (to find your children and) to make it to shelter. And the danger was much more acute in the southern Israeli towns near Gaza.

For a powerful personal account from a young U.S. activist who witnessed Gaza immediately after the bombing: "A small voice on a quick trip," http://smallvoiceonaquicktrip.tumblr. com/. Also see "Media Advisory: Middle East Children's Alliance Programs Address Trauma Faced by Children after 8 Days of Bombing in Gaza," (12/10/12), www.mecaforpeace.org.

99. Online petition from Other Voice, www.othervoice.org–originated 10/24/12 and continued during the assault on Gaza. Other Israeli peace groups placed an ad on *Haaretz*'s front page: "No to the Elections War! We refuse war and the spilling of blood..."; see Sarah Anne Minkin's article, 11/16/12, "Refusing the elections war," www.thedailybeast.com.

100. *Democracy Now*, (11/19/12), Live report from Gaza hospital: as civilian toll mounts, Israel again bombs Palestinian journalists. Although the 11/21/12 cease-fire agreement allowed for free movement by Gazans—including in border areas, and also allowing fishermen to fish six nautical miles offshore—Israeli soldiers and gunboats violated these agreements; see Phyllis Bennis' 12/1/12 article, "The Gaza ceasefire holds: a little bit to be thankful for," www.ips-dc.org; also 12/6/12, "Emergency Delegation to Gaza winds up week of witness to war's devastation, Gazan's resilience," Codepinkalert.org.

As a result of the cease-fire agreement, in late December 2012, for the first time in 5 years, Israel allowed 20 truckloads of building materials into Gaza for use by the private sector and pledged to continue these daily; 34 truckloads of gravel from Egypt were also allowed in, earmarked for housing. See Isabel Kershner's 12/30/12 article "Israel, in shift, lets building materials cross into Gaza," www.nytimes.com.

101. Bisharat, G. (6/7/10). Gaza occupation and siege are illegal. *San Francisco Chronicle*, http://articles.sfgate.com.

102. Zunes, S. (6/10/10). Democratic Party defends Israeli attack, www.huffingtonpost.com.

103. *Democracy Now*. (6/4/10). As Obama refuses to condemn flotilla assault, survivors recount shootings, beatings aboard Mavi Marmara, www.democracynow.org. As described to host Amy Goodman by flotilla participant Kevin Ovenden, journalist Nicci Enchmarch held the Turkish journalist as he died.

104. *Democracy Now*. (6/3/10). Flotilla passengers Huwaida Arraf of the Free Gaza Movement and retired army Colonel Ann Wright respond to Israeli claims on deadly assault, www.democracynow.org.

105. Chomsky, N. (6/8/10). *In These Times*. The real threat aboard the freedom flotilla, www.inthesetimes.com. In response to the allegation that one of the flotilla groups had terrorist links, Insani Yardim Vakfi (IHH), the Institute for Middle East Understanding, reports "The Intelligence and Terrorism Information Center, a think tank with ties to Israel's Defense Ministry, concluded that there is "no known evidence of current links between IHH and 'global jihad elements.'"

106. From an interview with Netanyahu broadcast on KPFA radio in Berkeley, CA, 6/2/10. I heard Netanyahu's insistence in an interview with him on KPFA radio in Berkeley, CA, 6/2/10. Then in March 2013, in conjunction with President Obama's first trip to Israel, Netanyahu apologized to Turkish Prime Minister Recep Tayyip Erdogan for "operational mistakes." He also agreed to pay compensation, but refused to comply with Erdogan's demand that Israel end its maritime blockade of Gaza. See "Behind Obama's

Turkey Win," by Lee Smith, 3/29/13, www.tablet.mag.com.

107. Bennis, P. (6/7/10). Israel's flotilla massacre: Made in the U.S.A., www.common-dreams.org. Also Zunes. Democratic Party defends Israeli attack. (Chap 10, Note 102)

108. Ibid. (Bennis).

109. Zunes S. Democratic Party defends Israeli attack. (Chap 10, Note 102)

110. Rosen, B. (5/31/10). *Ta'anit Tzedek: Jewish Fast for Gaza.* Open the gates: A rabbinical response to the Gaza freedom flotilla tragedy. As we go to press, the fastforgaza.net website is gone, but you can reach Rabbi Brant Rosen at his *Shalom Rav* blog, rabbibrant. com/. A personal note here: of course this was a horrific and unconscionable act by the Israeli government. Yet I was stunned to see how much more worldwide outrage there was to this one attack, which killed nine Turks, than to the three-week nonstop bombing of Gazans, which killed nearly 1400. Is this an indication of just how much Palestinians lives have been dehumanized?

111. *New York Times.* (6/1/10). Israel and the blockade (editorial), www.nytimes.com.

112. Levinson, C. (6/5/10). Leftist and rightist Israelis clash at Gaza flotilla protest in Tel Aviv, www.haaretz.com. An additional Israeli response: the Knesset stripped Palestinian Knesset member Hanin Zoabi (a flotilla participant) of privileges, such as her diplomatic passport, and verbally assaulted her. She also received death threats.

113. In June 2011, Egypt's Rafah crossing was opened, allowing essential supplies through and limited numbers of people; other needed goods were smuggled in through tunnels. And in late December 2012, Israel began allowing in construction materials, see Note 100 above. But as of early 2013, as a result of continued Israeli restrictions on imports, Gazan water systems remained crippled, people lacked steady electricity or electric fuel, and 95% of the water was undrinkable. The drastic Israeli limitations on exports impacts economic development, so 2012 unemployment in Gaza was at least 50%. What Gazans want most is mobility and freedom. See B'Tselem's "The siege on Gaza," also (the Israeli Legal Centre for Freedom of Movement) Gisha: Gaza Gateway, and Al Haaq for updates.

114. Kelly, M. (8/27/12). U.N.: Gaza won't be "liveable" by 2020 unless urgent action is taken. *Business Insider,* www.businessinsider.com. Also see Professor Noam Chomsky's powerful article from his October 2012 trip to Gaza: (11/6/12), "Noam Chomsky's reflections on his visit to Gaza," www.pchrgaza.org. An excellent source of information about the water crisis in Gaza is EWASH, the Emergency Water and Sanitation/Hygiene group, www.ewash.org.

115. Peter, T. (9/23/10). U.N.'s Gaza flotilla probe finds Israeli soldiers committed "willful killing." *Christian Science Monitor,* www.csmonitor.com.

116. *BBC News.* (6/13/12). Israeli report criticizes PM Netanyahu over Gaza flotilla, www.bbc.co.uk.

117. Siegman. H. (6/11/10). Israel's greatest loss: Its moral imagination, www.haaretz. com.

118. Yagna, Y. (9/28/10). "Jewish Gaza-bound activists: IDF used excessive force in naval raid," www.haaretz.com. The quote about the Gaza siege was from former Israeli Air Force pilot (and now refuser) Yonatan Shapira.

119. Ibid. Another passenger was Rami Elhanan who lost his daughter Smadar to a suicide bombing in Israel in 1997.

120. Tolan, S. (6/5/10). Israel and the psychology of "never again," www.salon.com. Tolan is not Jewish.

121. Leary, J. (2005). *Post traumatic slave syndrome: America's legacy of enduring injury and healing* (p. 195). Milwaukie, OR: Uptone Press. Leary notes that cortisol can be passed through the placenta to unborn infants as well. I realize this could contradict my earlier

contention that Jews are not born afraid, though I still believe my statement basically stands. And stress does not necessarily correlate with fear.

122. Steen, X. (1/1/09). Escaping the trauma vortex. *The Jerusalem Post*, www.jpost.com.

123. Ibid.

124. Gottlieb, L. (2009) Kavanah for erev Yom Kippur. *Danforth Jewish Circle*, http://djctoronto.com/explore/erevyk2009sermon.php. Gottlieb was among the first ten women rabbis in the U.S.

125. Waskow, A. (2001, September). Kotsker rebbe. *Shalom Center* listserve.

126. Wind, M. (9/13/09). Presentation at Jewish Voice for Peace chapter meeting, Berkeley, CA.

127. From a radio interview on KPFA-FM in Berkeley, CA, on 6/2/10, with host Brian Edwards-Tiekert.

128. For more info about Israeli children as soldiers-to-be, see New Profile's 2004 Report on Child Recruitment in Israel, www.newprofile.org.

129. Sherwood, H. (8/22/10). Israeli army's female recruits denounce treatment of Palestinians, www.guardian.co.uk.

130. Ibid.

131. Veteran Israeli soldiers speak out about service (6/6/12). Maanews.net., www.maannews.net. The Israeli group Breaking the Silence has collected testimonies from 800 Israeli soldiers who served in the West Bank and Gaza.

132. Feldman, Y. (2/5/09). Lieberman's anti-Arab ideology wins over Israel's teens, www.haaretz.com.

133. MC. (7/7/10). The writing on the Warsaw Ghetto wall—an interview with Yonatan Shapira. *Indymedia*, www.indybay.org.

134. Ibid.

135. "Munich" refers to the terror attack which murdered 11 Israeli athletes at the 1972 Olympics in Munich by Arab guerrillas of the Black September movement. My group of women was at the Maccabia to protest then-Prime Minister Ariel Sharon's anti-Palestinian policies. When he spoke, we rose up shouting "war criminal" in Hebrew and holding banners; we were then attacked by people sitting around us, and the police hauled us out of the stadium, arrested and interrogated us at the station, and later released us at 2 a.m.

136. Cole, J. (1/21/10). Ignoring Gaza's humanitarian crisis, www.salon.com.

137. *Democracy Now*, (3/5/12). Debate: attacking Iran, AIPAC, Israel-Palestine and Obama with Rashid Khalidi and Jonathan Tobin, www.democracynow.org. Quote is from Rashid Khalidi, who is not Jewish. Scott McConnell's 11/27/12 article in *The National Interest*, "Why Americans don't understand Palestine," also reports, "It is also true that Hamas leaders have expressed interest in a long-term negotiated truce."

Plus in a 2012 *Haaretz* poll, 53% of U.S. Jews said they would support a Palestinian state; see "62% of U.S. Jews would re-elect Obama," 4/3/12, by Natasha Mozqovaya, www.haaretz.com.

138. Zunes, S. (5/20/11). Two steps back, one step forward. *Foreign Policy in Focus*, www.fpif.org. And not just that. Many authorities agree that the most viable plan by far is the 2002 Arab League Peace initiative, signed on to by all 22 member Arab states and backed by the Palestinian Authority—which offers Israel recognition, full diplomatic relations and normalization with all members of the Arab League in return for a full retreat to the 1967 borders and a just resolution to the refugee issue—though Netanyahu and other Israeli leaders before him have consistently rejected it. See, for example, "U.S Must Engage with the Arab League Peace Initiative," by Carlo Strenger, (11/21/12),

www.haaretz.com.

139. Similarly, in 2011, the Gaza Youth Manifesto for Change stated: "We want three things. We want to be free. We want to be able to live a normal life. We want peace. Is that too much to ask?"

140. Freedman, S. (6/22/08). Culture of fear, www.guardian.co.uk.

141. See New Profile's Charter, www.newprofile.org.

142. Klein, N. (6/16/07), Gaza: Not just a prison, a laboratory. *The Nation*, www.countercurrents.org.

143. Ibid.

144. Ibid.

145. Cook, J. (7/12/10). Israel paves the way for killing by remote control. *The National*, www.thenational.ae.

146. Klein. Gaza: Not just a prison. (Chap 10, Note 142).

147. Klein, N. (2007). Losing the Peace Incentive: Israel as Warning (p. 541). In *The shock doctrine*. New York, NY: Picador.

148. Ibid.

149. Ibid., quote is from Len Rosen. New Profile cofounder Rela Mazali notes that half of Israel's land is "controlled...by security organizations"; see "Selling Israeli Militarism like toothpaste", (6/23/11), *the Real News*.

150. Another example: Israeli banks finance the occupation. See more at www.whoprofits.org/.

151. In providing checkpoint technology, Hewlett-Packard is serving a similar need now for the Israeli army as IBM and Polaroid did in supplying systems of population control for South Africa's apartheid regime.

152. Weingart, L. (11/11/04) The wrath of the Jews, www.zcommunications.org.

153. Bennis, P. (2003b). *Understanding the Palestinian-Israeli conflict*. Lowell, MA: Trans-Arab Research Institute.

154. Weingart. The wrath of the Jews. (Chap 10, Note 152)

155. These are, respectively, the Foreign Assistance Act and the U.S. Arms Export Control Act. I note that the Foreign Assistance Act ends, however, with the phrase "unless such assistance will directly benefit the needy people in such country," so perhaps the U.S. government justifies such aid by privileging Israeli perceived needs (not just for security, but for domination as well) over Palestinian human rights. The U.S. Campaign to End the Israeli Occupation reported in April 2011 that in the previous decade, the U.S. gave Israel more than 670 million weapons, valued at nearly $19 billion, which killed nearly 3000 unarmed Palestinians who were not participating in hostilities. See www.weaponstoisrael.org.

Significantly, in October 2012, 15 prominent U.S. Christian leaders wrote a letter calling on Congress to ensure military aid to Israel is consistent with U.S. law—bringing on cries of anti-Jewish bigotry from Jewish mainstream organizations, although rabbis signed a counter letter in support of the Christian leaders. See "Rabbinical support for the end of unconditional military aid to Israel," (10/15/2012), http://palestiniantalmud.com; also see Rabbi Brant Rosen's Op-Ed in JTA, (10/23/12), "Christian's letter was reasonable, worded sensibly," www.jta.org. In a 4/17/13 speech in Berkeley CA, Professor Angela Davis said that without this U.S. aid, the occupation would collapse.

However, Mitchell Plitnick argues,"The goal should not be to end aid to Israel, but to get Israel to cooperate with U.S. policy in order to get that aid"—referring to the two acts explained above—and so changing our relationship with Israel "into a more normal alliance"; see his 11/2/12 article, "Unseating the Israel Lobby," Souciant.com.

156. See also Note 99 in Chapter Three.

157. Bennis, P. (12/30/08). The Gaza crisis, www.zcommunications.org.

158. Ibid.

159. Guttman, N. (12/16/09). U.S.-Israeli arms cooperation quietly growing, www. forward.com. Also Bennis, P. (8/4/10), Why the U.S. won't cut ties with Israel, no matter how extreme its government gets, www.alternet.org. Qualitative Military Edge (QME) means Israel gets newer/better weapons than her Arab/Muslim neighbors. Also contributing to QME is the $680 million pledged to Israel in 2012 towards the Iron Dome Missile Defense System, made in Israel; see Bumiller, E. and Sanger, D., "Israel unveils iron dome missile defense system," (5/23/2011), *New York Times*.

160. *Democracy Now*. (1/9/12). Drones, Asia and cyber war: Pentagon shifts priorities in new review; budget still exceeds Bush era, www.democracynow.org. Quote is from William Hartung, author of *Prophets of War: Lockheed Martin and the Making of the Military-Industrial Complex*, referring to the $60 billion arms deal with Saudi Arabia, saying "there's not a deal that's ever come close to this." Plus, since QME means Israel gets the best weapons, "the result is a U.S.-generated arms race"; see Walter Pincus' 10/17/11 Op-Ed in the *Washington Post*, "United States needs to reevaluate its assistance to Israel."

161. Barrows-Friedman, N. (2/10/10). U.S. expanded weapons stockpiling in Israel, www.truth-out.org. *Truthout*. Stockpiling has been going on with Israel since 1990; South Korea has a similar arrangement. Also see Pincus, W. (10/17/11, *Washington Post* Op-Ed, "United States needs to reevaluate its assistance to Israel." In 2012, the stockpiling is expected to reach $1.2 billion.

162. *Huffington Post*. (10/28/12). Austere Challenge 2012: U.S. General Martin Dempsey In Israel to oversee military drill, www.huffingtonpost.com.

163. Bennis, P. (8/4/10). Why the U.S. won't cut ties with Israel, no matter how extreme its government gets, www.alternet.org. In June 2011, Congress awarded the "highest-ever level of funding to the joint U.S.-Israel missile defense program," to protect U.S. interests "in the volatile Middle East" from "dangerous regimes" in Iran, Syria, Lebanon, and Gaza, "and wherever America's troops and citizens are stationed"; see *Jewish Telegraph Agency*, (6/1/11), "Record amount approved for U.S.-Israel missile defense program." And U.S. academic institutions are profiting as well: in December 2011, Cornell University won a bid to partner with the Technion–Israel Institute of Technology; Technion develops military arms technology that Israel relies on to sustain the Occupation. As we go to press, the project still needs to be approved by the City Council; see "Cornell NYC Tech's Alarming Ties to the Israeli Occupation," (3/1/12), by Adam Hudson, www.thenation.org.

164. Zunes, S. (5/18/07). U.S. role in Lebanon debacle. *Foreign Policy in Focus*, www. fpif.org.

165. An example of how the U.S. is not an "honest broker" in Palestinian-Israeli negotiations: The Palestine Papers show that the U.S. coordinated positions with Israel in behind-the-scenes negotiations—and then pressured Palestinians to accept Israeli demands, relegating Palestinian rights to the background.

166. The U.S. (and Israel) opposed the U.N. statehood bid, saying this should not substitute for direct negotiations. A Pew Research Center poll in fall 2011 showed a plurality of Americans favored the U.S. recognizing Palestine, while a Hebrew University poll reported that about 70 percent of Israelis thought Israel should go along, if the U.N. recognized a Palestinian state. As of 2011, over 100 countries have recognized the state of Palestine, and a 2012 Public Religion Research Institute poll found that 53% of U.S. Jews supported a Palestinian state. As of early 2012, the U.S. has used its veto in the U.N. Security Council 41 times to block efforts to secure Palestinian rights, playing what many see as an obstruc-

tive role in reaching a just peace.

The new Palestinian status in the U.N. is now the same as that of the Vatican. Though some say the new status will not change facts on the ground, others point out that Palestinians can now gain access to U.N. agencies, could bring Israel to the International Criminal Court for violations of international law, and can sign treaties to protect its natural gas fields and air space. See George Bisharat's 12/3/12 Op-Ed, "Palestine's state status enables security," www.sfgate.com. Significantly, the U.N. resolution reaffirmed Israel "as a state among the nations with its right to self-determination while affirming that a Palestinian state has an equal right"; see Rabbi David J. Cooper's Op-Ed, 12/6/12, "Being a friend to the Jewish state means criticizing wrong-headed actions," www.jweekly.com.

Response to the vote illuminated cracks in mainstream Jewish consensus; although rabbis at a large Manhattan synagogue later wrote that their e-mail to their congregation had been premature—an e-mail applauding Palestine's new nonmember status—they did not retract their original words, that the U.N. vote was "a great moment...an opportunity to celebrate the process that allows a nation to come forward and ask for recognition." See Sharon Otterman and Joseph Berger's 12/4/12 *New York Times* article, "Cheering U.N. Palestine vote, synagogue tests its members," and Adam Horowitz's 12/6/12 article in www.mondoweiss.com, "One day later: B'nai Jeshurun leaders regret voicing support for Palestine U.N. bid."

Finally, for an excellent 2012 article about the changing/potential role of Europe, a major Israeli trade partner, to "have a decisive and positive influence on Israel," see "Making Europe Responsible," 12/14/12, by Mitchell Plitnick, souciant.com.

167. In response to the U.N. granting Palestine nonmember observer status, Israel authorized 3000 new Jewish-only homes in East Jerusalem/West Bank settlements, *plus* a plan to complete a settlement in the "E1" area, which will split the West Bank in half. The Israeli group Peace Now reports that Israel has authorized more settlements in 2012 than in any year in the past decade; see *Democracy Now*, 12/3/12, "Israel expands settlements, seizes PA funds after U.N. statehood vote" and "Israel advances settlement to bisect Occupied West Bank." U.S. Senator Dianne Feinstein responded, "It's an indication of Israel's continuing to stick a thumb in the eye of the Palestinians," and J Street called the move "a dagger aimed at the heart of a future Palestinian state"; see Churches for Middle East Peace Bulletin 12/8/12, "What does the E-1 announcement mean for a two-state solution?", e-mail info@cmep.org.

Meanwhile, 500 U.S. rabbis and cantors wrote Netanyahu asking him not to build settlements in the E1 area, a letter sponsored by Rabbis for Human Rights/North America, Americans for Peace Now, and J Street; see Laurie Goodstein's 12/20/12 *New York Times* article, "Religion: Rabbis oppose Israeli plan in disputed area." And while the Obama White House "publicly criticized Israel" about the settlement expansion, it "refused to take punitive action"; see *Democracy Now*, 12/20/12, "U.S. blocks bid to condemn Israeli settlement expansion."

In early 2013 a U.N. panel "called on Israel...to halt settlement expansion and withdraw all half a million settlers from the occupied West Bank," also telling private companies to "stop working in settlements if their work adversely affected the human rights of Palestinians": "the settlements contravened the Fourth Geneva Convention forbidding the transfer of civilian populations into occupied territory and could amount to war crimes." See "U.N. rights inquiry says Israel must remove settlers," by Stephanie Nebehay, 1/31/13, *Reuters*.

168. UNESCO is the United Nations Economic, Scientific, and Cultural Organization. 1990's U.S. law prohibits such funding, claiming Palestine lacks "internationally recognized attributes" of statehood; the U.S. had provided 22% of UNESCO funding. However, as of early 2012, Obama was seeking a congressional waiver to restore funding to UNESCO.

169. In a *New York Times* Op-Ed (11/22/11), "Israel and Pinkwashing," activist/writer Sarah Schulman described pinkwashing as "a deliberate strategy to conceal the continuing violations of Palestinians' human rights behind an image of modernity signified by Israeli gay life," see www.nytimes.com. In her excellent 7/3/12 article in *Tikkun*, "Revealing the truth behind the rainbow: Seattle's anti-pinkwashing success," Wendy Elisheva Somerson argues that "well-funded American Jewish institutions consistently use their power to shut down conversations about Palestine every chance they get."

Similarly, Rabbi Rebecca Alpert writes, "As a progressive Jewish lesbian, I resent the Israeli government's efforts to suggest that good policies toward one oppressed group can in any way mitigate horrific policies used against another group...when the Israeli government is ready to encourage American Jews to talk about Palestinian rights, I will welcome the dialogue that I hope will ensue." See "Readers Respond," *Tikkun*, Winter 2013, p. 4.

170. Somerson, W. (7/3/12), "Revealing the truth behind the rainbow," www.tikkun.org.

171. Cohen, R. (2/12/10). Hard Mideast truths, www.nytimes.com.

172. Ibid.

173. Levy, G. (11/1/09). America, stop sucking up to Israel, www.haaretz.com. Columbia University professor Rashid Khalidi echoes these words, in his 2013 *New York Times* Op Ed: "...the United States must forthrightly oppose the occupation and the settlements and support an inalienable Palestinian right to freedom, equality and statehood"; see "Is Any Hope Left for Mideast Peace?," 3/13/13.

174. Lerman. Must Jews always see themselves as victims? (Chap 10, Note 11)

175. In April 2011, dozens of Israeli artists and intellectuals signed a declaration calling for an end to Israel's occupation, and endorsing a Palestinian state on the basis of 1967 borders, to liberate both peoples; see Ethan Bronner's *New York Times* article (4/19/11), "Israeli intellectuals press for Palestinian state." In June 2012, more than 50 international aid groups and U.N. agencies, including the World Health Organization, Save the Children, and Amnesty International, issued a joint appeal to end the Israeli blockade of Gaza, citing the poisoning of 95% of Gaza's water. See *Democracy Now*, 6/15/12, "U.N., aid groups call for end of Gaza blockade."

176. Specifically within Israel: ending the system of ethnic privilege and racism, which only grants Palestinians second-class citizenship, recognizing some of their rights, but not their full equal rights as Israeli citizens, especially regarding housing and land ownership.

177. Beinart, P. (6/10/10). The failure of the American Jewish establishment. *New York Review of Books*, www.nybooks.com. Beinart's article is all the more powerful because he himself is a millennial, pro-Israel (liberal) Zionist.

178. Horowitz. Squaring the circle. (Chap 3, Note 114)

179. From Jewish Voice for Peace listserve, October 2009, used with permission. Admittedly, as I try to imply throughout this book, such healing from the Shoah is an ongoing journey, with many different layers and aspects, a journey different for each of the millions of Jews and others affected.

180. In her July 2012 *Tkkun* article "The Jewish community's drift towards the right," coproducer/director of the documentary *Between Two Worlds: The American Jewish Culture Wars*, Deborah Kaufman writes that "few national Jewish organizations...are organized democratically, where members actually vote for representative membership...Few remember the days when leaders were elected based on vision and commitment, making them accountable to members."

181. Chazan, N. (3/9/09). Critical currents: A tale of two polls. *Jerusalem Post*, www.jpost.com.

182. Beinart, P. (6/10/10). The failure of the American Jewish establishment. *New York*

Review of Books, www.nybooks.com. Beinart is quoting from pollster Frank Luntz.

183. Ibid., Similarly, in Dana Goldstein's 2011 *Time* article, "Why fewer young American Jews share their parents' view of Israel," she cites a survey of rabbinical students at New York's Jewish (Conservative) Theological Seminary: about 70% said they were "disturbed" by Israel's treatment of Arab Israelis and Palestinians, compared with half of those ordained between 1980 and 1994. Also see Jewish folklorist Steve Koppman's 9/27/12 powerful Op-Ed in *Jweekly.com*, "Protesting against Israel—valid or anti-Semitic?: Organized community conflates policy, values," where he writes about the "conflation of Judaism, the Jewish people and the policies of…Israel promoted sadly by the organized American Jewish community as it chronically subordinates Jewish values and teachings to whatever Israel's government does."

184. Ibid., (Beinart). Note: Beinart's 2012 book also argues that young liberal Jews are also turning away from establishment Zionism because the Jewish mainstream fails to foster open debate about Israel. Beinart edits the Daily Beast blog "Open Zion." In 2012, he called for boycotting products made in Israeli settlements. See his Op-Ed in the (3/18/12) *New York Times*, "To Save Israel, Boycott the Settlements."

185. Beinin, J. (2009, August). Rachel Corrie in Palestine…and in San Francisco. *Middle East Report*, www.merip.org.

186. Ibid.

187. Sokatch, D. (9/13/07). We must teach about Israel—warts and all. *Jewish Journal*, www.jewishjournal.com.

188. Ibid. Case in point: a young staffer at the San Francisco Jewish Federation was walked directly out the door the morning after the 2009 San Francisco gay pride march, where she marched in the official Jewish contingent carrying a sign "No Pride in Occupation." She was placed on forced leave until her previously announced departure.

189. Ettinger, M. (2010) Okupacia (pp. 14-15). In Adelfang, O. (Ed.), *Shifting sands: Jewish women confront the Israeli occupation*. Bellevue, WA: Whole World Press.

190. Ibid., p. 17.

191. Beliak, H. (2009, July). Quoted in Jewish Voice for Peace listserve.

192. In this initiative, officially known as the BDS Movement (Boycott, Divestment, Sanctions), Palestinians call for divestment from all Israeli companies, boycotts of Israeli products (since nearly the entire Israeli economy is linked to the Occupation), and international sanctions against Israel. This call from Palestinian civil society has three goals: to end the occupation, to promote equality for Palestinians living in Israel, and to recognize Palestinian refugees' right of return. Whereas some Jews and many mainstream organizations attack this strategy (the conservative Koret Foundation created a $6 million initiative to counteract BDS activities, calling these anti-Semitic), Jewish Voice for Peace and various rabbis and Jewish Israelis reject the idea that BDS is inherently anti-Semitic. See three useful articles: "BDS backer in hot seat at *shul* forum" in the *Boston Jewish Advocate*, October 2011; and "A statement in support of the Penn BDS Conference" by Rabbis Alissa Wise and Brant Rosen, (2/2/12), *The Palestinian Talmud*, http://palestiniantalmud.com; and "Judith Butler's remarks to Brooklyn College on BDS," (2/7/13) www.thenation.com. In the latter, Butler writes that the BDS movement's "stated core principles include the opposition to every form of racism, including…anti-Semitism." She differentiates BDS from clear anti-Semitism which is to be "unconditionally opposed": the election of national socialists to the Greek parliament, the National Party of Germany's "recirculation of Nazi insignia and rhetoric," and some Palestinian use of "anti-Semitic slogans, falsehoods and threats."

The Jewish Council on Public Affairs, the Israel Action Network, and others have accused the Methodist and Presbyterian churches of being anti-Jewish because of their growing campaigns to divest from U.S. corporations profiting from the Occupation. Meanwhile, the Israeli Knesset passed an antiboycott law in 2011 that applies severe penalties to Israeli groups and individuals supporting BDS, including the boycott of settlement products—a law criticized by a plethora of Jewish (including Israeli) groups as antidemocratic and violating free speech; as of 2012, various Israeli groups mounted an appeal to this law.

The reason for the BDS strategy? The 2011 Russell Tribunal in Cape Town, South Africa, "ruled that Israel has established an institutionalized regime of domination amounting to apartheid as defined under international law. Israel is discriminating against and eliminating an entire nation on racial grounds in a systematic and institutionalized way…" See "Civil disobedience against the Israeli government" by Nurit Peled-Elhanan, *Israeli-Academia-Monitor.com*, http://israel-academia-monitor.com/index.php?type=large_advic&advice_id=8403&page_data[id]=173&cookie_lang=en.

In June 2012, a watershed victory in the movement to divest from companies profiting from Israel's occupation: leading investment firm Morgan Stanley Capital International (MSCI) removed Caterpillar from its Socially Responsible Investing lists, saying Cat's role in Israeli human-rights violations was a key factor in the decision, following a major campaign by anti-occupation groups nationwide. Soon after, pension-fund giant TIAA-CREF divested shares of Caterpillar (CAT) stock worth $72 million from their socially responsible funds. Before that, the Quakers fully divested from Caterpillar. And a month later, after intense debate, the Presbyterian Church failed to pass similar divestment by only two abstaining votes. Some Presbyterians said they were swayed by testimony from young Jewish activists who had witnessed Palestinian suffering in the West Bank; see "Presbyterian Church votes steer clear of controversies," 8/8/12, by Benjamin Mueller, *Pittsburgh Post-Gazette*.

In 2013, when esteemed physicist Stephen Hawking decided to boycott Israel's Presidential Conference (an annual celebration of Israeli business, political, and military elites, dominated by the Israeli right wing), in solidarity with the BDS strategy, the *Boston Globe* editorialized, "The movement that Hawking has signed on to aims to lace pressure on Israel through peaceful means. In the context of a Mideast conflict that has caused so much destruction and cost so many lives, nonviolence is something to be encouraged." See (5/11/13), "Stephen Hawking makes a peaceful protest," www.bostonglobe.com.

193. Mackey, R. (8/27/10). Boycott of theatre in Israeli settlement grows. *New York Times*, http://thelede.blogs.nytimes.com/ 2010/08/27/boycott-of-theater-in-israeli-settlement-grows/. The quote is from dramaturg Vardit Shalfi. Also, as of 2012, other self-identified Zionist groups and individuals are supporting boycotting products made in settlements, like Americans for Peace Now (a member of the Conference of Presidents of Major Jewish Organizations), Rabbi Arthur Waskow, and Peter Beinart, who wrote a *New York Times* Op-Ed about what he called "Zionist BDS": "To save Israel, boycott the settlements," www.nytimes.com. In 2012 the U.S. Methodist and Presbyterian national bodies voted to join the boycott of products made in settlements; as of 2012, more than 600,000 settlers live illegally in Palestinian territory. Also in 2012, U.N. special rapporteur on human rights in Palestine, Richard Falk, submitted a report to the General Assembly calling for boycotting companies linked to settlements in the West Bank, saying these are complicit in the Israeli occupation; see "U.N. independent expert calls for boycott of businesses profiting from Israeli settlements," 10/25/12, un.org.

194. At the request of Israeli activists, Jewish Voice for Peace mobilized the campaign to get the U.S./UK showbiz professionals involved; see http://jewishvoiceforpeace.org/campaigns/making-history-support-israeli-artists-who-say-no-normalizing-settlements-4.

195. Guttman, N. (9/8/10 2010). Why some Jewish stars support Israeli artistic boycott, www.forward.com.

196. Abileah, R. (4/15/10). Showdown for human rights in Berkeley, http://mondoweiss. net. The two U.S. corporations targeted by this bill were United Technologies and General Electric, both of which manufacture arms used to kill Palestinian civilians by the Israeli army. For an illuminating Jewish panel discussion about these issues, see "Is BDS the Way to End the Occupation?" in the July/August 2010 *Tikkun*. See also Donna Nevel and Dorothy Zellner's article, "Why the BDS Campaign is effective and right," (Autumn 2012), *Jewish Currents*, pp. 4-5.

197. Alpert, R. (2011, Winter). Solidarity with Palestinian activists. *Tikkun*, 30. And in a 2012 interview with Mitchell Plitnick, Rabbi Brant Rosen explained "BDS is not anti-Semitic…If we think the occupation is intolerable and this call [the 2005 call from Palestinian civil society for boycott, divestment, sanctions] is a smart and ethical response to leverage power to get Israel to cease, then we must support it"; see "Wrestling in the Daylight: an interview with Rabbi Brant Rosen," 12/6/12, www.mitchellplitnick.com.

198. For example: the number of illegal settlements has tripled, the building of a Separation Wall, the two major attacks on and siege of Gaza, as well as increased limitations on Palestinian mobility.

199. Tutu, D. (5/1/12). Justice requires action to stop subjugation of Palestinians. www.tampabay.com.

200. Mozgovaya, N. (2/11/09). Pro-Palestinian Bronx expressway banner—a Jewish initiative, www.haaretz.com.

201. Levins Morales, A. (2003) Foreword (pp. 9-10). In Wineman, S., *Power under: Trauma and nonviolent social change*. Aurora Levins Morales' Foreword is powerful, and Wineman's book appears to be as well—focused on recognizing the humanity of the abuser and integrating this ability into our social change work. The book is downloadable for free at gis.net/~swineman/Power_Under.pdf.

202. Roy, S. (4/7/07). How can children of the Holocaust do such things? www.counterpunch.org.

203. Ibid.

204. Millennial activists Guy Izhak Austrian and Ella Goldman (2003) say the same, in "How to strengthen the Palestine solidarity movement by making friends with Jews": "Remember that Jews can hear anything you want to say about Israel/Palestine if it's obvious that you care about Jews and our safety." (Chap. 7, Note 10).

205. Hale, G. (2/26/09). Ni'lin pays tribute to Jewish victims of the Holocaust, www. commongroundnews.org.

206. Grossman, D. (11/7/06). A state of missed opportunities. Journalist's Speech at the Rabin memorial ceremony in Tel Aviv, translation by Haim Watzman. *The Guardian*, http://www.guardian.co.uk/world/2006/nov/07/israel. In a late 2012 mailing from B'Tselem, Grossman wrote, "The fact that the occupation has continued for forty-five years is infuriating and outrageous."

207. Gottlieb. Kvannah for erev Yom Kippur. (Chap 10, Note 124)

208. Ibid. Also see Rabbi Gottlieb's 2013 book, *Trail guide to the Torah of nonviolence*, (published in France), www.editionsterredesperance.com.

CHAPTER ELEVEN: ON THE FRONT LINES: An Activist's Vignettes

1. In September 1982, during the Lebanese Civil War, Christian Phalangist militia massacred approximately 2000 children, women, and men in *Sabra* and *Shatila* refugee camps in Lebanon (some estimates are as high as 3500)—while Israeli soldiers, who were in control of the area, allowed the militias into the camps, did nothing to stop the slaughter, and prevented civilians from escaping. Israeli historian Benny Morris says

Israelis agreed to authorize Lebanese forces to "mop up" these camps, in an effort to root out terrorists. Afterwards, 400,000 Israelis protested the massacre, and the Israeli Kahan Commission found that Israel was responsible for participating in the violence and recommended the dismissal of the army chief. Minister of Defense Ariel Sharon was also forced to resign, since the Commission concluded that he bore personal responsibility and should never again hold public office—though he then became prime minister in 2001. The U.S. nurse whose letter is referred to is Ellen Siegel, who was volunteering at Gaza Hospital. See "The Sabra and Shatila Massacre," http:// electronicintifada.net/bytopic/. Also see the animated Israeli film *Waltz with Bashir*.

2. Women in Black (WIB) was founded by women in Jerusalem in 1988, just after the outbreak of the first *Intifada*. They stand weekly throughout Israel, holding signs calling for an end to the Occupation (and also throughout the world, including in the U.S.). In the tradition of the Women of the Black Sash (South Africa) and the Mothers of the Disappeared (Argentina, many of whom are also Jewish), WIB is a feminist, nonviolent, international movement against militarism, war, and violence. See www.womeninblack.org.

3. Rosenwasser, P. (1992a). *Voices from a "promised land": Palestinian & Israeli peace activists speak their hearts* (p. 34). Willimantic, CT: Curbstone Books. All the quotes in this paragraph are from the interview with Veronika Cohen. This book is now out of print but can be ordered from my website, wwwPennyRosenwasser.com. This same interview is in another of my books, still in print, *Visionary voices, women on power: Conversations with shamans, activists, teachers, artists and healers*, which you can order from Aunt Lute Books in San Francisco.

4. In "Lives of Women under Occupation," the Haifa Feminist Center reports "A sharp increase in the rate of deadly domestic violence against women within Israeli households …as an indirect result of the military conflict. Nearly half of the women killed in domestic violence in Israel during...[recent] years were murdered by soldiers and security guards who carried licensed weapons that they turned on family members and partners." See also www.newprofile.org. From my experience as an activist, it's true worldwide: that wherever there is militarism, it breeds domestic violence as well.

5. Rosenwasser. *Voices from a "promised land,"* (p.152.). (Chap 11, Note 3). Approximately 20% of Israeli citizens are Palestinian. Note: although this book is out of print, you can order it on my website, www.pennyrosenwasser.com.

6. Ibid., p. 222.

7. Berson, M. (1987). A connection of spirit: An interview with Alice Walker. 1987 *Sisterfire! Festival Program Book*, (pp. 16-18). Washington, DC: Roadwork.

8. In Oakland it's the difference between white and multiracial middle-class communities, and poor/working class communities of color. Generally, within Israel at that time, worst off (most oppressed) were the Bedouins, next the other Palestinians, then the Jews of color—both Ethiopian and Mizrahi.

9. These last two sentences are from the Mission Statement of the (short-lived) Coalition of Jews for Justice, which we founded in the Bay Area at the beginning of the Second *Intifada*.

10. However, there was no proof that the settler had been killed by these cave dwellers. As of July 2012, Israeli army forces are still threatening to demolish most of the *Palestinian* village of *Susya*, in the South Hebron hills, although the Israeli peace movement is fighting to prevent the demolition; the nearby *Jewish* settlement of *Sussya* is built on *Susya's* lands.

11. From keynote address by Terry Greenblatt at the San Francisco Jewish Film Festival, July 2001 (at Wheeler Auditorium on the UC Berkeley campus).

12. Ibid. These words were also part of a speech Terry gave before the U.N. Security

Council, 5/7/02, http://coalitionofwomen.org/home/english/articles/terry_greenblatt_at_un/.

13. Thanks to Susan Freundlich for her perspective and description of this event.

14. *Warrior poet*, the name of Alexis DeVeaux's excellent biography of Lorde.

15. Lorde, A. (1997). *The cancer journals* (p. 15). San Francisco: Aunt Lute Books.

CHAPTER TWELVE: CRACKING THE CODE OF OUR CONDITIONING

1. Hagan, K., *Fugitive information*, (p. 88). (Chap 1, Note 1)

2. Ibid., p. 89.

3. From an "Art and Politics" panel Davis was on in Los Angeles, 11/6/11. I heard this on KPFA radio in Berkeley, a broadcast from Pacific Radio Archives.

4. Brown, C. (1995a, March/April). Beyond internalized anti-Semitism: Healing the collective scars of the past. *Tikkun 10*, 46.

5. Steinem. *Revolution from within*. (p. 102). (Chap 7, Note 19)

6. The specific methodology we used, Cooperative (or Collaborative) Inquiry, is well-suited for exploring internalized oppression. Part of action research, Cooperative Inquiry is designed for small groups to investigate compelling questions about our own lived experience — *with* each other, not *on* someone else. An excellent user-friendly resource: "A Short Guide to Cooperative Inquiry" by Peter Reason and John Heron (also called "A Layperson's Guide to Cooperative Inquiry") http://www.human-inquiry.com/ cishortg.htm. See also the introduction to the Action-oriented Reader's Guide in this book.

Significantly, sociologist Kurt Lewin is credited with formalizing action research and experiential learning in 1946, the forerunner of Cooperative Inquiry. Lewin had first-hand experience with anti-Semitism in Nazi Germany, which led to his passion for resolving intergroup conflict. He saw this process as a tool for resolving such conflict and eliminating minority self-hatred as well as injustice. See Lewin, K. (1948). *Resolving social conflicts* (G. W. Lewin, Ed.). New York: Harper & Brothers.

7. Also, see the Action-oriented Reader's Guide for examples of the actions we tried and useful questions for reflection.

8. Forster, E. M. (1910). *Howard's end*. London: Edward Arnold. "Only connect" is the motto of the book. Forster was not Jewish.

9. Lynne Gelzer, April 2010, personal communication, used with permission.

10. Berkowitz, G. (2002). UCLA Study on Friendship Among Women, *www.anapsid. org*. In (Melissa Kaplan's) *Chronic Neuroimmune Diseases*, http://www.anapsid.org/cnd/gender/tendfend.html.

11. Ibid.

12. Ibid.

13. Moragh. *Breaking silence*, (p. 180). (Chap 6, Note 49)

14. Ibid., p. 178.

15. Weingart. The wrath of the Jews. (Chap 10, Note 152)

16. Thanks to Cherie Brown for this idea.

17. Felman, J. (1996, July/August). Nurturing the soul. *Tikkun*, 11, 51.

18. Hidary. Excerpt from "The Hebrew Mamita." (Intro., Note 1)

19. Hagan, K., *Fugitive information* (p. 98). (Chap 1, Note 1)

20. Ibid., p. 88

21. Ibid.

22. Edut. Bubbe got back (p. 27). In Ruttenberg. *Yentl's revenge*. (Chap 1, Note 65)

23. Siegel, R. (1995) Jewish women's bodies: Sexuality, body image and self-esteem (p. 53), in K. Weiner & A. Moon, *Jewish women speak out*, (Chap 1, Note 62)

24. Thorne, L. (1994). Challenging racism. *Ruah Hadashah 8*, 50.

25. Shumofsky, M. (1994). Uprisings day 1994. Unpublished essay.

26. Rachel, N., On passing, (p. 15). In Beck, *Nice Jewish girls*, (Chap 2, Note 96)

27. Although articulated here by Amy, my thanks to Sonika Tinker and Dinyah Rein (*Loveworks*) for this concept, which I learned from them and brought to the group.

28. Roy, Arundhati. (1/27/03). Confronting empire. Porto Allegre, Brazil (World Social Forum), www.ratical.org. Roy is not Jewish.

29. Steinem. *Revolution from Within*. (p. 157.) (Chap 7, Note 19)

30. Wahba. Benign ignorance. (p. 65). In Khazzoom. *The flying camel*. (Chap 1, Note 34)

31. Rosenblum, A., "the past didn't go anywhere" (p. 31) (Chap 1, Note 129). I've said it earlier but want to reaffirm: this is an excellent, brief, resource for the topics in this book.

32. Ibid.

33. Jordan, J. (1994). A Powerful Hatred. In *Affirmative acts: Political essays*. Anchor Books: Doubleday. Jordan was not Jewish.

34. Thanks to Staci Haines for this concept in her book, *The survivor's guide to sex: How to have an empowered sex life after child sexual abuse* (1999), San Francisco: Cleis Press.

35. Piercy, M. (1973). (Excerpt from) The aim, the best that can be hoped for: THE MAGICIAN (p. 93). In *To Be of Use*. Doubleday: NY.

CHAPTER THIRTEEN: JEWISH-POSITIVE

1. Hidary. Excerpt from "The Hebrew Mamita." (Intro., Note 1)

2. Marder, D. (4/5/07). Black Jew illuminates diversity of Judaism. *Philadelphia Inquirer*, http://www.jewishresearch.org.

3. Ibid.

4. Cooper, David J. (9/8/10). On joy and redemption. (Erev Rosh Hoshana sermon), http://old.kehillasynagogue.org/article.php?story=20100915153320272&query=on%2Bjoy %2Band%2Bredemption

5. Rabbi Abraham Joshua Heschel referred to the Philosophy of Radical Amazement. Other spiritual traditions refer to this idea as well.

6. Saxe-Taller, J. (2010 September). Rosh Hashana 5771 sermon. Congregation Sherith Israel, San Francisco, CA. Unpublished essay, used with permission.

7. Ibid.

8. According to Wikipedia, collective effervescence is the basis for French sociologist "Émile Durkheim's theory of religion as laid out in his 1912 volume *Elementary Forms of Religious Life*." Thanks to Rabbi David J. Cooper's 2010 Erev Rosh Hoshana sermon which spoke of this concept, quoting Barbara Ehrenreich's book *Dancing in the Streets: A History of Collective Joy*, in which she cites Durkheim.

9. Cooper, David J. (9/8/10). On joy and redemption. (Erev Rosh Hoshana sermon), http://old.kehillasynagogue.org/article.php?story=20100915153320272&query=on%2Bjoy %2Band%2Bredemption

10. Bush, L. (9/21/11) Jewish women watching, http://jewishcurrents.org. The ad was in 2001. The group has also confronted the Christian Right, attacks on reproductive rights, and "Jewish racist voices" that protested the creation of the Khalil Gibran International Academy, focused on Arab culture.

11. The first woman rabbi was Regina Jonas, from Berlin, ordained in 1935. Rounded up by the Nazis, survivors said her sermons in Theresienstadt were uplifting. She was murdered in 1944 in Auschwitz.

12. Eden. A. (11/6/09). Women at Jewish organizations lag behind in promotions. The Forward, http://blogs.jta.org/ philanthropy/article/2009/ 11/06/1008990/forward-women-at-jewish-organizations-l. Overall, women make 78 cents for every dollar men earn (Grumm,

Patrick, and Ramdas, 3/9/09, Women can lead the way to recovery, *San Francisco Chronicle*). For more info, see the research report, "Cultivating the Talent: Women Professionals in the Federation System," by Didi Goldenhar and Sivanie Shiran, http://www.advancing-women.org/files/8/228.pdf. Thanks to Dana Schneider for this info. Also see "Federation making strides in improving its record on women, but kinks remain" by Dan Klein, 11/1/11, *JTA*; Klein notes of the "top speakers" at the 2011 Federation General Assembly, none were women.

However, at the end of 2012, Jill Jacobs of Rabbis for Human Rights reported that based on the annual Slingshot Guide, women direct more than half of the most *innovative* U.S. Jewish organizations; see 11/1/12, "Women lead more than half of most innovative Jewish organizations in America," http://www.rhr-na.org.

13.Thanks to Bonnie for sharing this with me. She teaches at George Washington and Georgetown Universities and for years coordinated the Jewish Womyn's Tent at the Michigan Womyn's Music Festival. Also check out the Jewish Women's Archive, www.jwa.org, which focuses on uncovering and transmitting "the rich history of American Jewish women."

14. Jacobs, M. (2010 September/October). Love the life—and activism—you're in. *Tikkun*, 81-82.

15. Fishkoff, S. (1/10/11). Singer-songwriter Debbie Friedman, inspiration to thousands, dies at 59. *Jewish Telegraph Agency*, http://www.jta.org. Friedman recorded 22 albums, composing feminist/spiritual folk and liturgical songs that revitalized Jewish worship.

16. Gottlieb, Kavanah for Erev Yom Kippur 5770, (Chap. 10, Note 124)

17. Kaye/Kantrowitz. *The colors of Jews*. (p. 222). (Chap 1, Note 52)

18. Cohen, S. & Kelman, A., assisted by Blitzer, L. (2007). Beyond distancing: Young adult American Jews and their alienation from Israel. The Jewish Identity Project of Reboot, http://bjpa.org/Publications/details.cfm?PublicationID=326. Peter Beinart's article referred to in Chapter Ten was partly based on this study.

19. Kaye/Kantrowitz. *The colors of Jews*. (p. 200). (Chap 1, Note 52)

20. Ravitz, J. (10/28/09). "New Jews" stake claim to faith, culture, http://articles.cnn.com. The last phrase quoted is from Ari Wallach—who used the term "Judaism 2.0" and was one of the forces behind "The Great Shlep," referred to in the following sentence.

21. Neuman, J. (8/26/10). So much for controlling the media. Heeb, www.heeb-magazine.com.

22. Lange/Levitsky, D. (2009 August). *Monthly Review*. Jews Confront Zionism.

23. Ravitz. "New Jews" stake claim. (Chap 13, Note 20). Paraphrasing Ari Wallach.

24. Ibid. The quote is from Andy Abrams.

25. The point is to first connect with your friend and communicate that this is the conditioning all non-Jews receive, just as all white people are taught racism, either directly or indirectly, by a white-dominant society. And fine to do it lightly, even with humor!

26. Dorf, J. (1/16/07). Jenny Schecter and Jewish visibility in the LGBT community. www.ourchart.com. juliedorf's blog.

27. Ibid.

28. Ibid.

29. Pogrebin. Anti-semitism in the women's movement. (Chap 1, Note 126)

30. Axner, M. (8/19/11). Why holding a picket sign is good for the Jews. *The Jewish Advocate*. Boston, MA.

31. Thanks to Rabbi Lynn Gottlieb and Sandy Butler who gave me ideas for this.

32. Khazzoom. Esther is *our* queen. (Chap 2, Note 22)

33. Rosenwasser & Gatmon. Crosscurrents of Jewish women, 119, (Chap 2, Note 2).

34. Wahba. Benign ignorance. (p. 65). In Khazzoom. *The flying camel*. (Chap 1, Note 34)

35. Susser, D. (10/30/09) A long way home: Local rabbi conducts ceremony of return for crypto-Jews. Jewish News of Greater Phoenix. http://www.jewishaz.com. The Conversos from the Spanish Inquisition (see Chapter One) were crypto-Jews, but there are also crypto-Jews from various countries and centuries. The Jews in this ceremony were all B'nei Anusim Hispanic Sephardi.

36. Kaye/Kantrowitz. *The colors of Jews.* (p. 159). (Chap 1, Note 52)

37. Gold, R. (11/16/11). What does a Jew look like? Ask Rabbi Capers Funnye, www. haaretz.com. Rabbi Funnye is the first African American member of the Chicago Board of Rabbis, works with the Pan African Jewish Alliance, cofounded the Alliance of Black Jews, and is a cousin of Michelle Obama. His congregation is not affiliated with any denomination, and includes Africans, African Americans, Ashkenazim, B'nai Anusim, Filipinos, Latinos, Sephardim, and Caribbean Jews.

38. Khazzoom. When Jewish means Ashkenazi. (Chap 2, Note 23)

39. Ibid. Khazzoom asks those who grew up in Iran, Syria, Ethiopia, Turkey, if they have told their children/grandchildren their stories, recorded the songs, folktales, traditions? She urges their children/grandchildren to record these stories, ask questions, and get the information while their older relatives are still alive.

40. Ibid. Later, Khazzoom directed a temple-affiliated project that normalized Jewish multiculturalism, as part of U.S. Jewish identity.

41. Khazzoom. United Jewish feminist front. (p. 178). In Ruttenberg. *Yentl's revenge.* (Chap 1, Note 65)

42. Ueshiba, M. (1992). The art of peace (p. 33) (translated by John Stevens). Boston: Shambala Books.

43. Amida prayer, 2007 Yom Kippur machzor (prayerbook), p. 17, Kehilla Synagogue, Oakland, CA.

44. Kaye/Kantrowitz, M. & Klepfisz, I., (with Mennis, B.) (1989.) In gerangl/In struggle (p. 339). In Kaye/Kantrowitz & Klepfisz. *The tribe of Dina,* (Chap 5, Note 27)

45. Excerpt from Leon Rosselson's song, "My Father's Jewish World." This song can be found as an individual download, and it is also on the CDs by Fuse Records: *Turning Silence into Song* and *The Last Chance* (an 8-song CD on Israel/Palestine).

46. Arditti, R. (1989). To be a Hanu. In Kaye/Kantrowitz & Klepfisz. *The tribe of Dina.* (pp. 334-346). (Chap 5, Note 27)

47. Bush, L. (4/13/12). Gracia Mendes Nasi, http://jewshcurrents.org. Quote is by Marianna D. Birnbaum, *The long journey of Gracia Mendes.*

48. Bush, L. (10/2/10). Groucho Marx, http://jewishcurrents.org.

49. Suhl, Y. (Ed.). (1967). *They fought back: The story of the Jewish resistance in Nazi Europe* (pp. 3-4). New York: Schocken Books. Hilberg lost twenty-six members of his extended family in the *Shoah.*

50. Ibid., p. 4.

51. Ibid.

52. Ibid.

53. Working with Frankl in Theresienstadt were Rabbis Leo Baeck and Regina Jonas.

54. Bush, L. (10/23/11). The dancer in Birkenau, http://jewishcurrents.org. The Nazi was Josef Schillinger, the woman was possibly "a former Warsaw dancer named Horowitz," as reported by Martin Gilbert in *The Holocaust: A history of the Jews during the second World War.*

55. Marans, N. (11/2/09). Op-Ed: Kristallnacht in Munich, then and now, http://jta.org.

56. Gilbert, M. (2000). The Holocaust: Maps (p. 160.) In Adams, Blumenfeld, Castaneda, et al. *Readings for diversity.* (Chap 1, Note 93)

57. Berenbaum, M., The world must know (p. 176.) (Chap 1, Note 40)

58. Historian Leonard Zeskin estimates of the 20-30,000 Jews who joined Soviet partisans, 20% survived. See "Commemorating the Warsaw Uprising and Jewish Resistance during the Holocaust," 4/18/08, http://www.leonardzeskind.com. See also the extraordinary documentary, *The Partisans of Vilna*, and read the powerful interview by Aviva Cantor, "She Fought Back: An Interview with Vilna Partisan Vitke Kempner," in *Lilith*, Issue # 16.

59. Gilbert, M. (2000). The Holocaust: Maps (p. 160.) In Adams, Bell, & Griffin. *Teaching for diversity*. (Chap 1, Note 2). And another story: in 1942, the Jews of the Byelorussian ghetto of Nieswiez set fire to their own homes to avoid a Nazi "selection," then fought guards with weapons they had gathered. Some escaped through the flames and formed a Jewish fighting force in the forests, battling the Nazis for two years, some even surviving.

60. Suhl. *They fought back*, (p. 6). (Chap 13, Note 49). Lawrence Bush reports in "Unarmed Resistance," http://jewishcurrents.org, *that* Lachva was one of the first ghetto uprisings. Half the Jewish population was killed, 90 survived the war.

61. Ibid., p. 221.

62. Berenbaum, M., *The world must know* (p. 176.) (Chap 1, Note 40)

63. Bush, L. (10/14/12). Revolt in Sobibor, http://jewishcurrents.org. Half of the camp's 600 inmates escaped, but most were killed by pursuers or while crossing minefields; 53 survived, some fighting as partisans.

64. Mark, B. (1967). The Warsaw ghetto uprising (p. 109). In Suhl, *They fought back*. (Chap 13, Note 49).

65. Edelman, M. (undated.) The ghetto fights (published in a pamphlet called "The Warsaw Ghetto: The 45th Anniversary of the Uprising"). Interpress Publishers, p. 31, http://www.writing.upenn.edu/~afilreis/Holocaust/warsaw-uprising.html. Edelman dedicates this pamphlet to the memory of Abrasha Blum, crediting Blum's composure and presence of mind as enabling them all to weather "the nightmare of those terrible times."

66. Ibid., p. 2.

67. Ibid.. p. 23

68. Litwoman, J. (1982). Some women in the resistance. Compiled for the San Francisco Jewish Feminist Conference, 1982. Unpublished essay, used with permission by Rabbi Jane Rachel Litman.

69. Suhl, Y. (1967). Little Wanda with the braids, (p. 51). In *They fought back*. (Chap 13, Note 49).

70. Suhl. *They fought back*, (p. 2). (Chap 13, Note 49).

71. Suhl, Y. (1967). Rosa Robota–heroine of the Auschwitz underground (p. 220). In *They fought back*. (Chap 13, Note 49)

72. Ibid., p. 222.

73. Ibid., p. 223.

74. Litwoman, Some women in the resistance. (Chap 13, Note 68). The quote by Korczak, as described by Litman, was from a talk Korczak gave to "a group of Labor Zionist women in Tel Aviv" (before her death in 1988).

75. Mendelsohn. *The lost*. (p. 403). (Chap 1, Note 30)

76. Berenbaum, M., *The world must know* (p. 157.) (Chap 1, Note 40). And: how tragic that *any* Jews who wanted to leave were left behind.

77. Their combined efforts were able to delay deportation until the tide turned against the Nazis. Based (mostly) on information from Michael Bar-Zohar's 1998 book, *Beyond Hitler's Grasp: The heroic rescue of Bulgaria's Jews*, Adams Media Corporation, Holbrook, MA.

78. Bush, L. (9/12/10). Varian Fry in Vichy France, http://jewishcurrents.org.

79. Mosque founder Si Kaddour Benghrabrit "used patiently woven networks of friendship to save lives." From Derri Berkani's documentary *The Mosque of Paris: A Forgotten Resistance*.

80. Setton, R. (2003a). Jew/Arab/woman: Notes toward an identity. In *Jewish women from Muslim societies* (p. 19). Hadassah International Research Institute on Jewish Women and American Sephardi Federation.

81. Mendelsohn. *The lost.* (p. 456). (Chap 1, Note 30)

82. Berenbaum, M., *The world must know* (p. 160). (Chap 1, Note 40)

83. Ibid., p. 159.

84. The article was written by congregant Alan Canton.

85. Fishkoff, S. (11/2/09). Hillel groups responding to hate acts by bringing together campus communities. *Jewish Telegraph Agency*, http://www.hillel.org. The quote is from Joe Gettinger.

86. See "Jewish group, Rabbis condemn charging of Muslim students by Orange County DA," 2/7/11, http://jewishvoiceforpeace.org/blog/jewish-group-rabbis-condemn-charging-of-muslim-students-by-orange-county-da.

87. Fletcher, T. (2004, October). Anti-Semitism Talk at KTA Conference (Kindertransport Association Conference, Burlingame, CA). Unpublished speech, used with permission.

88. Ibid.

89. Excerpt from Leon Rosselson's song, "My Father's Jewish World." I omitted the first two lines of the chorus, which are "It's not a nation, not a religion." Used with permission.

CHAPTER FOURTEEN: LIBERATORY HEALING

1. Greenspan, M. (2003, May-June). Healing through the dark emotions in an age of global threat. *Tikkun*, 18, 22.

2. Brooks, D. (3/7/11). The new humanism. *New York Times*, http://www.nytimes.com.

3. Steinem. *Revolution from within.* (p. 171). (Chap 7, Note 19). Collins is not Jewish.

4. Ibid., p. 170.

5. Ibid.

6. Ibid., p. 173.

7. Ibid., p. 172.

8. Ibid., p. 173.

9. Roth, C. (2/17/10). Bay Area holocaust survivors respond to "Mein Kampf" exhibit, www.sfgate.com.

10. Ibid.

11. Cameron. *Finding Water.* (Chap 8, Note 5). Cameron is not Jewish.

12. Ibid., p. 9.

13. Also martial arts, dance, Rosen work, more. Also the Feldenkrais Method of body-and-consciousness work, using exercise and bodily awareness for well-being and health; founded by Moshe Pinchas Feldenkrais, born in 1906 in Ukraine. His goal was not just more flexible bodies, but also more flexible minds.

14. Gottlieb. Kavanah for erev Yom Kippur. (Chap 10, Note 124)

15. Boskin, N. (2010 September). Yom kippur drash. Kehilla Community Synagogue, www.kehillasynagogue.org/article.php?story=20100927120543841.

16. Ibid.

17. Ibid.

18. Ibid.

19. Ibid.

20. Ibid.

21. Hanna, T. (1986). What is somatics? *Somatics: Magazine-Journal of the Bodily Arts and Science*, 5(4), 2. In Johns. We are self affirming soul healing Africans. (Chap 7, Note 40)

22. Johns. We are self affirming soul healing Africans. (pp. 128-129). (Chap 7, Note 40)

23. Steen, X. (1/1/09). Escaping the trauma vortex. *The Jerusalem Post,* www.jpost.com.

24. Levine, P. (2005). *Healing trauma: A pioneering program for restoring the wisdom of your body.* Boulder, CO: Sounds True. I do not know if Levine is Jewish.

25. Ibid., p. 39.

26. Steen, X. (2009, January 1). Escaping the trauma vortex, www.jpost.com.

27. Haines, S. (4/10/12). 2012 Somatics and trauma advance training information. (Listserve e-mail). See www.somaticsandtrauma.org. Haines is not Jewish.

28. Haines, S. (12/7/09). Somatics and Trauma 2010 Trainings. (Listserve e-mail). See www.somaticsandtrauma.org.

29. Haines, S. (1999). *The survivor's guide to sex: How to have an empowered sex life after child sexual abuse.* San Francisco: Cleis Press.

30. Haines, S. (12/7/09). Somatics and Trauma 2010 Trainings. In 2012, Haines' organization partnered with the Strozzi Institute to build the first national somatics organization that is majority people of color and majority queer, also accessible to working class and poor communities. They hope to mobilize well-intentioned projects and communities towards systemic change, who are outside the social justice movement. Participants will practice with community-based organizations that serve youth, survivors of violence, people with HIV/AIDS, and/or work for racial/environmental justice and violence prevention. See www.somaticsandtrauma.org.

31. Johns, T. We are self affirming soul healing Africans. (p. iv).(Chap 7, Note 40)

32. Johns, T. (3/3/08). Dissertation defense, California Institute of Integral Studies. Personal communication, also discussed beginning p. 288 of dissertation, see above.

33. Johns. We are self affirming soul healing Africans. (Chap 7, Note 40)

34. Ibid., p. 283.

35. Ibid., p. 280.

36. Johns, T. (2007). Learning to love our Black selves: Healing from internalized racism (p. 482). In P. Reason & H. Bradbury (Eds.), *The safe handbook of action research: Participative inquiry and practice.* Los Angeles: Sage. Also in Johns. We are self affirming soul healing Africans. (p. 280).(Chap 7, Note 40)

37. Johns. We are self affirming soul healing Africans. (p. 281).(Chap 7, Note 40)

38. Ibid., p. v.

39. Ibid., p. 288.

40. Brown, C. (2011 Winter). Unhealed terror, www.tikkun.org.

41. *Democracy Now.* (2/15/10) Interview with Gabor Maté: When the body says no, www.democracynow.org.

42. Ibid.

43. Abraham. I want my RC! (Chap 4, Note 10). Abraham is not Jewish.

44 King, M. L. (6/24/57). "On the Power of Peaceful Persuasion" (speech).

45. I am using pseudonyms here instead of initials, to make it easier to follow the story.

CHAPTER FIFTEEN: HOPE INTO PRACTICE: Choosing Justice Despite Our Fears

1. Surasky, C. (1/17/10). Jewish Voice for Peace listserve, used with permission.

2. Kaye/Kantrowitz. *The colors of Jews,* (pp. 198-199). (Chap 1, Note 52)

3. I'm borrowing this concept from Paul Kivel, in his February 1998 paper "I'm not white, I'm Jewish. But I'm white: Standing as Jews in the fight for racial justice" (p. 9), presented at the Whiteness Conference, University of California at Riverside.

4. For background and explanation of Rabbi Luria's cosmology myth, which transformed the meaning of *tikkun olam,* see Howard Schwartz's *Tikkun* article, 3/28/11, "How the Ari

created a myth and transformed Judaism," www.tikkunorg.

5. Wise, A. (2/1/12). Sell the Torah, put the kid in school, http://palestiniantalmud.com. Wise explains that Mussar comes from Proverbs 1:2 and can be found in the Torah, Gemara, Halakah (Jewish law), Jewish literature, and the history of Jewish labor and social justice activism. It was also an ethical, spiritual, and cultural movement founded in the 19th century in Eastern Europe by Rabbi Israel Salanter. See Wise's powerful story on this blog post.

6. Berg, A. (2007, December). A zionist changes his mind. *Tikkun*, 57.

7. The original from *Pirkei Avot 2:21//Verses of the Fathers* (a Talmudic compilation of rabbinical ethical teachings): "It is not incumbent upon you to complete the work, but neither are you at liberty to desist from it." See Chapter Eleven for another version.

8. Kaye/Kantrowitz, M. (2007, March.) Some notes on anti-Semitism from a progressive Jewish perspective, www.jewishcurrents.org/2007-mar-kayekantrowiz.htm.

9. Ibid.

10. Miller. *The drama of the gifted child.* (p. 4). (Chap 10, Note 2). In a 9/5/12, talk in Berkeley, CA, sponsored by radio station KPFA, physician/author Gabor Maté spoke of a similar idea, though framed differently: "How self-awareness within supports progress without." Also, check out the *UNtraining workshops*, a "provocative and compassionate approach" that focuses on healing personal and social oppressions. Trainer Rita Shimmin writes "Loving yourself is a political act. We are taught not to love ourselves, and from that place we are easily manipulated."

11. Lerner, M. (10/8/09). Say no to the war in Afghanistan and Pakistan. *San Francisco Chronicle*, http://articles.sfgate.com.

12. Rabbi Lynn Gottlieb also attests to this idea in (2009) Kavanah for erev Yom Kippur. (Chap 10, Note 124.) See also Buddhist teacher Pema Chodrun's book, *Comfortable with Uncertainty*, who says if we can see ourselves clearly, and feel good-hearted about ourselves, "there's no obstacle to feeling loving-kindness for others as well" (p. 12).

13. Windwood, A. (7/16/10). Oscar Grant, Israel and reaching for grace. Rockwood Leadership Institute Newsletter. www.rockwoodleadership.org. Windwood credits "my friend Roz" for this idea. Windwood is not Jewish.

14. Daphne Leef's Speech September 3, 2011. *Haaretz.com*, http://makom.haaretz. com/blog.asp?rId=275. She is referring to the 2011 summer protests in Tel Aviv, mostly for economic justice, the largest social protests in Israeli history up to that point. This was roughly 5.5% of Israel's population, equivalent to about 22 million in the U.S. There were up to 120 protest encampments in cities throughout Israel, along with the one-day demos.

15. Zinn, H. (1994). *You can't be neutral on a moving train: A personal history of our times* (p. 208). Boston: Beacon Press.

16. Source unknown, used with permission of Dr. Reagon. Reagon is not Jewish.

17. Ibid.

18. Berlet, C. (9/18/09). Conspiracy nation, www.indypendent.org.

19. "Obama Remarks on 40th Anniversary of the Assassination of Dr. Martin Luther King, Jr." (4/4/08), www.prx.org/pieces/25178-obama-speaks-in-indiana-on-the-40th-anniversary-of. Reverend King's words were based on the concept first articulated in 1858 by abolitionist minister Reverend Theodore Parker: "I do not pretend to understand the moral universe. The arc is a long one. My eye reaches but little ways. I cannot calculate the curve and complete the figure by experience of sight. I can divine it by conscience. And from what I see I am sure it bends toward justice."

20. Rosenwasser, P. (1992b). *Visionary voices, women on power: Conversations with shamans, activists, teachers, artists and healers* (p. 179). San Francisco: Aunt Lute Books. The quote is from an interview with the late activist/comedian Fran Peavey.

21. Pogrebin, L. C. (2011, Winter). Hard-won tips for twenty-first century activists. *Tikkun*, 60, 25th Anniversary Issue. Of course we get discouraged sometimes; the point is, to let ourselves really feel that when it comes up, to cry or write or talk to a friend so that it doesn't keep building up inside us—and then refocus on reasons to be hopeful. Also, Dr. Bernice Johnson Reagon reminds us that as crucial as working in coalitions is, to band together and win victories, working for a common goal with folks who we may also have significant differences with can be very hard—it's not a place where we get to feel comfortable: "You can't stay there all the time," she reminds us. Check out her excellent legendary article "Coalition Politics: Turning the Century" in *Home girls: A black feminist anthology*.

22. Ibid. (Pogrebin)

23. Smith, B. (2011, Winter). How we treat each other makes a difference. *Tikkun*, 68, 25th Anniversary Issue. A telling anecdote: in his 2010 *New Yorker* article "Small Change," Malcolm Gladwell reports that college freshman Ezell Blair was at that Greensboro lunch counter, to change Jim Crow segregation laws, because he was with two good friends from high school, plus his college roommate. For an excellent/short activist video that includes this theme, plus other (fun) organizing advice (such as "if you act like you belong, security won't notice you," or "when arrested, sing loudly"), see Rae Abileah's youtube video, http://bit.ly/UJhRXm.

24. Brown, R. (2011 September) Organizer reflection: July 19th in Philly. *JVP Organizing Newsletter*. Issue 3, http://www.scribd.com/doc/64716497/Jewish-Voice-for-Peace-Organizing-Newsletter-Sept-2011. Speaking of relationships, longtime organizer Elly Bulkin notes in her essay "Hard ground," in Bulkin, Pratt & Smith. *Yours in struggle*. (p. 192). (Chap 2, Note 20) "When my personal connections *to women of various identities* are extremely limited, these limitations are reflected in my thinking, my words, and my activism." (Italics added)

25. Klein, N. (10/6/11). Occupy Wall Street: The most important thing in the world now, www.thenation.com.

26. Ibid.

27. Levins Morales. Latinos, Israel and Palestine. (Chap 1, Note 23). Dorothy Miller Zellner, who worked for 20 years with the Southern Nonviolent Coordinating Committee (SNCC), said that half of the white folks who went south in 1964 to participate in the civil rights movement were Jews: "We all got the message from our parents, 'You must not stand idly by'" (from her talk at the Jewish Voice for Peace National Membership Meeting in Berkeley CA, 4/20/13). Zellner is featured in Debra Schultz's excellent book, *Going south: Jewish women in the civil rights movement*. Schultz points out, "In relation to the total U.S population, Jewish *women* participated in the civil rights movement in disproportionate numbers" (p. 18) (Italics added)

28. Surasky, C. (1/17/10). Jewish Voice for Peace listserve, used with permission.

29. Kaye/Kantrowitz. *The colors of Jews*. (p. 64). (Chap 1, Note 52)

30. Bush, L. (10/31/10). November 1: Women strike for peace, http://jewishcurrents. org. A 1977 Gallup poll named Abzug one of the 20 most influential women in the world. Rabbi Arthur Waskow called her "perhaps the toughest, smartest, bravest Jewish progressive of our generation."

31. Kaye/Kantrowitz. *The colors of Jews*. (p. 64). (Chap 1, Note 52)

32. Lubeck, S. (7/15/10). Tisha B'Av reflection on the Oscar Grant killing, www.jweekly. com. It's been true since I can remember: one out of every three black men will spend time in (U.S.) Juvenile Hall, jail, or prison in their lifetime.

33. Somerson, W. (2010, July/August). The intersection of anti-Occupation and queer Jewish organizing. *Tikkun*, 58.

34 Ibid.

35. Ibid., p. 73.

36. Ibid.

37. Horn, J. (10/13/11) Occupy Wall Street Jews to "Occupy Judaism," www.jpost.com.

38. Ibid., Jews held similar services at Occupy Boston, Philly, and D.C. Alex Sugerman-Brozan wrote in "Kol Nidre at Occupy Boston: We are the 99% and the 1%": "It is a core tenet of progressive social movements that we do not necessarily blame the individuals within institutions, but the institutions themselves, and the structures that give those institutions so much unaccountable power…to me, the 1% is in all of us. It is that part of us that is susceptible to greed and cynicism…Social movements must proceed on the belief that everyone can change…"

39. Personal e-mail, 10/10/11, used with permission. David Wilensky of *New Voices*, the national Jewish student magazine, wrote "Afterward, I felt like I was walking on air." The following Rosh Hoshana, Vilkomerson spoke more about this event, at a talk at her shul: "Suddenly, I understood the ancient tradition of call and response as it must have been in the days of the temple. And by the act of repeating what the leader said, I had to actually own and feel the words, even when they made me uncomfortable"—adding that when folks were invited to call out their own sins, "whether we agreed with them or not…we had to repeat them, and in so doing…we all became more human to one another." Personal communication, used with permission. Vilkomerson is executive director of Jewish Voice for Peace. See also her eloquent article for Passover, (3/18/13), on Forward.com, "Put Olive on Seder Plate for Palestinians and All Oppressed People"; she writes "If we personally remember that we were liberated from Egypt, doesn't that empathy obligate us to work to make sure that every person enjoys that same freedom?"

40. April 1: Occupy Interfaith Freedom Seder & Palm Sunday Processional, http://blog. occupyjudaism.org/post/19716936730/ april-1-occupy-interfaith-freedom-seder-palm-Sunday. Also see http:/www.kolotchayeinu.org/ ritual_processional. Participating were Occupy Faith NYC, Occupy Judaism, Occupy Catholics, Jews for Racial & Economic Justice, the Shalom Center, Congregation Kolot Chayeinu, and Judson Memorial Church. Both holidays are explicitly connected to themes of Occupy Wall Street.

41. Eisner, J. (10/13/11). Why "Occupy Judaism" is turning point, http://forward.com.

42. Ibid.

43. Horn. Occupy Wall Street Jews to "Occupy Judaism." (Chap 15, Note 37)

44. Cooper, D. J. (2008, May). How do we manage spiritually during hard times? *Kol Kehilla newsletter*. www.kehillasynagogue.org, Oakland, CA.

45. Others to check out: *Mazon, Jspot.org blog, Bet Tzedek Legal Services*, the *Jewish Campaign for Immigration Reform*, many more—including *Keshet*, which works for full inclusion of queer Jews in Jewish life and offers a "Jewish Guide to the Marking of the Transgender Day of Remembrance." Also including *Jews in ALL Hues*, a peer-driven grass roots group that creates community for dual (or multiple) heritage Jews; they note that 52% of all young U.S, Jews up to age 28 are dual/multiple heritage Jews (including having one Jewish parent, adopted Jews, Jews by Choice, etc.) And *Jews On First!* has defended the First Amendment against the Christian right, but since early 2013 is no longer updating their website. See later in the chapter for groups specifically focused on peace in Israel/Palestine.

An April 2012 survey of U.S. Jews about Jewish values by the Public Religion Research Institute found that: 84% said pursuing justice was "somewhat or very important," 72% said the same about *tikkun olam*, and 46% said a commitment to social equality was key to their Jewish identity.

See also Ezra Berkeley Nepon's wonderful 2012 book, *Justice, justice shall you pursue:*

A *history of New Jewish Agenda*, newjewishagenda.net—a must-read, with an eye to new 21st century possibilities. New Jewish Agenda was a multi-issue, national membership organization that practiced participatory grassroots democracy, with over 45 chapters and 5000 members, from 1980 to 1992. It included task forces on Middle East peace, LGB rights, nuclear disarmament, Central American solidarity, economic justice, Jewish feminism, ending South African apartheid, more. Agenda was "an explicitly Jewish voice in local, national and international justice movements," founded in an effort "to apply Jewish values, traditions and insights" to the problems and needs of the 1980s. This history, these lessons, are crucial for present-day activists. Also included is a fascinating summary of the origins of *"tikkun olam"* in an essay by Rachel Mattson.

46. This New York bill guarantees domestic workers overtime at time and a half, a day off every week, and a statement of hours, similar to other workers. In his essay in Ezra Nepon's 2012 book *Justice, justice shall you pursue* (Chapter 15, Note 45), Daniel Rozsa Lang/Levitsky notes that "JFREJ was founded in large part as a response to the 'mainstream' Jewish community's efforts to shun and discredit Nelson Mandela after his release from prison because of his support for Palestinian liberation." In the program book for JFREJ's 2012 awards dinner, Executive Director Marjorie Dove Kent wrote: "In partnerships with individuals and organizations, we have each other's backs without knowing for sure what the next challenge will be. Our liberation is bound up in each other's future."

47. Bend the Arc stated as one of its chief goals to bridge the gap "between the cautious voices of many [Jewish] institutions and the more diverse justice-oriented Jews on the street." May it be so.

48. Kaye/Kantrowitz. *The colors of Jews.* (pp. 122-123). (Chap 1, Note 52). Quote is from Linda Holtzman.

49. Petterson, S. (9/22/11). A Rosh Hashanah sermon, http://kehillasynagogue.org/2011/09/22/a-rosh-hashanah-sermon-2011-5772/.

50. LGBTI rights. Lesbian, Gay, Bisexual, Transgender, Intersex.

51. Renewal Rabbi Arthur Waskow founded the Shalom Center in 1983. Jewishcurrents.org explains that after Martin Luther King Jr.'s murder in 1968, "Waskow's experience of walking through the military-occupied District of Columbia led to his writing *The freedom seder*, weaving together Jewish, Black and other liberation struggles."

52. For example, see Adam Horowitz's *Mondoweiss* 12/17/12 article, "'Jews Against Islamophobia' condemns latest round of Geller ads in NYC."

53. Dreier, P. & May, D. (10/1/07). Progressive Jews organize, http://www.thenation.com/article/progressive-jews-organize. The four community networks are: Pacific Institute for Community Organizing, the Industrial Areas Foundation, the Gamaliel Foundation, and the Direct Action and Research and Training Center.

54. Ibid.

55. Ibid.

56. Kaye/Kantrowitz. *The colors of Jews.* (p. 125). (Chap 1, Note 52) The speaker is organizer Vic Rosenthal. JCA also runs noncongregational programs, including one for "Indie" Jews.

57. Ibid., p. 136.

58. Heschel. *I Asked for Wonder,* (p. 88). (Intro., Note 10)

59. *Jewish Week.* (6/13/08). 36 under 36. Also, *Jewish Philanthropy,* (6/16/10), 36 under 36: Visionaries for a new era, http://ejewishphilanthropy.com/36-under-36-visionaries-for-a-new-era/.

60. Slutsky, C. (5/15/09). 36 under 36: 2009, http://mochajuden.com/?p=562.

61. Lipman, S. (6/15/10). Making a space for Latin American Jews. *New York Jewish*

Week, www.thejewishweek.com.

62. Falk, M. (1996). "Vhavta" in *The book of blessings: New Jewish prayers for daily life, the Sabbath, and the New Moon festival*. New York: HarperCollins, (1999 paperback, Boston: Beacon Press).

63. Rosenblum, A. (2007). "the past didn't go anywhere" (p. 19) (Chap 1, Note 129).

64. Herbert, B. (1/29/10). A radical treasure, www.nytimes.com. At the 2012 Democratic National Convention, senatorial candidate Elizabeth Warren said something similar: "People feel like the system is rigged against them. And here's the painful part: They're right…Oil companies guzzle down billions in profits. Billionaires pay lower tax rates than their secretaries. And Wall Street CEOs, the same ones who wrecked our economy and destroyed millions of jobs, still strut around Congress, no shame, demanding favors and acting like we should thank them." See *Democracy Now*, 9/6/12.

65. Healey, J. (11/15/11) When hope comes back (A poem for the 99%). http://josh-healey.org/2011/11/16/when-hope-comes-back/. Reminds me of how I felt several months later, "locking down" (chaining ourselves to) Wells Fargo headquarters in downtown San Francisco, beneath a banner "We are unstoppable! Another world is possible." (With others, we succeeded in closing the bank headquarters for the day.)

66. Ibid.

67. Gottlieb, L. (1/1/09). Peace through understanding. Jewish Voice for Peace listserve, http://peacethroughunderstanding.blogspot.com/2009/04/jewish-voice-for-peace.html. Gottlieb was among the first ten women rabbis in the U.S.

68. Ibid. See near the end of Chapter One.

69. An excellent animated/brief resource is *Israel & Palestine: A Very Short Introduction*, http://www.youtube.com/watch?v=Y58njT2oXfE&feature=youtu.be, or http://www.jewish-voiceforpeace.org/.

Also, Aurora Levins Morales explains, "Israel needs to be pressured…in exactly the same way that the Congo needs to be pressured, that tortured country where millions have died in wars over the precious metal that makes our cell phones work, and the legacy of Belgian colonial rule, known for its extreme brutality, is reenacted…between Congolese people." See Levins Morales. Latinos, Israel and Palestine. (Chap 1, Note 23)

70. Rosenblum, A., "the past didn't go anywhere" (p. 21) (Chap 1, Note 129)

71. Ibid.

72. Ibid., p. 20.

73. "When a child's first wish is for clean water, the conditions under Israeli occupation become stunningly clear." Eda Gordon, in MECA News, Summer 2011, Middle East Children's Alliance newsletter. www.mecaforpeace.org. As of 2012, 95 percent of Gaza's water is still unsafe to drink.

And in the West Bank, Israel takes over 80 percent of the water from Ramallah's mountain aquifer each year; Israeli authorities have approved no new Palestinian wells in this aquifer since 1967. West Bank Palestinians are allowed 70 litres of water per person per day, while Israelis are given 300 litres of water per person per day, including West Bank settlers. The World Health Organization recommends 100 litres of water per person per day. See EWASH (Emergency Water Sanitation and Hygiene in the occupied Palestinian Territory), www.ewash.org/en/?view=79YOcy0nNs3Du69tjVnyyumIu1jfxPKNuunzXkRpKQNyIwQTTTGG.

74. Kamel, R. (2004). Jews, Israel, and the United States: Talking points for Jewish antiwar activism. U.S. Campaign to end the Israeli occupation, http://www.endtheoccupation.org/article.php?id=12.

75. Cattori, S. (2008, November 1). What is the lesson to be learned from the Holocaust?

An interview with Hedy Epstein. Information Clearinghouse, www.informationclearing-house.info/

76. Rothchild, A., *Broken promises* (p. 19). (Chap 1, Note 11)

77. Butler, J. (4/14/10). You will not be alone, www.thenation.com.

78. Butler, J. (2/7/13). Judith Butler's remarks to Brooklyn College on BDS, www.thenation.com. Read this entire eloquent speech, as well as the background info on Note 185, Chapter 1. Also see Butler, J. (8/27/12). Judith Butler responds to attack: "I affirm a Judaism that is not associated with state violence," http://mondoweiss.net.

79. Personal communication with Rabbi Margaret Holub, 7/22/12, used with permission.

80. Horowitz, A. (10/30/09). Palestinian equal rights joins the progressive agenda on "The Daily Show," http://mondoweiss.net.

81. Ibid.

82. *YoungJewishProud*. (2010). The young Jewish declaration, www.youngjewishproud.org.

83. Ibid.

84. *Ta'anit Tzedek* /Jewish Fast for Gaza, http://fastforgaza.net/. As we go to press, it looks like this website is for sale. In a 2012 interview, Rabbi Brant explained, "I see my Jewish liberation as inextricably bound up with Palestinian liberation." See Mitchell Plitnick's interview with Rosen, 12/6/12, "Wrestling in the Daylight: an interview with Rabbi Brant Rosen," www.mitchellplitnick.com.

85. Nobel Prize-winner Archbishop Desmond Tutu specifically cited "the brave rabbis of Jewish Voice for Peace" (for their letter in support of divestment from companies profiting from the occupation) in his 4/30/12 article, "Justice requires action to stop subjugation of Palestinians," www.tampabay.com.

86. Surasky, C. (7/2/07). Jewish Voice for Peace listserve, used with permission. In his 2/14/11 *JNews* article "Views of Egypt show new Jewish discourse in USA," Middle East analyst (and former JVP Policy Director) Mitchell Plitnick called JVP "the biggest and most effective grassroots Jewish political group in the country."

87. Surasky, C. (11/12/10). Jewish Voice for Peace listserve, used with permission. Young/Jewish/Proud is now the youth wing of Jewish Voice for Peace. Although these brave young Jews were booed and physically attacked, no charges were brought against them. Yet when ten Muslim students (nonviolently) interrupted Israeli Ambassador Michael Oren's speech at UC Irvine the previous February, in a similar though smaller action, they were convicted of two misdemeanors in criminal court. See http:// jewishvoiceforpeace.org/blog/jewish-group-rabbis-condemn-charging-of-muslim-students-by-orange-county-da.

88. Abileah, R. (11/9/10). Jewish values vs. Israeli policies: Why five young Jews disrupted PM Netanyahu in New Orleans, http://mondoweiss.net.

89. Miller, S. (11/8/10). Hecklers disrupt Netanyahu's speech at U.S. Jewish conference, www.haaretz.com. Jewish folklorist Steve Koppman makes a similar point, comparing Israeli treatment of Palestinians to traditional Jewish values; see his 9/27/12 Op-Ed in Jweekly.com, "Protesting against Israel—valid or anti-Semitic?: Organized community conflates policy, values."

90. Small, J. (11/18/10). King speaks out at Jewish assembly. *The Phoenix*, http://www.swarthmorephoenix.com/ 2010/11/18/news/king-speaks-out-at-jewish-assembly.

91. Occupy the occupiers: A Jewish call to action, (11/8/11), http://www.youngjewish-proud.org/occupy-the-occupiers-a-jewish-call-to-action/. Richard Silverstein documents the "decidedly Islamophobic" agenda of several extremist Jewish foundations: the Koret Foundation, the Fairbrook Foundation, and the Irving Moskowitz Foundation. He reports that they contribute "enormously to the current hostile atmosphere toward Muslims in the U.S. and Israel" (including hate-speech ads sponsored by Pamela Geller), turning

"the Israeli-Arab conflict into a religious holy war when it's really a battle over political power." See his 1/5/13 article, "Jewish foundations support Islamophobia at home, settler triumphalism abroad," www.richardsilverstein.com. See also Elly Bulkin and Donna Nevel's exposé of extremist Jewish groups' funding of U.S Islamophobia and right-wing projects in Israel, "Follow the money: From Islamophobia to Israel right or wrong," 10/3/12, www.alternet.org.

92. Weiss, P. (11/8/10). Five young Jews disrupt Netanyahu speech with call for new Jewish identity, http://mondoweiss.net. In her article "Progressive except on Palestine," in *The Hill*, JVP director Rebecca Vilkomerson wrote, "Many analysts, including Israelis, believe the occupation is the single greatest threat to peace in the region."

93. Cooper, D. J. (2011, October). Hillel, Israel, Palestine and me, http://www.kehillasynagogue.org/article.php/20111010161658470. Also in the bay area, Beyt Tikkun Synagogue frequently invites speakers to offer diverse perspectives on Israel-Palestine; Beyt *Tikkun* is led by Rabbi Michael Lerner, who cofounded *Tikkun* magazine, a long-time national journal (interfaith, but also Jewish-identified) that consistently advocates for a just peace for Israelis and Palestinians.

94. Rosen, B. (1/2/11). JRC in Israel/Palestine: My final thoughts. *Shalom rav*, www.rabbibrant.com.

95. Ellis, M. (1987). *Toward a Jewish theology of liberation*. Maryknoll, NY: Orbis Books.

96. Levins Morales. Latinos, Israel and Palestine. (Chap 1, Note 23). Also, in Guy Izhak Austrian and Ella Goldman's 2003 article, "How to strengthen the Palestine solidarity movement by making friends with Jews": "When Jews are struggling to articulate their experiences of an oppression that is kept so eerily invisible, your first response should not sound like a debate...Instead, value our trust in you and listen. Put thought and caring into appropriate ways to raise your points." (Chap 7, Note 10).

97. U.S. Palestinian Community Network. (3/13/12). Granting no quarter: A call for the disavowal of the racism and anti-Semitism of Gilad Atzmon, http://uspcn.org/2012/03/13/granting-no-quarter-a-call-for-the-disavowal-of-the-racism-and-antisemitism-of-gilad-atzmon/.

98. Ibid.

99. Weingart, L. (2005, March). Commentary: Speaking to the Presbyterians about selective divestment. *Jewish Voice for Peace newsletter*, http://www.jewishvoiceforpeace.org/content/speaking-presbyterians-about-selective-divestment.

100. In a 2012 interview with Mitchell Plitnick, Rabbi Brant Rosen encourages "real dialogue, which occurs when you focus on the painful issues you don't agree on instead of just celebrating the things you have in common." See "Wrestling in the Daylight: an interview with Rabbi Brant Rosen," 12/6/12, www.mitchellplitnick.com. Also check out "When Shmuley met Rae," 8/30/12, by Ron Kampeas, about a "surprisingly heartfelt talk between a leftist activist and a right-wing rabbi," blog.jta.org.

101. Pollack, L. (12/29/08). Outraged American Jews turn last night of Hanukkah into *shiva* for Gaza: Latkes and laments, http://mondoweiss.net.

102. Ibid.

103. Ibid.

104. Gottlieb, L. (2008, May/June). Refusing to be enemies. *Tikkun*, 23, 43. Just to reiterate: it in no way compromises our work for a just peace to have compassion for Israelis as well—for the fear they feel when the siren blasts, warning of a quassam rocket from Gaza about to hit, somewhere. It is so clearly in both people's interests to end the occupation, to ensure human rights and fairness for all.

105. This quote is often attributed to Lilla Watson, Indigenous Australian woman from

the Gangulu tribe, a visual artist, activist, and women's studies/aboriginal epistemology scholar. According to Wikipedia, Watson prefers the quote be attributed as I have done here, since it was born of a collective process.

106. From the February 2011 Jewish Voice for Peace statement on the uprising in Egypt: "Given the history of persecution and genocide Jews have survived, we understand the uneasiness that some Jews and Israelis feel at the prospect of unknown outcomes of revolutions among Israel's neighbors. We think the uprisings are cause for hope." See http://jewishvoiceforpeace.org/blog/jewish-voice-for-peaces-statement-to-the-egyptian-people.

107. Gottlieb, L. (2011, Winter). *Tikkun olam*: The art of nonviolent civil resistance. *Tikkun*, 43, 25th Anniversary Issue. This also includes not expecting Palestinians to moderate their words so that Jews will feel more comfortable; it is our responsibility as a Jewish community to help one another heal from our historical trauma, this is not the job of Palestinians.

108. Kaye/Kantrowitz, M. (2007, March.) Some notes on anti-Semitism. (Chap 15, Note 8).

109. Kaye/Kantrowitz. *The colors of Jews*. (Chap 1, Note 52)

110. Excerpt from "Red Sea: April 2002" by Aurora Levins Morales, from the forthcoming collection *Poet on Assignment*. Used with permission. For more about her work and ideas, see www.auroralevinsmorales.com.

111. Kaye/Kantrowitz. *The colors of Jews*. (p. 123). (Chap 1, Note 52)

112. Kaye/Kantrowitz. M. (1992c). While patriarchy explodes. In *The issue is power: Essays on women, Jews, violence and resistance*, (p. 226). San Francisco: Aunt Lute Books.

113. Used with permission. Dr. Reagon is also founder of the riveting African American a capella group Sweet Honey in the Rock.

114. Kaye/Kantrowitz. *The issue is power*. (p. 197). (Chap 7, Note 7).

115. From the irrepressible, extraordinary activist, and my late friend, Fran Peavey, in my interview with her "From the Heart," in Rosenwasser. (1992b). *Visionary voices*. (Chap 15, Note 20.)

116. Lorde, A. (1997). *The cancer journals* (p. 13), Special Edition. San Francisco: Aunt Lute Books. Lorde was not Jewish.

117. Klepfisz, I. (1990d). *Yom Hashoah, Yom Yerushalayim: A meditation*. In *Dreams of an insomniac: Jewish feminist essays, speeches and diatribes* (p. 128). Portland, OR: Eighth Mountain Press.

ACTION-ORIENTED READER'S GUIDE

In addition to my own experience and thinking, a few ideas for the questions and exercises in this Guide came from the following:

*Melanie Kaye/Kantrowitz, Irena Klepfisz, and Bernice Mennis in their groundbreaking 1989 handbook, Ingerangl/in struggle: A handbook for recognizing and resisting anti-Semitism and for building Jewish identity and pride. In Kaye/Kantrowitz & I. Klepfisz (Eds.). *The tribe of Dina*, (pp. 334-346). (Chap 5, Note 27).

* Irena Klepfisz's chapter "Anti-semitism in the Lesbian/Feminist Movement" in her 1990 book *Dreams of an insomniac: Jewish feminist essays, speeches and diatribes* (pp. 56-59). Portland, OR: Eighth Mountain Press.

*Stereotypes of Jews," p. 294, by Maurianne Adams & Katja Hahn D'errico in "Antisemitism and anti-Jewish oppression curriculum design, 2007, in Adams, Bell, & Griffin.

Teaching for diversity. (Chap 1, Note 2).
   * Dinyah Rein and Sonika Tinker (when they worked together as *Loveworks*).
   * Also Wendy Somerson, Joan Lester, and Sandy Butler.
   Huge thanks and appreciation to all of them.

1. For more information, also see Chapter 12, Note 6.
2. The original version of this exercise, "Stand Up/Sit Down: Anti-Semitism," was developed by Michael Taller and printed in Hugh Vasquez and Isoke Femi's 1993 *A manual for unlearning oppression and building multicultural alliances* (p. 164), Oakland, CA: TODOS Sherover-Simms Alliance Building Institute.
3. Thanks to Taj Johns and SASHA (Self Affirming Soul Healing Africans) for creating this idea in their work to heal from internalized racism, described in Johns' 2008 dissertation, *We are self affirming soul healing Africans.* (p. 286). (Chap 7, Note 40)
4. In this context, oppressor is used to refer to one group that systemically dominates, victimizes, exploits others in a harsh inhumane way for its own benefit.

Index

Acknowledgments

Although I quote from a plethora of activists, scholars, journalists, and friends, *this work in its entirety reflects no one's perspective other than my own.* That said, there is no way I could have transformed my Ph.D. dissertation into this book without the extraordinary help, generosity, and support of my community.

The book's subtitle is taken from a quote (see Chapter Fifteen), by the brilliant and passionate lesbian feminist Yiddish scholar and activist Irena Klepfisz, who as a child survived the Warsaw Ghetto Uprising that her father helped lead: Thank you, Irena. And appreciation to Elizabeth Seja Min for helping me craft the final book title.

My gratitude to those who sent articles and books; provided logistical, technical, or promotional know-how; supplied contacts, information, advice, support: Nancy Adess, Lisa Albrecht, Sina Arnold, Bob Baldock, Nora Barrows-Friedman, Dalit Baum, Joel Beinin, Daryl Berman, Rachel Biale, Sandy Boucher, the late Barbara Brenner, Karen Brodkin, Paul Curatolo, Chris Dunaway, Barbara Edwards, Sherry Gorelick, Lux Guacci, Barbara Higbie, Margaret Holub, Amy Horowitz, Taj Johns, Eryn Kalish, Ari Kelman, Jo Kent Katz, Alainya Kavaloski, Marjorie Dove Kent, Loolwa Khazzoom, Paul Kivel, Donna Korones, Wai Lee, Jane Litman, Lynn Marie Lumiere, Larin McLaughlin, Alec MacLeod, Sarah Anne Minkin, Bonnie Morris, Naomi Newman, Doug Paxton, Shana Penn, Andy Perham, Henri Picciotto, Karen Platt, Mitchell Plitnick, Joyce Ravitz, my cousin Gail Richardson, my brother David Rosenwasser, my niece Elizabeth Rosenwasser, Stephanie Roth, Alix Sabin, Dana Schneider, Moli Steinert, Donna Stoneham, Cecilie Surasky, Jane Suskin, Pat Washington, Liat Weingart, Judy Werle, Akaya Windwood, Noah T. Winer, and Stephen Zunes. Thanks also to hosts on Pacifica community radio station KPFA-FM, where I heard valuable interviews and songs.

I relied on the knowledge and perspective of those who helped me sort out my thinking: Sandy Butler, Sarah Anne Minkin, Paul Kivel, Aurora Levins Morales, Wendy Somerson, Cecilie Surasky, Mitchell Plitnick, Stephen Zunes, Jesse Bacon, Dalit Baum, Elizabeth Seja Min, and

Susan Freundlich. Big appreciation to Dyanna Loeb, Aurora Levins Morales, June Jordan's Literary Estate Trust, and Bitch, for permission to use excerpts of your poems, and to Marge Piercy, Aishe Berger and Nina Rachel for your poem excerpts as well; to Joan Bobkoff, Phylece Snyder, and Liat Weingart for your photographs; to Dr. Bernice Johnson Reagon and Leon Rosselson for permission to quote from your songs. And deepest thanks to so many for your precious stories.

This book could not have been written if Elizabeth Kasl had not first skillfully shepherded me through my dissertation, with empathy for and belief in my work. Through her films, Shakti Butler provided me opportunities that became life-changing, and Susan Freundlich cheered me on, with so much love. Early on, Amanda Saltzman and Noa Mohlabane let me know that my work made a difference, and Jackie Dennis provided vital support. The Four Dreds have been compassionate and inspiring teachers and friends: thank you Colette Winlock, Bola Cofield, Earthlyn Manuel, and especially, Taj Johns. Wendy Somerson devoured my dissertation and insisted that it become a book.

Huge thanks to those who read portions of this book and gave me useful feedback: Shoshana Simon, Akaya Windwood, Jesse Bacon, and Cecilie Surasky. Paul Kivel, Wendy Somerson, and especially Sarah Anne Minkin, read larger portions, providing critical information and analysis; Kaylie Simon read nearly all of it and kept me going with her boundless enthusiasm. Sandy Butler and Joan Lester read the manuscript several times over with painstaking care.

Cherie Brown introduced me to key concepts about internalized anti-Semitism and Jewish liberation; Julian Weissglass took me to Auschwitz/Birkenau and continues to inspire me with his vision, boldness and humility. They have both been irresistible teachers in helping me love and value myself as a Jew, along with Sandy Butler, Susan Freundlich, Ruth Hartman, Glen Hauer, Yeshi Sherover Neumann, Amy Horowitz, Aurora Levins Morales, Naomi Newman & Traveling Jewish Theatre, Chaya Gusfield, Deidre Hicks, Paul Kivel, Julie Saxe-Taller, Buz Bogage, Dawn Howes, Jessica Chen, Michael Taller, Jaime Jenet, Meg Weber, Denice Dennis, and Diane Balser.

And there are more than I can name here, who inspire me with their Jewish chutzpah, intelligence, and fierce commitment to justice, also for their humor, huge hearts, and friendship: a few include Rae Abileah, Deborah Agre, Lisa Albrecht, the late Barbara Brenner, Sandy Butler, Julia Caplan, Nancy Drooker, Kathy Engel, Sara Felder, Terry Fletcher, Stefanie Fox, Susan Freundlich, Lynne Gelzer, Lynn Gottlieb, Cindy Greenberg, Terry Greenblatt, Glen Hauer, Lev Hirschorn, Margaret Holub, Julie Iny, Sarah Jacobus, Melanie Kaye/Kantrowitz, Jo Kent Katz, Loolwa Khazzoom, Paul Kivel, Smadar Lavie, Aurora Levins Morales, Sydney Levy, Barbara Lubin, Ariel Luckey, Sarah Anne Minkin, Mirit Mizrahi, Naomi Newman, Dev Noily, Sara Norman, Liz Palmer, Mitchell Plitnick, Stephanie Roth, Alix Sabin, Julie Saxe-Taller, Ilana Schatz, Cindy Shamban, Nicky Silver, Kaylie Simon, Shoshana Simon, Wendy Somerson, Cecilie Surasky, Jane Suskin, Rebecca Vilkomerson, Noah T.Winer, Alissa Wise and Ari Wohlfeiler.

My dissertation, and so this book, never could have happened without the feisty, wise, and loving women who met with me for a year, exploring our stories and developing our thinking together. You know who you are. Thank you.

And when the chips were down, Ann Russo and Misha Klein immediately rallied my spirits with their concrete support, experience, belief in my work, and love. Ezra Berkeley Nepon, Diane Lofgren, Carla King, Margaret Mann, John Mark Schuster, and Joan Pinkvoss provided excellent counsel in helping this book to be born, along with the skills of Deb McCarroll, Vicki Gibbs, Linda Herman, Susan Taunton, David Sweet, Margo Dean, Irene Young, and Irene Elmer; and I was thrilled that Lorna of AK Press agreed to help distribute it. Immeasurable thanks to my longtime friend and creative consultant Elizabeth Seja Min, whose savvy, thoughtful strategizing helped me publish this manuscript.

Thanks also to the Occupy movement, especially Occupy Oakland, for offering hope, excitement, and a rebirth in showing what democracy could really look like.

There are no words to express my heartfelt amazement and gratitude to those who repeatedly shooed away my demons…who kept me going, who believed in me, who constantly offered their wisdom, and especially, their love: my gifted and enthusiastic editor Joan Lester; my ever-affirming long-time confidante, guide, and cherished friend Barbara Higbie; my brother David, always listening and encouraging, helping me laugh my way through anxiety; and my committed and tender activist/intellectual Jewish-expert friend Sandy Butler, who helped more than I can say.

About the Author

Transplanted to Oakland, California, from Northern Virginia/Washington, D.C., Penny Rosenwasser is the author of *Visionary Voices, Women on Power: Conversations with shamans, activists, teachers, artists and healers*, and *Voices from a 'Promised Land'; Palestinian & Israeli peace activists speak their hearts*. She earned her Ph.D. at the California Institute of Integral Studies in Transformational Learning & Change. Penny is a founding board member of Jewish Voice for Peace and former Jewish Caucus Chair of the National Women's Studies Association. She teaches an Anti-Arabism/Anti-Semitism class with a Palestinian colleague at the City College of San Francisco and belongs to Kehilla Synagogue.

Penny is also a member of the European American Collaborative for Challenging Whiteness, and works as an event organizer and fundraiser. A former performing folk musician, KPFA radio host/producer, women's music networker, festival organizer, and diversity workshop leader, she's been active on issues ranging from ending nuclear power and weapons, to feminism and queer liberation, to peace and racial justice, especially focusing on Israel-Palestine—including leading four women's peace delegations to that region. She has published in *Lilith, Tikkun, Bridges*, the *San Francisco Chronicle*, the *Feminist Studies Quarterly, Alternet, PlanetOut, Creation Spirituality, off our backs*, and the *San Francisco Bay Times*. And she loves fooling around on the ukelele, drumming on the dumbek, and snorkeling in search of sea turtles and spotted eagle rays. www.PennyRosenwasser.com

29800909R00255

Made in the USA
Lexington, KY
07 February 2014